G000116084

Internationalizing the Internet

NEW HORIZONS IN THE ECONOMICS OF INNOVATION

Founding Editor: Christopher Freeman, *Emeritus Professor of Science Policy, SPRU – Science and Technology Policy Research, University of Sussex, UK*

Technical innovation is vital to the competitive performance of firms and of nations and for the sustained growth of the world economy. The economics of innovation is an area that has expanded dramatically in recent years and this major series, edited by one of the most distinguished scholars in the field, contributes to the debate and advances in research in this most important area.

The main emphasis is on the development and application of new ideas. The series provides a forum for original research in technology, innovation systems and management, industrial organization, technological collaboration, knowledge and innovation, research and development, evolutionary theory and industrial strategy. International in its approach, the series includes some of the best theoretical and empirical work from both well-established researchers and the new generation of scholars.

Titles in the series include:

Internationalizing the Internet

The Co-evolution of Influence and Technology

Byung-Keun Kim

Professor, School of Industrial Management, Korea University of Technology and Education, Republic of Korea

NEW HORIZONS IN THE ECONOMICS OF INNOVATION

Edward Elgar
Cheltenham, UK • Northampton, MA, USA

© Byung-Keun Kim 2005

All rights reserved. No part of this publication may be reproduced, stored in a
retrieval system or transmitted in any form or by any means, electronic, mechanical
or photocopying, recording, or otherwise without the prior permission of the
publisher.

Published by
Edward Elgar Publishing Limited
Glensanda House
Montpellier Parade
Cheltenham
Glos GL50 1UA
UK

Edward Elgar Publishing, Inc.
136 West Street
Suite 202
Northampton
Massachusetts 01060
USA

A catalogue record for this book
is available from the British Library

ISBN 1 84376 497 0

Typeset by Manton Typesetters, Louth, Lincolnshire, UK
Printed and bound in Great Britain by MPG Books Ltd, Bodmin, Cornwall

Contents

Acknowledgements

This book originates from the research carried out in the SPRU (Science and Technology Policy Research Unit) under the guidance of Professors Robin Mansell (now London School of Economics and Political Science) and Edward Steinmueller. They have never failed to give me sincere and productive guidance for the research and have given me support throughout the process of writing this book. I am also deeply grateful to Christopher Freeman who has encouraged and guided me since I joined the SPRU in 1997. They kindly read almost the entire manuscript.

I would like to thank colleagues and friends at the SPRU, the SEI (Sussex European Institute), and KISDI (Korea Information Strategy Development Institute) for their challenging ideas and support: particularly, Nick von Tunzelmann, Martin Bell, Mike Hobday, Andrew Davis, Pablo D'Este Cukierman, Surya Mahdi, Jim Watson, Michele Javary, Francis McGowan, James Rollow, Jung-Tae Hwang, Joong-Bum Choi, Joo-Young Ock and Moo-Seuk Oh.

I am grateful to Cristiano Antonelli (University of Torino) and anonymous referees for their kind encouragement and advice. I have also benefited from institutional and financial support from the KUT (Korea University of Technology and Education). This book is finally completed at the KUT. Ki-Yung Om and colleagues deserve my special thanks for their help.

I thank Matthew Pitman and Karen McCarthy (Edward Elgar) for their patience and kind help in the process of editing and production of the book. I would also like to thank Cynthia Little for her editorial help.

Finally, and most importantly, I would like to thank my family: Bo-Min, Min-Choul and Sung-Raye for their endless love and support. This book is dedicated to my parents who taught me the value of challenge and courage.

1. Introduction

The Internet system, a global network of computer networks, emerges as one
of the core technological regimes in the current information and communication technology (ICT) revolution (Freeman and Louçã, 2001). A leading
contention in the Information Society debate[1] is that the Internet is becoming
increasingly important to societies and economic life because of its powerful
potential to change economic, social and cultural systems at both national
and global levels. Castells describes the fundamental, distinctive features of
the 'new economic system' brought about by the ICT revolution as 'informational, global and networked' (Castells, 2000: 77). It is seen as a major
driving force for the transformation of modern societies in that it is altering
the ways in which people come together, communicate with and control one
another (Rheingold, 1994; Cairncross, 1997; Slevin, 2000; Hoff *et al.*, 2000;
Smith and Kollock, 1999; Grossman, 2001).

This book aims to provide an alternative history of the development of the
Internet and the consequence of it. MacKenzie (1996: 7) points out that
'technologies may be best because they have triumphed rather than triumph-
ing because they are best'. In fact, the Internet system was neither the only
possible choice (Thomas and Wyatt, 1999) nor the best data network system
in terms of technological and economic performance (Parulkar and Turner,
1990) but we do not attempt to prove or contest the intrinsic or ex post
superiority of the Internet. We believe that the negotiation among social
groups in the design of a technology determines the realization of Arthur's
(1988: 590) 'increasing returns to adoption'. We will explore the design
processes of the Internet system, focusing on the way the different political
and economic interests between social groups and countries have shaped the
development of the Internet.

Analysing historical, economic and social factors contributing to the different performance of the Internet development system between countries is the
second theme of this book, which provides both historical and quantitative
analyses of the uneven development of the Internet system considered as the
important source of digital divides by many authors and policy makers. We will
look at the deep structure of the uneven growth of the Internet development
between countries and regions by examining dynamics of competition and
collaboration between the USA and other countries in the development of data

network technologies. We will also investigate the internationalization and localization processes of the Internet. The internationalization of the Internet system mainly by the USA and the localization of it in other countries are intertwined. The localization inevitably involves the competition and substitution between the Internet and other communications system. The socioeconomic factors influencing the localization of the Internet will be analysed in the co-evolution mechanisms of technology and other socioeconomic systems.

Many studies focus on the way the Internet system emerged from the US government's experimental network to become the most popular global computer network. This aspect has been explored by many authors, notably Hart *et al.* (1992), Hughes (1998), Abbate (1994), Hauben (1997) and Naughton (1999), all of whom have attempted to explain the economic, cultural and political context of the evolution of the Internet system. However most of these studies focus on the visions of heroic inventors, the triumph of the flat management practices employed by the US government R&D project in cooperation with universities, the decentralized structure of governance, the culture of the Internet and broader communities, and so on. Although these studies provide a detailed and interesting history of the political and cultural context surrounding the development of the US Internet system they fail to demonstrate how the Internet has triumphed as a global information infrastructure and, by the same token, ignore the digital divide that this triumph has created.

The development and diffusion of the Internet system is expected either to give certain countries the opportunity to catch up more quickly (and even leapfrog) the world's technological leaders or to widen the existing technological and economic gaps between these countries and the lagging countries. From a social and political perspective, the disparities in access to the Internet system at the national and global levels raise issues about the inclusion and exclusion of people and countries in a digital economy. International organizations and policy makers are having to acknowledge that the disparities in Internet access across countries arise from economic and social factors, most of the Internet system being concentrated in developed countries and in certain cities or regions.[2] For example, a UNDP (2000) report raises concerns about the growing disparity in the advanced communication systems, in particular the Internet system, despite public policy changes towards liberalization of the telecommunications market:

> The scale of the ICT challenge is immense. Despite the forces of market liberalization and globalization and efforts at public policy reform, the goal of achieving universal access to ICT and Global Information Infrastructure has remained elusive, and the disparity in access to ICT is growing. Today 96 per cent of Internet host computers reside in the highest income nations with only 16 per cent of the world's population. There are more Internet hosts in Finland than in the whole of

Latin America and the Caribbean, more in New York City than in the entire continent of Africa (UNDP, 2000: 1).

However, until recently, only a few studies had focused on the similarities and differences in the development of the Internet system across countries.[3] Most of the studies that have been undertaken argue that the development of the Internet in a country is influenced by economic and social variables such as income, human development, language, computer and telecommunications infrastructure and policy. Most of these efforts are based on an interpretation of the relations between possible economic and social variables and the diffusion of the Internet measured either by the number of host computers or by the share of the market for the technologies based on traditional diffusion models.[4]

In this volume the evolution of the Internet is examined along two streams of analyses, both of which view technology as a sociotechnological system. Technoeconomic approaches (Rosenberg, 1976; Freeman, 1982; von Tunzelman, 1995; Dosi *et al.*, 1988, 1990) and sociotechnological approaches (Mackenzie and Wajcman, 1999; Bijker *et al.*, 1987; Bijker and Law, 1992) provide theoretical and empirical frameworks for analysing the economic and social shaping of technology and the reciprocal shaping of economic and social processes by technology.

However there have been controversies over the technological trajectory or irreversibility even though they have some intellectual common ground (Freeman, 1994a; Mackenzie and Wajcman, 1999; Williams and Edge, 1996). Scholars adopting technoeconomic approaches emphasize that there is a certain pattern or stability that is achieved through the processes of harmonization, regulation, standardization and routinization of technological change to avoid chaotic instability and to reap the benefits of scale economies (Freeman, 1988b). Once its path has been selected and established, a technological system seems to take on a momentum of its own in which problem-solving activities and directions are defined.[5] For example, Sahal argues that 'the process of technological development typically leads to a certain pattern of machine design which remains unchanged in its fundamental aspects over long periods of time. The basic design in turn guides the course of the subsequent development of technology' (Sahal, 1981: 21). Arthur (1988) argues that the irreversibility is attributed to learning by using, by network externalities, scale economies, informational increasing returns and by technological interrelatedness.

However the concepts of technological trajectory and irreversibility have been criticized by those taking a sociotechnological approach on the grounds that technologies are socially and institutionally shaped by the expectations, theories, activities and self-interest of relevant social groups and their constituencies (MacKenzie, 1990; Bijker and Law, 1992). For example, Fleck *et al.* (1990) argue in their studies of Computer Aided Production Management (CAPM) that imperatives or trajectories of technological development are oversimplified and thus fail to illuminate the dynamics of the technology design processes.

Neither a simple technological trajectory (direction of development) nor a single paradigm apply, either to organizationally simple or complex technologies. Even where there appear to be clear-cut principles underlying the *design* of a particular technology, the *implementation* of these has not conformed to the stereotyped prediction which appeared in the early literature (Fleck *et al.*, 1990: 636–7). However, their argument that technological change is contingent upon local contexts has also been criticized. For example, Härd (1994) argues that the creation of black boxes at the local level is very important for design and production as practical work because some degree of local stability is needed for research, development and commercialization to function properly. The social choices made by relevant groups are also constrained by political and economic power relationships and historical experiences.

Technoeconomic perspectives and sociotechnological perspectives are not contradictory; they are complementary. Sociotechnological studies focus on the early stage of technological system development while technoeconomic perspectives mostly look into the later stages of innovation, often after a technology's commercialization. The former tend to stress the social implications of technology and of technological change while the latter tend to focus on the economic process of technological change. Social reasoning and economic reasoning cannot be separated in analysing technological change, particularly in the context of information and communication technologies (ICTs).[6]

Some scholars have suggested that the way to fill gaps between these economic and social approaches and global and local controversies is to develop a co-evolutionary approach (Nelson and Winter, 1974; Nelson, 1992; Freeman, 1995a) or a meso-level analysis (Misa, 1988; Sørensen and Levold, 1992). Freeman (1995a) emphasizes the co-evolution of science and technology, and economic, political and cultural systems in establishing or missing opportunities for confluence and congruence in the context of economic growth in a country. However, much of the analytical framework for their analyses is concerned with the co-evolution that is necessary to achieve this, which still needs to be developed. Misa (1994) points out that studies at a micro level generally attempt to deconstruct technological determinism, while analyses of the macro level tend to produce technologically deterministic accounts. He argues that perhaps meso-level studies of technology offer a middle ground between these two extremes. Sørensen and Levold also stress the importance of meso-level analysis because 'there are very important "intermediate" institutions and institutional arrangements (networks) involved in technological innovation' which are neither completely fluid (social constructivist perspectives) nor predetermined (technoeconomic approaches) (Sørensen and Levold, 1992: 14–15).

Chapters 2 and 3 comprise discussions on a paradigm of technological systems design based upon these two perspectives and the governance of telecommunications and the Internet systems. Chapter 2 discusses the economic and sociological approaches in studies of technological systems. The insights given by the 'technoeconomic' and 'sociotechnological' perspectives are applied to uncover conflicting political and economic interests in the design of the Internet and the negotiations between relevant social groups in the processes of development and global expansion of the Internet and to examine differences and similarities in the localization of the Internet between countries and regions.

In this book, as an alternative approach to the traditional diffusion models, the localization of technological systems is conceptualized as the social, economic and cultural process of the adaptations and accommodations undertaken when technologies are transferred to new social and cultural contexts. The localization of a technological system involves economic selection and social learning processes. The economic selection process is closely interrelated with the social learning process in that the various learning processes and continuous interactions between users and suppliers in competing technologies are influenced by the wider technological, economic and social systems of a country.

A technological system transfer can be said to follow the process of being 'localized' or 'tailored' to the specific conditions of a range of countries with varying economic, social and cultural characteristics and the localization process inevitably involves social change. The diffusion of technological innovation is fundamentally a social change, that is, 'the process by which alteration occurs in the structure and function of a social system' (Rogers, 1995: 10). Therefore localization involves a process of 'negotiated change' in which the transferred technology undergoes processes of adaptation to meet the requirements of the local context. In other words, it is very difficult to assess a priori the prospects of a particular technology because how local actors and local knowledge will interact during the transfer process necessary to achieve a negotiated outcome is unknown. On this point, it is particularly important to adopt an agnostic view regarding the suitability or applicability of any imported technology.

The evolution of a technological system cannot be fully appreciated in the absence of a political economy perspective. Conflict, power and interests are not just socioeconomic factors influencing the development of a technological system but are inherent qualities of it (Sørensen, 1996). As Sussman

(1997: 285) rightly points out, 'communication technologies are extensions of opportunity within the rules of the political economy that control the allocation of resources in society'. Hård argues that 'social conflict' should be treated 'as a cause of innovation, diffusion, transfer, and application – not only as a result of these processes' (Hård, 1993: 409). Therefore interaction between the various actors within the technological and social system at the local and global levels, together with the dynamics of these relationships, are central to the analysis of the evolution of Internet system. The political economy perspective provides the foundation for an integrated analysis of the local situation and the global power structure which will point to the economic and political interests that are embedded in the design and development of the Internet system. Noble rightly underlines the complexity and interdependence of the evolution of a technology:

> Although the evolution of a technology follows from social choices that inform it, choices which mirror the social relations of production, it would be an error to assume that in having exposed the choices, we can simply deduce the rest of reality from them. Reality cannot be extrapolated from the intentions that underlie the technology any more than from the technology itself. (Noble, 1999: 172)

Chapter 3 presents discussions about the economic, political and technological characteristics of the Internet and telecommunications systems, focusing on the academic discourses on public utilities, universal service, natural monopolies, network industries and infrastructure. Reconfiguration of the global telecommunications system during the last two decades is also reviewed from the international political economy perspective. As Lee (1996: 108) asserts, 'there is perhaps no other sector which has undergone a process of globalization as extensively and as rapidly as telecommunications'. The rationales for and possible consequences of the liberalization of telecommunications, which is claimed by many authors to be an important institutional factor in the development of the Internet system, are critically examined.

Chapters 4 and 5 present a critical view of the existing research in its analysis of the Internet system design. Apart from many historical analyses, the number of studies on the socioeconomic features of the Internet system is ever increasing. Many of these examine economic issues – in particular, Internet service pricing.[7] Others consider the politics of the governance of the Internet, public access and control.[8] These studies are mainly concerned with economic and political issues that have arisen in the transition of the Internet system from a private network of networks to a publicly accessible network; from a system of government-funded networks to a commercial network of public and commercial systems; from being subject to centralized governance (US-centric and/or computer scientist-centric) to achieving self-governance (global and/or major market players); from being a decentralized network architecture to becoming a centralized one; and the transition from a US-centric network topology to a global network.

Chapter 4 looks at the competition between different technological systems in the development of computer networks focusing on the public data network standard (X.25) and the Internet (TCP/IP). The analysis of micro politics in setting the direction of newly emerging computing network technologies within groups or networks of experts is developed, drawing on the concept of epistemic communities.

The generation and distribution of knowledge in a society are shaped by a sociocognitive structure and collectively. Using Foucault's (1973) concept of *epistemes*, Ruggie defines an 'epistemic community' as 'a dominant way of looking at reality, a set of shared symbols and references, mutual expectations and a mutual predictability of intention' (Ruggie, 1975: 569). Fleck also proposes the concept of 'thought collective' as 'a community of persons mutually exchanging ideas or maintaining intellectual interaction' and of 'thought style' as the readiness for 'directed perception with mental and objective assimilation of what has been so perceived' (Fleck, 1979: 39, 99). These observations on epistemic communities provide important insights for the mechanism of academic and research communities. For example, knowledge is usually created collectively by a particular scientific and technological community which maintains internal coherence even though its members may have different political and economic interests. The coordination process of epistemic communities in the interest of a specific situational problem is shaped by the encompassing power structure of a society and the scope of regulated authority (Holzner, 1968). Ruggie (1975) and Haas (1992) employ the concept of epistemic communities in the international policy coordination literature as networks of knowledge-based experts. Mansell and Steinmueller (2000) also apply this concept to analyse conflicts of interest in the transformation of telecommunication systems.

However these theories still leave some important questions unanswered. First, the boundaries of epistemic communities are not always clear. Second, every community may have a different internal coordination process. For example, as was explained above, technology communities are different from scientific communities in terms of both their internal structure and their external factors. The functional nature of epistemic communities also raises the question of conflicting identities of certain members and coordination processes between similar communities. Members of a particular community can be grouped as different members of a formal organization or social class or can even be members of similar or competing communities.

To complete the analysis of the dynamics of competition and collaboration between the USA and European countries, reflecting their different economic and political interests in the context of the development of computing networks, the broad power relations surrounding the evolution of the Internet are examined. The analysis of the collaboration and competition between the Internet system and the public data network focuses on the USA and European countries in the 1970s and 1980s.

There are four stages that can be distinguished in the Internet system's evolution: an experimental network, US national system building, global expansion and the global system building process; most of these are described in Chapter 5. Changes in system builders, the critical problems encountered, the technological innovations introduced and governance are analysed in the context of each of these different phases of development. In particular the politics of the global expansion process are explored, focusing on collaborations through international computer networking communities, political control and regional characteristics.

Together with qualitative analysis of the design and evolution of the Internet, quantitative analysis is used to examine the outcome of Internet system development in relation to economic and social factors at both country and global levels. Chapters 6 and 7 examine 'population dynamics', focusing on the uneven development of the Internet between regions and countries and looks at the similarities and differences between countries in terms of the relationship between the development and diffusion of the Internet system and economic and social factors.

Chapter 6 in this volume analyses the population dynamics of Internet system development across countries, using quantitative data and methods. The grouping of countries reflects their geographic, cultural and economic factors. The relationship between the Internet system and other advanced communications systems is also analysed, focusing on different technological choices in the face of the Internet challenge. To examine 'population dynamics' in the development of the Internet system on a global dimension, statistical methods are used. The patterns in the uneven outcomes of the Internet system's development and the different choices of ICTs between regions and countries are analysed using quantitative analysis. The empirical findings bring new evidence about the factors influencing the extent of the digital divide. It is argued that the localization of the Internet is influenced by different choices in terms of ICTs and non-linear relationships between competing technologies, reflecting firms' strategies. As one way to show this dynamics of localization, different outcomes of the competing technologies of the Internet and online consumer service (including videotex systems) between countries are illustrated.

Chapter 7 examines the interactive relationships among endogenous factors underlying Internet system development, that is, Internet host computers, personal computers (PCs) and telephone mainlines modelled as a system of simultaneous equations. A set of hypotheses is elaborated to examine the relationship between the Internet system and the information and communication infrastructure, and identify the most important socioeconomic factors in the development of the Internet in a country. While some aspects of the relationship are still open to question the analysis reveals some properties of systemic technological interrelatedness that are useful for understanding the evolution of the Internet system.

To highlight the similarities and differences in the outcome of the Internet system across countries it is necessary to elaborate hypotheses based on analysis of the history of the evolution of the Internet system and country and technology-specific socioeconomic factors. An analysis of the relationship between the localization of the Internet system and the economic and social system shows co-evolutionary features. A more comprehensive approach to utilizing indicators representing countries' capabilities in terms of knowledge system and global integration activities helps identify the main factors influencing different outcomes in Internet system development between countries.

Chapter 8 puts forward some conclusions of this book by re-articulating main findings. Currently we are experiencing the second wave of the Internet system development. In particular, the race for the development of high-performance broadband technologies between OECD countries and the competition and collaboration between major market players across geographical and industry boundaries have given a fresh impetus to the debate over social and economic implications of the Internet. As Dutton and his colleagues rightly point out, the social and economic potential of high-performance Internet systems is shaped by a co-evolving web of people, institutions and technology (Dutton *et al.*, 2004).

NOTES

1. Duff (2000) provides useful discussions on various versions of information society thesis.
2. See NITA (1999), OECD (2001a, b) and Alcántara (2001).
3. See, for example, OECD (1996c), ITU (1999a) and Hargittai (1999).
4. The main shortcomings of the traditional diffusion models in the studies of technological systems are presented in Chapter 2.
5. That is, a natural trajectory (Nelson and Winter, 1977), a technological trajectory (Dosi, 1982), a technological guide post (Sahal, 1985) and a technoeconomic paradigm (Perez, 1983; Freeman and Perez, 1988).
6. See, for example, Dutton (1996).
7. See, for example, Bailey *et al.* (1995), Lehr and Weiss (1996), McKnight and Bailey (1997), Apostolopoulos *et al.* (2000) and McKnight and Boroumand (2000).
8. See, for example, Kahin and Keller (1995, 1997), Gutstein (1999) and Akdeniz *et al.* (2000).

2. Socioeconomic design of technological systems

2.1 INTRODUCTION

Scholars from several different disciplines have explored the paradigm of technological systems design. During the 1980s and 1990s, many scholars, mainly specializing in economics and sociology, established theoretical grounds for examining the dynamics of technological systems development. Broadly speaking, these studies have challenged traditional concepts of technology (for example, exogenous factors of economic growth) and the relationship between technology and the socioeconomic system (for example, linear model of innovation). Their approaches can be categorized under two general perspectives: technoeconomic and sociotechnological. However one of the most distinctive characteristics of research within these traditions is its interdisciplinarity, thus it is difficult to distinguish between them on a disciplinary basis.[1]

A more detailed examination of these two perspectives is the subject of sections 2.2 and 2.3 of this chapter where they are compared and contrasted with the large technical systems (LTS) approach of Hughes (1983). Individual scholars within these perspectives argue that the evolution of technological systems involves inherently dynamic and complex interactions between technological factors and economic and social contexts. Section 2.4 discusses the main concepts and limitations of the LTS approach which have been used in many studies of electric power, telecommunications and transportation systems.

With insights from economic and sociological approaches, a political economy of the localization is discussed in section 2.5. The evolution of a technological system inevitably involves struggles for control over a system and raises issues of economic and political power distribution in a society and between societies. The localization of a technological system is influenced by the local and global interplay; this is particularly true in the case of technology with strategic or military value. The process of localization of a technological system and the case of adaptation of imported technologies engages a technological system transfer process involving continuous adaptation to the specific technological, economic and institutional contexts and the social environment of a country.

2.2   ECONOMICS OF TECHNOLOGICAL CHANGE

This section discusses the main features of the technoeconomic perspectives in the analysis of technological change and their limitations. Technoeconomic perspectives emphasize the importance of technology in economic growth, focusing on the dynamic and complex interactions between economic and technological systems. Scholars in this tradition view technological change as the process of dynamic adjustment to recurring or consistent states of disequilibria and emphasize the dynamic interactions between technological and institutional change, but they also argue that the development of a technological system involves a stable pattern (Freeman, 1988b: 2). They emphasize that technical change is shaped by dynamic competition through continuous innovations based on appropriability, partial tacitness, specificity, uncertainty, variety of knowledge bases, search procedures, technological opportunities, cumulativeness and irreversibility (Dosi and Orsenigo, 1988: 15–16).

The process of the development of a technological system has often been analysed as technological diffusion. Some of the scholars who favour this approach argue that diffusion and adoption require complex and painstaking learning and further modification of products, processes and corporate organizations. For example, Metcalfe (1988, 1995) argues that the dynamic nature of technological diffusion involves the absence of a single artefact with invariant characteristics and, instead, involves an emerging design configuration together with its artefacts and skills and with a knowledge-based dimension. The constraints and problems which identify a diffusion path are accompanied by the market incentives that are influenced by relative factor costs and user valuations of different performance characteristics. Design configurations are typically built in a cumulative fashion (diffusion through learning and learning through diffusion) through interaction with and positive feedback from their environment. Diffusion is shaped by the evolving pattern of competitive advantage between rival technologies and it can be said that relative factor costs and user valuations co-evolve (Metcalfe, 1988: 482–4; 1995: 562).

The international diffusion of technology is an important starting point for firms' technological capability-building processes in most developing countries and this starting point heavily depends upon the features of technologies originally developed in the more industrialized countries. Bell and Pavitt (1993) observe that the continuous process of technical change involves two steps in each successive application of a transferred technology: a technology-using capabilities stage and a technology-changing capabilities stage. Therefore the success of this starting point in relation to prior accumulation of skill and knowledge in the imported technology relies not only on the appropriateness (of knowledge, skills and effects), but also on the technology-using and technology-changing capabilities of importing countries in the adoption and assimilation process (ibid.).

Recently scholars working in this tradition have increasingly been emphasizing the importance of various kinds of knowledge flows (for example, inter-firm, intra-firm, intra-cluster, extra-cluster) involved in the accumulation of technological capabilities (that is, knowledge stocks and resources). Studies of systems of innovation (technological system or knowledge system) link the knowledge aspects of technology to the role of firms in the process of knowledge accumulation (Carlsson, 1995; Nonaka *et al.*, 2000; Bell and Albu, 1999). Carlsson (1995) puts forward the idea of elements of technological systems being knowledge/competence networks, industrial networks/development blocks and institutional infrastructure. Nonaka *et al.* (2000) view a firm as a knowledge-creating entity, and argue that the knowledge and capability to create and utilize such knowledge are the most important sources of a firm's sustainable competitive advantage. Bell and Albu emphasize the importance of various kinds of knowledge flows in understanding the process of accumulation of technological capabilities by firms. They argue that knowledge systems and production systems overlap, but they are not identical, in that actors in one may not be actors in the other and knowledge flows may not be carried along the same channels as those concerned with market transactions for goods.[2] In addition, it is important to recognize the informal knowledge networks in the innovation process, suggested by von Hippel (1988), that support the exploration of 'knowledge as community'.

Bell and Albu (1999) argue that the differences in knowledge systems across countries (in particular, developing countries) arise from differences in the complexity of technologies and the distance of the cluster from the international technological frontier, as well as institutional factors. Some scholars further emphasize the diversity of institutions and government policies in the technology transfer and assimilation process (Rosenberg and Frischtak, 1985; Wade, 1990).

Recognition of the diversity of institutions has led to studies of national innovation systems (NIS). NIS involve a dynamic network of research systems and education and training systems that supports the acquisition, production, transformation and distribution of new technological knowledge (Freeman, 1988a, 1995b; Lundvall, 1988, 1992; Nelson, 1993; Edquist, 1997). Infrastructure investments and institutional changes either support or block the sources of an intensive and successful learning process in both new and existing technologies. The acquisition of a new major technology is a very complex and widespread learning process at all levels of society, involving social and technological innovations. NIS are used in two senses: 'in a broad sense [the NIS] encompasses all institutions which affect the introduction and diffusion of new products, processes and systems in a national economy; and in a narrow sense it encompasses that set of institutions which are more directly concerned with scientific and technical activities' (Freeman, 1992: 169). For example, Lundvall (1992: 12) suggests a definition of NIS that involves 'all parts and aspects of economic structure and institutional set-up affecting learning as well as searching and exploring – the production system, the marketing system and the system of finance present themselves as sub-systems in which learning takes place'. The NIS approach stresses the central importance of path-dependent, institutional learning processes and policy formations. Patel and Pavitt (1994) suggest the following main components of NIS: the main national institutions (for example, business firms, universities, a mixture of public and private institutions and government), their competences and national market incentives and pressures. Certainly the rate and direction of technological development are strongly influenced by country-specific factors such as economic signals, the technological and institutional context, and macroeconomic and cultural factors (Dosi *et al.*, 1990).

However the technoeconomic approach focuses on the economic selection process of technical change and stresses the importance of firms as the main locus of technological accumulation even though several authors recognize the importance of institutions as the context that influences this process.

What the technoeconomic approach fails to analyse is the mechanisms of the generation of technology based on communities, the importance of design factors and the socialization process of technological knowledge (Constant, 1984, 1987; Callon, 1995; Sørensen and Levold, 1992). For example, Callon (1995: 442) argues that 'economists generally neglected the design factor in order to concentrate on the competition aspect and the chances of survival of the respective technologies'. Economists do, however, emphasize the importance of knowledge and various knowledge flows in technological knowledge accumulation: the functioning networks among heterogeneous market and non-market actors in building or failing to build a dynamic accumulation of knowledge and capabilities are not included in their analysis.

Constant (1984), following the sociocognitive perspective and the history of technologies (in particular, Kuhn, 1962, and Layton, 1974), points to knowledge and function, 'community' and 'organization' as the building blocks of the 'culture of technology' (Constant, 1987: 232).[3] Constant (1984: 38) argues that community and tradition are the primary loci of technological advance: 'technology's cognitive locus is in a relevant community of practitioners and in the traditions of practice which a community possesses'. He points out that the structural similarity between science and technology lies in a common set of cognitive processes, both individual and collective. He also argues that technology differs from science in that technology has a hierarchical systems structure; thus it is decomposable and, therefore, it can be changed or improved with much greater efficacy (Constant, 1987: 227). Constant (1984) stresses that technology is a social function because technological artefacts are subject to direct environmental elements; he emphasizes that the locus of technology as function is organization (for example, firms). From the cognitive perspective, Lauden (1984) also stresses the role and importance of communities (for example, communities of technologists) in technological change. Lauden argues that 'the cognitive change in technology is the result of the purposeful problem-solving activities of the members of relatively small communities of practitioners' in the face of a problem, including a problem produced directly by the environment and not yet solved by any technology; the functional failure of current technologies; extrapolation from past technological successes; imbalances between technologies in a given period; backward linkages, compulsive sequences, technological co-evolution and presumptive anomalies (potential failures) (Lauden, 1984: 85–6).

Although authors in this tradition do recognize the importance of institutions, it is not always clear whether these institutions refer to the organization or to the culture at large. The concept of institution is central to the NIS literature because 'on the one hand, institutions provide some stability in the patterns of social interactions, thereby reducing uncertainty for individual decision-makers ... On the other hand, institutions are flexible and will be recreated through continuing and new social interactions' (McKelvey, 1997: 146).[4] Edquist and Johnson (1997) suggest a distinction between organizational and institutional characteristics: institution refers to behaviours such as routines, norms, shared expectations and the ground rules for economic behaviour; organization refers to more specific and concrete formal structures, usually consciously created with explicit purposes (for example, firms, technical institutes, training centres, business associations).

On the other hand, culture is often interpreted and used in different meanings between disciplines and within them. For example, culture is a central and widely used concept within the anthropological discipline and it means 'a way of life' (Keesing, 1981). Using various scholars' definitions, Pedersen (1989: 10) summarizes different ways of defining culture as 'systems of meanings, systems of values, collective programming, systems of norm, myths and routines, learned set of solution or set of basic assumptions'. However, as Pedersen (1989: 11) also points out, there is a common base of agreement to the implications of culture despite different interpretations among scholars: culture is a social phenomenon involving cognitive processes and contributing to 'creating continuity, identity, control and integration'.

Authors working in the technoeconomic tradition are also confronted with difficulties in measuring the NIS (Patel and Pavitt, 1994).[5] In this context,

David and Foray (1994: 13) suggest that 'country specific factors such as economic and geographic size, the prevailing per capita income and wealth levels, the degree of economic integration with the international economy, and the density of involvement in international political arrangements' may be tested for national profiles.[6] They argue that the relationship between national systems and global systems is not clear in that most NIS are embedded within larger, more complex, transnational relationships. Mytelka (2000) also argues that NIS are shaped by the global innovation system in certain clusters, particularly the telecommunications sector.

2.3 SOCIAL CHOICES IN TECHNOLOGICAL CHANGE

Sociotechnological perspectives stress the importance of the social implications of technologies focusing on the analysis of the content and design process of technologies because they are part of larger sociotechnological systems (MacKenzie and Wajcman, 1999; Bijker *et al.*, 1987; Bijker and Law, 1992). The central concept of sociotechnological perspectives is negotiability or choice in the technological system design and innovation process:

> there are 'choices' (though not necessarily conscious choices) inherent in both the design of individual artefacts and systems, and in the direction or trajectory of innovation programmes … Different routes are available, potentially leading to different technological outcomes. Significantly, these choices could have differing implications for society and for particular social groups. The character of technologies, as well as their social implications, are problematized and opened up for enquiry. (Williams and Edge, 1996: 866)

These authors are, therefore, concerned with the processes of change by which stabilization or closure is achieved in technology. Bijker and Law (1992) summarize the five main assumptions that are generally made by those adopting sociotechnological perspectives as follows:

(i)   Technological change is contingent;
(ii) Technologies are born out of conflict, difference, or resistance;
(iii) Such difference may or may not break out into overt conflict or disagreement;
(iv) A technology is stabilized if and only if the heterogeneous relations in which it is implicated, and of which it forms a part, are themselves stabilized;
(v)   Both strategies themselves and the consequences of those strategies should be treated as emergent phenomena. (Bijker and Law, 1992: 8–11)

These perspectives provide grounds for investigating alternative technological development paths and the different interests of social groups in designing technologies and they stress the social responsibility for technological development, adaptation and adoption.

Within sociotechnological perspectives, theories such as Social Construction of Technology (SCOT) (Pinch and Bijker, 1984; Bijker, 1997), Actor–Network–Theory (ANT) (Law and Callon, 1992; Callon *et al.*, 1992) and LTS (Hughes, 1987) have been developed. These theories make some common assumptions about the social processes underlying technological generation and replication but their theoretical approaches are different. For example, similar concepts such as 'technological frame' (SCOT), 'translation' (ANT) and 'system' (LTS) are suggested for analysing the seamless web of technology and society.[7]

The SCOT model analyses the process of interaction and meaning of the artefacts of each group based on 'interpretative flexibility', focusing on the problems and associated solutions that 'relevant social groups' present about the artefacts until closure is achieved. Closure is the stabilization of technology as a system. Law argues that 'Closure is achieved when debate and controversy about the form of an artifact is effectively terminated' (Law, 1987: 111). However closure does not mean the end of change; rather it should be considered as facilitating the order that makes change possible (Misa, 1992b). Thomas and Wyatt (1999) argue that closure has been variously achieved and undone at different moments during the evolution of the Internet system.

The ANT approach stresses the heterogeneity and variability of associations of humans and non-humans focusing on certain integrated systems which the actors are related to, and produce, in the process of solving problems. The proponents of SCOT and ANT argue that systems and networks are shaped in contingent processes of interaction and negotiation among purposeful actors or groups of actors. The LTS approach 'tends to treat actors as units *within* the analysis', while the SCOT and ANT approaches 'view actors as the explicit units *of* their analysis' (Summerton, 1994: 4–5). Hughes (1983) defines the LTS approach in terms of technical and organizational components that can be understood as being connected by a network or structure to achieve a common goal. Such a system is often 'neither centrally controlled nor directed towards a clearly defined goal' (ibid.: 6). The internal dynamics of systems are based on the technological interrelatedness of the system which, in turn, is influenced by the environment.

SCOT and ANT are open to criticism with respect to their methodological and practical implications (Russell, 1986; Winner, 1993; Williams and Edge, 1996; Latour, 1999). This critique is related to the issue of micro–macro disputes in that micro studies have a tendency to ignore social and political influences occurring outside the micro context that can influence the processes of change. The LTS approach is relatively free from the micro–macro dispute. Russell (1986: 333) asserts, 'If we accept that arguments over technological options are socially constructed, then it follows that a relativist approach with respect to them leads us into relativism with respect to social interests – in other words, political neutrality.' These models are criticized as focusing on the observable behaviour of the actions of individuals and interactions in which the broader institutional context is fluid and largely unspecified. The possibilities of interpretative flexibility (of choice) seem endless, and SCOT and ANT studies 'remain skeptical about the nature and influence of broader social and economic structure of power and interests' (Williams and Edge, 1996: 870). This suggests that social constructivists have a problem in accounting for closure. Hård (1993) argues that the closure achieved is often the result of uneven power relationships reflecting the economic and social structure rather than struggling groups always ending up in agreement. He also criticized the fact that closure inevitably involves restructuring of power relationships but SCOT neglects to accommodate the analysis on social conflicts in their research. Despite criticism of their political ambiguity, the constructivist perspective provides a rationale for political considerations of technological development: 'Demonstrating interpretative flexibility makes it clear that the stabilization of artefacts is a social process and hence subject to choices, interests, and value judgment – in short, to politics' (Bijker, 1997: 281). The SCOT model employs 'a semiotic power structure' to explain the development of a new order constituted by a particular combination of technology and society (ibid.: 286). These politics, however, are very localized, and instruments for closure.

Sociotechnological approaches put emphasis on the social choices in the design of a certain technological system by examining alternative technological development paths and conflicts of interest among social groups in constructing technologies. They provide interactive models for investigating the relationship between technologies and contextual factors, such as political and social factors. With the exception of the LTS approach, however, all these models exclude the influence of the broader social and economic structure of power and interests from their investigation.

The next section discusses the main concepts of and limitations to the LTS approach as one of these sociotechnological models. The evolution of the telecommunications system has been analysed by many authors using the LTS approach, mainly because it provides a conceptual framework for integrating technological, social and political factors in the analysis of network and infrastructure systems, based on their common technological characteristics.

2.4   LTS APPROACH

The evolution of technological systems, in particular electric power systems, telecommunications systems and transportation systems, have been examined using what has come to be known as the LTS approach (Hughes, 1983; Mayntz and Hughes, 1988; La Porte, 1991; Summerton, 1994). The LTS approach has been used to examine the technical and political aspects of the development of a technological system. The basic tenet of the LTS approach, like other theories of sociotechnological perspectives, is that specific technologies are part of larger social and technological systems such as 'material technologies, organisations, institutional rule systems and structures and cultural values which support and sustain them' (Summerton, 1994: 3).

Main Concepts of LTS

Despite some ambiguity in the definition of 'large' and 'technological systems', most of the existing literature on the evolution of LTS focuses on traditional infrastructure systems including transportation, energy and telecommunications (Joerges, 1988; Summerton, 1994). These complex and large-scale technological systems appear to have similar technological, organizational and institutional characteristics such as technological interrelatedness, vertically (and/or horizontally) integrated monopoly, and economic and political attributes.

The LTS approach was initiated by Thomas P. Hughes (Hughes, 1983) and provides several concepts such as system builder, critical problems, reverse salients and momentum. Hughes defines system builders as the people who invent and develop the technological and organizational components of a technological system and have 'the ability to construct or to force unity from diversity, centralization in the face of pluralism, and coherence from chaos' (Hughes, 1987: 52).[8] Hughes argues that system builders changed from individuals (for instance, project managers) to 'the function within the context of organizations dedicated primarily to building systems', reflecting changes in the size of the organization and in the collective nature of the systems builders' activities (Hughes, 2000: 7–8). Hughes (1983, 1987) offers a general model of the evolution of a technological system based on his observation of the history of electric light and power between 1870 and 1940. He argues that the evolution of systems seems to evolve in accordance with a loosely defined pattern: invention, development, innovation, transfer, growth, competition and consolidation. These phases in the evolution of a technological system are not sequential. They may overlap and backtrack on each other. Electric systems evolved through three distinct phases: electric lighting systems, universal lighting systems and power systems, and large regional power systems (Constant, 1987). In each stage, different kinds of system builders emerged to solve different critical problems: inventor-entrepreneurs during the invention and development phases; manager-entrepreneurs during innovation, competition and growth phase; and financier-entrepreneurs and consulting engineers, especially those with political influence, during the consolidation and rationalization phases.

Hughes' view of the driving forces of the growth of LTS, including electric power and telecommunications, is different from that of Chandler (1977), who argues that the critical driving factor of the modern large-scale technological systems is throughput velocity, that is, the capability of managerial coordination to increase the rate of flows of goods through the stages of production, thereby enhancing the efficiency of both capital and labour inputs. Hughes, however, argues that economic factors should be considered as 'deterministic', not as determining the growth of systems (1983: 465). The growth of systems results in reverse salients: 'components in the system that have fallen behind or are out of phase with others' (Hughes, 1987: 73). These reverse salients emerge because technological systems inevitably expand unevenly. Critical problems are defined as problems whose solution would bring the system back into line – that is, correct the reverse salient (Hughes, 1983). Technological imbalance between interdependent processes (a technological bottleneck) is one of the main sources of technological change (Rosenberg, 1976). Reverse salients can be technical (technical inefficiencies that are limited in capacity, or arise from problems of reliability), economic (changing costs and wages, varying demand for system output), political (new regulatory legislation) or organizational (Rosenberg, 1976; Hughes, 1986; Summerton, 1994). The process through which reverse salients are identified and resolved reflects the different interests and interpretations of actors about the direction of technological systems development.

When an existing system fails to correct a reverse salient, a new and competing system may emerge, based on a radical innovation and the battle taking place between the existing system and a new competing one. New technological systems emerge gradually from this battle of the systems through a combination of coupling at a technological level and consolidation at the institutional level. However it is only rarely that radical innovations are introduced because of the conservative momentum of the system. Hughes points to the evolutionary process of innovation in that 'Invention is usually correction of a reverse salient or the bringing of a system into line with a salient' (Hughes, 1992: 115). Hughes (1987) distinguishes between radical and conservative inventions with respect to their relationship to existing systems. Radical inventions are unlikely to become components of existing technological systems; conservative inventions will contribute to, improve or expand the existing systems and predominate during the competition and system growth phase. This view is endorsed by Tushman and Anderson

(1986) and Henderson and Clark (1990), who suggest that incremental innovation (architectural innovation) is competence enhancing for existing firms and that radical innovation (modular innovation) is competence destroying in the sense that a firm's existing capabilities are no longer appropriate for the new environment. These categories are based on the continuous and discontinuous effects of innovation on the existing technological system or firms (or industrial structure). Hughes stresses that even radical inventions are often improvements on earlier, similar inventions that failed to develop. The cumulative process of innovation involves technologically complex systems which include an institutional setup. System builders are those that help to 'bring the product into use, often combining the invented and developed physical components into a complex system consisting of manufacturing, sales, and service facilities' (Hughes, 1987: 64).

As was stated in Chapter 1, the technological system takes on its own momentum once its path is established, in which problem-solving activities and direction are defined. Hughes (1983) argues that, even after a prolonged period of growth and consolidation, they do not become autonomous. He points out that momentum arises especially from the organization and people committed to it and their various interests in the system. This momentum is maintained by critical problems that constrain system growth being continually solved. Despite the seemingly established momentum of a technological system, contingencies such as war can push technological systems in new directions. The notion of momentum is similar to the concepts of natural trajectories (Nelson and Winter, 1977) and technological guideposts (Sahal, 1985) in that technological systems have direction but their momentum is not autonomous because it is shaped by social and institutional factors and other contingencies.

During the last 20 years of the 20th century, most of the LTS including energy, telecommunications and transportation systems were reconfigured, mainly in parallel with technological change and the growing prevalence of neoliberal ideas in public policy.[9] Summerton defines reconfiguration, as 'the dynamics of situations or periods in the development of technical system in which previously achieved closure is undone' (Summerton, 1994: 5). This reconfiguration is similar to institutional change (or governance change), such as deregulation and liberalization, but the term 'reconfiguration' is used to refer to both technological and institutional changes. Summerton points to several types of reconfiguration, including territorial expansion and interconnection of similar systems across political borders, transforming regional systems into national ones and national systems into transnational ones; the crossing of functional system boundaries by combining the parts of different systems that complement each other; and institutional border crossing: the reorganizing of previously monopoly systems into new configurations based on principles of competition and open access. The transformation of existing infrastructure systems may even create an entirely new system, as in the case of trans-border organ transplant systems, combined road and air transport, long-distance data transmission, and telephony (Braun and Joerges, 1994).

The process of reconfiguration of infrastructure systems, in particular of telecommunications systems, raises issues concerning the redistribution of economic and political power (Wyatt *et al.*, 2000). As Dutton and his colleagues point out, the outcome of the reconfiguring of access and communicative power will most likely mirror and reinforce existing social and economic divides as technology cannot in itself overturn entrenched and deeply rooted power bases and cultural and social influences; at the same time, the power shifts brought about by the Internet systems are opening up possibilities of a new social and economic order in both global and local dimensions (Dutton *et al.*, 2004: 36–7).

Limitations of the LTS

Hughes provides a useful conceptual framework for examining the complex process of technological system evolution, which integrates technological, social and political factors. He stresses the sociotechnological features of technology and argues that 'technological affairs contain a rich texture of technical matters, scientific laws, economic principles, political forces, and social concerns' (Hughes, 1983: 1). The systemic approach provides a framework for integrating dynamic relations between technology and social change in a coherent way. The technological style or cultural context also provide an explanation for differences in the direction of the development of LTS even though they may not explain the rate. However the LTS approach has certain limitations.

First, there has been no clear definition of what is 'large' and what the boundaries of 'technological systems' are (Joerges, 1988; Carlsson, 1995; Edquist, 1997). The least ambiguous boundary of LTS is apparent in the case of both network and infrastructure systems.

Second, even though Hughes emphasizes the sociotechnical aspects of technological systems, 'the system takes on a physical dimension corresponding to power lines that spread coextensively with the power system' (Bijker *et al.*, 1987: 192). Knowledge-centred perspectives on the definition of technological systems also need to be accommodated in the analysis of technological change because knowledge (competence) flow is more important than flows of ordinary goods and services in understanding the complex process of technological change (Carlsson and Stankiewicz, 1991).

Third, Hughes fails to consider the organizational aspects of the technological system. Hughes mainly focuses on the technological systemic aspects, such as technological interrelatedness; that is, a change in one component has an impact on the other components of the system. Therefore he does not consider knowledge community approaches to problem solving involving reverse salients or organizational approaches in specifying how systems and functions within systems are divided among organizations (Constant, 1987). These aspects are likely to be important in explaining the driving forces of growth and consolidation of an LTS. There is a variety of possible organization arrangements that seem to increase in number as a function of system scale and complexity.

Fourth, Davies argues that 'Hughes neglects to provide an analysis of the economic selection environment – that is, cost structure, scale of production and profitability – that structures the behaviour of those involved in a search for improved techniques' (Davies, 1996: 1150). He argues that internal growth and direction are reinforced by the cost structure (the high fixed costs) of LTS and, therefore, economies of scale and scope should be accommodated in any analysis of their evolution. The selection environments in Hughes's model are influenced primarily by technological factors based on technological efficiency, reliability, compatibility and political factors such as 'vested interests' although he does examine economic factors such as the load factor. In this sense, Hughes stresses the importance of non-market factors in shaping technological change:

> we should abandon the misconception that only economic values and forces shape technology. In our century, engineers and managers preoccupied with economics have dominated the design of technology for the market, but the primacy of economics has not always been the case nor will market economics necessarily play such a dominant role in the future. (Hughes, 1994: 436)

As Dosi (1982) suggests, however, economic factors such as marketability, profitability, reduction of production costs and the search for new markets are fundamental forces in capitalist economies influencing technological change.

Finally, the role of users in inducing innovation and forcing the transformation of systems is conspicuously absent in studies employing the LTS approach (Summerton, 1994). The innovation process is an interactive process, often involving both users and producers (von Hippel, 1988; Lundvall, 1988). On the basis of a study of Swedish factory automation, Carlsson and Jacobsson (1994) emphasize the role of advanced local user-firms with significant problem-identification and problem-solving capabilities in the diffusion of new technology in the local market. Antonelli (1999) also points to the important role of large users in the process of technological change in the case of telecommunications systems. Increasingly, large users have been actively involved in the battle to achieve control of networks.

From a different angle, Callon (1995) points out that first users are often closely associated with the design and early development stages of a new technological system. Therefore the identities and choice of the first users are extremely important in the context of technological development and competition. This may be one explanation for the irreversibility process in a technological innovation, that is the increasing returns to adoption (Arthur, 1988) based on economies of scale, network externalities and the learning process. Von Hippel (1988) and Porter (1990) also emphasize the importance of 'lead users' and 'domestic advanced users'. Von Hippel (1988) defines 'lead users' as those that possess particular real-world experience and those that expect high rents from a solution to a need because their needs become general in a marketplace months or years in the future.

In summary, the LTS approach provides a useful conceptual framework and model for examining the complex and dynamic process of technological system evolution, in particular, infrastructure systems, integrating technological, social and political factors. Owing to the ambiguity surrounding its boundaries, however, the LTS approach fails to accommodate economic factors such as economies of scale and scope and network externalities in explaining the growth of a technological system. The knowledge nature of a technological system and the consideration of the role of advanced users also need to be accommodated.

2.5   THE POLITICAL ECONOMY OF LOCALIZATION

In order to find a way to answer the questions of how certain technological systems develop in countries other than where they were invented and why the performance of the transferred technology varies between countries, the concept of localization needs to be articulated.

The process of the localization of a technological system has often been analysed as technological diffusion. A vast number of studies[10] in this field have established the general proposition that the diffusion curve when plotted over time follows a certain pattern; for instance, that of a cumulative normal curve (Mansfield, 1961; Griliches, 1957; Bain, 1964; Rogers, 1983; Bass, 1969) or a cumulative lognormal curve (Davies, 1979). With respect to the diffusion of technology, the epidemic model assumes that agents are boundedly informed about a new technology and that the diffusion process reflects the process of information acquisition; whereas the equilibrium diffusion model defines the process of diffusion in terms of a moving equilibrium defined by the existence of heterogeneous economic agents and some process of change (endogenous or exogenous) that alters the nature of what is being diffused (Karshenas and Stoneman, 1992, 1995).

Since the 1960s, international technology diffusion analyses have been heavily influenced by the product life-cycle approach (Vernon, 1966;

Hirschman, 1967) and epidemic model. These approaches have provided some insights into the differences in rates of technological innovation between countries. For instance, in a product life-cycle approach, the speed and extent of international diffusion of innovations is expected, first, to be dependent on the wealth and technological capacity of the adopting country and, second, to follow the pattern of domestic diffusion within advanced countries. However the product life-cycle approach has been criticized because it employs a linear model of the progress of technological change from invention to innovation to imitation and diffusion. Bell and Albu point out that the traditional diffusion model defines 'innovation as development of new kinds of machinery', and 'diffusion as acquisition and installation of new machinery, which has already been developed elsewhere' (Bell and Albu, 1999: 1716–18). These definitions suggest that technological innovations from developed countries will be passively adopted by developing countries after they have become pervasive in the developed countries. However the relationship between invention, development and innovation is not linear but involves a dynamic and interactive process (Kline and Rosenberg, 1986). In fact technological change is a cumulative, continuous and interactive process of development of technological skills among users and improvements in production capacities, and often needs time for problem solving and adaptation. The neoclassical diffusion models are mainly based on assumptions about equilibrium, infinite rationality and full information, assumptions that do not take account of the dynamic and evolutionary process of technological change (Metcalfe, 1988).[11] More importantly, the technology examined using these diffusion models is almost exclusively concerned with machinery (capital goods) or consumer goods.[12] There have been few attempts made to explain the systemic nature of technological innovation and diffusion.

Technoeconomic perspectives tend to view the localization of a technological system as a specific learning mechanism and an economic selection process. The learning process involves various interactions between suppliers and users. The economic selection process of a technological system mainly refers to the process of competition and collaboration between the existing and alternative technologies. The dynamics of the substitution and complementarity process are often related to a social learning process as technological innovation involves a change in behaviour and 'habits of thought' and, thus, changes in habitual modes of procedure for inquiry and problem solving, what Veblen called 'cumulative causation' (Veblen, 1919).

Sociotechnical approaches suggest that the localization of a technological system involves practical, symbolic, cognitive, organizational and social dimensions. For example, some scholars, including Sørensen (1996), Rip (1995), Deuten et al. (1997) and Silverstone and Hirsh (1992), extend the adaptive process to include sociocognitive aspects of the localization of a technological system focusing on the process of adaptation and use of new technology.

In the analysis of the evolution and the localization of a technological system, many authors include political economy perspectives in the analysis of the technology. For example, Sørensen argues that social learning is one of the basic features of sociotechnical change over time and that conflict, power and interests have to be assumed as inherent qualities of these processes of re-embedding universalized technology (Sørensen, 1996: 3). The adaptation is a response to a different environment and adaptation to the environment culminates in a distinctive style (Hughes, 1983). Therefore he emphasizes that the differences across regions and national systems arise from non-technological factors associated with the cultural context. The technoeconomic perspective also emphasizes the importance of the role of institutions in shaping technological change.

With economic and social reasoning, the political shaping of technology is critical in understanding the complex realities of the internationalization and localization of technological systems with strategic or military importance. Technological system transfer is influenced by technological capabilities and also the local and international economic and political structure (Rosenberg and Frischtak, 1985; Dyker, 1997). When, how and to what extent a techno-logical system is transferred often involves international politics and is influenced by a country's technology accumulation capabilities. The interna-tional transfer of technology has been controlled by export control regimes in both the military and commercial arenas, particularly for technologies that may have a potential military application (Walker, 1994; Andrews, 1995). The export of computers has been controlled by the USA since World War II and technology transfer of the Internet was also restricted to US military allies during cold war period (see Chapter 5).

The evolution of a technological system involves struggles for control over a system and raises economic and political power issues (Nelkin, 1979a, 1979b). Political forces often influence the priorities given to the use of science and technology and shape perceptions of their impacts and direct the means of control (Nelkin, 1979a). Technological development often raises political issues such as 'efficiency versus equity', 'benefits versus risks', 'regulation versus freedom of choice' and 'science versus traditional values' (Nelkin, 1979b). Hård (1993: 418) argues that 'the ability of a society to favor technical change is a result of conflicts taking place in a large number of arenas and concerning not only monetary gains but also property rights and the control of production processes, recognition, and legitimacy, as well as political power and authority'. In fact, economic power cannot be sepa-rated from political power (Skocpol, 1979). Mansell (1993) stresses that the dynamics of power relations in the appropriation and control of innovations are critical in influencing the direction of technological change and, thus, industrial change.

Strange (1988: 23) also points out that 'it is the power that determines the relationship between authority and market'. The biased, uneven and unequal power relations in the process of interactions between production and consumption, between states and markets, and between local and global interests, shape the dynamics of technological change (Silverstone and Mansell, 1996). Many scholars also examine the asymmetric power structure between countries which shapes economic, technological and political outcomes (Wallerstein, 1974a, 1974b; Strange, 1996; Czempiel and Rosenau, 1989). Historically the Internet system was developed as an efficient knowledge acquisition, transformation and distribution tool for applying the power of converging information processing and communication within science and technology communities. As is analysed in Chapter 5, the Internet system was developed as an arrangement of national research networks in the USA during the 1980s and its global expansion began in the late 1980s with the connection of national research networks in other countries as a result of collaboration among international academic communities.

In this sense, it is worth noting the structure of production and distribution of knowledge. Modern science and technology are increasingly shaped by local and global interactions (Disco and Meulen, 1998; Shrum and Shenhav, 1995; Watson-Verran and Turnbull, 1995; Turnbull, 1993; Schott, 1993). Disco and Meulen (1998) argue that implemented technology is a phenomenon emerging simultaneously at the local and global levels, rather than being the direct result of deliberate local actor strategies. They also argue that global orders emerge from heterogeneous local practices through the mechanisms of abstraction and aggregation, and that the global order includes various kinds of institutions such as 'markets, political regimes, five-year plans, legal systems, religious beliefs, the prevailing technological state of art or the current state of scientific theorizing' (Disco and Meulen, 1998: 325).[13]

Global and local interactions involved in generating and distributing technological knowledge are influenced by global knowledge systems. Watson-Verran and Turnbull (1995) stress the local–global tension of different knowledge systems between countries reflecting their local cultural contexts. Shrum and Shenhav (1995) and Schott (1993) put emphasis on the geopolitical features of science and technology communities, that is, uneven power relations in the global science and technology communities: 'the world technical community is now reality, but characterized by high level of differentiation and inequality' (Shrum and Shenhav, 1995: 632). Schott (1993) also argues that the global scientific community is informally organized by a global web of collegial ties, but in the structure of the centre and periphery reflecting uneven power relations in global knowledge systems. Turnbull asserts that 'the major differences between western science and other knowledge systems lie in the question of power' (Turnbull, 1993: 48). Strange points to the asymmetric structure of global knowledge systems:

> But just as the power to determine what shall be produced by whom and on what terms constitutes structural power in production, so the power to determine what knowledge shall be sought; how it shall be accumulated and applied; how and where knowledge once accumulated shall be stored; and to whom it shall be communicated and on what terms, constitutes another kind of structural power in the world society and in the world economy. (Strange, 1989: 168)

In this book, the localization of a technological system is defined as the continuous adaptation of a technological system to a different place and time and different economic and social contexts, rather than the passive diffusion – acquisition and installation of new machinery as proposed by traditional diffusion models. The localization of a technological system involves economic, social and cultural changes and is influenced by the power structure and dynamics of local and global interplays.

2.6 CONCLUSION

The design of a technological system involves dynamic interactions between technologies and cultural, social, economic and political developments. There are two main approaches to uncovering the complex and dynamic process of technological system development. The technoeconomic approach argues that technical change is shaped by dynamic competition through continuous innovation and disequilibria mechanisms, based on uncertainty, learning and path dependence. From a technoeconomic perspective the development of a technological system can be seen as the process of learning and continuous interaction between users and suppliers embedded in the system and knowledge accumulation in both firms and the wider technological, economic and social systems of a country, rather than the passive diffusion – acquisition and installation of new machinery. The process of competition among the existing and alternative technologies is argued to be mainly based on an economic selection process that produces a process of substitution and complementarity within technological development. Scholars working in this tradition argue that the different direction and rate of technological accumulation between countries are mainly attributed to the different knowledge systems (innovation systems) of a country for supporting the acquisition, distribution and generation of new technological knowledge.

However this approach fails to integrate the aspects of technology as communities, the importance of design factors and the socialization process of knowledge. The dynamics of global and local interplay of many factors need to be considered in the NIS. These approaches also encounter limitations in terms of the measurement of knowledge systems.

The sociotechnological approaches put emphasis on the choices in the design of a certain technological system among possible but different paths and, thus, on social responsibilities for technological change. Among these theories, the LTS approach provides a useful analytical framework for examining the complex and dynamic process of technological system evolution by integrating technological, social and political factors. However the LTS approach fails to integrate the economics of technological change, the knowledge nature of a technological system and the role of advanced users in the analysis of a technological system design paradigm.

The concept of localization discussed in this chapter will also be used to examine the dynamics of collaboration and competition between the Internet system and other technological systems which have been influenced by local and global tensions in both the geopolitical and the contextual sense. 'Localization' is the term used throughout this book to refer to the economic, social and political processes of adaptations and accommodations that occur when a technological system that has been invented and developed in one place is taken to another, and following innovations. Various factors influencing the performance of the localization are also identified and elaborated in Chapter 7.

NOTES

1. Freeman (1994a) and Williams and Edge (1996) include extensive critical surveys on theoretical and empirical work in this field.
2. The contention of Bell and Albu that it is possible to distinguish knowledge systems from production systems at firm level leads to the idea that the combination of internally organized capabilities and external knowledge resources produces a relevant unit of analysis, 'the associated materials-centered systems of production and trade' (Bell and Albu, 1999: 1718–23).
3. The knowledge features of technology are important because, as Layton (1974) stresses, without knowledge (know-how) tools are useless and they cannot be separated one from another. Technological knowledge formally originates from science, and tacitly from work processes (Jacot, 1997). Views on 'a technology as knowledge' can be divided roughly into the cognitive approach (relatively more focused on knowledge creation from science) and the organizational approach (relatively more focused on knowledge creation from work).
4. North (1994) also argues that the political and economic institutions are underlying determinants of economic performance as they form the incentive structure of a society.
5. Niosi *et al.* (1993) present some crude measures of national characteristics in innovation system in terms of units, flows and the performance.
6. David and Foray (1994: 13) introduce the concept of the 'distribution power' of an innovation system based on the degree of codification, completeness of disclosure and ownership status.

7. Detailed discussions about common theoretical ground and differences in these theories are well presented in Bijker and Law (1992) and Williams and Edge (1996).
8. System builders preside over technological projects from concept and preliminary design through research, development and deployment, in other words they play leading roles in designing systems that incorporate both organizational and technical components. However they are different from project managers in that they need to cross disciplinary and functional boundaries, for example, to become involved in funding and political stage setting (Hughes, 2000: 8).
9. Summerton (1994) argues that the reverse salients that led to the transformation of the existing infrastructure systems were negative externalities such as congestion, environmental impacts and risks and political ideologies – contingencies that produce changing competitive conditions among systems.
10. See the literature surveys by Rogers (1995), Sarkar (1998) and Geroski (2000).
11. Among many authors, Metcalfe (1988, 1995) and Gold (1981, 1988) provide excellent discussions on the limitations of these diffusion models in the studies of technology.
12. See Karshenas and Stoneman (1992).
13. Concepts of 'governance', 'regime' and 'order' have been used in the international relations discipline. For example, Rosenau (1992: 4) suggests the definition of governance as 'a system of rule that works only if it is accepted by the majority (or, at least, by the most powerful of those it affects), whereas governments can function even in the face of widespread opposition to their policies'. Krasner (1983) defines international regimes as 'arrangements – as sets of implicit or explicit principles, norms, rules, and decision-making procedures around which actors' expectations converge – for sustaining and regulating activities across national boundaries'. Young (1989: 13) distinguishes international order and regime, in that the former refers to 'broad framework arrangements governing the activities of all (or almost all) the members of international society over a wide range of specific issues' and the latter means 'more specialised arrangements that pertain to well-defined activities, resources, or geographical areas and often involve only some subset of the members of international society'. These concepts are also widely used in other disciplines. For example, Campbell *et al.* (1991) apply the concept of governance to the studies of government and industry relations. They argue that governance includes markets, bureaucratic hierarchies, associations and informal networks and the state plays the unique role in the governance transformation process (Campbell *et al.*, 1991: 3).

3. Economics and politics of telecommunication systems

3.1 INTRODUCTION

The Internet, a sub-system of telecommunications, consists of computer networks built largely upon the existing telecommunication infrastructure. The Internet can be defined as a network of interconnected computer networks, which communicate with each other globally using a common communications protocol: Transmission Control Protocol/Internet protocol (TCP/IP).[1]

This chapter discusses the technological, economic and political characteristics of telecommunications to understand the dynamic processes of the Internet system development and its implications for economies and societies. As discussed in Chapter 4, the inventions and growth of data network including the Internet have been either facilitated or restricted by the institutional changes in the traditional telecommunications system.

Many authors argue that the Internet is introducing a new industrial paradigm for telecommunications system and information infrastructure. For example, Kavassalis and Lehr argue that 'the Internet will eventually emerge as a significant force of a more open, less integrated industry structure' (Kavassalis and Lehr, 1998). However the future industrial structure of the Internet is closely related to that of the telecommunications system. The growth of the Internet system is tied to its integration into the telecommunications system by coupling technologies, and consolidation of market players is discussed in Chapters 4 and 5.

Section 3.2 reviews the governance of telecommunications. The governance and management of telecommunications have varied in different countries reflecting different historical experiences, traditions and legal system. Different governance of telecommunications between the USA and European countries affected the design of computer networks (see Chapter 4). Academic discourses on the governance of telecommunications in the USA which have influenced changes in the governance of telecommunications globally are presented.

Section 3.3 discusses technological, economic and social implications of the telecommunications system, focusing on network and infrastructure literature. Recently technological and economic characteristics of the telecommunications system have been analysed in the literature of network industries. The strategic importance of communications and information infrastructure to the societies and economies is also often examined in the literature of infrastructure.

Liberalization was initiated in the USA, and other countries have followed. Following discussion of the international political economy in section 3.4, the globalization of telecommunications is examined in section 3.5. Several authors maintain that the reconfiguration of the telecommunications system will be brought about as a result of the Internet system, but the direction of this reconfiguration is not as clear-cut as they foresee. Section 3.6 looks at two of the claims about how the Internet system is influencing the evolution of the telecommunications system.

3.2 GOVERNANCE OF TELECOMMUNICATIONS

Centralized governance emerged from the very early competition between private actors (and between private and public actors) in the process of the system building of telecommunications in the USA and European countries.[2] In the UK, Sweden and other European countries, early telecommunications services were set up by private companies but they were transformed into state monopolies. Most European countries created government agencies for the management of Post, Telegraph and Telephone (the PTTs), while the USA established a system of publicly regulated private monopolies.

These differences reflect the different historical experiences, traditions and legal systems in these countries. The USA has rarely elected to support public enterprise and has had a different legal and constitutional structure from that of the European countries (Steinfield *et al.* 1994). In the USA, private ownership of infrastructure has been justified on the basis of individualism and as a counterbalance to political excesses. Bonbright (1940: 1) argues that the social control of public utilities was designed and developed to enforce public interest, without fatal offence to the individualism that 'Government should stay out of business'. As Jacobson and Tarr (1995: 5) point out, public ownership regarding the provision of infrastructures has been implemented only where private provision seemed impractical or inadequate. Various forms of infrastructure ownership and financing over the years in the USA have been shown to reflect a complex federal political system with numerous partially independent policy-making authorities.

In most European countries, monopolies have existed in the form of public enterprises. Most European countries viewed the telegraph and telephones services primarily as 'government social services not to be supplied by private businesses in the normal market' (Melody, 1997: 13). There were also various economic, social and political concerns for the PTT regime, including a secure source of public finance (revenue), the importance to national security and defence, and social service.[3] Also European countries did not put as much emphasis on antitrust regulation.

In the USA, regulation was designed to ensure that the monopoly operator behaved in the public interest. This involved regulation of entry, price, quality and conditions of service, as well as the imposition of a universal service obligation (Kahn, 1970a). Kearney and Merrill (1998) point out that the original paradigm of regulation in the USA, which was established with the Interstate Commerce Act's regulation of railroads, beginning in 1887, characterized by legislative creation of an administrative agency charged with general regulatory oversight of particular industries, did not depend on whether the regulated industry was a natural monopoly, and it was designed to advance accepted goals of reliability and, in particular, non-discrimination.

The issues concerning the governance of telecommunications have often been discussed in the literature of public utilities,[4] natural monopolies,[5] common carriers,[6] and universal service differently over time by various academic disciplines, mainly in the USA. While the broader literature on the governance of telecommunications consists of a wide range of overlapping concepts and debates, perhaps the core element has been that of natural monopoly and its regulation.[7] It is worth examining competing discourses on deregulation of telecommunications in the USA as they have contributed to the debates on the issues of reconfiguration of telecommunications globally.

In the USA, the telecommunications sector has been regulated on the basis of the principle that public policy should accomplish economic efficiency and distributional equity.[8] As Kahn (1970a) points out, the public interest theory is the fundamental basis for regulation in the law and in economics prior to 1970. This assumes that the basic purpose of regulation was to correct some market failure. Regulation is a substitute for market competition and protects the consumer from arbitrary exercise of monopoly power by the producer. For example, Sanders (1987) describes why economic regulation was justified in the USA.

> Far from being a natural development, free markets require consistent exertion by government to establish and maintain, and social groups of great diversity fight to harness the power of the state in order to protect themselves from the slings and arrows of outrageous markets. (Sanders, 1987: 117)

However the public interest theory has been attacked and criticized by three groups of scholars. Many economists have focused on inefficiencies of the regulated monopolies. For example, Averch and Johnson (1962) propose the hypothesis that cost-of-service regulation gives an incentive to distort a regulated firm's input choices, usually overcapitalizing to expand its rate base.

Even though the hypothesis is fully supported by neither theoretical nor empirical observation, it has been used to investigate the alleged inefficiencies of cost-of-service regulation (Berg and Tschirhart, 1995).[9]

The regulatory capture argument was proposed by Stigler (1971) and Posner (1974) and developed by Peltzman (1976) and Becker (1983). They argue that the demand for regulation comes from firms' interests, and that firms can use regulation to enhance collusion, to erect barriers to entry, to restrict competition from substitute products or to obtain direct government subsidies, rather than from consumers who want regulation to protect them from a monopolist. Bernstein (1955) also argues that regulation by independent commissions in the USA 'encourages a showing of favoritism to the regulated groups, a narrow view of the public interest, an unrealistic concept of the democratic political process, and the maintenance of localism and particularism in Congress' (Bernstein, 1955: 7).

The theory of rent seeking (Tullock, 1967; Krueger, 1974; Buchanan *et al.*, 1980) also contributed to the debates on the deregulation of public utilities. The authors working in this tradition argue that monopolies are mostly created by the imposition of government regulations and it is worthwhile for people to invest resources to influence government decisions. Rent seeking can be defined as investment of resources undertaken by individuals or groups of individuals with similar interests in the expectation of 'obtaining an increase (avoiding a decrease) in their wealth as a result of securing (blocking) changes in legal rights; or maximizing the benefits (minimizing the cost) of earlier policy changes that created non-exclusive rights' (Hartle, 1983: 539).

In the early 1980s, the contestable market theory challenged some conventional wisdom in the theory of regulation (Baumol *et al.*, 1982). In a contestable market, where there are no sunk costs, and all firms including potential have access to the same opportunities, deregulation is sufficient by itself to bring about efficient industrial performance. The threat of entry disciplines incumbent firms to meet consumers' demands with maximum efficiency, and there is no need at all for government regulation. This theory has influenced public policies by offering some guidance to policy makers. However certain scholars have noted that conditions for a contestable market are highly unlikely to be satisfied in practice. For example, Shepherd (1984: 585) argues that Baumol and his colleagues 'treat a specialised, extreme set of conditions, which are probably found in no real markets which have significant market power'. Entry involves substantial sunk costs and dominant incumbents have at their disposal a range of instruments for strategic entry deterrence.

With these new thoughts about regulation, many authors point to changes in economic conditions and technological innovations as main causes of deregulation. For example, Joskow (1989) points to changes in economic conditions in which the efficiencies of public utilities and regulation were questioned. Perl (1997) argues that an important cause of deregulation in the USA is technical feasibility of competition due to the growth in market size and technological change which is interrelated to artificial price–cost disparities created by regulatory policies for assuring either distributional objectives or the recovery of historic investments. Centrifugal innovations had been threatening the strong centralized and integrated networks since the 1960s (Antonelli, 1999). The emergence and development of computer networking technologies, including the Internet, are an example of centrifugal technological innovations.

However Derthick and Quirk (1985) emphasize political shaping of the deregulation. Noll and Owen (1983) argue that the establishment of regulation and deregulation involves the creation of groups with special interests. Perl (1997) argues that performance of the regulated public utilities, particularly telecommunications, has been widely regarded as quite good. McCormick *et al.* (1984) also argue that the returns to deregulation are much lower than those suggested by the economists, including Harberg (1954) and Posner (1975). Kearney and Merrill (1998) have concluded that interest groups have discovered that regulatory change is in their interests, and that an ideological consensus has emerged among economists and other policy elites that the original paradigm entails risks of regulatory failure that exceed the risks of market failure under the new paradigm.

In Europe, in the 1980s and 1990s, with the beginning of market liberalization, regulatory bodies, whose goals included the public interest and universal service, began to emerge.[10] However, in most European countries, the regulatory regime was often shaped by developmental objectives because they were catching up with the US.[11] The concept of universal service emerged as one of the most important policy issues with liberalization of the telecommunications market. The concept of 'public service' has been stronger in European countries than in the USA, where concepts of 'universal service' had greater currency (Garnham and Mansell, 1991). Universal service principles in telecommunications were introduced in the EU by the Council resolutions of 7 February 1994 (94/C 48/01, OJ C48/1, 16.02.94). It set out the major elements constituting universal service at Community level and provided guidance as to the principles to be applied to the financing of universal service in achieving the goal of universal service in a competitive environment.[12]

Universal service policy has been an important battleground in the design of governance and regulation between policy makers and market players, and between market players in the liberalized environment and rapid technological innovation.[13] New regulatory frameworks for universal service in the fully liberalized environment were established in the USA and European countries in 1996. The goals of universal service were reviewed and mandated by the 1996 Telecommunications Act in the USA. The EU also proposed guidelines for the universal service policy in preparation for fully opening telecommunications markets to competition from 1 January 1998.[14]

In the process of liberalization, the policy design for ensuring the existing universal service provision has been one of the most important issues in designing new governance of telecommunications. Questions raised in implementing universal service in the liberalized environment are (a) whether it is desirable and/or sustainable, (b) how much it would cost and who should pay for the existing network and the expansion of the network and (c) to what extent the definition and components of universal services should be extended, reflecting technological advances.[15]

The universal service concept has been recognized in different ways over time. In general, sociopolitical approaches towards universal service discuss the realm of policy objectives and justification while economic approaches concentrate on how to implement it in practice. The former look at the demand side from social integration while the latter focus on the supply side in achieving the allocative efficiency. Hudson and Parker (1990) and Schement (1995) stress the importance of universal service to rural development and social integration. Graham *et al.* (1996) also argue that 'the availability of telecommunications services relates to the issue of social cohesion and citizenship'. Dinc *et al.* (1998) argue that universal service policy is aimed at high penetration rates using a subsidy mechanism that lowers rates in order to avoid drop-offs from the network. Milne (1998) focuses on the affordability of telephones and gives weight to the political will to achieve social goals. Hadden distinguishes 'fairness', which has a welfare component, from 'universality' which suggests a ubiquitous improvement of network functions (1994: 48). It is well known that the argument of a universal network was used for the justification of monopoly in the USA.[16] With explicit government subsidies the idea of cross-subsidy is historically acknowledged as a means of achieving universal service but it was challenged (or it was not sustainable) in the liberalized environment.[17] Economists often argue that the existing mechanism of the provision of universal services is not compatible with the liberalization of the telecommunications market. Mueller (1999) criticizes universal service policies as a form of wealth redistribution. Wolak (1996: 163) also argues that 'there appears to be little loss in household level welfare and little, if any, reduction in the number of households connected to the local telephone network, due to the projected reductions in this cross-subsidy brought about by an increasing amount of competition in all telecommunications markets'. Maher (1999) argues that local rates should be geographically de-averaged and based on costs,[18] since entry that would occur under these conditions would be efficient as opposed to being motivated by possibilities of cream skimming or the avoidance of usage-based access charges. Rosston and Wimmer (2000) argue that universal service programmes have little

effect on telephone rates and result in high taxes, which distort market outcomes and cause competitive distortions. They also argue that selective
programmes are cheaper and perform better than cost-based rules that pay a
subsidy to all customers in an area because low-income householders are
likely to live in both rural and urban areas.

The definition and the components of a universal service are still unde-
cided. Rapid technological advances in telecommunications, for example the
development of the Internet system, add difficulties in defining universal
services. In reality, the definition and components of universal services appear to be shaped by the power relations between stakeholders, particularly
between regulators and market players.

3.3   TECHNOLOGICAL AND ECONOMIC CHARACTERISTICS OF TELECOMMUNICATIONS

Recently academic discourses on network industries and infrastructure have
often been used to examine the governance of telecommunications, focusing
on various technological, economic and social features. The technological
interdependence and network externalities in both demand and supply of
telecommunications largely stem from a telecommunication system's physical network. Infrastructure literature from the developmental concern – not
only economic concern (importance to the market economy itself) but also
and more importantly social and political concerns (looking at socioeconomic features of telecommunications) – stresses the role of government in
developing and promoting telecommunications infrastructure and services,
considering their importance to the balanced and sustainable development of
society as a whole.

Network Literature

The network systems including telecommunications, electricity and power,
and transportation systems have fundamental technological characteristics in
common: interconnectedness, technological interdependence and control of
service flow.[19] They employ production and distribution facilities and the
technical performance of the networks depends on their interconnectedness
and the overall performance of the system depends on the structure and
control mechanisms. Such systems have a structure in which heterogeneous
components are bound together in a physical network and the coordination or
control of service flows (traffic, electrical power, communications signals)
within these systems is critical to their effective operation (Hughes, 1983;
David and Bunn, 1988; David, 1992). A typical telecommunications system

consists of four types of network components including terminal equipments, switches and transmission (long distance) networks, and access networks.

The technological performance of network systems involves interconnectedness imposing a need to achieve a minimum level of compatibility and interoperability among the components. This can be accomplished by 'ex ante design coordination through the adoption of standards, or the provision ex post of "gateways" connecting otherwise isolated subsystems' (David, 1992: 104). If compatibility problems can be overcome, the network can be expanded beyond a 'critical mass' or 'threshold' scale of activity consistent with economic viability, instead of remaining at a stable, equilibrium level of production that would be achieved by the operation of an unregulated, competitive market process (ibid.).

Network externalities support a fully interconnected network as the most efficient supply structure. However it is well known that the incumbent operator with a large network has little incentive to make itself compatible with new entrants or to offer access to subscribers. In the telecommunications industry, competitors cannot provide services to customers through the local loop without purchasing the access service from the incumbent operator. Thus regulation of interconnection is called for in order to achieve network externalities. The network externalities argument also justifies universal service provision: 'welfare is increased by subsidising additional subscribers, since the existing subscribers enjoy benefits of an extended network that marginal subscribers would not take into account when calculating private costs and benefits' (Michie, 1997:1).

Because of strong technological interrelatedness, technological change in network systems may also produce a high level of lock-in. The opportunities for change in each component of the network system may be constrained by the need for compatibility and interoperability with the rest of the components of the system (Antonelli, 1992). Therefore Antonelli (1986) points out that in network systems innovations tend to be introduced only after each component has been assembled and evaluated in the context of the entire network. Unbalanced technological advance between components often impedes system development.

The network systems have structural network externalities in terms of both demand and supply. The concept of network externalities has been employed by many economists to explain the economic characteristics of network systems.[20] Network externalities arise from demand interdependence and technological interrelatedness (Rohlfs, 1974; Katz and Shapiro, 1986). Katz and Shapiro (1986: 146) define demand network externalities as 'the benefit that a consumer derives from the use of a good [which] is often an increasing function of the number of other consumers purchasing compatible items'. They distinguish between direct network externalities, which arise from networked systems, and indirect network externalities (or network effects) that are associated with the provision of durable goods (hardware) and complementary goods or services (software). Network externalities are usually thought to be positive, in that increases in the size of the network are accompanied by an increase in the collective demand for network services.

The demand for telecommunications services can be split into two complementary parts; that is, the demand for access to the telephone system and demand for usage. Access externalities arise from the value of customers' ability to be reached via a network and are related to the number of customers on the network wanting to reach that customer while call externalities arise from the value of calling, again related to the number of people available to call (Rohlfs, 1974). The demand for access is closely linked to the market (both supply and demand) for telecommunications services (Stehmann, 1995). A service must be available to induce demand.

Supply-side network externalities affect the technical performance of a system as a whole and give feedback about the profits of other component suppliers. This is related to the system's performance and its user demand compared to alternative technologies (David, 1985). To realize positive externalities, there must be excess capacity in the network. Excess capacity is common in network systems because of their capital-intensive characteristics and their high level of technical and economic durability. Pecuniary externalities may arise from cost-minimizing behaviour in the presence of excessive capacities. However negative externalities also may arise if the growth of the network is accompanied by congestion or other overload effects (David and Bunn, 1988).

Achieving economic and social goals by the provision of telecommunications involves a high degree of coordination between a capital-intensive supply network and complex and diverse patterns of consumer usage. In particular, economies of scale and scope in production, large indivisibilities in capacities and technological efficiency have been a justification for a centralized organizational structure of networks. However this argument has been challenged by proponents of decentralized governance. For example, the argument for the centralized governance considers capacity investment as the first-order determinant of profit but proponents of competition argue that the margin is not in capacity but in its utilization. Economies of scale can be achieved not only by the extension of capacity but also by more efficient utilization. The proponents of competition also argue that the gains in operating efficiency assured by integrated supply through the centralized institutional network system may be made at the cost of inefficiencies in other areas resulting from monopoly supply and the variety of approaches that emerge to employ capacity, for example service competition.[21]

Infrastructure Perspective

The telecommunications system has been considered as an infrastructure, but the definition of 'infrastructure' is not clear. According to the World Bank (1994), the infrastructure includes public utilities (power, piped gas, telecommunications, water supply, sanitation and sewerage, waste collection and disposal), public works (major dam and canal works for irrigation and roads) and other transport sectors (railways, urban transport, ports and waterways, airports) and the social infrastructure which could include education and healthcare. Economists tend to define infrastructure with respect to concepts of public utilities, externalities, an essential minimum of services and natural monopolies (World Bank, 1994; Crandall, 1997). However there is no precise definition of an infrastructure.[22]

> Infrastructure is an umbrella term for many activities [that are also] referred to as 'social overhead capital' by such development economists as Paul Rosenstein-Rodan, Ranger Nurkes and Albert Hirschman. Neither term is precisely defined but both encompass activities that share technical features (such as economies of scale) and economic features (such as spillovers from users to non-users). (World Bank, 1994: 2)

Infrastructure – social overhead capital (SOC) – is essential for promoting growth in productivity and, as a consequence, producing increases in real income at the national level. Until recently, however, there have been few studies on the relationship between infrastructure and the economic growth.[23] After Aschauer (1989) included public sector capital in the aggregate production function, analyses on the relationship between infrastructure and economic growth have seen a sharp increase in concern over US growth and the quality, quantity and financing infrastructure capital (Holtz-Eakin and Schwartz, 1995). Cronin *et al.* (1993b) argue that investment in telecommunications infrastructure is causally related to the nation's total factor productivity and that contributions to aggregate and sectoral productivity growth rates from telecommunications advancements are both quantifiable and substantial. Esfahani and Ramirez (2003) also confirm that the contribution to GDP is substantial and generally exceeds the cost of those services. Despite controversies over techniques being used in the studies, infrastructure has been important to the economy (Gramlich, 1994).[24] Carlaw and Lipsey (2002) argue that conventional definitions of externalities miss many of spillovers that are both cause and consequence of the technological changes that underlie economic growth.

   As Jacobson and Tarr (1995: 3) point out, infrastructures are the structures and networks that frame and bind together modern societies and make it possible to undertake social and economic activity. The infrastructures such as telecommunications have important social goals including equity, human connectedness and the ability to bind a community together (Miller, 1986; Lundstedt, 1990; Graham *et al.*, 1996). Concepts of social capital and organizational capital suggested by Coleman (1988), Putnam (1993), Tomer (1987) and others capture the importance of intangible capitals embedded in social relationships and social resources enabling people to accomplish their purpose efficiently.[25] In developing countries infrastructure is more directly linked to overall development of the countries by integrating their economic and social resources and thus improving quality of life and competitiveness. In fact the social integration cannot be separated from economy as social relation is embedded within the economic activities (Polanyi, 1944; Granovetter, 1985).[26] The importance of these socioeconomic implications of telecommunications is often ignored by many economists who focus on issues of static efficiency in the provision of telecommunications services and networks.

3.4   THE POLITICAL ECONOMY OF GLOBALIZATION

The governance of telecommunications system changed dramatically during the last two decades of the 20th century.[27] The US initiated deregulation of finance, airlines and telecommunications in order to strengthen its strategic position and create competitive edge and demanded a free trade regime based upon the principles of market access, reciprocity, non-discrimination and most-favoured-nation applied multilaterally (Hulsink, 1996). Transnational firms were important to Public Telecommunications Operators (PTOs) in that generally they are the most profitable group of customers and the most advanced users of telecommunication services. Transnational firms, in particular in the financial sector, played a crucial role in the liberalization of telecommunications to enhance their international competitive and implement global strategies during the 1970s and 1980s. In the process of globalization of firms and economies, telecommunications have become a platform that provides a seamless advanced global communication network for them.[28]

In turn, the telecommunications sector itself has undergone an unprecedented globalization process.[29] For example, by 1993, the nine largest US telecommunications network operators (excluding AT&T and MCI) had 265 programmes in 52 different countries.[30] By the end of 1996, some 44 PTOs had been privatized, raising US$159 billion, and the vast majority of these privatizations involved foreign investors.[31] In 1994, the big four PTO global alliances including Concert Communications (the BT–MCI alliance), Global One (the French Telecom–Deutsche Telekom-Sprint alliance), WorldPartners (the equity partners of which include AT&T, Unisource, KDD and Singapore Telecom) and the Cable & Wireless Federation controlled about 68 per cent of the world outgoing international traffic.[32] Most PTOs in developed countries have expanded their geographical reach and operations into new domains through acquisitions and mergers and strategic alliances.

Globalization of PTO activities began in order to respond to economic globalization in general and liberalization of the telecommunications market led by the USA, in particular.[33] The rapid convergence between telecommunications, computing and broadcasting has also influenced PTOs' global expansion activities. PTOs in the USA and some other developed countries who initiated the liberalization pursued global expansion activities in order to obtain better profits or to make up the loss brought about by the new entrants in the domestic market. The profit margin for a basic telecommunication service was decreasing in most developed countries because of the mature basic telecommunications service market and relatively low profit margins from enhanced telephone services and bulk discount options. The increased level of competition also caused lower revenues for PTOs. The aggressive global activities of these PTOs and new entrants put competitive pressure on all PTOs in other countries and they also began global expansion. The motivation for globalization of PTOs includes creating a defensive shield to minimize the losses of customers in the domestic market and exploiting new commercial opportunities created by competition and privatization consortia, alliances, partnerships or distributorship.[34] The OECD (1995) describes a sequence of the globalization of telecommunications:

> Market liberalization triggered the growth of the 'chaos' through PTO globalisation. Globalisation thus may be seen as a way for PTOs to adjust to ever-increasing competition in both domestic and international markets. Once started in some countries the impacts of market liberalization are integrated in the globalizing economy, and put the pressure on other countries for (further) liberalization. (OECD, 1995: 65)

The institutional change on a global scale in the telecommunications system has been shaped by asymmetric international power relations (Cowhey, 1990; Dyson and Humphries, 1990; Strange, 1996; Sussman, 1997; Comer, 1998).[35] As Thatcher (1999) points out, regulatory reforms in the USA indirectly influenced changes in Europe by providing an example of change and sources of ideas in telecommunications and modifying the competitive dynamics of telecommunications. There was also direct pressure from US firms and policy makers for regulatory reform in other countries (Waverman and Sirel, 1997).

Dyson and Humphries (1990: 242) argue that the USA has, with its economic and technological power, forced other countries 'to transform the agenda of international political economy of communications towards deregulation to match the domestic characteristics of its own economy'. Cowhey

(1990) argues that the USA, Japan and the UK had enough market power to push through the transformation of the global telecommunications regimes when they unilaterally changed their national telecommunications policies. Strange contends that the 'structural power' beneath the market power exercised by the USA forced the liberalization and privatization of the rest of the world (Strange, 1996: 105).[36] For example, the USA used the power of trade sanctions where a bilateral agreement on opening foreign market was not successful (not effective). In 1988, the Telecommunications Trade Act was passed which included provisions for the US government to retaliate against unfair trade practices under section 301 of the Omnibus Trade and Competitiveness Act 1988. Japan, Brazil, Canada, South Korea, Taiwan and European PTTs were identified as particular targets.

As Lee (1996) stresses, along with major countries and private interests, international organizations, notably the ITU, OECD, WIPO (World Intellectual Property Organization) and GATS (General Agreement on Trade in Service), have contributed to the globalization of telecommunications. Lee (1996: 177) argues, 'hegemony has come about through the material dominance of core state and private interests, the ideological dominance of neoliberalism in the theory and practice of international organization, and the institutional maintenance and reproduction of this dominance by the ITU'. Freeman and Louçã point to the contradiction in the behaviour of the technology leaders, in that the UK in the 19th century and the USA in the 20th century typically advocated liberalization of the world market to expand their economic territory and, at the same time, tried to 'restrict access to technological know-how, through change in the intellectual property regime (IPR)' (Freeman and Louçã, 2001: 366). Ernst and O'Connor (1989) also point to these two different strategies of OECD countries (led by the USA). However the strategic behaviour of the technological leaders has often been confronted by challenges from followers in the conflicts brought about by radical technological innovations.[37]

3.5 NATURAL PATH ARGUMENTS AND THE INTERNET SYSTEM

The Internet is viewed as a major driving force of the technical and institutional changes in the telecommunications system. The growth of the Internet calls for radical technological and operational capability shifts, that is, shifts from circuit switching to packet switching, from centralized control to distributed intelligence and from a voice-centric service to multiservices (see, for example, Kavassalis and Solomon, 1997; Kavassalis and Lehr, 1998).[38] The growth in Internet use has resulted in a huge increase in data traffic.[39]

This requires substantial bandwidth beyond the existing telecommunications networks and new technological and operational capabilities for handling packet switching and multiservice. The growth of the Internet system is also changing the landscape of the international telecommunications infrastructure and the international revenue settlement regime (see Chapter 5). For example, Canada, Mexico and Sweden have emerged as new regional gateways to the Internet (OECD, 1999b). As Lehr and Kiessing (1998) point out, the emergence of the Internet reduces the validity of the existing regulatory jurisdiction based on geographic boundaries.

As discussed in Chapter 4, institutional changes in telecommunications have facilitated the development of the Internet. Most countries began to transform their telecommunications markets by introducing and promoting competition and privatization during the 1990s. Three major related events occurred during this period: the World Trade Organization (WTO) agreement on telecommunications services, the European Union (EU) policy on full liberalization of telecommunications services and the US Telecommunications Act 1996 (Melody, 1999). The chairman of the Federal Communication Commission (FCC) in the USA suggested certain policies, based on a neoliberal principle, for building a global information network, saying:

> I have been guided by four basic principles which I believe have global applicability, and may be particularly significant for developing countries: (a) privatization, liberalization and competition; (b) deregulation as competition develops; (c) universal access to communications services and technology; and (d) opportunity for underserved populations. (Kennard, 1999: 2)

However, in the face of the technological innovations brought about by the Internet system, the future evolution of the telecommunications system (that is, towards decentralized control, prevailing diversity and competition) is not so clear. Some of the recent research on the telecommunications network assumes a 'natural' evolutionary path. For example, it is argued that telecommunications have evolved from the traditional monopoly, through a transition period, into a highly competitive market structure (Noam, 1994a: 286). Many researchers have focused on the way rapid technological changes lowered entry barriers and how competition in telecommunications has benefited the economy, consumers and suppliers. For example, Baumol and Sidak (1994) argue that the market structure has evolved from a natural monopoly towards something closer to perfect competition or perfect contestability, as a result of technological change. Rosston and Teece show that technological innovations significantly lower entry barriers and that 'the distinction between local and long distance will disappear in its entirety, and the distinction between telephone, computer and television will also evaporate' (1995: 813).

The Internet system, the 'network of networks' (Noam, 1994a), has become the centre of this 'natural path' argument. It is expected to transform telecommunications systems fundamentally. For example, the technological and market convergence driven by the growth of the Internet system is expected to integrate global telecommunications systems in an essentially new way, and ultimately to transform them into open, flexible and decentralized systems (Kavassalis and Solomon, 1997; Kavassalis and Lehr, 1998). The 'natural path' of telecommunications evolution argument suggests, on the one hand, that technological changes are facilitating decentralized control of networks and, on the other, that these technological changes are being accomplished by an institutional transformation towards greater reliance on the competitive market mechanism.

However, the evolutionary pattern of the telecommunication system has been differently interpreted by other writers. For example, Trebing (1996) argues that telecommunication systems are following a 'natural path' due to network economies resulting from economies of scale and scope and network externalities. In this case, the technological and market convergence brought about by the Internet is expected to reduce competition rather than to strengthen it. Katz (1996: 1080) points out that 'increased economies of scope, the increased use of multi-service bundling strategies and a rise in the importance of network effects [network externalities] lead to greater concentration of industry'. Gong and Srinagesh (1996) maintain that vertical and horizontal integration may be a 'natural' outgrowth of competition in the converging industries because of increased complexity in a system of systems environment which is increasingly deregulated. In reality, despite liberalization and pro-competitive policies, access markets in the USA and UK are still controlled by the traditional PTOs.

Recent estimates of local market competition show a 98 per cent monopoly in the USA and 89 per cent in the UK. Given the persistence of monopoly control over final customer access, strong oligopoly in major service areas, and dominance of the traditional PTOs in major competitor positions in one another's markets, it would appear that the effect of competition may be quite limited (Melody, 1999: 22). The global integration of telecommunications systems, which is accompanied by liberalization and privatization, may provide the basis for the creation of a supranational network operator and therefore more *centralized control* over the telecommunications systems. In this regard, Kiessling and Blondeel (1998) admit that a centralized regulatory authority needs to be enforced, as it is very import in the light of industry convergence and globalization driven by the growth of the Internet.

From an institutional and political economy perspective, some scholars have sought to uncover the complex reality of technological and institutional changes. They focus on analysing the power relations embedded in the design process of new technologies. For example, Mansell (1993) argues that the evolution of telecommunications systems has been controlled by a handful of actors, in particular the strategies of corporate actors in the early 1990s. Technological changes in telecommunications, for example the introduction of fibre-optic transmission technology in combination with the digitalization of switching, may have reinforced integrated monopolistic control of national long-distance operations by a small number of oligopolistic firms.[40]

Actors with different goals reflecting their different interests often collaborate or compete with each other (Cawson *et al.*, 1990). Cawson and colleagues argue that various types of interactions between two basic conflicting forces, competition and collaboration, at levels differing from the local to the global, are critical for understanding the dynamics of industrial change. There have been numerous studies examining how telecommunications systems have been shaped differently by economic and political factors reflecting the interests of actors in the context of particular countries.[41]

Melody (1985) argues that national monopoly control regimes of telecommunications systems are being transformed into an intensified, but intermediate, unstable, oligopolostic rivalry among transnational corporations supported by their home country governments. Long before Melody's observation, Marx had noted capitalism's tendencies towards centralization, the merging of existing capital and concentration of capital and change in the distribution of capital that were discernible in the 19th century.[42]

Arnbak points to market failures or significant imperfections: 'A paradox would appear to emerge; even if market disciplines can now be relied upon for core/long distance networks, the benefits of a direct choice between such networks are hardly enjoyed by the majority of individual users or new entrants' (Arnbak, 2000: 486). As a consequence Levi-Faur points out: 'Because competition is always "imperfect" ... the competition state (and neo-liberalists) faces a paradox: *the greater the commitment of the competition state to the promotion of competition, the deeper its regulation will be*' (Levi-Faur, 1998: 676).

Mansell (1993) argues that the economic and social aspects of the selection process of ICTs may reflect institutionalized biases in market power which may result in a widening of the existing disparities in the capabilities of production and usage of ICTs among users across and within countries. Without the enforcement of global governance, telecommunications liberalization will inevitably be shaped by the forces of centralization at the global level and, as a result of the economic and political characteristics of telecommunications, the rate and direction will be influenced by the biased global power relations and tensions between the state and market (Tarjanne, 1999).

In summary, there are two versions of the evolution of telecommunications systems. One describes recent developments including the advent of the

Internet, in terms of growing diversity, decentralized control and intense competition as a result of a large number of players with very low barriers to market entry. The other explains the same developments pointing to the growing influence of a small number of key players, centralization tendencies and fierce oligopolistic rivalry. This explanation suggests increasingly higher barriers to entry as consolidation of the Internet occurs as a consequence of the 'system of systems' evolutionary process. A political economy perspective is needed to reveal the complex realities of the Internet's evolution and the dynamic relationship between this and the telecommunications system.

3.6 CONCLUSION

We have examined the technological, economic and political characteristics of telecommunications in order to understand the evolution of the Internet. As discussed in Chapter 4, the inventions and growth of the data network including the Internet have been either facilitated or restricted by the institutional changes in the traditional telecommunications system. The different accounts of the governance of telecommunications in the USA and other countries have influenced the different technical choices on telecommunications. Academic discourses and policy debates on the regulation of telecommunications from various disciplines have been developed in the USA where government regulation was introduced to control private monopolies. There have been rigorous debates between groups of scholars and others who support government regulation to constrain market power and assure universal access to telecommunication services and those who share a common belief in the supremacy of the free market over regulatory intervention. The governance of telecommunications in the USA is argued to have been politically shaped.

Recent network literature provides insights into the sectoral characteristics of a telecommunications system, such as its technological interrelatedness, economies of scale and scope and network externalities. One of the most important characteristics is its 'systemic' nature. Infrastructure literature captures the socioeconomic implications of telecommunications.

Some scholars point out that there have been different strategies on the market liberalization policies between countries, reflecting their relative technological powers. The liberalization and globalization of telecommunications that have been pursued reflect stakeholders' interests under the uneven international power structure.

The Internet system is considered to be a driving force of institutional change towards market governance. However it is also argued that relationships between the Internet and the telecommunications systems are shaped by technological and institutional changes which, in turn, are likely to be shaped by conflicting interests among actors within a country and the uneven global power structure.

Chapter 4 implements the research agenda introduced in the previous two chapters by considering the battles between the systems in the development of computer networking technologies, focusing on the Internet and the X.25 systems.

NOTES

1. For a description of the technological and organizational components of the Internet, see also Comer (1991), Werbach (1997), Quarterman and Carl-Mitchell (1994), Cukier (1998) and OECD (1998a, 1998b).
2. See Brock (1981), Noam (1992) and Davies (1994).
3. See, for example, Steinfield *et al.* (1994).
4. Miller (1995: 273) argues that the concept of public utility was originated in the USA in order to provide social control for preventing abuse of private market power by firms providing essential services. The most critical issue in defining a certain sector as a public utility was whether the sector was 'affected with a public interest' (Bonbright *et al.*, 1988: 7). Bonbright (1940) and Kahn (1970a) put an emphasis on economic and political rationale for a unique status of public utilities as the regulated monopolies: essential nature of services, the size of importance to other industries and economy (infrastructure) and natural monopolies. Dimock (1933) argues that the concept of public utility is very old in the UK but it has not been developed to a systemic theory. He points out that the main reason that public utility doctrine has emphasized more in the USA than in the UK is to be found out in the American system of judicial supremacy as contrasted with the British regime of Parliamentary omnicompetence (Dimock, 1933: 24).
5. One of the classical definitions of natural monopoly was proposed by Kahn (1970a: 2): 'the technology of certain industries or the character of the service is such that the customer can be served at least cost or net benefit only by a single firm (in the extreme case)'. The allocative efficiency can be achieved by a single entity to minimize the value of resources used to supply the market. He argues that the long-run decreasing cost is an indispensable condition for natural monopoly. Since then, Kahn (1970a) argued that economies of scale have been considered a key property of natural monopoly. Technical features of natural monopoly were extended to a multiproduct. Baumol (1977) proposed subadditivety of the cost function as a new concept in testing for natural monopoly in the multiproduct firm. This implies that every output combination is always produced more cheaply by a single firm.
6. See, for example, Noam (1994b), Frieden (1995) and Grieve and Levin (1996) for the concept of common carriers in telecommunications in the USA.
7. Hägg (1997) provides a brief survey of the core theoretical literature on the economics of public regulation and recent contributions on political and regulatory intuitions in the USA and Europe.
8. See, for example, Crew and Kleindorfer (1986).
9. Many different types of inefficiencies of regulated monopolies have been suggested. See, for example, Crew and Kleindorfer (1986: 156–7) and Winston (1998: 91–2).
10. See Thatcher (2002) for an analysis of independent regulatory agencies (IRAs) in the UK, France, Germany and Italy after deregulation. Kiessling and Blondeel (1998) investigate the telecommunications regulatory framework in the European Union (EU).
11. Chang (1997).
12. The Council Resolution of 22 July 1993 set the liberalization of all public voice telephony

services a major goal for its telecommunication policy, while maintaining universal service.

13. The volume of research on the universal service is ever increasing. See Melody (1999) and Tarjanne (1999) for universal service policy issues in the process of regulatory reform in general. Martenson (1998), Hart (1998) and Kiessling and Blondeel (1998) examine the universal service policy in the European Union. Prieger (1998), Noll (1998), Dinc *et al.* (1998), Rosston and Wimmer (2000) and Garcia-Murillo and MacInnes (2001) analyse conflicting interests and policy issues following the Telecommunications Act of 1996 in the USA.

14. EU, Universal Service for Telecommunications in the Perspective of a Fully Liberalised Environment: COM(96)73 of 14/3/96.

15. See, for example, Nett (1998), Weller (1999), Panzar (2000), Valletti (2000), Choné *et al.* (2002) and Madden *et al.* (2000).

16. See Dordick (1990), Mueller (1993) and Schiller (1998).

17. See Makarewicz (1991), Dordick and Fife (1991), Gabel (1995) and Prieger (1998).

18. The exisiting (previous) local rate was based upon the geographically averaged principle regardless of differences in the cost of providing telecommunication services and a uniformed tariff regardless of differences in consumers' usage – it should be changed reflecting actual cost of service provision in different areas and consumers' usage.

19. Despite some common features, each technological system has its own particular technological and economic characteristics. For example, alternative technological distribution systems, such as wireless or landlines, are enabled by technological changes and are not always complete substitutes for one another. The extent of systemic features also varies. Heterogeneity and changes in the characteristics and preferences of both final and intermediate consumers must also be considered in understanding the evolution of telecommunications systems.

20. According to Antonelli (1992) the relevance of externalities or external economies can be traced back to Marshall (1920) and Scitovsky (1954). Scitovsky (1954: 143) defines external economies as 'services (or disservices) rendered free (without compensation) by one producer to another'. Antonelli defines externalities as 'all forms of direct interdependence among the members of an economic system that do not operate through the market mechanism or that are not fully mediated by prices' (1992: 7).

21. See Stehmann (1995) for economic analysis on the controversies over monopoly versus competition and facility-based competition versus service competition.

22. Cain (1997: 118) argues that the term 'infrastructure' came into current use in the 1950s, when the military applied it to their permanent installations: their 'underlying' structure.

23. Cronin *et al.* (1993a) provide summaries of the previous studies investigating the relationship between telecommunications and economic growth.

24. However the relationship between infrastructure and economic growth has been controversial. See Esfahani and Rameriz (2003), Gramlich (1994) and Holtz-Eakin and Schwartz (1995).

25. See Dasgupta and Serageldin (1999), Sobel (2002), Dolfsma and Dannreuther (2003) and Carroll and Stanfield (2003) for more recent discussion on the issues of 'social capital'.

26. The concept of 'embeddedness' was suggested by Karl Polanyi (1944) and developed by Granovetter (1985). Holton (1992:19) points out: 'According to Polanyi, economists have neglected the first three types of economy in favor of a market-based economy, as the basis of their conceptualization of the economy. As such, economists have neglected the way in which the economy has been embedded in wider social relations where reciprocity, redistribution, and the household have been dominant. Instead economists have focused on the market which is the sole type of economy sharply differentiated from the remainder of society.'

27. See Dicken (1999) for the transforming processes towards a globalized world economy.

28. See, for example, Langdale (1989).

29. Kurisaki (1997) points to three different forms of PTO globalization: (1) new service options in the provision of existing international telecommunications service, (2) foreign direct investment (FDI), and (3) off-shore services provided by alliances between PTOs.

30. Trebing (1996).
31. ITU (1999a).
32. Ibid.
33. See OECD (1995: 33–41) for domestic and international factors of PTO globalization. They include globalization of large firms, market saturation in OECD countries, asymmetry in the level of liberalization between countries (for example, regulatory prohibition from entry to specific service areas and preparation for possible competition in the home country), exploiting economies of scale, increased opportunities for foreign investment, liberalization of, and competition in, international telecommunications, and technological advances and opportunities.
34. See Ioannidis (1994), OECD (1995), ITU (1997a), Chamoux (1997) and Kurisaki (1997).
35. The world system is based on the 'imbalance of international power' or 'asymmetrical dependences' (Wallerstein, 1974a, 1974b; Strange, 1996).
36. Strange defines structural power as 'the power to shape and determine the structures of global political economy within which other states, their political institutions, their economic enterprises and (not least) their scientists and other professional people have to operate' (Strange, 1988: 24–5).
37. See, for example, Ernst and O'Connor (1992).
38. Intellectual property (IP) has become a basis for engineering extensions to the telecommunication networks while other protocols provide alternative envelopes for carrying IP packets. Equipment supporting IP has gained significant competitive advantage in inter-office and long-distance transmission thanks to its falling price and robust performance, but other protocols and equipment continue to be important.
39. According to ITU (http://www.itu.int/journal/200102/E/html/indicat.htm), in many European countries Internet dial-up traffic accounts for around a third of local telephone traffic and, in most countries, Internet dial-up traffic far exceeds international telephone calls. Wellenius *et al.* (2000) also point out that about 7 per cent of the annual growth of the fixed network in the world during the period 1990–99 is attributable to the explosion of Internet service and predict that the Internet will carry as much traffic as voice telephony by 2003 and three times as much by 2010.
40. Davies (1996).
41. See Levy and Spiller (1996), Lehr and Kiessing (1998), Flynn and Preston (1999), Cherry and Wildman (1999), Abramson and Raboy (1999), Singh (2000), Xavier (2000), Abdala (2000), Samarajiva (2000), Petrazzini and Guerrero (2000), Onwumechili (2001) and Thatcher (2002).
42. Marx and Engels (1970), *Capital*, vol. 1, p. 645, cited in Giddens (1971: 58).

4. The design of data network systems: competing and collaborating technologies

4.1 INTRODUCTION

We have reviewed the paradigm of a technological system's design and the governance of telecommunications in Chapters 2 and 3. Most technology inventions result from problem solving rather than being pure chance. The design of technologies is shaped by negotiations among the different interests of social groups, and closure is the outcome of a process involving uneven power relationships between actors that also reflect economic and social structure. This chapter applies this view in an analysis of the struggle between proponents of alternative computer networking architectures. The advent and development of computer systems led to the invention of computer networking technologies, in particular packet switching technology. Packet switching technology has different technological and economic characteristics from circuit switching technology, which was applied for the traditional voice network. The Internet system started as an experimental network, which implemented for the first time a radical invention, packet switching technology, in a large-scale project.

The emergence of packet switched data networks provoked a battle for control of their development between network operators and computer manufacturers and for control of the network between telecommunication operators and advanced users, for example computer scientists. In this analysis, the expert networks of these social groups are known as telecommunications communities, computer communities and Internet communities, as discussed in Chapter 1 with respect to epistemic communities.

This chapter looks at competition between different technological systems in the development of computer networks, reflecting the interests of their system builders, focusing on the public data network standard (X.25) and the Internet (TCP/IP). Section 4.2 describes the history of computer networking and the different designs and paths of packet switching technology development. Battles between the computer and telecommunications communities and between the Internet and telecommunications communities over the international standards for data communication are analysed in section 4.3. Competing interests and institutional differences in the development of computer networks between European countries and the USA have also contributed to the battle of the systems. Section 4.4 examines government policies that fostered the creation of a 'developmental block' favouring a public data standard and the Internet systems in Europe and the USA, respectively. Government policies are crucial to understanding the triumph of the Internet system over public data networks.

Competition between systems is seen as a battle over technological leadership in ICTs. It is argued that the development of data communication technologies was shaped by different interests of stakeholders, and governments played an important role in the battles between them (Section 4.5).

4.2 THE DEVELOPMENT OF EARLY COMPUTER NETWORKS[1]

One of the earliest computer communication systems was SAGE (Semi-Automatic Ground Environment), a computer and radar-based air defence system of the 1950s.[2] During the 1960s, computers were introduced into telegraphic message switching systems to replace manually punched paper tape. Technological fusion between computer technologies and communications technologies led to the invention of computer network technologies. Lawrence Roberts, a pioneer of computer network technologies, stresses the importance of computer scientists in the development of computer network technologies:

> Packet switching technology was not really an invention, but a reapplication of the basic dynamic-allocation techniques used for over a century by the mail, telegraph, and torn paper tape switching systems ... What was required was the total reevaluation of the performance and economics of dynamic-allocation systems, and their application to an entirely different task. Thus it remained for outsiders to the communications industry, computer professionals, to develop packet switching in response to a problem for which they needed a better answer: communicating data to and from computers. (Roberts, 1978: 1307).

The Invention of Packet Switching Technologies

As commercial time sharing became widespread in the late 1960s, many communication networks, including INFONET and GE (General Electronic) Information Services, NASDAQ (National Association of Security Dealers Automated Quotation), NFCU (Navy Federal Credit Union), AUTODIN (Automatic Digital Network) and SITA (Société Internationale de

Télécommunications Aéronautiques) were established, using concentrators to reduce the cost of remote access (Paoletti, 1973; Chretien *et al.*, 1975; Schwartz, 1977; Gerla, 1985; Wood, 1985). Private networks for specific communities, for example SITA for airlines and SWIFT (Society for World-wide Interbank Financial Telecommunication) for banks, also began to adapt to packet switching technology.[3] SITA had been providing telecommunications for international air carriers since 1949. By 1963, the SITA network had expanded to cover the world.[4] In 1969, SITA began its redesign with the replacement of major nodes of its message switching network by high-level network nodes interconnected with voice-grade lines organized to act like a packet switching network (Roberts, 1978).

These computer networks were based on analogue circuit switching technology used in the public voice network. Traditional telephone networks, from the terminal equipment through to switching and transmission, were designed to accommodate the special requirements of human conversation. However computer traffic occurs sporadically, in that the intervals between short segments of transmitted data are relatively long (Tobagi *et al.*, 1978). Technological and economic factors led to the radical invention of packet switching technology. Data switching on the voice network was technically inefficient and the cost of long-distance telephone calls was very high. Technical inefficiency resulted from 'the long delay set-up, the lack of line error recovery, the inefficient use of the facilities by bursty users, and the speed selection limitation' (Gerla, 1985: 223). The principal spur of packet switching technology development was the search for a technology to use expensive computer facilities together, thus at relatively low cost. For example, time sharing services companies (for example, GE Information Services and Tymshare, Inc) were also set up in the 1960s to enable customers to access host computers owned by these companies at a relatively low cost (Schwartz, 1977).

Packet switching was independently invented by two computer scientists, Paul Baran of the Rand Corporation in the USA and Donald W. Davies of the National Physical Laboratory (NPL) in the UK to solve these critical problems. The first study on packet switching technology was conducted by Paul Baran for the US Air Force to accommodate all military communications, but it remained largely ignored until the Advanced Research Project Agency Network (ARPANET) was planned (Roberts, 1978). The distributed network proposed by Baran incorporates many redundant pathways for the delivery of messages while a centralized network has aggregating nodes and thus is vulnerable to military attack. A more decentralized structure and geographically highly dispersed network model were designed for military purposes (Baran, 1964). However Naughton (1999) argues that Baran's idea was not sophisticated enough for a military purpose communication system:

The idea [of a distributed network] was duly presented to the US military. The top brass were distinctly underwhelmed. Such a primitive system might be okay for the President, they observed, but *they* needed much higher bandwidth. It is ancient law of military life that high-ranking officers need secure, high-capacity communications channels not only for communicating with their superiors but also for the more subtle nuances required for messages to wives and mistresses, champagne importers and so on. (Naughton, 1999: 97; emphasis in original)

The idea of packet switching was also being developed by Leonard Kleinrock and Lawrence Roberts at the Massachusetts Institute of Technology (MIT).[5] J.C.R. Licklider, the first head of the computer research programme at the United States Department of Defense Advanced Research Project Agency (DARPA) established in October 1962, encouraged computer scientists to develop networking. Under the direction of Licklider, the Advanced Research Project Agency (ARPA) sponsored and substantially furthered the development of time-sharing computer systems after 1962.[6] The ARPANET project, which grew out of the development of the time-sharing computer and Licklider's special interests in computer networks (Roberts, 1978), was developed in the search for the efficient use of computer systems.

The stated motive for ARPANET was an economic one. By networking ARPA's computer systems together, the users of each computer would be able to use the facilities of any other computer on the network; specialized facilities would thus be available to all, and it would be possible to spread the computing load over many geographically separated sites. (Campbell-Kelly and Aspray, 1996: 289)

However, the designers of the Internet system were able to ignore the cost of using the network because it was being funded by the US government. Although ARPANET had been governed by military computer scientists and engineers controlling the project's focus on increased computer utilization and the development of computer networks, the management and engineering style changed from a hierarchical management structure to a decentralized one.[7]

The first actual computer network development projects were conducted by Donald Davies in the UK and Lawrence Roberts in the USA. The ARPANET project was initiated by Lawrence Roberts, who took over the management of the computer research programme under the sponsorship of ARPA in 1967. The Information Processing Techniques Office (IPTO) team needed to connect three ARPA-supported time-sharing systems at MIT, SDC and the University of California. However these computer systems were incompatible with one another; thus a request was made for the ARPANET packet switching equipment to enable the operation of the network in 1968.

Donald Davies had circulated his proposal on the packet switching network throughout the UK in late 1965 and 1966 (Davies, 1986; Roberts,

1978). The term 'packet' was coined by Donald Davies to describe the 128-byte blocks being moved around inside the network. Davies's aim to build a national packet switching network was not accomplished; instead his idea and vision were the foundation for a local area network at NPL (Davies, 1986). However the work of Davies and his colleagues on packet switching technology in NPL gradually began to have an influence in the UK and much of Europe.[8] Even though his plan was not accepted, Donald Davies's discussion with the British Post Office (BPO) on packet switching influenced the UK's early commitment to this new technology.[9]

> By 15th September 1965 I had collected these ideas together and argued them more cogently in a paper 'Proposal for the Development of a National Communication Service for On-line Processing'. This 8-page paper was sent to a number of people in the telephone service (then the British Post Office) and telecommunication industry ... A few comments came back, none destructive but none very enthusiastic. The most common remarks were (a) that it was only message switching, which we know about, or (b) that it would be fine, but nobody could build the necessary 'message switches' ... A lecture was announced for 18th March 1966 in our regular series of lectures, open to interested people .... The discussion was brisk and a few Post Office people dominated it. These few were to become the main proponents of packet switching and to develop the experimental network, EPSS, for the Post Office. (Davies, 1986: 3–4)

In addition to the NPL network and the ARPANET, CYCLADES, an academic and research experimental network, also played an important role in the development of computer networking technologies. The CYCLADES project was initiated under the auspices of the French government's Délégation à l'Informatique (DaI) for the purposes of resource sharing and conferencing, and as an object of research and a platform for other research (Pouzin, 1973). In 1973, the first hosts were connected to the CYCLADES network, which linked several major computing centres throughout France. An international connection to the NPL in the UK was established in August 1974 (Pouzin, 1982). CYCLADES grew out of the communication sub-network, CIGALE, which only moved disconnected packets and delivered them in whatever order they arrived without any concept of messages, connections or flow control. The CYCLADES structure provided a good testbed for trying out various protocols (Davies, 1973).[10] Several of the researchers involved in CYCLADES later became principal players in the early development of the International Organization for Standardization (ISO) Open Systems Interconnection (OSI)[11] layering model (Quarterman, 1990).[12]

In Germany, the early experimental networks, HMI-NET 1 (1974–6) and HMI-NET 2 (1976–9), contributed to the development of BERNET and DFN. HMI-NET is similar to CYCLADES in its development of a community of experienced people and its effect on widely used standards and networks. For example, Professor Karl Zander, who was involved in HMI-NET, became one of the first proponents of what later became COSINE (Quarterman, 1990).

Packet switching technology was not invented and developed by a heroic individual or visionary entrepreneur. Rather it was an example of collective invention by an independent group of computer scientists (mainly working for public research and development (R&D) laboratories) in some technology leading countries. The USA and the UK especially, had strong capabilities in computer science (Mowery, 1996). Researchers who established and worked on the experimental networks in the USA, the UK, France and Germany contributed to creating new communities, 'computer networking profession-als', in their own countries which gradually became a global community.[13] They exchanged knowledge and expertise by various means, including conferences, publications and face-to-face meetings. However, before their ideas could lead to a 'new technological order' – computer networking – there was a need for technological developments in related sectors.

The Technological and Institutional Changes

Up to the early 1970s, packet switching technology for computer-to-computer communications was not embraced by the telecommunications community, for technological and economic reasons (Burren, 1991; Davies, 1973). Packet switching had no perceived technical merit at the time and did not fit in with the existing telephone system. It was also not expected that computer traffic would achieve significant volume compared to telephony. The telecommunications community believed that 'in any case in time the telephone network would be converted to digital operation and this would meet all requirements' (Burren, 1991: 119). With the start of digitization of telephone networks, the concept of an Integrated Services Digital Network (ISDN) began to be developed in the early 1960s (Gagliardi, 1986).

However, the rapid advances in computer technology during the period of the late 1960s and the early 1970s, and especially the advent of transistor minicomputers,[14] and the rapid growth of distributed computing,[15] removed the limitation on implementing packet switching and made it possible to have reliable economic and flexible networking systems (Roberts, 1978: 1307). Before the advent of computers, dynamic-allocation systems, that is, packet switching systems, were necessarily limited to non-real time communications, since many manual sorting and routing procedures were involved in the passage of a message. The advent of minicomputers and the growing performance of distributed computing technology demonstrated the potential for computer-controlled packet traffic networks (Steinmueller, 1996). Distributed computing technology, which was developed in the late 1960s, had its greatest impact during the 1970s. The ability to develop entirely new computer system architectures in which tasks were distributed offered the possibility for networked computing, a means of combining computers of different sizes and computational capabilities and optimization of the system in terms of both computational performance and response time. Minicomputers also made it possible for small organizations to begin to purchase and use their own computers. Digital Equipment Corporation (DEC) pioneered the minicomputer with the introduction of the PDP-8 in 1965 (Chandler, 1997).[16]

The rapid development of computer technologies influenced the economics of telecommunications systems (Saunders *et al.* 1994).[17] The costs of switching (computer) have decreased to a greater extent than the costs of communication systems (network) since the 1960s. These rapid technological innovations in the computer system meant that packet switching became more economic than circuit switching technology. The price of routers (switches) in 1960 was about ten times higher than that of communications systems in the early 1960s. After 1970, the relative cost of routers to communications systems measured as US$1 per million bits became much cheaper (Mackie-Mason and Varian, 1996).

In general, there is a trade-off between transmission facilities and switches in the design of the physical network architecture (Roberts, 1978; Huber, 1987). If the relative cost of transmission facilities is less than that of switches, a hierarchical, centralized network architecture is generally more economic than a decentralized one with more switches:

> the packet systems require both processing power and buffer storage resources at each switch in the network for each packet sent. The resulting economic trade-off is simple: if lines are cheap, use circuit switching; if computing is cheap, use packet switching. (Roberts 1978: 1307)

This observation explains changes in the economics of two different switching technologies and network architecture. However it ignores the important fact that the 'spillover' from microcomputer production to routers was more effective than the spillover to switches. It is not just that transmission costs fall relatively slowly compared to switching costs but rather that a particular kind of 'switch' can much more effectively utilize existing transmission capacity.

More importantly, digital processing technologies blurred the traditional distinction between communication function of transmission and switching, and computers were rapidly assimilated as part of the communication process (Pickens and Hanson, 1985). Technological convergence was building up pressure for changes in the governance of telecommunications. Tensions and conflict over control between telecommunications network operators and computer manufacturers increased with the technological convergence of the computer and communications systems in the USA in the 1960s. Brock (1994) argues that these conflicts were a principal reason for the liberalization of the telecommunications market.

Regulatory changes favouring competition were implemented following the FCC 1966 First Computer Inquiry. In 1971, the FCC concluded that data-processing services should not be regulated and could only be offered by carriers through a separate data processing subsidiary. The FCC also concluded in the Specialized Common Carrier Inquiry in 1971 that the introduction into the market of new specialized communications services and competitive carriers was beneficial to the public and would be permitted in the future (Ungerer and Costello, 1988). As a result, various new types of specialized carriers were authorized, including those that built microwave facilities, those that offered primarily private line voice-grade point-to-point analogue communication channels and value added carriers. This decision also expanded Microwave Communications Inc. (MCI)'s rights, granted under the decision by the FCC[18] in 1969, to build and operate a small 200–mile microwave station between Chicago and St Louis to offer private line communication services in competition with American Telephone and Telegraph (AT&T) (Mathison, 1978: 1529–31). By January 1973, MCI and several dozen other companies (Data Transmission Company, United Video, Inc., Western Tele-Communications, Inc., Southern Communications Co., and Nebraska Consolidated Communications Corp., and so on) filed applications for more than 40 intercity routes having some 1900 microwave relay stations.[19] Among these specialized carriers, Datran (Data Transmission Company) proposed to build and operate a nationwide, all-digital switched network specifically designed for data transmission that would initially interconnect 35 metropolitan service areas. Datran, a subsidiary of University Computing Company, filed an application for a nationwide common carrier system using digital microwave and computer switching in November 1969 and became the first common carrier devoted exclusively to data transmission in April 1972, when the FCC granted its construction permits for the western half network covering Palo Alto, California to Houston, Texas. As Brock (1994) points out, the results of the 1971 enquiry encouraged competition in the supply of private line (or leased line) services, which was very important for the development of private computer networks (including the Internet) in the USA.

In September 1970, the Office of Telecommunications Policy was created by an executive order in order to formulate new policies and coordinate government use of telecommunications. One of OTP's responsibilities was to examine the effects of the convergence of computer and communications and recommend policies in the area (Enslow, 1972). OPT and the commerce department's Office of Telecommunications (OT) was reorganized and became the National Telecommunications and Information Administration (NITA) in 1978.[20]

The Different Paths

Technological advances in computer technologies and institutional changes in the telecommunications sector in the USA provided a turning point for the further development of the early computer networking technologies which were originally developed for research applications in academia involving experimental networks. After the successful demonstration of ARPANET in 1972, a number of private and public networks based on packet switching technology began to emerge in some of the developed countries (see Table 4.1).

However the directions of technological development in packet switching were diverse. Different types of computer network technology design were involved: decentralized (datagram) versus centralized (virtual circuit) and open system (public network) versus proprietary system (private network). Most of the experimental computer networks, such as ARPANET, NPL and CYCLADES, were built on decentralized network intelligence and most public data networks were built by Public Telecommunications Operators (PTOs) on centralized network intelligence. These data networks were open systems. Most firms whose networks were private used proprietary protocols provided by computer manufacturers.

Pioneering Experimental Networks

Technologies continued to develop out of the pioneering academic experimental computer networks. Following the success of the ARPANET trials, the Internet project was established to connect 'the individual networks that may be separately designed and developed', each of which 'may have its own unique interface which it may offer to users and/or other providers including other Internet providers' (Leiner *et al.*, 2000: 5). Gateways were essential to connect heterogeneous networks designed in accordance with the specific environment and user requirements of a particular network. The heterogeneity of computer equipment in universities and US public research laboratories arose because of (a) the generous support of academic computing through the willingness of scientific funding agencies to pay computational costs; and (b) the absence of centralized procurement at the federal level. Langlois and Mowery (1996) describe the US computer manufacturers' efforts to collaborate with universities by offering them discounts, research grants, free computer time and cash contributions. In addition, 'a federal agency like ARPA could not prevent researchers from buying computers from different manufacturers

Table 4.1   Some computer networks in the USA and Europe in the 1970s

	Country	Date operational	Switching technique	Type of service
Public data network				
Telenet	USA	1975	packet	virtual circuit
Tymnet	USA	1976[1]	packet	virtual circuit
EPSS	UK	1977[2] (experimental) 1979 (public service)	packet	virtual circuit
RETD	Spain	1973[3]	packet and message	virtual circuit
Infoswich	Canada	1978	packet	virtual circuit
Datapac	Canada	1976 (experimental) 1977 (public service)	packet	virtual circuit
Transpac	France	1978	packet	virtual circuit
DDX-1	Japan	1977 (experimental) 1979 (public service)	packet	virtual circuit
Private computer network				
ARPANET	USA	1971	packet	virtual circuit, datagram
NPL	UK	1973	packet	datagram
CYCLADES	France	1975	packet	datagram
SITA	worldwide	1969	message	message switched
Semi-public				
EIN	Europe	1976	packet	datagram
EURONET	Europe	1979	packet	virtual circuit

Notes:
1. An earlier version of TYMNET was in operation as a private network starting in 1969.
2. Non-standard protocols.
3. Network being modified to include international standards such as X.25

Sources: Adapted from Wood (1975, 1985) and Kelly (1978).

because all US firms had to be given equal opportunities to tender' (Naughton, 1999: 84).

Internet systems were designed from the perspectives of hosts rather than networks. The decentralized intelligence was designed to connect geographically dispersed and heterogeneous computer systems and allowed computer scientists to control computer networks using their expertise in computer technologies, rather than ceding control to the centralized Public Switched Telephone Network (PSTN) operators. The Internet community, just like computer manufacturers, regarded telecommunications network operators as suppliers of transmission facilities. Goode (1997) points out that the goal of the Internet community in designing the computer network was to rely on the processing power of the host computer to control the network.

The Internet community represented interests of advanced users in research communities in the connections (virtual circuits) versus connectionless (datagrams) debate after the CCITT approved X.25 as the international standard of public data networks. The suggestion of adopting TCP/IP as a standard for public data networks by American representatives to the CCITT was rejected (Abbate, 1999). Roberts (1978: 1311) stresses that 'Even with universal adoption of X.25 and the virtual circuit approach by public networks throughout the world, there is currently a vocal group of users [in particular the Internet community] requesting a datagram standard.' The Internet community continued to develop its own computer network system. Unlike the Internet, the early experimental research networks in Europe changed their datagram network systems to X.25.

The development of packet switching technologies in NPL and CYCLADES contributed to the establishment of academic and public data networks in the UK, France and other European countries. In Europe, regional computer networks such as the European Informatics Network (EIN) (originally COST-11) and EURONET were designed to connect major computer science centres to facilitate research in computer networking, to allow resource sharing between research centres and to provide a model for a public data network in some European countries. The COST 11 project had been initiated by ministers from eight European countries: France, Germany, Yugoslavia, Italy, Portugal, Switzerland, Sweden and the UK in November 1971 (Barber, 1975b). The project director was Derek Barber of NPL, one of the original investigators of packet switching in the UK. Roberts (1978: 1309) argues that 'given freedom from the red tape of multinational funding, this project would have been one of the earliest pace-setters in packet networks in the world'. The EIN, which provided a datagram service between subscribers' computers, began operations in 1976 with nodes in France, Italy, Switzerland and the UK and at Euratom (Wood, 1985). Wood points out that there were coordinating problems among member countries and these contributed to delaying the operation of the EIN. Nine Common Market countries (Belgium, Denmark, France, Germany, Ireland, Italy, Luxembourg, the Netherlands and the UK) collaborated to develop EURONET, which became operational in 1979 and was provided jointly by the nine PTOs (Wood, 1985: 165). EURONET was a distributed network using the packet switching technology of the French TRANSPAC X25 network (Carpentier *et al.*, 1992).

Private Networks of Computer Manufacturers

IBM with its Systems Network Architecture (SNA) and Digital Equipment Corporation with DECNET were the first proprietary protocols offered (Quarterman and Hoskins, 1986). IBM announced SNA in 1974 and the first reasonably complete implementations appeared around 1980 (Kapoor, 1992).[21] DECNET announced DECNET Phase I which was delivered in 1976 to connect PDP-11s running RSX-11.[22]

The computer manufacturers, in particular IBM, intended to expand their territory to the newly emerging computer networks by providing incompatible systems. Based on its huge share of the world computer market, IBM could have made its SNA protocol a de facto standard. David and Steinmueller (1990: 9) argue that 'in practice, IBM's actual products serve to define the "standard" by which data communication can be achieved where IBM is the sole vendor. Other vendors may define entry points into SNA and devise interfaces that conform to IBM standards'.

The computer manufacturers had a history of using standards as a weapon in competition, whereas telecommunications system operators had employed compatible standards within the framework of public ownership or state regulation (Jagger and Miles, 1991). Campbell-Kelly and Aspray (1996) describe the 'lock-in' strategy traditionally adopted by leading computer manufacturers in the development and implementation of packet switching technologies:

> The computer manufacturers, in particular, developed their own systems such as IBM's System Network Architecture (SNA) and Digital Equipment Corporation's DECNET. By reworking a very old marketing strategy, the manufacturers were hoping to keep their customers locked into proprietary networks for which they would supply all the hardware and software. (Campbell-Kelly and Aspray, 1996: 296)

Public Data Networks

As packet switching technologies became increasingly technologically and economically efficient, PTOs introduced experimental and operational networks. The growth of private networks became a threat to PTOs' revenue.

In the early 1970s, the PTTs readily supplied telecommunication facilities to corporations implementing private networks. The revenue generated by these facilities was perceived by the PTT as beneficial. As these networks grew in capacity, the concerns of the PTTs increased. In lieu of providing increased revenue, these networks, owing to their highly efficient use of the available frequency spectrum of leased line facilities, were considered to be a threat to PTT revenue (Tenkhoff, 1980: 59).

In 1976, AT&T introduced the packet switching network based on the Transaction Network Service (TNS) specially designed for high-volume users.[23] However AT&T showed little interest in packet switching during the period of development of the relevant technology (Roberts, 1978). Two explanations for AT&T's refusal to adopt packet switching technology are offered in the literature. The first, put forward by Naughton (1999), was management resistance. Naughton maintains that there were technical and strategic reasons for AT&T's resistance to Baran's idea, including a problem of vulnerability concerning the AT&T network (something that was denied by AT&T) that precluded the introduction of radically different technology into the plant. Moreover the development and implementation of a radical technology would reduce AT&T's monopolistic position in the market (ibid.: 107). The second explanation put forward by Larry Roberts was that AT&T showed even less interest in packet switching than PTTs in many other countries. This explanation suggests that AT&T's understanding may have been limited. Roberts (1978) stated that 'AT&T, and its research organization Bell Laboratories, have never to my knowledge published any research on packet switching. ARPA approached AT&T in the early 1970s to see if AT&T would be interested in taking over the ARPANET and offering a public service, but AT&T declined' (ibid.: 1310).

With changes in regulation, the new market players such as Telenet and Tymnet entered the public data network sector as value added service providers. Bolt Beranek and Newman (BBN), the primary contractor for the ARPANET, had felt strongly that a public packet-switched data communication network was needed. The FCC's new policies encouraged competition, so BBN formed the Telenet Communication Corporation in late 1972. In October 1973, Telenet filed with FCC for approval to become a carrier and to construct a public packet-switched network, and six months later this was granted. Telenet introduced the first public packet network service in August 1975, based on BBN's ARPANET experience.

Some European countries had begun to plan and operate public data networks. The UK started an early public packet network through the BPO's planned Experimental Packet Switched Service (EPSS). Donald Davies's 1966 briefings with the BPO on packet switching encouraged the UK's early commitment to this new technology. The BPO prepared the specification and contracted with Ferranti Ltd in 1973 (Wood, 1975). In November 1973, the French PTO announced its plan to build a national public data network, TRANSPAC. France began operation of the Réseau à Commutation par Paquets (RCP) as a testbed for TRANSPAC in 1974. Also in 1973, the Spanish National Telephone Company (CTNE) began operating a hybrid packet and message-switching network oriented primarily to computer communications applications in banking (Mathison, 1978). They changed their system by using the X.25. After international standards were approved by the ITU's Consultative Committee on International Telegraphy and Telephone (CCITT) in 1976, several countries introduced public data networks.

In Canada, the Trans-Canada Telephone System (TCTS) started to operate a public packet network, Datapac, in 1979 (experimental service in 1977). The Canadian National/Canadian Pacific Telecommunications (CN/CPT) introduced Infoswitch in 1978. In Japan, the Nippon Telegraph and Telephone (NTT) announced plans to build a public packet-switched data network and, in 1977, the Dendenkosa Data Exchange – DDX-1, an experimental switching system – came into operation.

All the initiatives of the PTOs were based on circuit switching technology, reflecting their core capabilities. Their different technological decisions also reflected their different vision of the development of data networks compared to the computer community. The telecommunications community developed the concept of an Integrated Digital Network (IDN) for the provision of voice and data services through digitalization of switching and transmission equipment. In 1972, the ITU CCITT offered the first definition of ISDN as follows: 'An Integrated Services Digital Network (ISDN) is an Integrated Digital Network (IDN) in which the same digital switches and digital paths are used to establish connection for different services' (Gagliardi, 1986: 4). Burren (1991) thus argued that X.25 standards were conceived by the telecommunications community as a short-term measure to accomplish a digital network and to gain control over the network against the computer manufacturer community.

In sum, packet switching technology was invented and developed for the emerging computer network because the telecommunications community failed to address the problems raised by computer networking over the traditional telecommunications system. The computer community took the initiative in the early development of packet switching technologies and their activities ultimately created an incentive for the telecommunications community to develop and provide computer network services. They designed the computer network to be controlled using the processing power of a host computer. The rapid advances in computer technology contributed to making packet switching technology cost-effective and technologically feasible. To face the challenge from the computer networking community, the telecommunications community also started to develop packet switching technology, but it was based on a virtual circuit interface so as to ensure their control of the network. Major computer manufacturers started to develop their own proprietary systems to increase their market positions in computer technologies. The different technological designs of the computer networks increasingly raised tensions between these communities as the computer became popular.

4.3   THE BATTLES OVER INTERNATIONAL STANDARDS

Standards are extremely important in the development of telecommunications systems. Hawkins asserts that 'communication systems cannot function without standards' (1996: 157). Standards are not confined to technological matters but also may involve features of a culture. Silverstone and Mansell (1996: 216) point out that standards provide a starting point in that 'it is in the establishment of common procedures and protocols, common both technically and in the widest sense also linguistically, and common to all those with desire and resources to gain access to the system that emerges, that communicative networks become possible'.

The battle between the Internet system based on the TCP/IP and the public data network system began in the 1970s. The protagonists were the PTOs, the computer manufacturers and large users who were struggling for control of the data networks through the design of a standard. Standardization inherently embodies many political and economic biases (Hawkins, 1996). In particular, a technological capabilities bias in the telecommunications industry and the computer industry between the USA and Europe made the battle over international standards even more political. The different institutional arrangements in the development of data networks between the USA and Europe (and other developed countries) also offer one plausible explanation for the causes and consequences of the battles between the Internet system and the public network communities (David and Steinmueller, 1994).

CCITT Standards: Computer Community versus Telecom Community

The first battle over data network standards occurred between the telecommunications network operator and the computer manufacturer communities. Tensions and conflicts between the PTOs and computer manufacturers led to the establishment of an international standard for data communication. In fact the battle over computer networks began at the early stage of packet switching technology development. In late 1967, Special Study Group A was established at CCITT for data communication and its members formulated questions for the 1968–72 period. Davies (1986) describes the position of the computer manufacturers' on the data network, expressed at one of their meetings:

A long lecture was given to 'Special A' by Fred Warden of IBM, concluding with the theme 'Don't you, the PTTs, trouble yourself about the special needs of data networks – just give us large bandwidths at low cost to join up our main frames and we'll do the rest.' This was the very opposite of our [PTT] views. (Ibid.: 11)

In 1968, CCITT had set up a special working group, the Nouveau Réseau de Données (NRD) to prepare procedural standards (Recommendations) applying to public data networks (Kelly, 1978). The early work of the NRD focused on the establishment of recommendations applicable to circuit switched data transmission, and some initial recommendations of CCITT had been issued by the ITU in 1972. CCITT upgraded the NRD working party to group status – SGVII – in order to accommodate the need for the establishment of a data network for offering a wide range of services and facilities. PTOs in some developed countries, also in the early 1970s, had been conducting R&D to develop public data networks and planned to add data transmission to their array of services. The establishment of an international standard for data networks was required because of the need to interconnect national public data networks. This would encourage PTOs to invest in the establishment of national public data networks which connected each other globally. More importantly public network operators were reluctant to be locked into specific protocols provided by a single manufacturer. They wanted protocols compatible with a variety of computer equipment so that they could interconnect their systems to handle international data traffic. PTOs in Europe, Canada and Japan were especially against accepting the computer manufacturers' proprietary protocols because the computer market was dominated by US manufacturers, in particular, IBM.[24]

In October 1974, a dispute between Bell Canada and IBM in building a public packet switching network, Datapac, arose (Abbate, 1999). The former began to build the TCTS (Trans-Canada Telephone System), developing its own protocols, but shortly after IBM's SNA protocols became available. Even though the Datapac network used most IBM computers, the Canadian government sought a non-proprietary system:

While TCTS tried to persuade IBM to modify its protocols to meet Canada's requirement [for ensuring compatibility with computer systems produced by other manufacturers], IBM urged the carrier to accept SNA, arguing that it did not make sense for a huge corporation to tailor its product for such a small segment of the world market. (Ibid.: 153)

This conflict between Bell Canada and IBM and the rapid development of public data networks in other countries led the CCITT to the creation of its own protocols for public data networks.[25] In 1975, an ad hoc group within the CCITT began work on a set of protocols which became Recommendation X.25. The first draft of X.25 was produced in March 1976 and the plenary CCITT's Recommendation X.25 was approved by the majority of members in September 1976. CCITT Recommendation X.25 is a standard interface protocol between packet-switched data terminal equipment (DTE) and packet-mode data circuit-terminating equipment (DCE).[26] Public network operators generally agreed that Recommendations were 'implementation independent', so as not to be forced to purchase a particular system to match that used in another country (Kelly, 1978: 1540). Therefore they concentrated on developing the host–network interface. The X.25 protocol provides virtual circuits interface including independent flow controls on each virtual circuit to offer the network (and the user) protection from congestion and overflow (Roberts, 1978).

However X.25 was criticized by expert users and users' communities, in particular the Internet community. For example, the X.25 standards were prepared in haste to meet the timing of the CCITT's standards approval process and they were incomplete.[27] They claimed that 'the X.25 had been set up in direct opposition to the Internet's TCP/IP protocols' (Abbate, 1999:155). The controversy between supporters and opponents of X.25 led to the heated debates of datagram versus virtual circuit protocol schemes. X.25 and TCP/IP have their respective technological advantages and disadvantages.[28] X.25 and TCP/IP protocols were not technically mutually exclusive, but they followed different paths of development. Different perceptions of computer networks design between the telecommunication community and the Internet community drove them to pursue different network design goals. The Internet community put higher priority on robustness and autonomy in the design of the Internet, while the X.25 community stressed accountability and controllability (Sunshine, 1989). A critical difference in network design between X.25 and TCP/IP was over which part of the system would control the quality of service: the communications subnet (X.25) or host computers (TCP/IP). In other words, the main difference was over control of the network: by telecommunications network operators or by expert users (computer scientists and engineers).

The CCITT was important in supporting the telecommunications community, not only by technical collaboration, but also by facilitating bilateral monopolistic bargaining, reinforcing national monopolies and limiting the rights of private firms in the global market (Cowhey, 1990). After X.25 became the official international standard, virtually all public packet network operators started development of interfaces to allow them to provide X.25 service to their customers (Gerla, 1985). The establishment of X.25 as an international standard contributed to the telecommunication operators' power over computer manufacturers in developing the computer network. The X.25 standard was designed to allow 'packets of data to be sent and reassembled over public networks without relying on the specific vendor implementations like those of IBM and DEC' (David and Steinmueller, 1990: 11).

Underlying the international standards-setting process there was also strong economic and political interest in revitalizing Europe's domestic computer industry in the face of the dominance of US manufacturers (David and Carpenter, 1998). For example, Science Engineering Research Council Network (SERCnet) UK (later renamed the Joint Academic Network – JANET), a national computer network which was designed to connect wide area networks (WAN), was built on the switches provided by 'British-made GEC midi-computers with software written at Rutherford Laboratory, a research institute in the academic community' (Rosner, 1986:79).[29]

ISO Standards: Telecom Community versus Internet Community

A few years after the CCITT began to work on the X.25 standard, a group of computer experts within the ISO launched a campaign to create a set of network standards that would be usable with any computer system. CCITT standards were confined to national data networks. Internationally two organizations, CCITT[30] and the ISO,[31] were responsible for networking standards, which were adopted by many countries.[32] The ISO historically represented primarily the interests of computer manufacturers and users while CCITT focused on the priorities of PTOs (Piscitello and Chapin, 1993).

In 1977, ISO Technical Committee 97 on Information Processing created a new Subcommittee (TC 97/ SC 16) to specify an architecture to facilitate the interconnection of heterogeneous systems. There was growing demand for interoperability between different computer systems as many computer manufacturers had begun to provide communication systems based upon proprietary protocols. At the same time, developing specific software to support the communications between or among heterogeneous systems (different manufacturers, different models of same manufacturer) became too costly to be accepted (Stallings, 1987). SC 16 represented primarily the interests of computer manufacturers and users (Piscitello and Chapin, 1993). SC 16 agreed to coordinate their efforts to develop a single reference model for Open Systems Interconnection. They worked closely with Study Group VII of CCITT on the development of public packet switching standards even though the two organizations had different perspectives on the data network development.

ISORM (ISO Reference Model) was designed to maximize flexibility and minimize the impact of technological changes. ISO defined a 7 Layer Reference Model and adopted X.25 as an official protocol for the network layer. Compromise on different approaches to data network technologies between the telecommunication community and the computer community led to ISORM. The concept of a layered communication architecture of ISORM was much along the lines of IBM's SNA and architectures of other computer manufacturers. The Basic Reference Model of Open Interconnection was approved in May 1983. Transport and session protocol standards to provide the OSI Session Service were agreed jointly by the ISO and CCITT in 1984 (Jardins, 1986). As Jardins points out, all major countries started national OSI architecture, and implementation of OSI, and computer manufactures also began publicly to declare their strategic turning towards OSI support.

However this was not the end of the battle between the X.25 community and the Internet community, but the beginning. Under the pressure of accepting an international standard, the Internet community could carry out their own technical development by claiming that the Internet met unique needs for the military system. The DoD argued that the need for operational readiness, mobilization and war-fighting capabilities were extreme and their operational and technical needs included survivability, security, precedence, robustness, availability and interoperability (Padlipsky, 1982b). For example, the Internet community argue that DoD could not wait for the proliferation and vendor implementation of an international standard because of a need for operational readiness.

At the same time, the Internet community also criticized the international standard, X.25, on the basis of military concerns, but the heated debates between proponents of the international standard and the Internet community went beyond controversies over technical design of data networks (Padlipsky, 1982a; 1982b). For example, Padlipsky (1982b) describes his motivation for writing a paper criticizing the international standard:

> Some zealous ISORM [ISO Reference Model] advocates suggested that the DoD research community suffers from a 'Not Invented Here' syndrome ... At least one or two zealous members of the research community have asserted that the problem is not *Not Invented Here*, but *Not Invented Right*, so an assessment of the apparent keystone of the ISORM suite, X.25, from the perspective of whether it's 'good art' ought to be appropriate. That's what we're up to here. (Padlipsky, 1982b: 1) (emphasis added)

During the 1980s, led by the American National Standard Institute (ANSI) and the National Bureau of Standards (NBS), the Americans participated in the technical committee of the ISO and lobbied for acceptance of the Internet protocols as OSI standards. Even after the Internet protocols failed to be adopted as the official standard, they shared the view on the needs of computer users and a commitment to supporting heterogeneous network systems. They worked together to bring the standards into close alignment. As a result of this, OSI has created an Internet working sub-layer within the network layer to accommodate the datagram Internet working approach. Many core technologies related to the Internet system, for example most of the features of TCP, were incorporated in the design of TP4; the main local area network (LAN) standards, Earthnet, token ring and token bus, became the official standards for the link layer; and ISO-IP which was based on ARPA's IP, was adopted (NRC, 1985).

However standardization itself is not enough to cause the interested parties to commit themselves to a given technology. Even though X.25 protocols became international standards of public data networks via the CCITT, and further officially confirmed by the ISO, we saw the decline of X.25 over TCP/IP protocols in public data networks in 1990s. Most corporate networks were also still based on these proprietary protocols. For example, over 60 per cent of large US companies were using IBM's SNA as the primary method for computer networking in 1992.[33] Major computer manufacturers, including IBM, Digital Equipment Corporation and Honeywell, did not give up their proprietary protocol strategy (Reardon, 1988). In fact, IBM, DEC and other computer manufacturers announced their plans for support of OSI products after 1985 (Jardins, 1986). Despite the fact that they announced that they would support X.25 in addition to their own protocols and planned to offer X.25 software for their systems, they did not actually bring X.25 products to the market until years later, when customer demand for the X.25 protocol had become too strong to ignore.[34]

Reardon (1988) gives the reason for the persistence and growth of proprietary architecture: a fully supported end-to-end solution is more cost-effective and provides a better technical performance than a self-supported 'pick and mix' approach; a specific implementation often provides a more efficient solution with better integrity, security and operational management facilities than more generalized approaches; specific implementation can and will tend to react faster to new user requirements. Minoli (1991: 533) points out the complex knowledge required for 'data communication in that approximately 100 key standards are required by a sophisticated contemporary network to undertake data communication'. They include file transfer, transaction processing, messaging, virtual terminals and Internet working. Also a private network does not need a high level of compatibility and interoperability and operators tend to customize technologies to suit their particular needs. Therefore, even where an international standard was established, limited user capabilities and fast technological change made room for the major computer manufacturers' 'lock-in' strategy by retaining their influence with users to promote proprietary protocols. In addition, Piscitello and Chapin (1993: 29) complained that 'ISO and CCITT standards are difficult to identify, hard to acquire, challenging to read, and hideously expensive'.

Beyond some Conjectures

There have been attempts to explain the success of the Internet as the triumph of the user-centric and decentralized network over the supplier-dominant and centralized network. However, to describe the battle between the X.25 and Internet protocols as a battle between network suppliers and network users is not entirely accurate. Computer owners (users of networks) can be divided according to their capabilities to use computers. Roughly speaking, expert owners (such as computer engineers) may want diversity in the control of the network while others may want reliability requiring little effort on their part. For example, BITNET, which provided relatively simple functions, was more popular with academic users than was the Internet at the end of 1987. Kahin (1992) points out that most non-computer scientists appeared to have been satisfied with less complicated and customized computer network services. Therefore, if computer network services based on X.25 protocols could provide satisfactory services to most of the non-expert users, the foregoing argument about the conflict over control between providers and users is overly simplistic. One of the reasons for the popularity of the Internet among US academic users was that the funding provided by the US federal government favoured technologies such as the Internet. High-end application development attracts federal funding and infrastructure, and in turn attracts other users who have been using more costly alternatives. For example, universities shifted their BITNET traffic onto the Internet at fairly modest cost (Klingenstein, 1993). In fact relatively less sophisticated global computer networks such as BITNET, USNET and FIDONET[35] were adopted more widely than the Internet in 1991.[36]

The Internet community won the battle over the international official standard supported in Europe. Hartley (1990) explains the different approaches of the USA and Europe as the promotion of de facto versus official standards which was based on cultural differences. The European style in standards development was to seek perfection both technically and politically, in particular, in an 'attempt to satisfy all interests and nationality groups' (ibid.: 155). The US approach is 'what you apply to something that has become, over a long period of development and evolution, universally accepted as worthy of standardization' (ibid.). The American approach (de facto) may be more suitable for computer networking than the European approach (official) because of the considerable time needed for development of interrelated technologies and components and the complexity of technologies (Hartley, 1990; David and Carpenter, 1998).

However it is not sufficient to explain the reason for the relative demise of X.25 protocols and the ISO standards and the success of the Internet protocols in terms of a cultural difference or preference for official versus de facto decisions by European countries and the USA. For example, the so-called European style of standardization has won over the American approach in the race for the second generation of mobile communications systems.[37]

Many authors also argue that decentralized control of the network was more conducive to technological innovation communication. Centralized control tended to reduce specialization (user-defined service offerings using third party equipment), which is a source of technological innovation in data communication systems (David and Steinmueller, 1994). The conservatism embodied in centralized network control could not accommodate 'the vital significance of the close relationship between workstations, computers, and data networking' (David and Carpenter, 1998: 11). However this may not always follow. For example, the success of Minitel in France may provide a different view.[38] The centralized telecommunications authorities introduced new services but focused on widespread benefits in line with their 'public service principle'. Also, in theory, a single public switched network can generate larger network externalities than unconnected private networks. Therefore the issue perhaps is how to continue technological and economic innovation while embracing the public service principle of developing 'universal access', in the face of rapid technological change.

4.4 GOVERNMENT POLICIES

The choices of X.25 and the Internet between Europe and the USA was influenced by different governance of telecommunications between Europe and the USA. The more centralized telecommunication network regime in Europe, compared to the more distributed ones in the USA, appears to have been the reflection of different political values, policy goals and regulatory environments and these differences prompted the different developments of data communication. In the USA, packet data communication was developed, using leased lines supporting enhanced (or value added) network services, while other countries predominantly adopted the public switched network principle in the development of data communication.

Different government policies in the development of data network and institutional arrangements had contributed to the outcomes of competition technologies between the USA and Europe. The vested interests and power embodied in these policies shaped the development of data network technologies.

The Development of Private Networks in the USA

The historical experience of the USA in the development of the telecommunications system gives some insight into the virtuous circle of the development of private networks, the main source of Internet growth. Promoting private networks utilizing leased lines paved the way to high-performance data communication systems. Prices for leased lines were kept low, often even below direct costs, in order to provide businesses with a lower-cost alternative to the public switched telecommunication network (Mansell, 1993). David and Steinmueller explain leased lines as 'an artefact of the US tariff system that allows users to purchase point-to-point connectivity for voice or data services' (1994: 232).[39] They stress the importance of relatively low-cost leased lines for the direction and rate of the development of data networks in the USA in that the utilization of private networks contributed to creating an entire industry devoted to high-performance data communication equipment used to construct mutually incompatible wide-area networks (ibid.: 223). The unique institutional setting up of leased lines in the USA resulted from the liberalization of the telecommunications system which was brought about in part by the convergence of communications and computer technologies.[40]

The use of leased lines contributed to the growth of the Internet system. On the user's side, they encouraged greater utilization of the network and, in some cases, even overutilization as a result of their flat tariff structure and the unique practices of the WAN management.[41] The flourishing of private networks contributed to the growing incompatibility of networks, thereby increasing the usefulness of TCP/IP, which is capable of integrating heterogeneous computer networks.

Tables 4.2 and 4.3 demonstrate the relative development of various private data networks in the USA. The size of the private data network was almost twice that of the public data network in 1986, measured by number of nodes. There were more than five times as many private data networks, including private corporate, state and federal government networks, than public networks. The total network capacity of the private networks was more than twice that of the public network.

The liberalization of the telecommunications market from the 1960s contributed to the development of private networks, including the Internet, because competition contributed to a decrease in the price of some network components and improved the quality for corporate users, and also contributed to increases in the productivity of the network operators (Stehmann, 1995). In particular, the divesture of AT&T resulted in network competition and the entry of private carriers focusing on reselling capacity. The USA took a big step in its liberalization of telecommunications, enforcing competition in long-distance business by divestiture of AT&T in 1982. Anti-competitive behaviours of AT&T resulted

Table 4.2   Estimated public and private data network nodes in the USA (1986)

Network operators	Number of nodes
Public data network	1 932
Tymnet	450
Telenet	400
CompuServe	200
Infonet	105
Mark Net	400
MCI Datatransport	110
Alaskanet	17
AT&T	100
Autonet	150
Private data network	3 600

Source: Adapted from Huber (1987: 5.6).

Table 4.3   Packet switching: estimated installed networks and capacity (1986)

	Number of networks	Capacity (million kilo characters / month)
Private networks		
Federal government networks	14	More than 500
Private corporate and state government networks	50	More than 200
Public national networks	14	400
Local exchange carriers (LECs)	10	100
Total		More than 1 200

Source: Adapted from Huber (1987: 5.4).

in a series of challenges from new entrants (MCI and Sprint). The liberalization policy in the USA concerned AT&T's efficiency and monopoly power, increasing pressures from other sectors to enter the telecommunications sector, and increasing demands from large firms for advanced telecommunications service. The separation of AT&T's long-distance business from the natural monopoly segment (local telecommunications) was designed to remove the ability and incentives of discrimination among suppliers of long-distance services. The divestiture process was completed and became effective on 1 January 1984. It encouraged greater competition and investment in the tele-communications sector. However the argument of economies of scope in a unified network concerning technological innovations became more persua-sive than the structural separation policies concerning the loss from the monopoly provision. Computer III, adopted by FCC in 1986, paved the way to dismantling the structural boundary between monopoly local telecommu-nication segment and competitive information services. During the 1980s, policy concern shifted from problems of controlling monopoly power to problems of enhancing productivity and international competitiveness (Brock, 1994). Stehmann (1995) shows that up to one-third of total investment in telecommunications networks in the USA in the early 1990s was accounted for by the new types of private carriers.

The Influence of the US Government in the Development of Data Networks

The influence of the US government on the direction and rate of the develop-ment of data networks in the USA was due to its being one of their major users. Teske (1993) points to the importance of the US government in the telecommunications sector:

> The federal government is by far the largest single employer in the United States. In addition, more than one in seven working Americans are employed by state or local governments. Government workers make up a very large percentage of employment in the American economy, and in other nations. Not surprisingly, then, a very large share of telecommunications usage is generated by governments at all levels. A broader conception of the public sector, including public universi-ties, public health care facilities, libraries, and other related public and not-for-profit enterprises, makes public sector choices even more important to telecommunica-tions providers. (Teske, 1993:1)

Indeed, in 1968, the private networks of the US federal government were bigger than all the national public data networks put together (see Table 4.3). The US General Service Administration (GSA) had managed the Federal Telecommunications System (FTS) and overseen the purchasing of equip-ment and leasing of lines since 1964.[42] Before competition was introduced, the government used AT&T's TELPAK tariff for leased lines which only provided basic direct dial service and low-speed data transfer. As a result many customers left the GSA system and paid more for better services as they were offered by other providers. Several federal and state government agencies in the USA built their own private networks for economic and technological reasons.

Several governments have established private networks to consolidate traffic over one network, to achieve cost savings by avoiding access charges, and for other reasons [to enhance security and/or privacy for sensitive operations, and/or to make efficient use of the existing separate networks, and/or to achieve special functionality such as redundancy and provide better service to their clients]. Sometimes governments actually own all or part of a network, including switches and lines, but most often they lease facilities or services from telephone providers. (Ibid.: 2)

On 7 December 1988, GSA awarded two ten-year fixed-price contracts for FTS2000 services totalling $25 billion over ten years to AT&T (60 per cent) and US Sprint (40 per cent).[43] These contracts allowed AT&T and Sprint to sell services to their assigned agencies: the more services they sold, the more revenue they could generate. The US DCA operated a separate network for the US defence agencies across the world, involving annual expenditure of more than US$3 billion.[44]

The US federal and state governments were relatively sophisticated users with capabilities similar to those of the more advanced parts of the business sector.[45] However US government agency networks were built upon different data network systems and thus were fragmented. There was little pressure for these individual networks to be compatible because they were designed for and restricted to closed communities of researchers (Leiner *et al.*, 2000). For example, HEPNet was extended to most countries with High Energy Physics (HEP) communities, using the DECNET protocols.[46] It provided important sources for the development of the Internet system as it was designed to operate on heterogeneous network systems.

The US Government Policies on Internet System Development

There were several policies deliberately designed to promote the Internet system in the USA. First, NSF made TCP/IP mandatory for the NSFNET programme. TCP/IP was the protocol used on the ARPANET and the protocol was most favoured by the computer science and DoD (Department of Defense) user communities. However TCP/IP was not the only non-proprietary protocol that NSF could have chosen. The X.25 standard communication protocol was in use in the public packet-switched networks, for example, Tymnet and Telenet. DECNET also could have been a viable option for NSFNET because it was a connectionless protocol that was the core of almost all of the high-energy physics networks and was widely used in ESNET (the Energy Sciences Network) and SPAN (the Space Physics Analysis Network) (Mandelbaum and Mandelbaum, 1992). There were several reasons for the choice of DECNET protocols in these global networks: digital equipment was widely used by physicists; TCP/IP was not used because the huge files physicists needed to exchange made the early ARPANET and Internet impractical, and there was no developed TCP/IP in Europe; DECNET higher-level protocols could run over a variety of network protocols and media, most importantly Ethernet and X.25 (which is particularly important in Europe).[47]

The choice of TCP/IP over X.25 for the NSFNET had major consequences. Mandelbaum and Mandelbaum point out that the decision in favour of the TCI/IP protocols led to 'the establishment of the system of specialized, private academic networks we have today, rather than to reliance by the academic and research community on the public, commercial networks that are the mainstays of the business world' (ibid.: 62). This decision not only provided interoperability with ARPANET but also meant that TCP/IP should be adopted by most research networks. The choice of TCP/IP, a non-proprietary protocol suite, provided a common platform for developing applications and instantly enabled connections to the ARPANET and CSNET, the NSF-funded computer science network (Kahin, 1992). The NSF also elected to support DARPA's existing Internet organizational infrastructure, hierarchically arranged under the IAB. The public declaration of this choice was the joint authorship by the IAB's Internet Engineering and Architecture Task Forces and by the NSF's Network Technical Advisory Group of RFC 985 (Requirements for Internet Gateways), which formally ensured interoperability of DARPA's and NSF's parts of the Internet. It contributed to the consistent and stable technological development of the Internet.

The critical decision was made by NSF that NSFNET would be built by supporting the creation of regional or intermediate-level networks. The NSF strategy for building a national research network by creating a backbone network was aimed at exploiting economies of scale in using the Internet system. The backbone strategy promoted demand for the Internet system and encouraged establishment of independent regional and intermediate-level networks. NSFNET gained further momentum from the aggregation of users at university campus level (ibid.).

The Internet had been subsidized by the US government either directly, through the NSFNET backbone, or through grants to users.[48] With the advent of distributed computing in the early 1980s, university campus computer centres had begun to shift the focus from mainframe computers to cross-campus connectivity via high-speed data networks (ibid.). End users of the Internet system paid virtually nothing, thanks in part to the flat structure of the leased line tariff. Large subscribers were connected on a flat fee basis, so that, for most individual users, there was no usage charge, which also contributed to the Internet's rapid growth. This unique charging principle came from the fact that the Internet was mainly used in academic communities. Leiner stresses the charging principle:

The scientific user should not have to worry about the costs of data communications any more than worries about voice communications (his office telephone), so that data communications become an integral and low-cost part of our national infrastructure. This implies that charges for network services must NOT be volume sensitive and must NOT be charged back to the individual. (Leiner, 1987: 2)

Following the model of distributed computing usage was free; campus network costs applied at the institutional level but were only rarely charged to the departments of end users. The cost of these networks was frontloaded in the initial installation, in the same way as department-level investments in microcomputers and workstations. Colleges and universities also invested hundreds of millions, possibly billions, of dollars in wiring for campuses, thereby providing almost universal access to the Internet (Kahin, 1992).

Most importantly, the US government strategically delayed adoption of OSI protocols because of the national interest in the Internet system. The US National Bureau of Standards (NBS) established a Program in Open Systems Interconnection, which sponsored workshops to help computer manufacturers implement the OSI protocols (Blanc, 1987). The NBS and the Department of Defense, anticipating the clash between the OSI (X.25) and Internet protocols as the OSI protocols had gained a following, particularly in Europe, commissioned a study to provide recommendations on 'Transport Protocols for Department of Defense Data Network' (Spanier, 1986). In February 1985, the Committee on Computer–Computer Communication Protocols (CCCCP)'s final report concluded that: 'the DoD has a large and growing commitment in operational TCP networks, and this will increase by 50 to 100% in the next 18 months. This rate of investment will probably continue for the next five years for new systems and the upgrading of current ones' (NRC, 1985: 10). Elsewhere in the report, the committee states that 'if DoD does not make a firm commitment to TP-4 (the OSI transport protocol) by mid-1985, the number of systems that will move ahead with TCP will probably constitute almost half of the growth of the DDN in the next five years'. In other words, delaying the decision to move to TP-4 (ISO-IP) until 1986 would have meant that most of the DDN sub-nets that existed in the late 1980s would be based on TCP (Spanier, 1986: 142).

The DoD did not commit itself to a decision to use the OSI protocols until late 1986 (Spanier, 1986).[49] This was enough to send the signal to manufacturers to invest in and develop products related to the Internet system. The US government's role also was critical in incorporating the Internet system into the OSI model with the X.25 protocol. Finally US government policies had encouraged the creation of a critical mass (a development block) for the development of the Internet system and, as a result, it became a de facto standard. The US government started the commercialization of the Internet system. In 1986, it organized a conference between scientists and engineers from the DARPA Internet research community and vendors, to promote understanding and cooperation. Leiner *et al.* (2000) describe the meeting in which around 250 vendors came to listen to 50 inventors and to look at the experiments initiated by the DARPA research community. This meeting between the Internet inventors and experimenters and commercial vendors became a regular event and participation in it expanded.

European Policies

During the 1970s, European countries increasingly came to realize the importance of telecommunications for industrial policy.[50] Nora and Minc (1980) influenced both information and communication policy in France and also the European Commission's policy for these sectors. Nora and Minc contrasted Europe's weakness in information technology and microelectronics with its strength in the telecommunications sector. In 1979, the European Commission published a policy report aimed at strengthening its position in the face of the US large domestic market and Japan's coherent industrial policy. It made several proposals: a coordinated European industrial policy; an initiative to improve the qualifications of the workforce; the creation of a common market for telematics services (for example, ISDN); the establishment of a European information industry; and the fostering of coordination and cooperation between producers and users (Schneider and Werle, 1990). However the recommendations of this report were not acted on until the mid-1980s. At the country level, specific technology policies such as the 'Plan Télématique' (1978) in France, and the joint 'Programme Technical Communication' of the postal and research ministries (1978) in West Germany were adopted. The UK government introduced its videotex system, Prestel, and its 'teletext initiative'. As a result of this, in most European countries national data networks focusing on public services began operation in the 1970s. These national public data networks were interconnected and based on X.25 standards. A total of 68 600 public data network ports were installed throughout Europe by the end of 1984 (see Table 4.4).

European countries had focused on the development of the videotex system while the Internet system was being built in the USA. The videotex system was designed to allow low cost and user-friendly access via public switched data networks based on the X.25 standard. France had achieved remarkable success in the development of the videotex system. By the end of 1987, subscribers to Minitel, in France, exceeded 3 million (Ungerer and Costello, 1988). However the UK, Germany and other European countries failed to create a mass market.[51] The strategy in Europe to provide low-cost advanced data communication systems for homes and businesses by using the public switched data network achieved some success, however.

Table 4.4   Public packet switched networks in Europe (installed ports, year end 1984)

Country	Service	System(s)	Manufacturer	Ports	Carrier
Austria	Internat. 'I	EDX-P	SIMENS	160	RADAUS
Austria	DATX-P	SL-10	NT	1 000	ÖPTV
Belgium	DCS	EDX-P	SIMENS	3 928	RTT
Denmark	DATAPAK	TP-4000	GTE	400	PT
Finland	DATAPAK	DSP-25, TP-4000	BTMC, GTE	1 000	PTT, HTV
France	TRANSPAC, NTI	CP-50	SSA, TRT	21 000	PTT
Germany	DATEX-P	SL-10	NT	13 000	DBP
UK	PSS, IPSS	TP-4000 DPS-25	BTMC, GTE	13 000	BT
Greece	HELPAC		SESA	100	PTT
Italy	ITAPAC	EDX-P	SIMENS	2 500	SIP, PT
Ireland	EIRPAC	SL-10	NT	300	PTT
Iceland	ISPAC	Eripac	LME	300	PTT
Luxembourg	LUXPAC	DPS-25	BTMC	300	PTT
Netherlands	DATANET 1	DPS-1500	BTMC	1 400	PTT
Norway	NORPAK	TP-4000	GTE	1 000	TV
Portugal	TELEPAC	SL-10	NT	1 000	CTT
Spain	IBERPAC, NID	HW716 TESYS	HONYWELL SECOINSA	5 500	CTNE
Sweden	TELEPAK	Tymnet Engine	TYMNET	1 300	TV
Switzerland	TELEPAC	SL 10	NT	500	PTT
Total				68 800	

Data: Adapted from Gabler (1986), 'Packet switching in the Federal Republic of Germany (with a view to the situation in CEPT countries), in Csaba *et al.* (eds), *Computer Network Usage: Recent Experiences*, Amsterdam: Elsevier Science Publishers B.V., North-Holland.

Liberalization of the telecommunications market initiated by the USA challenged the PTTs national champions regime in Europe. Carpentier *et al.* (1992: 85) describe two immediate consequences of deregulation in America for Europe: 'a tariff war and American pressure to rapidly penetrate the European market and this pressure was exerted simultaneously by firms and the Administration'.[52] It contributed to building up a consensus on the establishment of single European telecommunications governance by introducing liberalization of the national telecommunication market. As a consequence, power was shifted from the PTTs to the Commission during the 1980s.

Increasingly more complex and extensive telecommunication and related technologies also contributed to achievement of a consensus on regional collaboration
in R&D programmes. The convergence of ICTs made telecommunication systems even more complex. Increased demand for telecommunications services
resulted in larger systems. The more complex, larger systems required greater
investment in R&D.

From the early development of packet switching technologies, regional
network projects including COST 11, ERONET and Diane were established.
However these European regional networks were short-lived; they did not
have a large set of computers and had no long-term funding (Kirstein, 1999).
From the mid-1980s, under the initiative of the European Commission, various R&D programmes in ICTs were launched (Peterson, 1993). The COSINE
(Cooperation for OSI Networking in Europe) Project was adopted as a part of
the Eureka programme at the second Eureka Ministerial Conference in Hano-
ver in November 1985.[53] The European Commission programme for Research
on Advanced Communication in Europe (RACE) and ESPRIT (European
Information Technologies for R&D) were established in order to develop
broadband network technologies and information technologies (see Table
4.5). In particular, RACE aimed at stimulating advanced transmission techniques for voice and data networks, such as ISDN and Asynchronous Transfer
Mode (ATM).

The EC's policy directive on ICTs was based on the arguments that they
could promote information technologies (their weakness) through telecommunications (their strength) and that they could foster telecommunication
technologies through network integration. The network integration strategy
appears to have had two objectives: creating greater market demand by establishing regional networks, and integrating data and voice services through
ISDN and Integrated Broadband Networks (IBN). This policy direction was
quite different from the US approach towards network fragmentation even
after European countries introduced competition. The policy choice in the
USA was for network competition, while in Europe service competition was
preferred.[54]

The objective of the COSINE project was to provide the European academic and industrial research communities with a computerized open
communication infrastructure based on OSI protocols. In building a pan-
Europe data network the aim was to create a critical mass for OSI products,
thus giving European industry an opportunity to be at the leading edge in the
supply of open systems for data communication conforming to international
standards. To achieve this policy goal, Decision 87/95/EEC made it mandatory for public purchases of over ECU100 000 to be OSI-based.[55] The COSINE
project aimed to provide network services based upon international ISO
Standards and CCITT Recommendations for Open Systems Interconnection

Table 4.5 Selected Europe R&D Programme for ICTs

Programme	Focus	Period	Total cost (million ECU)
COST 11	Implementation of the European informatic networks	1971	
Euronet/Diane	European data-transmitting network linking approximately 300 databases	Euronet since 1975, Diane since 1980	
FAST	Planning science and technology	Since 1980	
RACE0	Broadband network R&D	1985–86	22.10
RACE1		1987–92	550.00
RACE2		1991–94	554.00
ESPRIT0	Information technology	1983	11.50
ESPRIT1		1984–88	750.00
ESPRIT2		1987–92	1 600.00
EUREKA COSINE	Pan-European computer-based network (OSI)	1985–93	36.93
			18.10
EUREKA EUROCAIRN	Upgrade pan-European computer networking infrastructure	1993–96	0.92
Telematic systems	Trans-European networks for cooperation in administration, education and training, libraries, linguistic, transport, health care, rural service	1991–94	430.00
FRAMEWORK 4C	Telematic	1994–98	898.00
	Communication technologies	1994–98	671.00
	Information technologies	1994–98	2 057.00

Source: CORDIS RTD-PROJECTS/© European Communities, 2000; EUREKA (http://www3. eureka.be); Schneider and Werle (1990: 98).

(OSI) together with functional standards as prepared by European standard organizations such as ETSI and EWOS (Olthoff, 1988).

From the early 1980s, in most European countries a national academic and research network had been established. These networks, which were typically based on leased lines controlled by national monopoly operators, used X.25 protocols reflecting the European network operators' interests and strategies to compete with TCP/IP. This mainly resulted from the different strategic selections of data network technologies in the USA and Europe. In Europe, a switched packet data network based on X.25 was the standard for computer networking. Until the early 1990s, because of the relatively high cost of leased lines in Europe compared to costs in the USA, it was still common to find institutes with connections of 64 kilobit, or even less, in Central and Eastern Europe (Neggers, 1991; David and Carpenter, 1998), because leased lines were very expensive. The networked universities and research institutes paid an average annual fee to cover operational costs. In the face of development of high-speed network technologies in the Internet system of the USA, the European Community had to adopt multiple protocols to accommodate the TCP/IP protocols.

The Réseaux Associés pour la Recherche Européenne (RARE) had been created in 1986 as a forum for the national networking organizations to discuss matters of common interest and, in particular, to resolve the problems of interworking between national services that had been independently created. One of RARE's first major tasks was to coordinate the technical work to support the COSINE specification phase. COSINE developed more slowly than planned, mainly because, for 'organizational reasons, consensus between representatives of the eighteen countries involved had to be reached before each major decision was taken' (Davies, 1993: 1). 1988 saw the Implementation of COSINE. The first concrete result of the project was the creation of the IXI (International X.25 Infrastructure), a pilot network which provided service between all the COSINE countries, starting in July 1990.

Despite all these efforts, countries in Europe eventually had to introduce the Internet system and subsequently had to transform their data networks to accommodate the Internet system for various technological and contextual reasons. First, technological development focusing on network design may have been an obstacle in keeping pace with the fast development of PCs as a powerful terminal for data communications. This was partly because, in general, advanced PCs were only distributed in Europe after they had become widespread in the USA (Mansell and Steinmueller, 2000). Furthermore David and Carpenter (1998) argue that the conservatism of the telecommunications operators and manufacturers in Europe meant that X.25 products were not into the market quickly enough. More importantly, despite substantial R&D efforts at both national and regional levels, Europe failed to create a similar cluster of advanced users to that which emerged from collaborations between the US academic, research and business communities with the support of their government (ibid.).[56]

Second, different perspectives and history of telecommunications system development contributed to the European countries and their communities of actors focusing on the technological development of network integration rather than on specific network technologies. The 'public infrastructure principle' upheld by the telecommunications community, and a commitment to telecommunications as being within the government domain, also restrained efforts to introduce liberalization in Europe. Therefore the costs to users of establishing private networks using leased lines were much greater in Europe than in the USA. Busquin and Liikanen stress the institutional barrier to the development of research networks in Europe:

> The major problem with European data research networking has always been its cross-border connectivity, due to the high price of interconnection circuits. This is neither a technical problem nor an infrastructure one, it was only due to the lack of competition in the cross-border European telecommunications market. (Busquin and Liikanen, 2000: 5)

The development of computer network technologies in European countries had been led by the telecommunications community while research communities (advanced users) played a critical role in the development of computer network technologies in the USA. Third, the effectiveness of regional R&D programmes and their coordination among countries was also questionable. Without any actual commitment from member countries, the effectiveness of regional R&D programmes was limited. Peterson (1993) argues that, in addition to the technical complexities involved, the strength of vested national interests and the underdevelopment of international standards organizations contributed to the slow progress towards setting up and implementation of OSI systems. Also nationally specific data network establishments, for example, in the UK (Coloured Book protocols) delayed the implementation and development of OSI systems (Hartley, 1990). The limitations imposed by European policies in the adoption of OSI and on R&D into ICTs were the result mostly, not of the technology, but of institutional and political coordination problems. As David and Steinmueller (1994) argue, it was not any inherent defect in the X.25 standard which was alleged to lead to its demise, rather there were very few potential adopters of X.25 as there were alternatives which could serve a great variety of user needs and they were so widely adopted.

However, the common experiences, common interests and the power shift from the national PTOs to the European Commission in the telecommunications sectors provided the opportunity to catch up with the USA (Busquin and Liikanen, 2000).

4.5   CONCLUSION

The visions of individuals and computer networking communities in the USA and European countries were shaped by the power relations between users and suppliers of network facilities, on the one hand, and by the institutional bias in computer and telecommunications systems between the USA and European countries, on the other hand. This chapter has analysed the technological, economic and political aspects of the battle over data communication development between the telecommunications operators, computer manufacturers and the Internet community in the context of the emergence of an international standard for data network systems.

Computer networking communities composed of researchers working on early experimental networks became established in some advanced countries, particularly the USA, the UK and France. These pioneering researchers had collaborated with each other in establishing the global order of computer technologies, but established different paths of computer network development in line with what they perceived to be their country's best interests (and in line with their own visions). They were actively involved in national and regional research network-building processes and disputes between expert groups involved in international standards setting. In the USA, computer scientists, who led the development of data networks, and users together established the Internet community, while in European countries it was the telecommunications community that dominated the development of data networks.

Network technology developed along three different routes, reflecting the interests of the parties involved. First, most of the private networks for computer networking and research deployed the datagram network architecture which allowed control of the network through information processing power. Second, all packet switching networks developed by PTOs in Europe were based on virtual circuit switching technology in a bid to enforce centralized control of the network. Third, computer manufacturers in the USA sought to enter the newly emerging information and communication market by providing their own proprietary protocols such as SNA (IBM) and DECNET (Digital Equipment Corporation). The development of data communication was influenced by competition between the telecommunications, computer and Internet communities. The battle between the telecommunication and the Internet communities for control of the network in the context of the *de jure* (X.25) versus *de facto* (Internet) protocols was the focus of the discussion in this chapter. The use of these two protocols, which were based on different principles, resulted in 'public switched' and 'private' networks reflecting the difference between the institutional arrangements in Europe and US government policies. These differences fuelled the controversies over technological leadership in the new ICT markets up to the end of the 1980s. The motivation for intervention was associated with achieving technological leadership in the new ICT markets.

The collision between the telecommunication and computer communities led to a battle over system standards, that is, between de jure and de facto standards. The battles over the data communication system were largely between the USA and the European countries, since the computer market had been dominated by US firms. The battle for control over the data network which raged between the telecommunications and Internet communities, was not only between network operators and users (computer scientists) for the control of the technology but was also about technological leadership between the USA and the European countries. The failure of X.25 (and the success of the Internet) was not attributable to technological factors but rather was the result of institutional bias.

NOTES

1. Computer communication networks have been classified differently. Soi and Aggarwal (1981) present the six major types of classification schemes, including the functional view (remote access networks, value-added networks and mission-oriented networks), the designer's view (circuit switching, message switching, packet switching and hybrid switching), the manager's view (centralized, decentralized and distributed), an operational view (deterministic algorithms, stochastic algorithms and flow control algorithms), a communication view (resources sharing, distributed computation, remote communication) and a hybrid scheme combining routing and topological classification.
2. See Hughes (2000).
3. The network originated in the late 1960s, when it was realized that effective use of the banks' computing power was essential in the face of the considerable growth of international banking. In May 1973, 239 banks from 15 countries became founder members of SWIFT. On 26 September 1977, the initial phase of implementation was completed (OECD, 1979).
4. Chretien *et al.* (1975).
5. Leonard Kleinrock at MIT published the first paper on packet switching theory in July 1961 and he convinced Roberts of the theoretical feasibility of communications using packets rather than circuits (Leiner *et al.*, 2000).
6. 'the first concrete proposal for a geographically distributed network of computers was made by Licklider in his 1960 Man-Computer Symbiosis paper' (Campbell-Kelly and Aspray, 1996: 288). For a description of Licklider's vision and his activities in the establishment of the ARPANET project and the historical description of the ARPANET project in general, see Campbell-Kelly and Aspray (1996: 288–90) and Naughton (1999: 77–91).
7. Hughes (2000) shows how systems engineering and systems approaches were adopted by the ARPANET project, based on experience from a series of large-scale projects including SAGE and Atlas. The experience in large-scale government projects provided the innovative environment for Internet development.
8. For example, Derek Barber of NPL became the project director of the COST II Project (Roberts, 1978).
9. Spratt (1987) provides a historical background and describes issues involved in computer networking development in the UK academic community.
10. CYCLADES went further, following in part the lead of ARPANET researchers, for instance

in multiple routing of packets that could be delivered out of sequence. CYCLADES also emphasized the necessity for careful layering of software and the development of a layering model.

11. Most English-speaking people regard ISO as an acronym for International Standards Organization but ISO emphasizes that its short name is not an acronym, rather it is a word derived from the Greek ΙΣΟΣ, meaning 'equal' (Brebner, 1997).

12. CYCLADES researchers, including Louis Pouzin, Hubert Zimmermann, and Gérard LeLann, created a national community of experts of international reputation. This community interacted with researchers in other countries. CYCLADES also influenced the TCP/IP protocol developers on such aspects as size of the unit to be retransmitted on packet loss. Vint Cerf derived the early TCP window scheme from discussions with Louis Pouzin and Gérard LeLann (Quarterman, 1990), who influenced the networking technologies used in the development of the ISO–OSI model.

13. See, for example, Pouzin and Zimmermann (1978) and Owen (1982).

14. The development of the integrated circuit in 1958, an operating system that allowed machines to run many different programs at once with a central program that monitored and coordinated the computer's memory, accelerated the development of computer technologies. The Intel 4004 chip, developed in 1971, took the integrated circuit one step further by locating all the computer's components (central processing unit, memory, and input and output controls) on a miniscule chip (Gaines, 1998).

15. In particular, the advent of transistorized minicomputers and rapid growth of distributed computing technologies, which eclipsed the older model of mainframe time sharing.

16. PDP went on the market in 1961, followed by PDP 5 in 1963. It was quickly followed by PDP-6, the first commercially available time-sharing system, and PDP-8, the first mass-produced minicomputer and the first to use integrated circuits (Chandler, 1997). By compromising speed in order to achieve very low cost, the PDP-8 tapped user needs that were not well served by the competing technological solution, time sharing, which had foundered in the late 1960s (Steinmueller, 1996).

17. Saunders *et al.* (1994) argue that cost reduction in telecommunications systems had been achieved by a combination of technological change and economies of scale (in both supply and demand).

18. A FCC decree in 1969 that granted MCI Communications Inc. the right to compete with the Bell System by providing a long distance service over its own private lines. It enabled MCI (now WorldCom) to connect to its customers through the Bell network, which was one unified system at that time.

19. Walker and Mathison (1973: 324–5).

20. NITA, A Short History of NITA (http://www.nita.doc.gov/opadhome/history.html).

21. SNA was developed in the 1970s with an overall structure that parallels the OSI reference model (Gurugé, 1992).

22. Phase II was announced in 1976 and delivered in 1978; Phase III was announced and delivered in 1980; and Phase IV was announced in 1982 and delivered in 1984 (Mosher, 1992).

23. See Brock (1981).

24. For example, according to Datamation (1 June 1989), of the market share of 15 leading computer hardware and software firms in 1984, US firms held 78.7 per cent in the computer mainframe sector worldwide, 82.0 per cent in minicomputers, 88.3 per cent in microcomputers, 81.2 per cent in peripherals and 83.3 per cent in the software market (cited in Malerba *et al.*, 1991).

25. Protocols are common tools designed for controlling information transfer between computer systems made up of sequences of messages with specific formats and meanings (Pouzin and Zimmermann, 1978).

26. See Burg (1992).

27. The approval of Recommendations should be voted by the entire CCITT membership at four-yearly intervals.

28. The main advantages of virtual circuit design – X.25 (compared to the datagram) are the reduction in header overheads, improved controllability of data flow by the network, and

accountability. The main advantage of the datagram (Internet) over the virtual circuit was the efficient use of bandwidth. However a datagram requires a battery of rather sophisticated flow and congestion control techniques to achieve fair bandwidth allocation and congestion prevention during peak periods. See, for example, Gerla (1985) and Sunshine (1989).

29. See Bryant (1984) for the history and development of the UK SERC network.

30. CCITT was one of seven ITU groups which were reorganized to become the International Telecommunications Union Committee on Telephony (ITU-T) in the early 1990s. The duties of CCITT were to study technical and operating questions relating to telegraphy and telephony. Most of its members were representatives of national telecommunications carriers, the PTTs. It was officially represented by the US Department of State. CCITT maintained liaison with carriers, ISO and ANSI. Many standards were harmonized with ISO (Minoli, 1991).

31. The ISO is an international organization dedicated to the writing and dissemination of technical standards for industry. More than 70 per cent of ISO member bodies are government standards bodies or are incorporated by public law. The most important technical committee relevant to telecommunications is ISO/IC JTC (Minoli, 1991).

32. Besides CCITT and ISO, major standards bodies exist, including, in the USA, ANSI (American National Standards Institute), IEEEE (Institute of Electric and Electronics Engineers), and NIST (National Institute of Standards and Technology) and, in the UK, CEPT (the Conférence Européenne des Administrations des Postes et des Télécommunications), EWOS (the European Workshop on Open Systems) and ETSI (European Telecommunications Standards Institute).

33. *Financial Times*, 13 Oct. 1992.

34. Abbate (1999).

35. The FidoNet network is a Usenet type of network developed by Tom Jennings in San Francisco in 1983, and released in June 1984. FidoNet implemented a packet-based, store-and-forward capability for email and bulletin board systems, and paralleled the growth of the Usenet and BITNET. Unlike other networking systems, FidoNet originally ran on normal IBM PC-compatible computers running the DOS 2.0 operating system or higher. This provided FidoNet system administrator capability to tens of thousands of users with home systems, and greatly assisted its early growth. FidoNet was incorporated as a company in 1986, and the network broke up into a number of separate groups when many users disagreed with this decision. Many FidoNet administrators continued to use the FidoNet software to establish sites. In 1987, UUCP (Unix to Unix Copy Protocol) software was released for the DOS operating system, enabling the connection of FidoNet to the Usenet. Many Usenet groups began to be carried on the FidoNet, but few FidoNet groups were carried on the Usenet. According to Odd de Presno, in June 1993, there were 24 800 FidoNet sites around the world, serving an estimated 1.56 million users. In 1998, FidoNet had about 30 000 nodes worldwide (http://fidonet.fidonet.org/).

36. A total of 31 countries were connected to the Internet in September 1991, while 47, 79 and 49 countries were connected to BITNET, USENET and FIDONET, respectively (http://www.funet.fi/index/FUNET/history/internet/en/)

37. See, for example, Sung (1997).

38. See, for example, Mayntz and Schneider (1988).

39. 'Leased circuits refers to a two-way link for the exclusive use of a subscriber regardless of the way it is used by the subscriber (e.g. switched subscriber or non-switched, or voice or data). Leased circuits, also referred to as leased lines, can be either national or international in scope' (*The ITU Telecommunication Indicators Handbook* (http://www.itu.int/publications/world/material/handbk-e.html)). 'The term "leased lines" owes its name to the manner in which telecommunication carriers historically sold private lines' (OECD, 1999b: 16).

40. In the USA, historically, the special arrangement of some users had been met through self-supply or private networks. In fact, even before competitive network operators had become established in the USA, it was AT&T which was the greatest proponent of bypass solutions … It was when AT&T, and later the RBOCs, saw the first inroads into their market

that the threat of bypass was used to argue that regulated competition would lead to the segmentation of the public network infrastructure and to the erosion of the systemic integrity of the US public telecommunication network (Mansell, 1993: 55–6).

41. David and Steinmueller (1994) point to the unique feature of WAN management practices in the externalization of surge requirements on the switched telecommunication network. To reduce negative congestion, companies construct smaller WAN capacity than needed for surge capacity. When a surge occurs, these companies dial into the switched network to absorb the overflow.

42. National Communications System Technology & Standard Division (1996: F-21).

43. Teske (1993).

44. Slye (1988: 357), cited in Teske (1993).

45. As Teske (1993: 2) puts it, American federal and state governments are relatively sophisticated users of information technology. For example, in terms of computer access, recent data show that the federal government is on top and state governments are about in the middle of the pack, while local governments trail, compared to businesses' access to computers. As service operations that specialize in information rather than the production of physical goods, governments must use information technology to advantage.

46. MFENet and HEPNet were established by the US Department of Energy (DOE) for its researchers in Magnetic Fusion Energy and High Energy Physicists, respectively. These networks merged to become ESNET (the Energy Sciences Network). NASA Space Physicists followed with SPAN (the Space Physics Analysis Network).

47. See Quarterman (1990: 228–9).

48. In 1992, the network backbone received US$29 million from the NSF, $13 million from the state of Michigan and $60 million from IBM and MCI (Teske, 1993).

49. 'Feds Weighing OSI Compatibility in All Net Buys', *Computer System News*, 8 September 1986, cited again in Spanier (1986). The DoD declared in 1987 that OSI protocols would be adopted. In July 1987, it announced that it would adopt OSI protocols as a full co-standard with the DoD protocols when GOSIP was formally approved as a Federal Information Processing Standard (Latham, 1988: 1).

50. See Carpentier *et al.* 1992 for the early development of information technology policy and projects at European Communities level.

51. Mayntz and Schneider (1988) provide a comparative analysis of videotex in France, Germany and the UK.

52. See Carpentier *et al.* (1992: 85–7).

53. Olthoff (1988), The COSINE Project, *Network News*, no. 27, Nov. 1988.

54. See Preissel and Higham (1995).

55. Gladwyn (1988).

56. Peterson (1993) points to a limitation of the Cosine programme in that it was a government-led not industry-led, project.

5.   The evolution of the Internet system

5.1   INTRODUCTION

We have examined the history of the invention and development of the Internet system as the selection process of packet network technologies which was shaped by visions of inventors and different interests of social groups and countries. The major stakeholders, including the telecommunication, computer and Internet communities, competed with each other to achieve control over the direction of evolution of computer network technologies. The battles were shaped by political, economic and technological power relationships, mainly between the USA and European countries through their competition for technological leadership in newly converging communication and information technologies.

This chapter examines how the Internet system emerged as the popular global data network from a network designed for military and academic research purposes in the USA. The evolution of the Internet system is analysed according to the model suggested by Hughes (1987). Its evolution can be divided into four different development phases: experimental period, Internet system building in the USA, global expansion and global Internet systems building. The governance and technological innovations during the experimental period and period of Internet system building in the USA were examined in Chapter 4.

This chapter is devoted to the history of connecting national research networks in developed countries through the collaboration of the international academic communities. Sections 5.2 and 5.3 review and reconstruct historical accounts of Internet development with the aim of expanding on issues that are relevant to the internationalization of the Internet. In the USA, the establishment of a backbone network (NSFNET), with government support for the building of regional and campus networks, contributed to the expansion of the Internet into the research and academic communities. The problems this raised, such as fragmentation of the networks, technical limitations of technological components, weakness of gateways between networks, lack of training and support for users, and lack of information about the networks connected to the Internet, foreshadowed some of the issues encountered in the internationalization process. System builders worked to upgrade the NSFNET to build the NERN (National Research and Education Network).

Section 5.4 examines the history of collaboration between the USA and other countries in the development of the Internet system, to illustrate how the USA exercized political and economic control in the global expansion of the Internet. Global expansion of the Internet began in earnest after the international coordination networks were established. Section 5.5 analyses the global expansion of the Internet system, focusing on regional differences between Western Europe, Asia and Eastern and Central Europe. Section 5.6 describes the global Internet system building phase, focusing on its integration into the telecommunications system through consolidation and establishment of global governance.

5.2   NATIONAL RESEARCH AND ACADEMIC NETWORK BUILDING

In the early 1980s, computer networks to connect scientists and researchers in the USA flourished. In addition to the ARPANET, networks were emerging to connect researchers within government departments, such as MFENet, HEPNet and SPAN. Academic communities also started to connect their computers through CSNET, BITNET and USENET. USENET, based on the UNIX built-in UUCP (Unix to Unix Copy) communication protocols, was established in 1980 (Quarterman and Hoskins, 1986). Most of these government agency research networks were eventually connected and integrated into the Internet system in the national research network building process.

The very success of ARPANET and the fast-growing research networks of government agencies and universities led to changes in the governance system to accommodate the needs of the broader research community. There was also an increasing need for institutions to be reorganized to accommodate and coordinate technological and managerial problems because ARPANET could not respond to the burgeoning demand from the building of regional and special-purpose computer networks such as Merit, Inc. and BARRNET (Hart *et al.*, 1992). These access nodes were expanding beyond defence agencies and defence contractors.

Between 1983 and 1988, the Internet became accessible to the academic and research community with the establishment of NSFNET. The NSF emerged as one of the main Internet system builders and was a member of the governing bodies. The Internet system started to expand to the wider research and academic community as control was handed over to the NSF. NSF made critical decisions that resulted in the US research and academic networks being built as specialist private networks based on Internet technologies rather than on public networks.

Technological innovations multiplied as more networks became connected to the Internet. In 1982, DARPA was funding Jon Postel at the Information Science Institute at the University of California to coordinate the allocation of Internet Protocol addresses and to assign networking parameters. Two years later the DNS, also funded by DARPA, was created to translate IP numbers into user-friendly names, with .mil, .gov, .edu, .org and .com suffixes.[1] The increase in the size of the Internet was challenging the capabilities of routers. Originally a single distributed algorithm for a router was replaced by a hierarchical model of routing with an Interior Gateway Protocol (IGP) inside each region of the Internet, and an Exterior Gateway Protocol (EGP) used to tie the regions together so that different requirements for cost, rapid reconfiguration, robustness and scale could be accommodated.[2]

The Construction of NSFNET

The Computing for Education and Research (CER) Program was established at the NSF in the late 1970s: this programme did not initially include supercomputing (Hart *et al.*, 1992). The NSF funded the THEORYNET project designed to provide an electronic mail system for theoretical computer scientists in the late 1970s and initiated a five-year project to construct a computer science research network, CSNET, in 1981 (Comer, 1983).

In the early 1980s, NSF became increasingly concerned about access for university researchers to supercomputers. The USA had far more supercomputers than the rest of the world combined: in 1982, there were about 61 Class VI supercomputers worldwide: 42 in the USA, seven in the UK, six in Germany, four in France and two in Japan (Dallaire, 1984). However supercomputers in the USA were largely concentrated in government laboratories for mission-oriented work (for instance, atomic weapons research, fusion energy research, aerodynamics and fluid dynamics studies and atmospheric science) and only a limited number of researchers could gain access to them. As Wilson (1984) witnesses, the Japanese Super-Speed Computer project generated strong pressures for a response in the USA.[3]

As a result of intense lobbying by the research community in the face of the Japanese supercomputing challenge, the NSF in 1984 received congressional approval for the construction of five supercomputing centres (Mandelbaum and Mandelbaum, 1992). These new supercomputing centres were built in 1985–6 at Cornell University (the Cornell National Supercomputer Facility), Princeton (the John Von Neumann Center), Pittsburgh (the Pittsburgh Supercomputing Center), the University of Illinois at Urbana/Champaign (the National Center for Supercomputing Application) and the University of California at San Diego (the San Diego Supercomputer Center). There were only five initially because of the high cost of the new machines.[4] Four Engineering Centers of Excellence (at the University of Delaware, Purdue University, the University of Washington at Seattle and the University of Minnesota) were included in the NSFNET networking plans for 1986–7.[5]

However this still did not make supercomputing power available to the vast majority of researchers. To improve this situation, NSF took steps to link these supercomputers and regional and university computer centres because scientists who were not based at the universities near the centres also wanted access to them. NSF made two critical policy decisions which led to the building of a national research network using the Internet system: the establishment of the NSFNET using TCP/IP and support for DARPA's existing Internet organizational infrastructure.

In 1985, NSF established NSFNET as the backbone network to link supercomputers and regional and university computer centres. The NSFNET consisted of several leased telephone lines connecting supercomputer centres. The NSF backbone was initially implemented using gateways (systems used to route traffic) developed at the University of Delaware and links operating at the ARPANET speed of 56 Kbps in 1986 (Hart *et al.*, 1992). This backbone was expanded to include 13 nodes, each of which was the hub of a regional network, composed, in turn, of interlinked university campus networks.[6] The NSFNET consisted of three different levels: the transcontinental backbone connecting the NSF funded supercomputer centres and mid-level networks; the mid-level networks themselves; and the networks. This hierarchical structure included a large fraction of the research and education community and even extended into a global arena via international connections.

NSF awarded a contract to Merit Network, Inc. (a consortium including IBM, MCI and the State of Michigan) to upgrade and operate the NSFNET backbone using 1.544Mbps T-1 leased lines connecting six regional networks, the National Center for Atmospheric Research (NCAR) in Boulder, Colorado, the five existing supercomputer centres, and Merit. NSFNET replaced ARPANET as the main Internet backbone in 1989.[7] In September 1990, Merit, IBM and MCI spun off a new independent non-profit organization, Advanced Network and Service, Inc. (ANS), to operate this NSFNET backbone and to tackle the challenges of moving to 45Mbps backbone speeds. IBM and MCI contributed US$4 million, and ANS acted as subcontractor to Merit. The backbone was expanded to 16 sites and the final T-3 router was installed in November 1991.[8]

National system building and critical problems
The national Internet system building process in the USA began with the separation of MILNET from ARPANET. The transition of ARPANET from

NCP to TCP/IP meant it could be split into a specialized network – MILNET – supporting military operational requirements and a network supporting research needs. This was accomplished in 1983. MILNET was integrated with the Defense Data Network (DDN) that had been created a year earlier.

With the removal of military restrictions, other groups such as CSNET added their networks to the growing network of networks. CSNET provided computer scientists with access to all the nodes on the ARPANET through agreement between CSNET, NSF and DARPA and allowed CSNET traffic to share the ARPANET infrastructure on a non-metered basis (Comer, 1983; Ruthfiled, 1995).

At the same time, the management structure of the ARPANET was reorganized. ARPANET had graduated to production use, but it was still an evolving experimental testbed under the leadership of DARPA and DCA. In 1983, ICCB was replaced by a number of task forces, each focused on a particular area of the technology (routers, end-to-end protocols and so on) to lead the technological development of the Internet system (Cerf, 1989). The IAB (Internet Activities Board) whose members were the chairs of the task forces was established in order that the Internet would be controlled in a consistent way. Changes to the coordination of engineering features were needed as the Internet system expanded to other government agencies, including NSFNET and various US and international government-funded activities. Interest was also beginning to grow in the commercial sector. In 1986, the Internet Engineering Task Force (IETF) was created from one of the task forces to serve as a forum for DARPA contractors to achieve technical coordination in their work on ARPANET, US DDN (Defense Data Network) and the Internet core gateway system.

The growth of the Internet continued, resulting in further changes to the substructure within both the IAB and the IETF. In 1989, IAB changed its setup from task forces to the IETF and then the Internet Research Task Force (IRTF).[9] The IAB recognized the increasing importance of the IETF,[10] and restructured the standards process to recognize explicitly the IESG as the major standards review body. The IETF combined working groups into areas, and designated area directors. An Internet Engineering Steering Group (IESG) comprising the area directors was established. The IAB was also restructured so that the task forces were eventually combined into the IRTF. The role of the IRTF was to continue to organize and explore advanced concepts in networking under the guidance of the IAB and with the support of various government agencies. With the establishment of NSFNET, the Internet had become a national system, being managed collaboratively by several government agencies. The Federal Research Internet Coordinating Committee (FRICC) was made up of key managers responsible for computer networking R&D in US government organizations, including DARPA, NSF, the DOE and

NASA.[11] The aim of FRICC was to coordinate US government support for, and development and use of, the Internet system (McClure *et al.*, 1991). FRICC was attached to the Office of Science and Technology Policy (OSTP) in the Executive Office of the President. FRICC sponsored most of the US research on the Internet system, including giving support to the IAB and its subsidiary organizations (Cerf, 1990c). Federal agencies shared the cost of a common infrastructure, for example the transoceanic circuits, and jointly supported and managed interconnection points for inter-agency traffic, the Federal Internet Exchanges (FIX-E and FIX-W) being built for this purpose. To coordinate this sharing, the Federal Networking Council (FNC) was formed from FRICC. The FNC cooperated with other international organizations, such as RARE in Europe, through the Coordinating Committee on Intercontinental Research Networking (CCIRN), to coordinate Internet support for the research community worldwide.

Even though FRICC (and later FNC) were established to coordinate the connection and management of the various fragmented private networks, below federal level there was virtually no management structure for the Internet (McClure *et al.*, 1991). Decision-making and policy-making authority for governing access and use were located in individual networks and host sites. The different concerns and interests of individual network and governance traditions and cultures emerged as critical problems in the further development of the Internet. Users' access to and use of the Internet were dependent on the individual networks to which they belonged, and the sophistication of users regarding the complexities of communication protocols and procedures. McClure *et al.* argue that the explosive growth in the absence of a unified logic or plan brought problems, including the fragmentation of networks, limited capacity of existing networks, technical limitations on hardware and software, weakness of gateways between networks, need for training and support for users and lack of documentation about the number of networks and their procedures.

National Research and Academic Network Building

Faced with the need to solve these critical problems, the US government launched the construction of a national research and academic network by upgrading the NSFNET. The US government was concerned about competitiveness in the area of supercomputers and this led to debates about the building of NREN (National Research and Education Network).[12] After lengthy and vigorous debate, and congressional deliberations, the High Performance Computing and National Research and Education Network Act of 1991 became law on 11 September 1991. According to this law, NSF was to take overall responsibility for managing NREN, while FCCSET continued to play a role in its planning. The legislative programme started in June 1986, when the Supercomputer Network Study Act of 1986, S.2594 was introduced by Senator Al Gore.

The White House Office of Science and Technology Policy was required to report to Congress on the role of the federal government in promoting supercomputing and high-speed networking. After policy reports issued by OSTP in 1987,[13] and by the National Research Council of the National Academy of Science (NAS),[14] the High Performance Computer Act was introduced on 18 May 1989.[15]

FRICC had the lead role in the process of building NREN. FRICC suggested a three-stage plan to create NREN:

Stage 1   to upgrade and interconnect existing agency networks by a jointly funded and managed T1 (1.5Mbps) National Networking Testbed,
Stage 2   to integrate national networks into a T3 (45 Mbps) backbone by 1993,
Stage 3   to instigate a technological leap to a multigigabit NREN starting in the mid-1990s.[16]

T1 lines had a speed of 1.544 megabits per second and these were considered to be high-speed lines; a T3 line had a speed of 45 megabits per second, which represents an increase in transmission speed by a factor of 30 (Quarterman, 1990: 134). It would integrate 'four levels of increasingly complex and flexible capacity': physical wire/fibre optic common carrier highways; user-defined, packet switched networks; basic network operations and services; and research, education, database and information services accessible to network users.[17]

This complex architecture was the outcome of a compromise between different actors lobbying for services for their infrastructure needs in the policy-making process of national networking policy initiatives.[18] Therefore problems remained, such as the priority of network service provision and coordination. Actors involved in NREN had their own views on implementation strategies. These included the research and education communities, librarians and other information providers, information technology manufacturers and other members of the information industry, federal and other policy makers and policy analysts and scholars (McClure *et al.*, 1991).

The updating of the NSFNET had been pursued in order to build NREN. The Internet came to be considered as an important tool for the competitiveness and technological leadership of the US economy. During the debates on the High Performance Computing and the National Research and Education Network Act, policy concerns about information technology extended from scientific research to the competitiveness of the economy. NREN became one part of the High Performance Computing and Communications Program as a result of the enactment by both Houses of Congress of S.272, the High Performance Computing Act of 1991.[19]

> In an era of partisan politics and deep anxiety about the underlying strength of the US economy, the NREN has become a rallying point for cooperation in the national interest – among scientists, among agencies, across sectors, and across the political spectrum. (Kahin, 1992: 6)

NREN was one of the four integrated components of the HPCC programme. It included development of the technology necessary for a scalable parallel computing system capable of performing trillions of operations per second; ASTA (Advanced Software Technology and Algorithms) focusing on the development of software technology and algorithms for research applications and for realizing the potential of networking high-performance computing systems; NREN to provide high-speed computer networking capability on a nationwide scale to scientific and education institutions; and Basic Research and Human Resources (BRHR) providing support for long-term research in many disciplines, in their efforts to increase the pool of researchers and in supporting efforts towards accelerated technology transition (Bostwick, 1991). In 1990, the agencies involved proposed a US$638 million budget for the HPCC programme, an increase of 30 per cent over the fiscal year 1991. NREN represented only 14 per cent of the total HPCC budget proposed for 1992, while HPCS, ASTA and BRHR accounted for 25 per cent, 41 per cent and 20 per cent, respectively. Most HPCC programmes were designed to promote, directly and indirectly, the development of the Internet system. The responsibilities of each participating HPCC Program agency are summarized in Table 5.1.

The central goal of the HPCC Programme was to accelerate significantly the commercial availability and use of the next generation of high-performance computers and networks. In detail it aimed to extend US leadership in high-performance computing and communication technology, disseminate and apply this technology widely to speed innovation and encourage US productivity and competitiveness. NREN was pursued through the cooperation of agencies reflecting the diverse communities of interest and the remarkable breadth of the programme. Table 5.2 presents the diverse policy objectives.

Transition and Commercialization

The building of NREN involved commercialization of the Internet. It facilitated the development of commercial products implementing the Internet technology and the development of competitive, private network services. By

Table 5.1   *The responsibilities of government agencies in the HPCC programme*

Government agency	Responsibility
DARPA	Technology development and coordination for gigabit networks
DoE	Energy development mission facilities and gigabits application research; with NASA, coordination of activities in HPC system evaluation, testbed development
NASA	Aerospace development mission facilities; coordination of accumulation and access to the HPC software base
NSF	Facilities coordination of broad deployment of the NREN working with other agencies' requirements
Department of Commerce, National Institute of Standards and Technology	High-speed network research; coordination of activities in HPC system instrumentation, in evaluation, and in standards issues
Department of Commerce, National Ocean and Atmospheric Administration	Ocean and atmospheric mission facilities
Environmental Protection Agency	States environmental mission assimilation
National Institute of Health, National Library of Medicine	Medical mission facilities

Source: Data adapted from Bostwick (1991).

the mid-1980s, the Internet was being used in the research, education and defence communities and companies such as Cisco Systems, Proteon and, later, Wellfleet (now Bay Networks) and 3Com became interested in manufacturing and selling routers and gateways.[20]

NSF gradually relaxed restrictions on commercial traffic and commercial ISPs emerged. As the network was increasingly opened to academic and research institutions, its commercial utility was recognized but was limited by the Acceptable Use Policy (AUP).[21] Under the draft AUP regime, between 1988 and mid-1990, there were regular requests from commercial players to

Table 5.2   Policy justification for the NREN

Objective	Examples and analogy	HPCA charges to individual agencies; other applicable HPCA actions
Tool	ARPANET; ESNET; MILNET	HPCA charges to DOE [Section 203(a)(4)] HPCS charge to DOC/NOAA [Section 204(a)(2)]
Basic research	ARPANET; traditional NSF programs	HPCA charge to DARPA [Section 102(d)]
Applied R&D	Mission agency research activities	HPCA charge to POE [Section 203(a)(1) and (b)(2)]
Research/ technology platform	Enabling technology (Advanced Technologies Programme)	HPCA charge to DOE [Section 203(b)(1)–(3); Section 102(c)(4), (9)–(10)
Knowledge infrastructure	NSFNET; library programmes, ERIC (Dept. of Education); Cooperative Extension Services (Department of Agriculture); Corporation for Public Broadcasting; NTIS; NLM; Depository Library Programme; Patent Office	HPCA charge to NSF [Section 201(a); Section 102(c)(2)]
Information infrastructure	Federal programmes in transportation infrastructure: highway, railroads, airports, waterways	HPCA charge to Section 102(c)(4), (10)
Equity	Public telecommunications facilities programme (DOC/ NTIA); rural electrification administration	HPCA charge to NSF [Section 201(a)(2)]; Section 102(a) and (b); Section 201(a)(1)

Source: Adapted from Kahin (1992: 12).

be included, but they were turned down because of the risks of overburdening network resources and of unfair competition with private network service providers (Kahin, 1990).[22]

In 1988, the Corporation for National Research Initiatives (CNRI) approached FRICC for permission to experiment with the interconnection of MCI Mail to the Internet. An experimental electronic mail relay was put into operation in 1989 and, shortly after, Compuserve, ATTMail and Sprintmail became operational. NYSERNET (New York State Regional Network) was the first to spin off to become a for-profit company, Performance System International (PSI). Other Internet providers began as independent entities; one of these was UUNET, which started as a private non-profit organization and began offering an Internet service called ALTERNET; another was CERFNET, a for-profit operation initiated by General Atomic in 1989; a third was NEARNet, which started in the Boston area and was absorbed into a cluster of for-profit services operated as BBN Planet. BBN was the original developer of the ARPANET IMP protocol and BBN also created the Telenet service which it sold to GTE and which subsequently became Sprintnet.

In the early 1990s commercial ISPs entered the Internet market. Some mid-level networks such as CERFnet provided interconnection services for private business for a fee consistent with NSFNET AUP. In the 1990s, as the AUP was relaxed, the first commercial Network Access Point (NAP) was established in the USA. In 1991, the Commercial Internet Exchange (CIX), by then the leading industry association of the ISPs, became the first entity to establish an exchange point for commercial users. The rationale for a commercial NAP was to enable companies using the Internet to have more flexible routing. Prior to the establishment of the CIX, while one division of a company might have access to the Internet, other divisions of the same company might not have the same access rights because of the AUP. In this situation, the company would have to route the traffic of these excluded divisions via another network. The establishment of a commercial NAP allowed the original CIX members to route all company traffic over the same network without fear of violating NSFNET or Internet AUPs.

NSFNET next began transition to the commercial Internet system. In May 1993, NSF issued a request for bids (NSF 93–52) designed to radically alter the architecture of the Internet. The NSF designated a series of NAPs in the place of NSFNET, quite similar to the CIX concept, where private commercial backbone operators could interconnect at different points on an intermediary backbone, and would directly connect at a series of single points.

The new network architecture was designed to favour big network operators (Davies, 1995b). Network service providers were not financed directly by NSF. Instead, NSF funded regional network attachments to these providers, but only for those present at all NAPs over four years. This encouraged scale and favoured the big operators who could exploit economies of scale. Control of the Internet was handed over to major telecommunication network operators. At the same time, NSF designed a very high-speed Backbone Network Service (vBNS) at 155Mbps, the usage of which was restricted to research organizations that required high speeds for applications such as scientific computation and visualization. NAPs could interconnect the vBNS and other backbone networks, both domestic and foreign.

In February 1994, NSF announced that four NAPs would be built. There were two Federal Internet Exchange points: FIX-East at the University of Maryland in College Park, Maryland, and FIX-West at the NASA Ames Research Centre at Moffet Field between Sunnyvale and Mountainview, California. These FIXs largely existed to interconnect MILNET, NASA Science Net and some other federal government networks. Therefore the NSFNET was transformed into a network with 11 major interconnection points, four official NAPs, three historical NAPs (CIX, FIX-East, and FIX-West) and four de facto NAPs. In 1995, NSFNET was retired and the US backbone traffic was routed via interconnected commercial networks. These networks continue to use the four original NSF-sponsored NAPs, now commercially funded, and the CIXs.

The backbone concept was adapted in order to exploit economies of scale in both demand and supply for the design of a national Internet system in the USA. As was explained in the previous section, the NSFNET was established on the basis of a multitiered service model which aggregated networks at regional levels and connected the regions with an interlinking superstructure based on a 'backbone' concept. This hierarchical network topology of the NSFNET backbone directly reflected the cost structure where many cheap routers are used to manage a limited number of expensive lines (Mackie-Mason and Varian, 1996). The centralization of the network infrastructure, at least at regional level is becoming increasingly inevitable in order to exploit economies of scale. To aggregate demand it is necessary to exploit economies of scale on the demand side and thus share the cost among the parties involved. As a result of this, Internet networks increasingly moved towards a centralized network structure.

A transition policy also encouraged the centralization of control in order to create a market of some scale for Internet services (Davies, 1995b). When NSFNET was retired, NSF decided to fund regional network attachments to Network service providers (NSPs) for four years, but only those that had been present at all the Network Access Points (NAPs). As a result, major US telecommunications operators such as MCI, US Sprint and ANS emerged as key players in the Internet commercialization era. All these major US telecommunication network operators had already been involved in Internet service provision. Moss and Townsend (2000) point out the effect of this policy on the network architecture:

> the commercial Internet backbone system is highly selective, concentrating the bulk of capacity and connections in a handful of metropolitan areas. In many ways, the present structure of the Internet backbone has largely erased the decentralizing objectives of earlier networks. (2000: 39)

When control was handed over from the public sector to commercial players, system builders adopted a strategy favouring a few major telecommunication operators to create a market and to nurture it. In the next section, the process of the global expansion of the Internet system is examined.

5.3 THE GLOBAL EXPANSION OF THE INTERNET SYSTEM

Early Collaborations

The Internet system was extended to Europe for scientific purposes from an early stage in its development. The first international connections to ARPANET were established in the UK (University College London (UCL)) and Norway (Royal Radar Establishment) in 1973. The Atlantic Packet Satellite Network or SATNET was jointly sponsored by ARPA, the BPO in the UK and the Norwegian Telecommunications Authority, and was used both for research and to transmit seismic data.

The implementation of packet switching in the ARPANET was achieved by collaboration between scientists in the USA and the UK. One of the important computer scientists who contributed to the internationalization of the Internet, Peter Kirstein, describes the early experiences with the ARPANET and the Internet in the UK and Europe in the middle of conflicts between European standards and the US dominance in the development of data networks.

In 1966, ARPA established a set of three seismic arrays in Alaska, Montana and Kjeller in Norway, known as NORSAR, based on a formal bilateral treaty between the USA and Norway. The arrays were operated for ARPA under the auspices of their Nuclear Monitoring Research Office and a communication link between Washington, DC and NORSAR was established. This channel was transmitted by satellite to London where it was connected via cable to Kjeller, where the NORSAR array was located. In late 1970 a proposal was made by Larry Roberts, who was in charge of the ARPANET project, to Donald Davies at NPL in the UK to link their two networks. This was not accomplished, mainly for political reasons (Kirstein, 1999).

In late 1970, Roberts proposed to Davies that it would be very interesting to link their two networks. The existence of the Washington to NORSAR line would make it comparatively cheap to break the connection in London and link in the NPL network ... The problem was that the British government had just applied to join the European Community; this made Europe good and the United States bad from a governmental policy standpoint. NPL was under the Department of Technology, and Davies was quite unable to take up Roberts's offer. He had to concentrate on European initiatives like European Informatics Networks. (Ibid.: 39)

Kirstein observed that, soon after, UCL set up a project to link to UCL (rather than NPL) as the primary node, based on a technological justification to overcome the political barrier. He described how ARPANET accepted this proposal and promised the necessary equipment and some financial support to allow UCL to use an expensive transatlantic link. However the project came up against problems, in that UCL failed to obtain financial support from the Science Research Council (SRC) and the Department of Industry (DOI) in the UK. Eventually support from the BPO, and Davies at the NPL, kept the UCL project alive. The BPO was interested in the SATNET project because it would promise to 'allow significant reduction in the number of channels required and hence, a reduction in cost' (ibid.: 41). In the late 1970s, groups in Italy, Germany, Norway, Comsat and the UK were also participants in the SATNET project.

From the outset, the aim of the UCL–CS (Computer Science) project was not only to carry out innovative research but also to provide network services to the UK and US groups that wished to cooperate. Kirstein observes that, as early as 1975, there was strong collaboration between several groups in the UK and the USA. UCL–CS continued to run the Internet–UK interconnection services until 1986, when 'the service had become an accepted part of the British research scene' (ibid.: 42). Because of political barriers and technological uncertainty, the project was established by a small number of 'key people [who] could make individual decisions and investments for a speculative project' and run by a private organization (by UK 'government intervention in the form of the Customs and Excise') (ibid.).

Despite the limited scale of the project, the early collaboration contributed to technological innovations of the Internet. For example, in late 1974, the experiments in TCP protocol were conducted for the first time by Vinton Cerf (at that time an assistant professor at Stanford) and Paal Spilling (a visiting scholar from Norway at UCL) (Kirstein, 1999). Kirstein also points to the important role of the computer scientists of the UK in the design process of international data network standards and a UK standard favouring the Internet system:

The UCL group played a prominent role in all this Standards formulation – partly because we were one of the most expert and partly to try to ensure that the British activities did not diverge too violently from the U.S. ones. With the one exception of the ordering of domains – where the UK decision was to use the reverse procedure to the Arpanet policy – we largely succeeded in keeping reasonable similarity. For example, the Grey Book for mail protocols was almost identical to its Internet equivalent. (Ibid.: 42)

Unlike the UK, academic communities in other European countries could have no significant academic involvement with their US colleagues until the mid-1980s. Global computer networks such as USENET and EARN contributed to the collaboration between the US and other countries' science and technology communities and encouraged them to support the Internet system later.

Computer scientists had built a computer communication community to exchange their knowledge and experience and thus were demonstrating the technological and economic efficiencies of packet switching globally. Their ideas and vision had been spread through global computer networks including BITNET, USNET and FIDONET which connected research and academic communities globally. Global expansion of the computer networking community contributed to the development of the Internet technologies.

Establishment of Global Collaboration Networks

To facilitate the global expansion of the Internet, the Coordinating Committee on Intercontinental Research Networking (CCIRN) was set up in 1988, and included FNC and its counterparts in North America and Europe. Co-chaired by the executive directors of the FNC and the RARE, the CCIRN provided a forum for cooperative planning and management of the global Internet between the principal North American and European research networking bodies (Cerf, 1989).

CCIRN had its first meeting in Washington, DC in November 1987, but, until May 1988, the Committee was known as the Necessary Ad Hoc Coordinating Committee. One of its main aims was to

stimulate cooperative intercontinental research by promoting enhanced interoperable networking services; specifically these include: promoting the evolution of an open international research network and coordinating and facilitating effective use of the international networks to enhance the quality of research and scholarship. (Wood, 1989: 9)

Between 1988 and 1991, CCIRN held two meetings per year, and regional CCIRN groups were formed, EuroCCIRN and North American CCIRN. North American CCIRN (NACCIRN) consisted of representatives from the USA, Canada and Mexico. From the USA, representatives included the CREN (Corporation for Research and Educational Networking), agencies participating in the FRICC (initially, DARPA, NASA, DHHS, DOE and NSF) and an observer from the IAB. From Canada, representatives included the Canadian Defence and the Canadian Research Agencies. From Mexico, representatives included the Consejo Nacional De Ciencia Y Tecnologia (CONACYT, the Mexican National Council of Science and Technology). EuroCCIRN, an initiative of RARE, included members of RARE, COSINE, EARN, EUNET, HEP-CERN, SPAN-ESA, CEC and ICB.[23]

To provide a structure for engineering and technical support to the CCIRN management activity, the Intercontinental Engineering and Planning Group (IEPG) was established in November 1990. The main role of the IEPG was to ensure that planning and engineering activities relating to the global Internet were commensurate with various national and regional requirements. In this way it was hoped that the Internet would continue to grow within an overall framework of engineering stability and effectively managed connectivity.

CCIRN focused on the management and policy levels and on the formulation of common policy and practices across various research support networks within the Internet.

At a more practical level there was collaboration between the USA and Europe on the expansion of the Internet system. For example, meetings on the network and infrastructure user requirements for transatlantic research collaboration were held in Brussels and Washington, DC in July 1990. They were designed to enable effective cooperation between the US and European research teams for participation in the planned ESPRIT–DARPA/NSF programme of collaborative research in information science and technology.[24] One of the important recommendations concerned the transatlantic and continental distribution of facilities. They set out to plan higher-speed transatlantic links by using the existing collaboration mechanism; to set up a European and US DARPA/NSF task force for sharing them; and to aggregate data transmission facilities. The USA has actively collaborated with Europe from an early stage of Internet system development through its military and scientific networks. However technological transfer to other countries began in earnest with the global expansion through the establishment of the CCIRN and RIPE NCC (Réseaux IP Européens – Network Control Centre) after RIPE was established.

In 1992, the Asia–Pacific joined CCIRN formally with the formation of APCCIRN (Asia Pacific region at the Coordinating Committee for Inter-Continental Research Networking), whose name was subsequently changed to APNG (Asia Pacific Networking Group). Observers from Africa joined CCIRN in 1995, and Latin America and the Caribbean joined CCIRN, and ENRED represented the region, in 1997.[25]

Economic and Political Control

The global expansion of the Internet system was controlled by the USA for economic and political reasons. NSF had made efforts to connect the US research and education communities with their counterparts and resources in Europe. This led to NSF assisting other countries in connecting to NSFNET through the International Connections Management (ICM) project (1991–6). ICM was the result of the effort to help US scientists at NASA to gain access to the SIMBAD (Set of Identifications, Measurements and Bibliography for Astronomical Data) database created and maintained by a French government agency.[26]

The ICM project helped about 25 countries to connect to the NSFNET during the period 1991 to 1996 by sharing the cost of links, for example international circuits and/or paying a port management fee. For example, when NSF established a satellite teleport gateway for Latin America in Homestead, Florida to deal with Internet traffic from Latin America through PanAmSat, NSF asked Sprint to put a router for PanAmSat Teleport and extend the connection to the Washington POP (point of presence). The port fee is the bundled average fee for a network operator (for example, Sprint) to recover the cost of bringing the signal to the Washington POP and router and managing the connection. In general, if a foreign country was connected to a US service provider, it would cost more (usually in the form of membership fees) than the 'port fee' paid by NSF.[27] The amount of financial support from ICM appears to have varied with respect to US economic and political interests. The ICM grant was focused on the connections for countries with advanced research capabilities, such as France, the UK and the Nordic countries, and those of political interest such as Latin America and Mongolia.

Steve Goldstein argued in his interview for the *Cook Report* that other countries rushed to connect their academic research networks to NSFNET mainly because the USA was the location of Internet resources, the USA had a better Internet infrastructure and there were cheaper international circuits between the USA and other countries.[28] It was much less expensive to transmit traffic by connecting to NSFNET than to connect other countries directly because the US network operators' international leased line prices were substantially lower than those of other countries. More importantly, however, the Internet was designed with the USA as its topological centre. APIA (the Asia Pacific Internet Association) argues that most Internet links were connected directly to sites within the continental USA with international Internet traffic typically being routed through the USA prior to reaching its final destination, even when the destination was in the same region (or, in some cases, even the same country) as the source.[29]

Connections to the US Internet also appear to have been influenced by political concerns. For example, from the early connection between the UK and the USA, there was extensive monitoring and access control because of security issues (Kirstein, 1999). This is partly because, during the cold war era, access to Internet technology was limited to US military allies. In particular, the technological transfer of the Internet system was subject to the COCOM (Coordinating Committee for Multilateral Export) regime restrictions.

> Before one can obtain a so-called supercomputer (at least from the United States which still ships most of these wonders), a Supercomputer Safeguard Plan (SSP) has to be worked out. While these plans may differ quite a lot in detail, most of them contain a phrase saying that the supercomputer must not be used by COCOM proscribed country nationals, and that it must have no direct ties to the networks of COCOM proscribed countries. (Greisen, 1990: 178)

In August 1994, NSF restrictions were still in place on traffic between some countries, including Bosnia-Herzegovina, Iran, Iraq, Libya, Macedonia, North Korea, Sudan, the Syrian Arab Republic, Vietnam, Yugoslavia (that is, Serbia and Montenegro), and NSFNET-sponsored sites and networks.[30]

5.4   DIFFERENT REGIONAL CONTEXTS

The research communities in most countries played an important role in the localization of the Internet system, a relatively complex and sophisticated technological system.[31] In particular, the localization of the Internet system required more advanced user capabilities than other ICTs because it is controlled by the users. The building of regional networks (for example, backbone networks) by connecting national research networks was extremely important in that this enabled economies of scale to be realized, particularly in the early stages of localization. More importantly, regional collaboration in building regional networks accompanied technological, economic and political activities which shaped the localization of the Internet.

European Countries

European countries competed and collaborated with the USA in the development of data networks. As discussed in Chapter 4, the X.25 community in Europe competed with the Internet community in the USA over the control of the technological development of the data network. At the same time, computer scientists and researchers in the USA and Europe were collaborating through international computer networking communities. In this sense, the

European Academic and Research Network (EARN) community had contributed to the collaboration among its members.

EARN was established in 1983 in order to serve the broader academic research community and associated industrial research community in Europe (and the Middle East and Africa: Jennings, 1990). EARN originated as an international version of BITNET sponsored by IBM and it maintained close cooperation with BITNET and CERN. From the beginning, EARN included some 15 west European countries and, from 1990, east European countries were connected.[32] By the mid-1980s, most European countries had had experience of the Internet technology indirectly through EARN. EARN was based on one hub site per country, normally a major academic computing centre. Other sites in the country had to lease a low-speed line to the hub. IBM funding terminated at the end of 1987.[33] After that, most of EARN's funding came from annual fees paid by the attached institutes.[34] An important advantage of EARN was its deployment of robust, what might be considered 'old-fashioned', technology. This made it easy for countries in Central and Eastern Europe and North Africa to join the EARN at reasonable cost.

The European Unix Network (EUNET) grew out of USENET in the USA, originally offering dial-up connections to an informally run network for electronic mail and news and then graduating to professional operation. It had access to a very wide set of news groups covering many fields of interest. It was the easiest data network for the research department of a commercial company to join. In Europe, by the early 1980s, most countries had national research networks, for instance JANET in the UK, SURFnet in the Netherlands, Renate in France and WiN (Wissenschaftsnetz) in Germany.[35] These networks typically were based on lines leased from the PTOs, and their operation was often the responsibility of a small team reporting to the ministry responsible for research or education (Williams and Carpenter, 1998). These national academic and research networks used OSI standards (X.25 protocols) reflecting the European PTOs' interests and strategies in competing with TCP/IP. Williams and Carpenter observe that some scientific disciplines had a tradition of operating on a pan-Europe level, for example, weather forecasting, particle physics and space science, all of which have an associated European Treaty Organization that acts as the main data source and as a natural communications hub.

Since no pan-Europe networks of the required performance existed, all of these disciplines set up their own networks which they paid for and operated. They cooperated with other networks, both for European leased lines whose cost was often shared and for intercontinental lines. Until the early 1990s, because of the high cost of European leased lines, it was common to find institutes in Central and Eastern Europe (CEE) with 64 kilobit/s connections, or even slower (Neggers, 1991; Williams and Carpenter, 1998). The networked universities and research institutes typically paid an annual fee to cover operational costs.

From the early stage of computer network development, European countries made efforts to build a regional network. However these activities were not very fruitful until the mid-1980s, when the European Commission emerged as a major actor in integrating European telecommunications networks. As the research benefits of such networks nationally became apparent there was considerable pressure to extend their scope to allow international cooperation among researchers. International partnership has long been a feature of cooperative R&D sponsored by the European Commission. Thus, in November 1985, the National Research Networks in Europe, as part of the Eureka programme and with support from the European Commission, established the COSINE (Cooperation for OSI Networking in Europe) project to develop a pan-Europe approach to research networking in providing an infrastructure for the academic, government and commercial communities based on the use of OSI protocols (Olthoff, 1988; Peterson, 1993).

RARE was created in 1986 as a forum for national networking organizations to discuss matters of common interest and, in particular, to resolve the problems of cooperation between national services that had been created independently. One of RARE's first major tasks was to coordinate the technical work necessary for the COSINE Specification Phase.

The IXI (International X.25 Infrastructure) pilot network was built as a result of the COSINE project in July 1990. IXI provided an X.25 service at 64 Kbps to 18 access points and also had connections to public X.25 services in nine countries where tariff arrangements could be agreed with the national PTOs. Although the technical characteristics of the IXI service were not advanced even when the service started, IXI nevertheless represented a significant step forward as a managed network providing a common service between many European countries. However the progress of the COSINE project was slower than planned mainly because of the complex process of coordination between representatives of the 18 countries (Davies, 1993). Therefore COSINE was overtaken to some extent by the explosion in European usage of TCP/IP and the higher-level protocols that they supported (Davies and Bersee, 1994). TCP/IP had been adopted as the basis of the national network service in a number of countries, notably Switzerland and the Nordic countries in the early 1990s. Since other countries were also introducing TCP/IP for at least part of their national services, it was essential that the new pan-Europe backbone could handle multiple protocols. In October 1992, EuropaNET was built to offer a 2 Mbps multi-multi-protocol (X.25, IP, CLNS) service in all COSINE member states. The large TCP/IP users set up Ebone92 as an IP backbone service with access points in five countries. Ebone92 was later transformed into Ebone93 with a greater

number of participants and higher speed lines to provide a backbone service between networks in different European countries and a neutral
interconnect service between the participating service providers, including
commercial networks. To connect different regional networks, EuropaNET
and Ebone, in 1993 gateways were set up between them (Davies and Bersee,
1994). The Nordic countries relied on Ebone for their international connections, while Germany and Italy had connections to EuropaNET, but not to
Ebone (Davies, 1993).

The Operation Unit Ltd of EuropaNET set up in April 1993, which later
became DANTE (Delivery of Advanced Network Technology to Europe Ltd)
was established to build and manage a single European infrastructure in June
1993. The goal of the company was 'to rationalise the management of otherwise fragmented, uncoordinated, expensive and inefficient transnational
services and operational facilities'.[36] In March 1994, ownership of DANTE
was transferred from RARE to the shareholders, national research networks.

In 1994, EuroCAIRN (European Cooperation for Academic and Industrial
Research Networking) was established as a Eureka Project to improve network facilities for European researchers by providing the framework for
organizing the pooling of national funding resources, promoting cooperation
between national networking activities and involving the information technology and telecommunications service industries (Davies, 1994b). As
explained in the previous chapter, high-speed European research networks
were funded by EU R&D programmes.

TERENA (the Trans-European Research and Education Networking Association) was formed in October 1994 by the merger of RARE and EARN
(European Academic and Research Network) 'to promote and participate in
the development of a high quality international information and telecommunications infrastructure for the benefit of research and education'.[37]

The European Internet system building process started with the establishment of RIPE (Réseaux IP Européens) in 1989.[38] The objective of RIPE was
to ensure the necessary administrative and technical coordination to allow the
operation and expansion of a pan-Europe IP network. The first task was
exchange of information and the implementation of a database in order to
have a central place to store operational data for network operators in Europe.
National and international IP network operators such as BelWü, CERN,
EASInet, Eunet, GARR, HEPnet, NORDUnet, SURFnet, SWITCH and
XLINK were to participate in the RIPE Coordinating Committee (Blokzijl,
1989a, 1989b). This voluntary organization became an official organization.
In 1991, the RIPE Network Coordination Centre (NCC) was established in
order to support and coordinate the management of a pan-Europe IP network
and act as a building block for the global administrative framework of the
Internet currently being developed (Blokzijl, 1990).

Of the European countries, the Nordic countries were quickest to adopt Internet technology. NORDUnet was a regional network project to provide the national research and education communities with an efficient networking service. From 1980, conferences were organized to promote cooperation and exchange of information among the Nordic national university projects (Carlson, 1987). Based on these experiences, the NORDUnet programme was set up in 1985 for four years and financed by the Nordic Council of Ministers (Villemoes, 1996). NORDUnet was fully implemented in 1989. It had direct circuits to NSFNET in the USA, and EUnet and CERN in Europe. In 1989, the network was handed over to the Nordic National Research Networks (NRNs), which set up and funded the NORDUnet organization to operate it. NORDUnet adopted a multi-protocol structure with TCP/IP as the primary service. At the beginning of the project, it seemed clear that it would be built on X.25 in that 'NORDUnet already in 1984 had defined its goals and objectives in a way which is congruent to RARE and COSINE projects and contains threads of activities and projects' (Carlson, 1987: 201). However, in the end, TCP/IP was selected as the primary protocol. Villemoes (1996) explained the political process in the selection of technological system as follows:

> After a difficult period of network protocol evaluation the program decided, in collaboration with the Nordic national research networks (NRNs), to interconnect them by a multi-protocol structure with TCP/IP as the primary service. This decision, which looks obvious today, was *a bold decision at a time when the rest of Europe was busy implementing OSI networks*. (Villemoes, 1996; emphasis in original)

Central and Eastern Europe

Until the 1980s, Central and Eastern European (CEE) countries were restricted in their connection to computer networks (including the Internet) as they were COCOM proscribed countries.[39]

In the second half of the 1980s the first talks with foreign partners took place with the aim of connecting certain research institutes to France and Germany. However the binding legal and administrative regulations concerning hi-tech transfer ruled this possibility out. A partial solution was found; it consisted of making use of accounts in machines abroad which could be reached via modems. This system, however, proved unreliable and not cost-effective. Nevertheless it gave access to international computer networks. Such accounts were opened, as far as I am aware, in Germany, Switzerland and Denmark. A funny thing is that I received the official refusal from the French side to establish a permanent communication line with Paris in 1987 by e-mail in Warsaw.[40]

Political transformations in the CEE countries made it possible to overcome this institutional barrier. EARN and BITNET played an important role in getting political restrictions relaxed and finally eliminated. In March 1989, EARN opened discussions with the US Department of Commerce (DOC) which issues Supercomputer Safeguard Plans (SSP) (Greisen, 1990). In January 1990, DOC allowed EARN, BITNET and CERN to connect COCOM proscribed countries, including Eastern Europe, under special conditions.[41]

The Internet system transfer and localization in Eastern Europe was supported by European Union and NATO projects. In particular, international connectivity was established by financial support under the PHARE (Poland and Hungary: Action for the Restructuring of the Economy) R&D Networking Programme and Internet technologies were transferred by the INSIGHT (Information Systems Integrated by using Global Hypermedia Technology) project.[42] The development of the Internet in Eastern Europe started with financial support under the PHARE project which was designed to support the processes of economic transition and institutional reform in the CEE.[43] There were two projects under the PHARE R&D Networking Programme: PHARE (91) and PHARE (94). The PHARE (91) project (the PHARE/COSINE Programme) covered Bulgaria, the Czech Republic, Hungary, Poland, Slovakia and Romania. In the PHARE (91) project, the aim was to establish international interconnectivity. The outcome of the PHARE (91) project was that Romania, Hungary and the Czech Republic were connected to the EMPB (European Multi Protocol Backbone) by 1993 (Tétényi, 1996). The PHARE (94) project commenced in November 1994 and covered 11 countries. DANTE took over management of the PHARE 1994 R&D Networking Programme. DANTE also managed INSIGHT, part of the EC's COPERNICUS Programme designed to set up information systems based on hypermedia technology (World Wide Web – WWW) in the CEE countries. Technology transfer was one important element of the project, while the establishment of a national information server in the language of each of the participating countries was another.[44] Technological support was provided by TERENA (Trans-European Research Network Association). CEE countries have now been integrated into Western Europe regional Internet backbones.

Some specific network development projects received funding support from the USA and from individual European countries, notably the Nordic countries which offered support to the Baltic Republics, and from Germany (Sterba, 1993; Rastl, 1994). The CEE countries were connected to the Internet by three service providers, EBONE, Europanet and NORDUnet. EBONE and NORDUnet connections were funded by national or other (non-PHARE) funds. The PHARE programme aimed to provide international connectivity to IXI, the COSINE X.25 infrastructure and Europanet. The Austrian government allocated financial support for leased lines to neighbouring countries in order to offer them immediate connectivity to the Internet via the ACOnet (Austrian Academic Computer Network) and provided (jointly with IBM and DEC) technical training to several hundred specialists from CEE countries (Sterba, 1993).

Most of the financial support from European countries and the USA has been concentrated on the establishment of research and academic networks. For example, NATO's Outreach programme was designed to improve computer communication between scientists in the NATO countries and cooperation partners, focusing on two main activities: one on policy by organizing workshops and the other on improving the infrastructure by the provision of support to improve connectivity.[45] During the period 1993 to 1996, 188 projects across NATO and CP countries were supported by NATO, of which the advanced network workshop (ANW) provided 27 per cent, the computer networking supplement to linkage grants (CNS) 21 per cent and the networking infrastructure grants (NIG) 52 per cent.[46]

Therefore most of the Internet development in these countries occurred in research communities. Table 5.3 shows the share of research and academic communities in total Internet system use in CEE countries. As a result, the research and academic communities, with the exception of the Czech Republic, constituted most of the usage of the Internet system until 1996.

Table 5.3   Share of research and academic community

Country	Number of academic hosts/total number of hosts
Czech Republic	3%
Romania	38%
Bulgaria	60%
Estonia	62%
Slovakia	62%
Slovenia	72%
Hungary	80%
Latvia	84%
Lithuania	87%
Poland	94%

Source: Adapted from Kalin (1997).

Asia–Pacific Region Countries

The Asia–Pacific region includes countries that are very diverse from a political, economic, social and religious point of view (Davies and Stover, 1998).

The lack of homogeneity between countries has contributed to a low level of regional cooperation on economic and social matters. The region includes developed countries such as Japan, Australia, New Zealand, South Korea, Taiwan and Singapore. With regard to East Asian countries, the cultural differences 'within those countries inhibit and perhaps preclude its promoting regional economic integration like that in Europe and North America' (Huntington, 1993: 28). Rather the major Asian countries have more direct connections with the USA both economically and socially.

Table 5.4 shows a comparison of the highest-volume international telecommunication routes between Asia and Europe in 1991. The Asia region including 12 countries (Australia, China, Hong Kong, India, Indonesia, Japan, South Korea, Malaysia, New Zealand, Philippines, Taiwan and Thailand) shows more international traffic with the USA than between these 12 countries and major European countries. The busiest international traffic routes within the Asia region were between Hong Kong and China, Japan and South Korea and Australia and New Zealand. International traffic between the advanced countries in Asia was less than that between them and the USA.

Table 5.4   Asia and Europe international telecommunication traffic routes: highest volume routes (1991)

Asia		Europe	
Route	Traffic	Route	Traffic
Hong Kong–China	720	USA–UK	1 182
USA–Japan	549	USA–Germany	816
USA–Korea	259	Switzerland–Germany	630
USA–Taiwan	194	Austria–Germany	586
USA–Australia	191	Germany–UK	582
Japan–Korea	180	France–Germany	559
Australia–New Zealand	153	France–UK	508
		Netherlands–Germany	472

Note: The unit of traffic is Mitt (Minutes of Telecommunication Traffic); data are for two-way traffic.

Source: Data adapted from TeleGeography Inc. (1992).

Historically major Asian advanced countries have collaborated closely with the USA in science and technology areas, including the Internet. The collaboration between the research and academic communities in some Asian countries and the USA has been at both individual and organizational levels. For example, most researchers and university faculty members in South Korea and Taiwan studied in the USA.[47] The development of the Internet system in Asia reflected these regional economic and social characteristics. The Asia–Pacific region's Internet connectivity is almost exclusively via the USA, including traffic exchange among entities in the same country and all transit traffic destined for, or originating in, Europe (OECD, 1998a). However most Asia–Pacific countries were connected to the USA on low bandwidths. Only Australia had a T1 link with the USA in 1994.[48]

In the Asia–Pacific region, ad hoc meetings on computer networking among some scientists who were interested in Internet technologies were held during the Academic Net Workshop (ANW) in Dublin in 1984.[49] The Asia–Pacific Coordination Committee for International Research Networking (APCCIRN) started during INET '91 in Copenhagen in June 1991.[50] Three years later it became the Asia–Pacific Networking Group (APAN).[51] APAN, representing the Asia–Pacific region at CCIRN, has spawned several Asia–Pacific organizations, including the Asia Pacific Network Information Center (APNIC), the regional Internet number resource allocation body. This was initiated as part of the APNG and was authorized by IANA in 1994 to commence allocation of resources regionally. APNIC covers 62 countries in the Asia–Pacific region, including South and Central Asia, South-east Asia, Indochina and Oceania.

The early Asia–Pacific regional networking activities had been led by Japan, South Korea and Taiwan. These countries already had national research and academic networks, which had been established in the 1980s, similar to other developed countries in Europe and North America. The Japanese National Centre for Science Information Systems (NACSIS) operated the Science Information Network (SINET) from 1986. The education network, KREN (the Korea Education Network), was initiated in December 1983 by Seoul National University to connect universities and education institutes in South Korea. As early as 1990, TANet grew out of the original BITNET in Taiwan. Japan, South Korea and Taiwan initiated the Consortium of Asian Research and Educational Networks (CAREN), the first regional network in the Asia–Pacific region in 1991, through an agreement between the Japanese BITNET Association, the Korea Education Network and the Ministry of Education in Taiwan. However the bandwidth between Japan and South Korea and Japan and Taiwan was only 9.6 Kbps.[52]

By 1993, there were still virtually no intraregional links between the Asia–Pacific countries except those transiting North America. The exception was a leased line between South Korea and Japan. In August 1994, a 64 Kbps line between Europe and Korea became operational which provided a direct link between KREONet (the Korea Research Environment Open Network), the

Korean national R&D network and EuropaNET. Between 1994 and 1996, many new intraregional links and links to Europe were added. However not only were the number of direct links to the USA increasing, but also the size of these connections. In terms of large-scale connectivity, by the first half of 1996 there were only three connections with 34 Mbps or higher capacities. Two of these were from Japan to the USA and one from Australia to the USA. In the second half of 1996, the first regional link of 34 Mbps or higher was added between South Korea and Japan, as well as one additional link between Japan and the USA. In 1998, the connectivity between Asia and the USA amounted to 13 links of 45 Mbps (Cukier, 1998). However there was only one intraregional link on this scale (between South Korea and Japan) and no similar direct link from the Asia–Pacific region to Europe.

The major problems in localizing the Internet in the Asia–Pacific region were the consistent lack of content and low level of regional networking activities (Davies and Stover, 1998). The lack of content was partly due to the technical difficulties involved in converting the Internet into the local language. For example, the National Computerization Agency (NCA) in South Korea points to the deficiency in language engineering technology: 'The most difficult thing in the domestic application software firms is the deficiency in language engineering technology, which is needed in the development of the Korean language processing system' (NCA, 2000: 53).

Regional collaboration efforts to overcome the language problem in adapting the Internet system started in the 1990s.[53] The lack of content and low level of regional networking activities reinforced the US-centric Internet traffic rather than contributing to the building of regional networks. In addition to the lack of regional traffic and lack of funds, the pricing structure, which favours direct links to the USA, has discouraged the building of regional backbone networks. The uneven development of the Internet between countries also retarded regional collaboration in localizing the Internet system. The international telecommunication infrastructure and its financial arrangement were different in Asia and the CEE region from those in Western Europe. Davies (1998a) points out that the telecommunications infrastructure, in particular the international private leased circuits (IPLC), underlying the basic links between national research and education networks was not 'so extensive and was of low quality in CEE and the Asia region' (ibid.: 1). The HJK (Hong Kong–Japan–Korea) cable system, the first optical fibre undersea cable network in the Asia–Pacific region, started commercial operation in 1990 (see Table 5.5). During the period 1990 to 1995, several optical undersea cable systems were launched, including APC (Asia Pacific Cable), C–J (China–Japan) and RJK (Russia–Japan–Korea). Their capacities were between 280 megabytes and 560 megabytes per second. All cable systems in the Asia region were built under a common carrier scheme which requires

Table 5.5   Underseas optical fibre cable systems in Asia and Pacific region

Name of cables	Capacity	Ready for service date	Note
TPC-3	280M[1]	1989	
GPT	280M[1]	1989	
HAW-4	280M[1]	1989	
HJK	280M[1]	1990	First optical fibre undersea cable network in the region (Hong Kong–Japan–Korea)
TPC-4	560M[1]	1992	
Pac-Rim-East	560M[1]	1993	
APC	560M[1]	1993	Asia Pacific cable
CJ	560M[1]	1993	China–Japan
HAW-5	560M[1]	1993	
Pac-Rim-West	560M[1]	1994	
SMW2	560M[1]	1994	
RJK	560M[1]	1995	Russia–Japan–Korea
TPC-5	5G[2]	1995	
APCN	5G[2]	1997	Asia Pacific cable network
FLAG	10G[2]	1997	Privately financed cable
SEA-ME-WE3	20–40G[2]	1999	planned
JH	100G[2]	1999	planned
China–US CN	89G[2]	1999	planned
PC-1	80G[2]	2000	planned
Japan–US CN	80–400G[2]	2000	planned

Notes:
1.   Mega bytes per second.
2.   Giga bytes per second.

Source: Adapted from 'APIA News Letter' no.3, October–November 1999.

cooperation and investment among telecommunications entities from the relevant countries, except FLAG, a privately financed cable system (Davies, 1998a, b).

In contrast to Western Europe, most international telecommunication facilities in the Asia region have been exploited 'according to traditional correspondent arrangements[54] by the incumbent telecoms operators in the countries which lie along their path' (ibid.: 3). In Western Europe, the alliances formed by the PTOs (for example, BT and its strategic partners, Global One and Unisource) and new players (for example, Hermes and WorldCom) have installed fibre systems over which they have complete control and which cover several countries as a result of EU telecommunication liberalization.

So far, different regional contexts in the process of the global expansion of the Internet system have been analysed. Even though European countries had competed with the USA for the control of the data network, with strong regional collaborations in building national and regional research networks based on economic and political concerns, and collaboration channels with the USA through international computer networking communities, European countries were able to transform their data network system to support multi-protocols to accommodate the Internet system from the end of the 1980s. CEE countries were in a relatively better position in localizing the Internet system compared to other developing countries because of the technological and financial support from the NATO countries, which was a reflection of economic and political interests. They could be integrated into the European Internet communities. In contrast, some Asia–Pacific countries that had maintained strong ties with the USA had difficulties in localizing the Internet system because of the low level of regional networking activities and the lack of content resulting from the low level of regional cooperation on economic, cultural and political matters.

5.5   GLOBAL SYSTEM BUILDING

After the NSFNET was privatized, control of the Internet system was increasingly handed over from the NSF (and FNC) to commercial players. Most countries were connected to the Internet through collaboration between the USA and other regions and countries. The global system-building process also appears to be being driven by technological, economic and political forces. In this section, the global system-building process is examined with the focus on the high-end sector (that is, global advanced research networks) and changes in the Internet system governance reflecting its commercialization, globalization and localization.

Global Network of Advanced Research Networks

National and regional efforts to foster the development of ICTs through massive investment by either direct public subsidies or private investment have contributed to the development of ICTs. The concerns over competitiveness and technological leadership (developed countries) and catching up (developing countries) have justified the heavy investment in ICTs since the 1980s. Most of these efforts came to focus on broadband technologies and, in particular, on a high-performance Internet in the 1990s. The Internet became a global data network with accumulated technological innovations, in particular the WWW.

The vision of a National Information Infrastructure (NII), the national initiative of improving the network infrastructure in the USA[55] (and elsewhere) and a Global Information Infrastructure (GII) have boosted the diffusion of the Internet in a way that encourages multi-media usage and improved network facilities. These kinds of efforts have provided a foundation for the development of advanced information and communications services and eventually boosted the development of advanced communication services based on the Internet. For example, universal broadband service including the Internet service appeared on the NII and GII agenda.[56] The US Telecommunications Act of 1996 provided a forum for discussions on the extension of the universal service obligation for broadband services including the Internet service. However the Internet service was not included as a 'core service' subject to universal services.[57] Instead financial support for schools and libraries for telecommunications services including the Internet was recommended by the Federal–State joint board.[58] Under the joint board's recommendations, ISPs would be able to provide these services and receive subsidies, but most of them would be exempted from contributing to the universal service funding mechanism.

As a result of the NII and other broadband network and applications development policies, national research and academic networks have been developed as high-performance networks through broadband testbeds and interconnected through regional backbones and global transit access points. Global interconnection of advanced research networks has been led by the USA. The ICM project was followed by the Science, Technology and Research Transit Access Point (STAR TAP) for interconnecting the NSF's vBNS with advanced networks[59] and the High-Performance International Internet Services (HPIIS) project for sharing some of the costs of the high-performance connections, including TransPAC,[60] MirNET,[61] AMPATH[62] and Euro-Link.[63] In 2000, some 20 foreign advanced research networks as well as the US Next Generation Internet (NGI)[64] networks and Abilene[65] were connected to STAR TAP (see Figure 5.1).

The International Networking activity also supports the Network Startup Resource Center (NSRC, http://www.nsrc.org), a user-driven technical support activity for enhancing connectivity between the US research and education community and countries recently undertaking Internet startup activity. NSRC maintains an on-line database of country networks, sends publisher-donated Internet reference books on request and often provides instructors for networking workshops in developing countries.

The building of a high-speed network for the European research community started in 1995 with the launch of the TEN-34 project for interconnecting the national research networks (NRNs). The TEN-34 project was carried out

Key: *STAR TAP* connected ✳ ITN connected○

Source: http://www.startap.net/NETWORKS/.

Figure 5.1   STAR TAP networks

by a consortium of European National Research Networks, with DANTE as the Coordinating Partner.[66] Between February 1997 and December 1998, TEN-34 provided the European academic and research community with a stable IP-based pan-Europe network service. TEN-155 is the current European research network and has supplied researchers in 19 countries with access capacities of up to 155 Mbps since 1 December 1998 (see Figure 5.2). To implement TEN-155, the QUANTUM Project, cofunded under the Telematics Applications, Esprit and ACTS Programmes of the European Commission, was established.[67]

TEN-34 had two principal technology policy goals (Davies, 1996). The first was to establish a 34 Mbit/s IP service based on an underlying infrastructure of ATM (Asynchronous Transfer Mode) and leased lines. In this context the ATM technology was only used as a multiplexing mechanism. The second goal was to pilot the use of ATM technology to seek to exploit the practical benefits that it promised. The European Commission placed ATM at the centre of its ambitions to build an information infrastructure (the EII) to rival those of the USA and Japan. The European Commission's 1993 White Paper[68] explicitly states that the advanced pan-Europe telecommunications networks would be based on ATM.

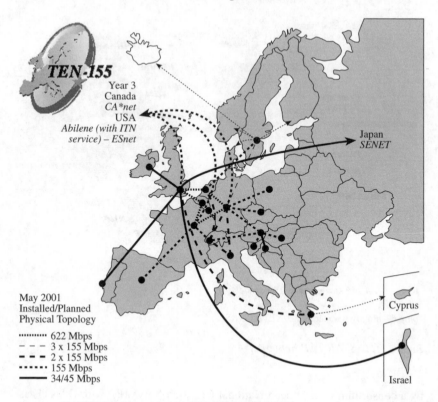

Source: DANTE (http://www.dante.net/ten-155/ten155net.gif).

Figure 5.2   TEN-155 network topology map

With regard to the networks that serve to carry the information (voice, data, images), the objective would be to consolidate the integrated services digital network and to install the high-speed communications network using advanced transmission and switching techniques (ATM), which will help digitalized multimedia services to make a breakthrough (EC, 1993).[69]

ATM is a connection-oriented approach which derives from the ordered world of PTOs rather than from the 'precious anarchy' of the Internet (Davies, 1995b). BT, France Télécom, Deutsche Bundespost Telekom, STET, Iritel and Telefonica signed an MoU in November 1992 to build an ATM pilot.[70] ATM was adopted mainly by either research and academic users or companies with highly specialized requirements, including CERN, SUPER-JANET and SITA (Ablett *et al.*, 1994). The Internet technologies have been coupled with telecommunication technologies mainly through the marriage of ATM and IP.[71]

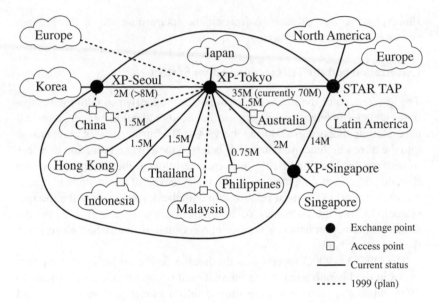

Source: APAN (http://www.singaren.net.sg/apps/apan_doc/appendixA.htm).

Figure 5.3   APAN network links

A high-speed network, Asia–Pacific Advanced Network (APAN) was founded by four countries (Australia, Japan, South Korea and Singapore) and two liaison member countries (Canada and the USA) in 1997. It was expanded to cover ten countries in the Asia–Pacific.[72] APAN is a high-performance research network for connecting national testbed networks and research networks (see Figure 5.3). In the Asia–Pacific various gigabit testbeds have been developed in many countries and regions, including Australia, China, Japan, South Korea, Malaysia, Singapore, Taiwan and Thailand (Chon, 1999). In other countries in Asia, such as Thailand, Indonesia and Hong Kong, there are similar arrangements through the Asia Internet Infrastructure Initiative (AI3), the satellite-based research network.

Changes in Internet System Governance

The Internet system is in transition from a private network for research and academic purposes towards a publicly accessible network; from networks mainly subsidized by governments towards mainly commercially provided networks; from the US-centric system towards a global system; from engineering community-centric governance towards commercial community-centric governance.

However, it is very difficult to forecast the future direction of the Internet system because it is still evolving.

Localization and the Telecommunication System

The localization of the Internet system has been intertwined with the institutional changes in telecommunications, that is, liberalization, privatization and deregulation, that occurred during the 1990s. The introduction of competition into the telecommunication market is believed to deliver a reduction in prices of network facilities and better performance in using the Internet. However liberalization (including changes in the management of the incumbent operator) does not exhibit a linear relationship with the development of the Internet system. In fact the outcomes of liberalization are shaped mainly by the dynamic interaction between various players such as the market players and the regulatory body.

The OECD (1999a) asserts that the Internet is the single most important factor in the liberalization of the international telecommunication market. In 1995, when the Internet system moved into a global system-building and localization process, leased lines accounted for only 17 per cent of the total active capacity between the USA and other OECD countries, but this grew to 51.8 per cent in 1997 (ibid.). The rate of leased line capacity increases in countries during this period differed considerably. For example, Canada, Mexico and Sweden emerged as regional gateways and they have experienced the highest growth rates (ibid.).

However the growth of the access networks tends to take relatively more time than that for the leased line segment because network competition requires substantial amounts of investment for the construction of the network and the competitive advantage of the incumbent operator is not reduced easily. Furthermore competition in telecommunications does not always encourage use of the Internet. For example, tariff rebalancing has led to increases in rental and local call usage costs for residential users in some countries. In many cases the price of international and long-distance calls has declined but the price of local calls has increased because of tariff rebalancing after competition was introduced (ITU, 1999a). Liberalization, in the short term at least, increases the cost of local dial-up access. Petrazzini and Guerrero. (2000) also point out that privatization of the telecommunication sector in Argentina delayed the development of the Internet system by increasing some prices and enforcing the private players' market dominance.[73] With government intervention focusing on price cutting in some sub-markets and competitive market pressures from the rising number of ISPs, there has been a rapid decline in Internet access charges. For example, Petrazzini and Guerrero emphasize that the recent rapid development of the Internet system in Argentina is attributable to two specific policies aimed at price reductions for leased lines and reductions in local call prices through the creation of a special dialling scheme for Internet-related calls. Most countries show a similar pattern. In this regard, the growth of demand for the Internet has facilitated access of new entrants to the telecommunication market and enforced competition by inducing alternative network operators to enter the market and encouraging policy makers to widen and deepen competition in network provision.

Consolidations

As the Internet has become a publicly accessible network, the network architecture has been increasingly integrated into the existing telecommunication system. The public Internet consists of a myriad of leased lines woven together by a common protocol, that is, TCP/IP, and the Intranet employs this protocol over leased lines to make up private networks. PTOs provide most of this capacity. New types of network providers such as IXC, Qwest or Williams Communications in the USA emerged in order to provide wholesale capacity for the Internet (Pospischil, 1998). Some network operators such as WorldCom and Global One provide a transport service for IP traffic by buying bandwidth from other network operators.

Most PTOs started to offer Internet access service during the period 1994–6. Examples are as follows:[74]

Taiwan: Chungwah Telecom (Hi Net) – March 1994,
South Korea: Korea Telecom (Kornet) – June 1994,
Singapore: SingTel (SingNet) – July 1994,
The Netherlands: KPN (Planet Internet) – June 1995,
UK: BT (BT Internet) – February 1996,
Germany: Deutsche Telekom (T-Online) – February 1996,
Spain: Telefonica (InfoVia) – March 1996,
USA: AT&T (WorldNet) – March 1996,
Italy: Telecom Italia (acquires ISPs Vodeo On Line and Telecom On Line – April 1996) (TIN) – March 1997,
Hong Kong: Hong Kong Telecom (Netvigator) – April 1996,
France: France Télécom (Wanadoo) – May 1996,
Switzerland: Swiss Telecom PTT (Blue Window) – September 1996,
Japan: NTT (Open Computer Network) – December 1996.

Consolidations between market players have increased dramatically since 1996. Most of the independent ISPs have been bought by PTOs, with the notable exception of PSINET (OECD, 1999b).[75] Consolidation through mergers and acquisitions and strategic alliances is aimed at expanding geographical coverage, brand value or capabilities.[76] For example, Cable & Wireless acquired Digital Island, one of the USA's leading Web hosting companies, in May 2001. Cable & Wireless has also taken over 13 European ISPs since 1999 to expand its geographical coverage. PSINET emerged from one of the first independent ISPs in the USA to become a global ISP, having more than 800 points-of-presence and operations in the USA, Canada, Europe, Latin America and Asia mainly through acquisitions.[77]

Financial Settlement Regime

The peering agreement model for the financial settlement of exchanges of traffic between ISPs is being replaced by interconnection agreements. The peering agreement model was common in the early Internet system which was built and maintained mainly by subsidies from the US government. The traditional financial settlement model for exchanging traffic between ISPs is the peering agreement, whereby traffic is not measured and there is no settlement between ISPs. A peering agreement means that two ISPs exchange the necessary routing information so that traffic can be exchanged between their networks at no charge. However these peering agreements raised tensions between ISPs, mainly because of asymmetrical traffic exchanges, and are therefore being replaced by interconnection agreements (Fischer & Lorenz, 2000). Since 1996, some of the largest ISPs have started to change their peering agreement policies. Peering agreements could not be sustained when the traffic exchanged became asymmetrical because the large ISPs obtained little benefit from being connected to small networks.[78] The peering model could not be sustained because the ISP market is becoming more concentrated as a result of mergers and acquisitions. Traditional small ISPs are being consolidated into bigger ISPs, while new types of ISPs are entering the market.[79] Another model for Internet traffic exchange is transit agreements, where one ISP will agree to transport traffic via its own network from another ISP to a third network, normally for a flat monthly charge (OECD, 1998b; Fischer & Lorenz, 2000). In fact Internet traffic is exchanged in several ways. Two ISPs may exchange traffic bilaterally by establishing a transmission channel. Multiple ISPs may exchange traffic through public exchange points.

Mismatches between traditional financial arrangements in international telecommunication and the peering model raise tensions and conflicts between the USA and other regions, in particular in Asian countries. The pressure to change the traditional financial settlement for international connection to the US Internet based on the peering model has increased (OECD, 1998b). In most cases, organizations in foreign countries paid the full cost of international links and the Internet service/port charge for connecting to the

USA, unless they were supported by special arrangements such as NSF's ICM. Under the peering financial settlement regime individual ISPs generally pay the telecommunication carriers the full cost of the circuits connecting their networks to international peering points. Therefore ISPs that own international network facilities, such as Telstra (Australia) and KDD (Japan) argue that, in shifting the financial mid-point to the US Internet exchange points, they are paying the full cost of international facilities for both their customers and the customers of ISPs based in the USA, because the Internet model for financing international infrastructure shifts the financial mid-point for traffic exchange from oceans (as in the case of cables) and geostationary orbit (as in the case of satellites) to Internet exchange points. The Asia and Pacific Internet Association (APIA) argues that ISPs in the Asia and Pacific region paid substantial amounts of money under the international financial settlement regime of the Internet.

With the 1Gbps bandwidth from the AP region to the USA around the end of 1997, the total cost for the circuits amounts to around US$150million, estimated from the international leased circuit pricing. Judging by the current growth rate, the total cost for the circuits would be over US$1billion per year by the year 2000. With increased demands on information in the AP region, the ISPs in the USA in effect are free-riding on the circuits paid for by the AP region ISPs. On the basis of the estimation above, the subsidy being provided by the ISPs in the AP region amounted to US$30 million at the end of 1997, and would be more than US$200 million by the year 2000. With increasing shifts in the traffic flow from the AP region, the amount of subsidy provided by the AP region ISPs in year 2000 will be a lot more than US$ 200 million.[80]

The financial settlement based on the peering model was justified by the observation that 'most of what people wanted to connect to the Internet for generally existed within US based networks and it was backed up with traffic statistics which observed tremendous disparities in the amount of the US-outbound traffic as compared to US-inbound traffic, with data leaving the US vastly outweighing data destined for US sites'.[81] APIA, however, argues that the disparity in international traffic between the USA and other regions has reduced significantly, as the Internet system has become increasingly localized. It stresses that the Internet traffic increasingly shows bidirectional flows because of Internet telephony, web casting and push technologies and multimedia applications. It argues that alternative international infrastructure financing, such as cost-sharing arrangements, is needed to replace the peering model. However European countries have different interests because they built regional networks in order to localize the Internet traffic and integrate Internet traffic from neighbouring regions. They also invested in the USA's international network operators and thus want to share in the benefits. In October 2000, a new ITU-T recommendation (D.50) called on companies to negotiate with each other to find more equitable ways of sharing the cost of international Internet circuits.[82]

The international Internet bandwidth in 2000 shows a different structure from the interregional telecommunications traffic flow in 1997. Figure 5.4 shows the international traffic flow in 1997, measured by the total annual traffic on the public networks. The international Internet bandwidth shows the uneven development of the Internet system between regions and countries. Figure 5.5 shows the US and Europe-centric structure of the global Internet system which has been built on international private networks (leased lines). In 2000, the international Internet bandwidth between North America (the USA and Canada) and Europe was about three times greater than that between North America (the USA and Canada) and the Asia and Pacific region.

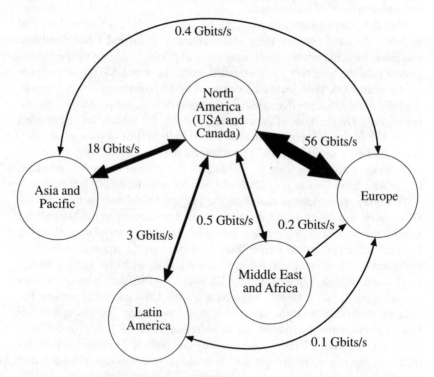

Source: Adapted from ITU, *News* (no. 2/2001).

Figure 5.4   International Internet bandwidth (2000)

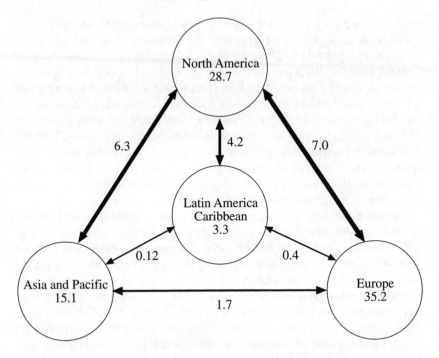

Notes:
1. All figures are given in billions of Minutes of Telecommunications Traffic for the public telephone network.
2. Numbers in a circle indicate the total amount of international traffic for countries within a region.

Source: Adapted from TeleGeography (1999: 225).

Figure 5.5   Interregional traffic flow (1997)

Global Technological Governance

The Internet Society was formed in 1991, primarily in order to provide financial support for the Internet standards process, by a group of people with long-term involvement in the IETF (Cerf, 1995). They needed to prepare long-term financial support for the standards-making activity of IETF in the face of the commercialization of the Internet system. Their activities were supported by agencies of the US government (notably ARPA, NSF, NASA and DOE). In 1992, the Internet Activities Board (IAB) was reorganized as the Internet Architecture Board operating under the auspices of ISOC. Starting in 1993, ISOC assumed its responsibilities under RFC 1602, and participated in various reviews of that process. Finally a cooperative and mutually supportive relationship was formed between the IAB, IETF and ISOC, with ISOC taking on as a goal the provision of service and other measures which would facilitate the work of the IETF.

Every Internet computer has a unique IP number. In December 1988, the Internet Assigned Numbers Authority (IANA) was established to coordinate the allocation of blocks of numerical addresses to regional IP registers. IP address blocks were originally allocated by IANA directly. Most allocations of IP address tasks have been transferred to three regional bodies: APNIC, ARIN and RIPE NCC. These organizations subsequently reallocate or assign IP addresses to individual organizations, such as ISPs or national bodies coordinating IP address space for a country. The recipients of those address blocks then reassign addresses to smaller ISPs and end users.

Domain names had been managed by SRI under contract with DARPA and DCA which took over the SRI contract in 1975. After DNS was introduced in 1984, NSF was awarded the domain names .int .com .org .net and .edu contract with SRI in 1987. In 1990, new Top Level Domains (TLDs) were created for countries based on the top-letter country abbreviations of the ISO. DNS management was also transferred to the private sector. The Defense Data Network NIC (domain name .mil and .gov) contract was awarded by DISA to Government Systems Inc. who took over from SRI in May 1991. NSF created InterNIC in 1993 and awarded DNS registration services to AT&T (directory and database services), CERFNet (information services) and Network Solutions Inc. (DNS registration service for .org .net .com .edu .int- the latter two were subcontracted to IANA). The registration and propagation of these key gTLDs were performed by NSI, under a five-year cooperative agreement with NSF. This agreement expired on 30 September 1998. In 1995, NSFNET contracted Network Solutions Inc. to manage certain gTLDs and authorized the company to charge users for registration from September 1995.

Global expansion and commercialization of the Internet system increased the pressure for changes in the monopoly of domain name registration. ICANN (the Internet Corporation for Assigned Names and Numbers) was formed to coordinate the technical management of the Internet's domain name system, the allocation of IP address space, the assignment of protocol parameters and the management of the root server system in October 1998.[83] However the structure of ICANN shows that power was shifting from engineering communities to commercial players (Froomkin, 2000).[84]

5.6 CONCLUSION

The evolution of the Internet system can be mapped according to the economic and political forces and policy tools operating in each stage of its development (Table 5.6). As discussed in Chapter 4, the invention of the computer networking technology and Internet system under the guidance and financial support of DARPA was to develop a reliable and cost-effective computer network. The managerial and technological capabilities accumulated through experience in computer technologies contributed to the successful establishment of the ARPANET project. The military restrictions of the ARPANET project provided an environment of maintaining the coherence to concentrate learning and experience in the experimental stage of the Internet system. The design concepts of the Internet system to connect heterogeneous computers provided a powerful potential for its future development after computer-networking technologies stabilized and the cost effectiveness was proven.

The success of the NSFNET in connecting the existing research networks across the USA, and encouraging the establishment of regional and campus networks, meant the Internet system was faced with conflicting interests as national system-building efforts developed. The national development stage of the Internet involved complex political processes. The outcome of these processes was the decision to build a national research and academic network by enhancing the existing NSFNET backbone and also encouraging the commercialization of the Internet. During this period, global expansion of the Internet began. From a US viewpoint, a principal aim at this stage was to connect US researchers to research sources in other developed countries.

As the building of the national research and academic network of the USA was consolidated and the commercialization of the Internet began in earnest, the global expansion stage was initiated. The US government's efforts to connect the Internet system to research networks in developed countries provided the basis for the Internet system to emerge as a global research network. The global expansion of the Internet system was backed by collaborations between the US and European research communities. These interregional collaborative activities have gradually extended to other regions. At the same time, international cooperative efforts inevitably had to deal with competing technologies: Internet systems and public data network systems based on OSI (see Chapter 4). The so-called 'battles of the systems' accelerated technological innovation and led to a coupling of competing technologies. The accumulated technological innovations in ICTs and the Internet system, in particular the WWW, and the US government's efforts to facilitate commercialization, accelerated the growth of the Internet system.

After control of the Internet system was handed over from the NSF to commercial players, and when most countries were connected in the mid-1990s, the Internet system entered a global system-building phase. The outcome of the battles of the systems was the integration of the Internet and

Table 5.6 The economic and political forces in the evolution of the Internet system

Stage	Experimental	US national system building	Global expansion	Global system building
Major features of the Internet system's evolution	Invention development	Innovation (battles of system)	Technology transfer & competition Localization	Growth consolidation
Economic forces	Reliable and cost-effective computer network	Economy of scale, network externalities		Economies of scale and scope, technological interrelatedness
Major policy concerns	Military R&D	Technological leadership Competitiveness Military		Global information infrastructure Universality
Major policy tools	APANET and the Internet project	Standardization (e.g. IAB) NSFNET National coordination (e.g. FNC)	Commercialization Global coordination (e.g. CCIRN) HPCC programme (including NERN)	NGI (the US Next Generation Internet) Liberalization of telecommunication market

Source: Elaborated by author.

telecommunications systems by coupling technologies and through consolidations of organizations. As the Internet system became localized, tensions between the Internet system and the local telecommunication system increased. This coincided with institutional transformations in these sectors. The liberalization and privatization of the telecommunication sector during the 1990s facilitated global expansion of the Internet system. Intercontinental networks expanded dramatically and regional networks became established. Competition and collaboration between countries in the development of a high-performance Internet system are leading to global advanced research networks. Global expansion and commercialization of the Internet system increased the pressures for changes to Internet system governance. The global Internet system was built upon battles for network control on a global dimension between centralized and decentralized forces, but the localization of the Internet system, including institutional setups, can be shown to have been influenced by the global system and also to have shaped it.

Policy concern about technological leadership in the face of challenges from Japan and the European countries contributed to building national research networks based on the Internet system. The Internet system was chosen from other computer networking technologies as a tool to connect the computer systems of universities and research institutions and funded by DARPA and NSF because it was the most popular with computer scientists. In connecting national research resources by means of a computer network, the backbone concept was adopted to exploit economies of scale by the establishment of the NSFNET.

The search for cost-effective technologies was accomplished and enforced by exploiting economies of scale in the phase of US national Internet system building. The Internet system began its expansion in the USA with the establishment of NSFNET. The multitiered architecture based on a backbone concept was designed to aggregate networks at the regional level and to connect regions through an interlinking superstructure. To aggregate demand, it is necessary to exploit economies of scale on the demand side. Individual demand for computer networking was integrated into the Internet by connecting the established networks, and additional demand was generated by this integrated demand. In this regard, the global expansion of the Internet system also contributed to the growth of the US Internet system. In Europe, regional networks were built by integrating the existing national networks through arrangements for cost sharing and the building of these regional networks encouraged further national and local network expansion.

The sources of uneven development of the Internet system are found in the internationalization of the Internet system. They include asymmetric development of research networks between regions and countries, different economic and political relationships between the USA and other countries; international

financial settlement based on the peering regime; and the existing technological and economic gaps between countries and cultural differences. For example,
in the global expansion phase, international networks were built by integrating existing national networks and these international networks encouraged
further national and local networks through the arrangements for cost sharing
among international networks. There were positive feedbacks between backbone networks and regional and local network building and between
international networks and national and local networks.

The role of the computer networking communities appears to be very
important in the battles of the systems and the transfer of the Internet system.
The early networks of collaboration between computer networking researchers contributed to establishing channels of Internet system transfer. The global
expansion of the Internet was coordinated by these global networks of computer networking communities. Computer networking communities and the
broader research communities were also very important in the localization of
the Internet system, particularly in the early stages. The asymmetric power
structure of global computer networking communities and the unevenness of
capabilities across countries appear to have been the reasons for the uneven
development of the Internet system. In particular the structure of the global
computer network communities in the early phase of global expansion of the
Internet was important after the global Internet network structure was formed:
it appeared to be very difficult to change.

The global expansion of the Internet system and its localization were
followed by a process of integrating competing technologies by coupling
technologies and through consolidations between market players. The complexities of Internet localization partly resulted from conflicting interests and
strategic behaviour in transforming the telecommunication system in order to
adapt to Internet technologies.

NOTES

1. The original naming system based on a single table of hosts was changed to a new naming
    system having a large number of independently managed networks (for example, LANs).
    The DNS was introduced around 1984 but it took almost four years before it was fully
    implemented on the Internet (Lottor, 1992). For example, DDN/MILNET started its
    transition from the existing host table (simple, flat namespace) to domain system in
    December 1986 and it was planned to be completed by October 1989 (Lazear, 1987).
2. Network Working Group and Network Technical Advisory Group NSF, 1986
3. American scientists and industry were alarmed by the Japanese supercomputing chal-
    lenge. Following the announcement by the Ministry of International Trade and Industry
    (MITI) in October 1981 on two computing projects including the Fifth Generation Com-
    puter Project and the National Superspeed Computer Project, Japanese manufacturers
    (Hitachi, Fujitsu and the NEC) entered into the supercomputer market dominated by the
    American computer companies. European countries followed America and Japan in

understanding the importance of high-performance computing for science and industry. See ACM (1984) and Wilson (1984) for the issues on the access to supercomputers in the USA at that time.

4. For example, DOE's James Decker estimated the cost of running a single supercomputer centre with one supercomputer to be about US$10 million per year, based on his experience in administrating in DOE's magnetic fusion energy network (Dallaire, 1984). Therefore he suggested that centralizing the supercomputers, that is, setting up a few supercomputer centres, each centre containing several supercomputers, and connecting these centres and with university users via data networks would be cost-effective. The NSF's report (*A National Computing Environment for Academic Research*) published in July 1983 proposed the creation of ten supercomputer centres (*Communications of the ACM*, vol. 27, no. 4, p. 301).

5. High Performance Computing and Networking for Science Advisory Panel (1991), 'A Background Paper', Office of Technology Assessment, Washington, DC.

6. Mid-level networks were established around a number of existing regional networks and some new ones. The establishment of the regional networks was to some extent a reaction to the decommissioning of the ARPANET. See Merit (/nsfnet/nsfnet.overview), Mandelbaum and Mandelbaum (1992) and Hart *et al.* (1992) for the detailed process of building NSFNET by connecting the existing regional networks and creating new ones.

7. MERIT (/nsfnet/nsfnet.overview).

8. Mandelbaum and Mandelbaum (1992).

9. The IAB 'sets Internet standards, manages the RFC publication process, reviews the operation of the IETF and IRTF, performs strategic planning for the Internet, identifying long-range problems and opportunities, acts as an international technical policy liaison and representative for the Internet community, and resolves technical issues which cannot be treated within the IETF or IRTF frameworks' (Cerf, 1990a: 4).

10. ITEF's mission includes the following:
 1 Identifying, and proposing solutions to, pressing operational and technical problems in the Internet;
 2 Specifying the development or usage of protocols and the near-term architecture to solve such technical problems for the Internet;
 3 Making recommendations to the Internet Engineering Steering Group (IESG) regarding the standardization of protocols and protocol usage in the Internet;
 4 Facilitating technology transfer from the Internet Research Task Force (IRTF) to the wider Internet community; and
 5 Providing a forum for the exchange of information within the Internet community between vendors, users, researchers, agency contractors and network managers (Malkin, 1994: 2–3).

11. As described earlier, the beginning of the 1980s marked the expansion of US government agency interest in networking, and by the mid-1980s the Department of Energy (DOE) and NASA had also become involved.

12. Policy debates started in the Panel on Large Scale Computing in Science and Engineering in 1982 (the report pointing out that the US research community was seriously lacking in access to high-performance computing), followed by the FCCSET report (1983a and b) (Hart *et al.*, 1992).

13. The OSTP's 1987 report recommended that the government establish a long-range strategy for basic research on High Performance Computing (HPC), to encourage joint business–university–government research in advanced software technology, and to coordinate the building of a research network 'to provide distributed computing capability that links the government, industry, and higher education communities' (Hart *et al.*, 1992).

14. The NAS report argued that government funding of advanced computing research was necessary for preserving US competitiveness in an industry which accounted for as much as 10 per cent of the GNP and almost 10 per cent of all capital investment (National Research Council of the National Academy of Sciences, 1988: 7).

15. S. 1067, National High-Performance Computing Technology Act of 1989, U.S. Congress, Senate, 101st Congress, May 18, 1989.

16. U.S. Office of Technology Assessment (1989: 34).
17. U.S. Office of Technology Assessment (1989: 23)
18. McClure *et al.* (1991) examine the process and provide detailed discussions of NERN.
19. S.272, High-Performance Computing Act of 1991, U.S. Congress, Senate, 102nd Congress, January 24, 1991.
20. For example, Cisco was established in 1984 by Mr Len Bosack, director of computer facilities for Stanford's Computer Science Department, and Sandy Lerner, director of computer facilities in the Graduate School of Business who recognized the commercial potential of their work. Cisco's monthly revenues increased from approximately US$250 000 in 1987 to US$340 million in 1992 (Kehoe, 1992, Survey of Computers and Communications (14): 'Not prepared to play second fiddle – Profile of Cisco', *Financial Times*, 13 Oct. 1992).
21. NSFNET, The NSFNET Backbone Services Acceptable Use Policy, June 1992 (ftp:// nic.merit.edu/nsfnet/acceptable.use.policy) and Electronic message of 24 May 1991 from Eric M. Aupperle, President of Merit Network, Inc., to Stephen S. Wolff, Division Director of NCRI, National Science Foundation, acknowledging confirmation of NSF–Merit agreement on the flow of commercial traffic across NSF-sponsored gateways to the T3 network (ftp://nic.merit.edu//nsfnet/nsf.agreements/commercial.traffic).
22. This report (RFC, 1192: November 1990) written by B. Kahin (1990) is based on a workshop held at the John F. Kennedy School of Government, Harvard University 1–3 March 1990 by the Harvard Science, Technology and Public Policy Program. Sponsored by the National Science Foundation and the US Congress Office of Technology Assessment, the workshop was designed to explore the issues involved in the commercialization of the Internet, including the envisioned National Research and Education Network (NREN).
23. CCIRN Message 9 from Phillip G. Gross, 'Proposed RFC on CCIRN International connection guidelines', 13 March 1990 (ftp://cs.ucl.ac.uk/ccirn).
24. See Cerf *et al.* (1991).
25. CCIRN History (http://www.ccirn.org/history.html).
26. Steve Goldstein's interview in *The Cook Report*, 1995.
27. Ibid.
28. Ibid.
29. See APIA (http://www.apia.org/IIIF%20CFP%209710.htm).
30. MERIT (<NIC.MERIT.EDU> /nsfnet/restrict.nets, 4 August 1994).
31. See DANTE (http://www.dante.net/about/dante-brochure.html).
32. In 1993, 32 countries were connected to the EARN (Bovio and Greisen, 1993).
33. 'Until the end of 1987, IBM paid for some of the national communications links as well as all the international ones. The cost of those international links was about Ecu1.5 million a year. In addition, both IBM and Digital Equipment Corporation (DEC) have supplied much of the equipment and expertise needed to get the network up and running. After 1987, the Canadian telecommunications manufacturer Northern Telecom donated four data switches to change the network over from the IBM standard to the X25 standard' (*Financial Times*, 29 July 1988).
34. Cooper (1988: 3).
35. DANTE (http://www.dante.net/about/dante-brochure.html).
36. DANTE (http://www.dante.net/about/dante-brochure.html).
37. TERENA (http://www.terena.nl/info/mission.html).
38. RIPE (http://www.ripe.net/ripe/about/history/index.html).
39. COCOM members comprised the NATO countries, Japan and Australia (Greisen 1990). Export control for computer products had been a part of US law and foreign policy since the end of World War II. There were both unilateral controls and multilateral controls through COCOM (Goodman, 1982).
40. Hofmokl and Gajewski (http://www.ceenet.org/ceenet_cbyc_anicaee.html).
41. Letter from the US DOC to CERN (18 January 1990).
42. DANTE (http://www.dante.net/phare/phare-intro.html).
43. PHARE, the acronym for the original programme: 'Poland and Hungary: Action for the Restructuring of the Economy'. The programme was established by Council Regulation

(EEC) N° 3906/89 of 18 December 1989 (OJ N° L 375, 23.12.1989) for economic aid to the Republic of Hungary and the Polish People's Republic. Within two years the programme was extended, in terms of countries and budget, to cover 14 partner countries: Albania, Bosnia and Herzegovina, Bulgaria, Croatia, the Czech Republic, Estonia, the Former Yugoslav Republic of Macedonia (FYROM), Hungary, Latvia, Lithuania, Poland, Romania, Slovakia and Slovenia. (However Croatia was suspended from the PHARE Programme in July 1995) (http://europa.eu.int/comm/enlargement/pas/phare/wip/phareprogr.htm).

44. The INSIGHT project participant countries include the Czech Republic, Estonia, Hungary, Latvia, Lithuania, Poland, Romania, Slovakia and Slovenia. Managers of web sites of the National Research Networks (as well as other organizations) in these countries are being trained to provide a high-quality web service to their community. INSIGHT addresses technical as well as content-related requirements of a WWW information service. The project started in January 1995 and lasted two years (http://www.dante.net/phare/phare-intro.html#insight).

45. NATO countries included the USA, Canada, Belgium, Denmark, France, Germany, Greece, Iceland, Italy, Luxembourg, Netherlands, Norway, Portugal, Spain, Turkey and the UK. Cooperation Partner countries were Albania, Armenia, Azerbaijan, Belarus, Bulgaria, the Czech Republic, Estonia, Georgia, Hungary, Kazakhstan, Kyrgyzstan, Latvia, Lithuania, Moldova, Poland, Romania, the Russian Federation, the Slovak Republic, Slovenia, Tajikistan, Macedonia, Turkmenistan, Ukraine and Uzbekistan (Nadreau, 1997).

46. ANW had two types of workshops with two different aims: increasing the levels of harmony among the various network policies at national and international levels; and training network managers. CNS was a grant to fund the purchase of small equipment such as PCs and modems and provide LAN and communication service fees to allow full access to the Internet. During the period 1993 to 1996, some 130 CNS were awarded to CP research teams. NIG aimed at improving the infrastructure for larger research communities such as the 'Black Sea riparian country WAN' and the 'Yerevan Research and Education network' while CNS was focusing on individual teams. One of the other projects included a contribution to the establishment of the Uzbekistan Science Network, the establishment of a fibre optic local area network at the Ioffe Physical-Technical Institute of the Russian Academy of Sciences and support towards the international connectivity of the R&D Computer Network, BASNET, of the Academy of Sciences of Belarus in Minsk. Because of the size of the projects, NIG were joint ventures among several granting agencies (Nadreau, 1997).

47. See KREONET (Korea Research Environment Open NETwork (http://www.kreonet2.net/01.html)) and TANet (Taiwan Academic Network) (http://www.tanet2.net.tw/english/about/index.html#a)).

48. See APNG Database on International Links of APNG-007.8 (8 June 1994).

49. ANW lasted until 1989 and became INET in 1991 (with no meeting in 1990 to prepare the first INET in 1991) (http://www.apng.org/history.html).

50. APCCIRN-001 (1992.6.16: http://www.apng.org/apng/001.overview).

51. APANG (http://www.apng.org/history.html).

52. The link between Seoul National University in Korea and the Science University of Tokyo in Japan was upgraded to a 56 Kbps TCP/IP link in December 1993. A 56 Kbps TCP/IP link is planned between the Beijing Institute of Chemical Technology in China and the Science University of Tokyo in Japan.

53. Some countries, including Japan, Korea and Taiwan, significantly developed and supported local languages (APCCIRN Meeting Minutes 12–13 January 1993).

54. Correspondent arrangements refer to the procedures by which a customer leases an international circuit by paying a monthly charge to the PTOs at each end of the circuit. These two PTOs can be in any countries that provide transit (Davies, 1998b).

55. In September 1993, the Information Infrastructure Task Force (IITF) of the US government issued the 'National Information Infrastructure: Agenda for Action'. The purpose of this agenda was to provide a coordinated development of advanced high-capacity, interactive communication facilities which would include means for the Internet, other

telecommunications and a variety of special media services to be made available on a large scale (http://www.ibiblio.org/nii/NII-Executive-Summary.html).

56. 'National Information Infrastructure: Agenda for Action' identified nine specific principles and goals to guide government action, including promoting private sector investment, extending the 'Universal Service' concept to ensure that information resources are available to all at affordable prices (http://www.ibiblio.org/nii/NII-Executive-Summary.html). Vice President Al Gore introduced the US vision for the Global Information Infrastructure (GII) at the first World Telecommunication Development Conference in March 1994. He called upon every nation to establish an ambitious agenda to build the GII, using five principles as the foundation including encouraging private sector investment, promoting competition, providing open access to the network for all information providers and users, creating a flexible regulatory environment that can keep pace with rapid technological and market changes and ensuring universal service (http://www.iitf.nist.gov/documents/docs/gii/giiagend.html#APPENDIX A).

57. The Federal–State joint board, set up in accordance with the 1996 Act, recommended that Internet access not be considered a 'core service' subject to universal service support under section 254(c)(1) (Joint Board Recommended Decision at 37, p. 69).

58. The joint board recommended a system of discounts, between 20 per cent and 90 per cent, for schools and libraries that purchased telecommunication and other services under this provision, to be financed by a fund of up to $2.25 billion per year (Joint Board Recommended Decision at 224–5, pp. 438–40). NITA (National Telecommunications and Information Administration US Department of Commerce) announced the 'E-rate proposal' to fulfil the mandate of section 254(h) of the 1996 Telecommunications Act (FCC CC Docket 96–45).

59. By early 1999, about 15 country nets as well as the US Next Generation Internet (NGI) networks and Abilene were interconnected to STAR TAP.

60. This project is managed by the University of Indiana to facilitate the connection of the Asia Pacific Advanced Network (APAN) to STAR TAP. APAN members include Australia, Japan, Korea and Singapore.

61. This project is managed by the University of Tennessee at Knoxville to facilitate the connection of Russia's MIRnet to STAR TAP.

62. AmericasPATH, or AMPATH, is a Florida International University (FIU) and Global Crossing (GC) collaborative project to connect the Research and Education (R&E) networks of South and Central America, the Caribbean and Mexico, to networks in the USA and other countries (http://www.startap.net/NETWORKS/).

63. This project is managed by the University of Illinois at Chicago to facilitate the connection of Israel's IUCC, The Netherlands' SURFnet, France's Renater2, the Nordic countries' NORDUnet, and the European Particle Physics Laboratory CERN, to STAR TAP (http://www.startap.net/NETWORKS/).

64. The NGI initiative is a multi-agency federal research and development programme to develop advanced networking technologies and revolutionary applications. NGI is led by and focuses on the needs of the federal mission agencies, such as DoD, DoE, NASA, NIH and others. The Federal NGI initiative and the university-led Internet2 work together in specific programmes, for example through participation in an NSF NGI program (http://www.ngi.gov/pubs/).

65. Abilene is a backbone network used by the Internet2 community. Internet2 is a consortium involving over 180 universities working in partnership with industry and government to develop and deploy advanced network applications and technologies (http://www.internet2.edu/html/about.html).

66. TEN-34 was a Research & Development project coordinated by DANTE and supported by the European Commission through its Telematics Applications Programme (Research Sector, 1996–1998 Contracts, Project RE 1009) (http://www.dante.net/ten-34/index.html). However it took more than two years from the first meeting for the backbone finally to become available. The reason for this was that standard PNO (public network operator) services in Europe could not fulfil the requirements of the R&D community in Europe, and, to some extent, in 1997 they still could not (Behringer, 1997).

67. DANTE (http://www.dante.net/quantum/).
68. European Commission (1993).
69. This view was subsequently reinforced by the report of the Bangemann Group. This committee, composed of leading representatives of the telecommunication equipment sector, PTOs and users, was set up to advise the European Council of Ministers and the EC on the requirements for pushing Europe into the lead in the creation of the information society. The Bangemann report also emphasized the role of ATM in the creation of high-speed, integrated pan-Europe networks as a building block for the information society (see European Commission, 1994).
70. All European PTOs were invited to participate and others have now joined, including Belgacom, PTT Telecom and Telecom Finland; there were 18 members as of 15 July 1993.
71. The ATM Forum argues that roughly 80 per cent of the world's carriers use ATM in the core of their networks. ATM has been widely adopted because of its unmatched flexibility in supporting the broadest array of technologies, including DSL, IP Ethernet, Frame Relay, SONET/SDH and wireless platforms. A number of standards have been developed to map IP over ATM networks (http://www.atmforum.com/).
72. The members are divided into primary members (Australia, Japan, Korea, Singapore, USA, China, Malaysia), associate members (Thailand), affiliate members (CGIAR), liaison members (Canada, Europe) and others (Hong Kong, Indonesia and the Philippines) (http://www.apan.net/info.html).
73. Argentina introduced some radical changes in its telecommunication sector, including privatization in 1989, but this led to increases in telecommunication service prices and resulted in a private monopoly. Because private investors demand a period of market exclusivity in the provision of basic services under conditions of economic and political uncertainty, privatization results in only the handover of control of the network from public to private market players (Petrazzini and Guerrero, 2000).
74. Adapted from IDATE (http://www.idate.fr/).
75. PSINet became a PTO in that its wholly owned subsidiary, PSINet Telecom Limited, received a licence from the FCC to provide facilities-based telecommunications services (OECD, 1999a).
76. Detailed consolidations chronicles are provided by IDATE.
77. PSINet has established PSINet Japan (1994), the Canadian subsidiary PSINet Ltd (1995) and PSINet UK (1995). The list of ISPs who were acquired by PSINET during the period 1997 to 2000 includes: iSTAR (Canada, 1997), InternetWay (Switzerland, 1997), LinkAge (Hong Kong, 1998), Interactive Network Gmbh (Germany, 1998), SCII-CalvaPro (France, 1998), ioNET internetworking Services (US, 1998), Inet (South Korea, 1998), Rimnet Corp. and TWICS (Japan, 1998), HKIGS (Hong Kong, 1998), Tokyo Internet (Japan, 1998), SpiderNet HugeNet and AsiaNet (Hong Kong, 1998), Openlink, Horizontes Internet, STI, and Domain Acesso e Servicios Internet (Brazil, 1999), Internet de Mexico and Datanet (1999, Mexico) TIC (Switzerland, 1999), Caribbean Internet (Puerto Rico, 1999), TIAC (US, 1999), Intercomputer and ABAFORUM (Spain, 1999), Global Link (Hong Kong, 1999), Argentina Online (Argentina, 1999), Netline Comunicacions S.A (Chile, 1999), Elender (Hungary, 1999), Infase Comunicaciones and Ciberia Internet (Spain, 1999), ServNet Servicos de Informatica e Comunicacao (Brazil, 1999), Vision Network (Hong Kong, 1999), TotalNet (Canada, 1999), Zircon Systems Pty Ltd (Australia, 1999), Netgate (Uruguay, 1999), JoinNet (Taiwan, 1999), alpha dot.net (US, 1999), PacWan (France, 2000), CorrerioNet (Brazil, 2000), New Com SAL (Lebanon, 2000), SSD, Interserver and Powernet (Argentina, 2000), GlobalNet and Pontocom (Brazil, 2000), Interactive Network (INX) (Germany, 2000), Internet Exchange Europe b.v. and Unix Support Netherlands b.v. (Netherlands, 2000) and Interactive Telephony Ltd (Jersey, 2000) (IDATE http://www.idate.fr/; PSI http://www.psi.com; http://boardwatch.internet.com/isp/summer99/bb/psinet.html).
78. The asymmetric traffic volume between GTEI (having its own network) and Exodus (web hosting ISPs) is the main reason for the disputes over the peering agreement between them (http://www.zdnet.com/intweek/daily/980810h.html).

79. As the ISP market is developing, new types of ISPs are emerging; Cukier (1998) suggests that there are four kinds of ISPs: backbone ISPs, downstream ISPs, online service providers and web site hosting ISPs. Furthermore some of the current ISPs are virtual ISPs that focus on marketing and customer services while buying the actual connection to the Internet infrastructure for customers and basic hosting facilities from another ISP.

80. APIA (http://www.apia.org/IIIF%20CFP%209710.htm).

81. Mr Hur (Inet, Inc. Seoul Korea) explains that 'the justification for this charging model [peering model] was acceptable in the initial phase of commercial Internet development. It was based on the fact that most of the information and content was based in the US, and most of the Internet users wanted to access the information in the US. The traffic flow between the US and the AP region had been in the order of 90:10 or even more' (http://www.apia.org/IIIF%20Inet%20response%209709.htm).

82. ITU (http://www.itu.int/journal/200102/E/html/indicat.htm).

83. ICANN (http://www.icann.org/general/fact-sheet.htm).

84. Moreover the *Cook Report* claimed that 'ICANN is the illegitimate offspring of IBM, and the Clinton Gore Administration – with the assistance of the Internet Society (ISOC) and Vint Cerf' (http://www.cookreport.com/icannoverall.shtml).

6. Internationalization and digital divide

6.1 INTRODUCTION

The previous two chapters examined the dynamics of the evolution of the Internet system. The biased and uneven political, economic and technological power relations between countries, notably the USA and other countries, appear to have shaped the competition between the Internet system and the X.25 data network system. At the same time, from the earliest stage of development, Internet technologies have extended to some countries via the international science communities to facilitate collaborative research and technology development. The expansion of the Internet and the global system was shaped by these competing and collaborating activities. They were intertwined with national and regional research network-building processes. The uneven global expansion of the Internet system does appear to reflect the different political and economic contexts that are embedded in the building of regional research networks. Despite the explosive growth of the Internet, there are huge discrepancies worldwide in terms of accessibility. These differences are far greater than for other ICTs and far greater in terms of disparities in the wealth of economies. As a result, there are economic and political concerns about the consequences of Internet system development for the existing world economic order. The uneven development between countries of ICTs, including the Internet, is said to be contributing to changes in the international division of labour and in technological leadership.

Economic and political concerns have been expressed about the consequences that the uneven development of the Internet system will have, particularly in terms of whether Internet system development will help to reduce the disparities that exist in economic and political power relationships both between advanced economies and developing economies and within countries, or whether it will contribute a different form of asymmetry.[1]

This chapter examines the outcome of global expansion and localization of the Internet, focusing on convergence and divergence phenomena. Section 6.2 discusses convergence and divergence issues in the development of the Internet. Section 6.3 examines global expansion of the Internet in terms of time of connection to the NSFNET, using a classification based on the cultural, economic and regional characteristics of countries. Section 6.4 analyses the patterns of the system in different regions and countries by comparing electronic switching systems. Section 6.5 examines technological substitution and complementarities by analysing competing technologies of the Internet and videotex (online service). The localization of the Internet system involves transformation of the videotex (online service) system. Section 6.6 analyses the pervasiveness of the Internet in terms of number of users, and disparities in access to it compared with other ICTs. Differences in the choices between the Internet system and the cellular phone system among regions and countries are also highlighted. Section 6.7 presents the conclusion to this chapter.

6.2   ECONOMIC AND SOCIAL IMPLICATIONS OF THE UNEVEN INTERNET SYSTEM DEVELOPMENT

The uneven development of the Internet system raises the issues of economic convergence (or divergence) and digital divide (or social inclusion). The evolution of the Internet system is often said to be leading the information and communication technology paradigm. Certain types of technological innovation such as ICTs may result in changes in the 'technoeconomic paradigm', in that their effects are pervasive throughout the economy (Freeman and Perez, 1988).[2] The authors argue that a technological revolution (that is, changes in the technoeconomic paradigm) is accompanied by a major structural adjustment in which social and institutional changes are necessary to bring about a better match between the new technology and the system of social management of the economy or the regime of regulation. Castells (1996) also points out that innovations in ICT changed the modes of production and development of capitalism and the role of the state from the 1980s. Economists regard the Internet as a general purpose technology (GPT) (Harris, 1998).[3] It is now generally accepted that ICT is a radical innovation that unlocks important growth potential for the world economy (OECD, 2000b).[4] Among many reports, OECD (2003) also provides evidence on the contribution of ICTs to the economic growth at both country and firm level.

The question of convergence (or divergence) in economic growth between countries and of its causation has been explored by many economists, notably Harrod (1939), Domar (1946), Solow (1956), Kaldor (1957), Myrdal (1957) and Hirschman (1958). These works provide important insights into uneven economic growth. However most of these models do not include the technological factor. Technology gap theory, proposed by Posner (1971) who extended Schumpeter's innovation cycle model into international trade, argues that new products and processes offered a temporary monopoly advantage to the producing country. Subsequent research by many scholars established the existence of imitation lags, dynamic economics of scale, process innovations and R&D in a variety of industries. Among many authors, Gomulka (1971) and Abramovitz (1979) argue that the existence of technological gaps between countries contributes to different economic growth rates.

From the mid-1980s, there have been controversies among scholars over technology gaps and economic growth.[5] For example, Baumol (1986) argues that convergence in the economic growth rate of advanced countries over the period 1870–1979 is best explained by technological spillovers, while Abramovitz (1986), although giving some weight to spillovers, places greater emphasis on 'social capability' in trying to explain why only some countries seemed to have been able to catch up. The new growth theorists, following Solow's work, also agree that economic growth depends positively on the volume of resources available for development of new technologies (for example, human capital and R&D) and the extent to which the new technologies are appropriate.[6]

However the neo-Schumpeterian argues that growth paths are in most cases highly dependent on structural features related to sector composition. Thus the possibilities for sectoral specialization, combined with different learning possibilities and demand patterns, induce differences in growth rates among countries.[7]

As stated in Chapter 2, scholars working in this tradition emphasize the partial tacitness, cumulativeness and idiosyncrasy of technological accumulation, the importance of technological capabilities in economic growth and the importance of firms in technological accumulation. They argue that economic growth is a process of transformation and not convergence to a steady-state growth path and that the transformation of capitalism involves co-evolution of the economic system and other sub-systems, for example science, technology and social and cultural systems. Technology is a key factor in shaping economic growth and changes in growth rate, but the effects of technological change on economic growth vary. The process of economic growth is characterized by structural changes brought about by radical and incremental innovations, and the dynamics of the economic selection process (for example, competition) shape economic growth (Verspagen, 2001: 6). Scholars working in this tradition believe that international differences exist and that they have consequences for convergence. Some suggest that the NIS explains differences in the direction and rate of technological accumulation between countries.

Studies of technological change and economic development suggest that 'catching up' is not impossible, but is only applicable to a few countries that have built the relevant technological capabilities and introduced institutional change and are able to exploit the window of opportunity brought by the current ICT revolution. Freeman and Soete (1990) and Freeman (2001) argue that convergence and divergence are related to the long wave of technical change and that there is a difference between the two phenomena with respect to timing. They claim that the phenomenon of divergence occurs in the period of establishment of a new technological regime by the technological innovation leaders. Those countries with strong capabilities for assimilating complex new technological systems have to overcome 'the major barriers in the form of intellectual property rights as well as barriers in the availability of finance, skills, and market access' (Freeman, 2001: 160). Steinmueller also points out that the corequisites for catching up (and leapfrogging) in the ICT sector include 'the development of absorptive capacities, access to equipment and know-how, complementary capabilities and the capability to meet downstream integration requirements' (Steinmueller, 2000: 1).

Convergence issues are also dealt with in the discourses on new ICT capabilities and the north–south divide and social exclusion and inclusion within a country.[8] For example, O'Brien and Helleiner (1983) stress that technological development of ICTs could produce new forms of dependence (that is, in the form of inequality of control and access to information) instead of enlarging the independent capacities of developing countries, and new dimensions of inequality and poverty when balanced against the opportunity cost of investing in other sectors. As Haywood (1998) argues, the access to the Internet may simply be laid over the same old patterns of geographic and economic inequality rather than contributing to the spread of information and knowledge to many more citizens, allowing them to share in political and economic influence.

6.3   GLOBAL EXPANSION OF THE INTERNET

This section will analyse cultural, economic and regional routes of global expansion of the Internet. Chapter 5 demonstrated that the internationalization of the Internet was shaped by economic and political factors by the US and regional context.

The Early Adopters

After the NSFNET was established in 1987, the Internet system entered the global expansion phase and, by the end of 1991, had achieved a global presence. Only eight countries were connected to NSFNET at the end of 1988. They were advanced western countries: the USA, Canada, France and the five Nordic countries, Finland, Norway, Denmark, Sweden and Iceland.[9] Table 6.1 groups countries by year of connection to the NSFNET (between 1988 and 1991). They are grouped by similarities of culture, economic and

Table 6.1 Countries grouped by the year of connection to NSFNET
(between 1988 and 1991)

		1988	1989	1990	1991
Western advanced	Europe	France, Demark, Finland, Iceland, Norway, Sweden	Netherlands, United Kingdom, Italy, Germany, Israel	Switzerland, Belgium, Austria, Greece, Ireland, Spain	Portugal
	Other region	United States, Canada	Australia, New Zealand		
East Asia advanced		—	Japan	Korea	Singapore, Hong Kong, Taiwan
Europe		—	—	—	—
Eastern & Central Europe		—	—	—	Czech Republic, Hungary, Poland, Croatia
Asia & Pacific		—	—	India	
Africa		—	—		South Africa
South Asia & CIS		—	—	—	Tunisia
Middle East & North Africa		—	—	—	—
North and South America		—	Mexico, Puerto Rico	Chile, Brazil, Argentina	—
Total		8	10	11	10

Note: Israel is included in Europe.

Source: Data adapted from Merit (<NIC.MERIT.EDU> /nsfnet/statistics/).

regional characteristics, based on Huntington (1993), Kedzie (1995) and Mansell and Wehn (1998). A total of 22 countries out of 40 are in the western hemisphere. Even though European countries followed different technological trajectories, they were the first group to join the global expansion of the

Internet. They made the change from X.25 to multi-protocol networks and, subsequently, in the late 1980s, to the TCP/IP protocol (see Chapter 4).

By December 1991, 39 countries were connected to the NSFNET. They were distributed across most regions: North and South America (7), Europe (18), East Asia (5), Eastern Europe (4), Oceania (2), the Middle East and North Africa (1), South Asia (1) and Africa (1). During the period 1988–91, global expansion of the Internet system was led by the western countries: the USA, Canada, Australia, New Zealand, Israel and the countries of western Europe.

The Followers

By May 1995, 87 countries were connected to the global Internet system. During the period between 1991 and 1995, Eastern Europe, the Asia–Pacific and the Americas[10] and many other developing countries led its global expansion. The number of developing countries from Eastern Europe, the Asia–Pacific and the Americas that were connected increased from 4, 0 and 5, respectively, in January 1991, to 14, 11 and 16, respectively, in May 1995.

By January 1999, 191 countries were connected to the global Internet system. In the Africa region, between May 1995 and January 1999, 34 developing countries were newly connected to the global Internet system. In the Americas region 23 developing countries, in the Asia–Pacific region 13

Table 6.2   Global expansion of the Internet system, number of countries

		January 1989	January 1992	May 1995	January 1999
Western advanced	Europe	7	17	18	18
	Other region	2	5	5	5
East Asia advanced		0	5	5	5
Europe		0	0	3	8
Eastern & Central Europe		0	4	14	20
Asia & Pacific		0	0	11	24
Africa		0	1	9	39
South Asia & CIS		0	1	5	15
Middle East & North Africa		0	1	7	17
America		0	6	17	40
World		9	40	94	191

Source: Data adapted from Merit (<NIC.MERIT.EDU> /nsfnet/statistics/); Network Wizard (http://www.nw.net/).

developing countries, and in the South Asia and the CIS (Commonwealth and Independent States) region 10 countries became new joiners of the global Internet system. Table 6.2 presents figures for the global expansion of the Internet in terms of regions and income and time of connection to the NSFNET (and global network after the NSFNET was 'retired').

Global Expansion Routes

Analysis of the global expansion of the Internet suggests that it appears to have followed certain paths from western countries to other countries (cultural route); from advanced countries to developing countries (economic route); from countries near the USA to countries distant from the USA (regional route). These three different paths overlap.[11] This confirms the development patterns discussed on an impressionistic and a quantitative basis in the studies of Internet diffusion.[12]

Scholars hold differing views about the cultural features of the Internet system. For example, Leoussi argues that 'the Internet is a flower of the Western mind – not a *fleur du mal* but rather a product of the most deeply rooted, humane and cherished values of Western civilization: freedom of speech and freedom of association – the value of classical democracy' (Leoussi, 2000: 14). On the other hand, Dutton *et al.* point out that the Internet reflects 'important historical American values of sharing, generosity, and neighbourliness which are the antithesis of market values' (Dutton *et al.*, 1994: 31). The notion of culture has been used to analyse differences between social groups, nations and regions because 'culture determines the identity of a human group in the same way as personality determines the identity of an individual' (Hofstede, 1980: 25–6). Williams (1983: 89) suggests that we should 'speak of "culture" in the plural: the specific and variable cultures of different nations and periods, but also the specific and variable cultures of social and economic groups within a nation'. Some scholars focus on national differences at national level (for example, Hofstede, 1980) and regional level (for example, Huntington, 1993), while others talk of social groups in a society (for example, Thompson *et al.*, 1990).

Cultural aspects are also related to economics. For example, as O'Brien and Helleiner (1983) pointed out, advanced ICTs have evolved under the leadership of western countries, in particular the USA, in response to the needs of transnational corporations (and defence and surveillance) to overcome the major imperfections of market exchange by internalizing their information (and other) flows.

As analysed in Chapter 5, the Internet backbone was built by integrating existing local and regional networks and this encouraged the growth of further local and regional networks. In the global expansion period, international networks were built up by integrating existing national networks and the building of these international networks in turn encouraged further national and local networks through the arrangements for cost sharing for international networks. There were positive feedbacks between backbone networks and regional and local network building and between international networks and national and local networks.

The Uneven Growth of the Internet System between Regions

This section looks at the influence of the regional route, focusing on the balance of Internet traffic between the USA and other regions and the intensity of use of the Internet system. Analysis of the Internet traffic between regions and countries is focused on the global expansion period, but, because of availability of data, is confined to the period between January 1992 and May 1995. In this period, the European countries started to build regional networks and Eastern European countries were connected to European regional networks, while most other regions were still connected to the NSF backbone network directly.

Table 6.3   The network growth between January 1992 and May 1995

		January 1992		May 1995	
		Number of networks	Share (%)	Number of networks	Share (%)
Western	Europe	681	20.7	9 220	18.2
	Oceania	131	4.0	2 231	4.4
	North America	2 286	69.6	33 265	65.5
	Total	3 098	94.3	44 716	88.1
East Asia advanced		136	4.1	3 100	6.1
Europe		0	0.0	125	0.0
Eastern & Central Europe		10	0.3	1 473	2.9
Asia & Pacific		0	0.0	221	0.4
Africa		13	0.4	439	0.9
South Asia & CIS		1	0.0	20	0.0
Middle East & North Africa		1	0.0	41	0.1
America		26	0.8	624	1.2
World		3 290	100	50 760	100

Source: Data adapted from Merit (<NIC.MERIT.EDU> /nsfnet/statistics/).

Some 3285 networks were connected to NSFNET in January 1992, 69.6 per cent of which were in the USA and Canada, while the number of networks connected to non-western countries was less than 6 per cent (see Table 6.3). During the period January 1992 to May 1995, East Asian advanced countries and Eastern European countries showed the highest increase in terms of numbers of networks.

North America (the USA and Canada) accounted for about 90 per cent of the total traffic on the NSFNET in the first quarter of 1992, measured by average total traffic (see Table 6.4). After the establishment of the regional backbone networks, EuropaNet and Ebone, in 1992 the Internet traffic in Europe became progressively localized. Jouanigot *et al.* (1993) argue in their study on the IP traffic of CERN that the 'intra-European traffic flows dominate, which has not always been the case in the past' (ibid.: CBC-4). As was shown in Chapter 5, most of the international Internet traffic from other

Table 6.4   The growth of Internet traffic between 1992 and 1994

	Average between January 1992 and March 1992		Average between October 1994 and December 1994[1]	
	Traffic[2]	Share	Traffic	Share
Western Europe	232.8	7.6	2 702.6	7.1
Oceania	40.6	1.3	603.9	1.6
North America	2 744.7	89.7	33 439.2	88.5
Total	3 018.1	98.6	36 745.8	97.2
East Asia advanced	32.5	1.1	653.6	1.7
Europe	0.0	0.0	15.5	0.0
Eastern & CIS	0.6	0.0	136.4	0.4
Asia & Pacific	0.0	0.0	41.2	0.1
Africa	0.8	0.0	27.8	0.1
South & Central Asia	0.2	0.0	7.1	0.0
Middle East & North Africa	0.0	0.0	9.2	0.0
America	8.2	0.3	166.1	0.4
World	3 060	100.0	37 803	100.0

Notes:
1. From December 1994, traffic started to migrate to the new NSFNET architecture.
2. Gigabyte, per month.

Source: Data adapted from Merit (<NIC.MERIT.EDU> /nsfnet/statistics/).

countries was, except in Europe, transmitted through the NSFNET. Internet traffic was more concentrated in western countries, in particular the USA, than appears to be the case as measured by the number of networks (see Table 6.3 and Table 6.5).

Table 6.5 shows the balance of traffic as a ratio of incoming and outgoing traffic through the NSFNET and average traffic per network. The balance of traffic through NSFNET for most of the world was negative between 1991 and 1994. In the first quarter of 1992, only Finland shows a positive balance of traffic (2.38) with NSFNET. Four countries – Switzerland (1.55), Taiwan (1.30), France (1.23) and Sweden (1.11) – exhibit a positive traffic balance. Only Finland and Switzerland show a positive traffic balance between the

Table 6.5 Traffic balance and traffic per network (1992–4)

		Average between January 1992 and March 1992		Average between October 1994 and December 1994	
		Traffic balance[1]	Traffic per network[2]	Traffic balance[1]	Traffic per network[2]
Western	Europe	0.39	0.41	0.71	0.55
	Oceania	0.67	0.41	0.61	0.84
	North America	1.09	1.53	1.06	2.09
		(1.13)[3]	(1.58)[3]	(1.10)[3]	(2.17)[3]
	Total	1.01	1.27	1.02	1.70
East Asia advanced		0.39	0.30	0.50	0.51
Europe		—	—	0.19	0.28
Eastern & Central Europe		0.11	0.06	0.58	0.18
Asia & Pacific		—	—	0.26	0.42
Africa		0.29	0.07	0.30	0.17
South Asia & CIS		0.22	0.19	0.26	0.54
Middle East & North Africa		0.27	0.02	0.14	0.37
America		0.63	0.39	0.33	0.48
World		1.00	1.17	1.00	1.55

Notes:
1. The ratio between the incoming and the outgoing traffic through the NSFNET.
2. Total traffic (one month) divided by the number of networks.
3. USA.

Source: Data calculated by author from Merit (<NIC.MERIT.EDU>/nsfnet/statistics/)

USA and themselves during the period between January 1991 and December 1994. Total incoming traffic from Finland to the NSFNET during the period 1992 to 1994 was 1628.88 gigabytes and total outgoing traffic from NSFNET during the same period was 1269.09 gigabytes.[13] Jouanigot *et al.* (1993) argue that those countries showing a positive balance are 'either "net" exporters of data or they are well organized in terms of mirroring popular anonymous ftp servers located in the US and elsewhere'.[14] The balance of traffic between other countries and the USA improved slightly from 1992 to 1994. For example, Western Europe and NSFNET improved from 0.39 in the first quarter of 1992 to 0.71 in the fourth quarter of 1994.

Table 6.5 presents other indicators of the intensity of Internet usage in terms of monthly traffic per network. Monthly traffic per network transmitted through NSFNET in the first quarter of 1992 was 1.17 gigabytes and this had increased to 1.55 gigabytes by the end of 1994. Monthly traffic through the NSFNET per network in Europe at the end of 1994 was 0.55 gigabytes, which was less than the average of Australia and New Zealand because some of the traffic in Europe was transmitted within the region through two regional backbones rather than through NSFNET. This indicator also confirms that there was a difference in the Internet system with respect to regional and economic factors. The regional differences in Internet system development in terms of volume and balance of Internet traffic were in part the result of regional network-building efforts. In sum, analysis of regional network growth during the period January 1992 to May 1995 shows regional convergences in terms of number of networks connected to the NSFNET and traffic balance. The extent of convergence appears to differ depending on time of regional network building and adoption of the Internet system. For example, the Nordic countries had already caught up to the USA in terms of traffic balance during that period because in 1989 they had implemented NORDUnet which adopted a multi-protocol structure with TCP/IP as the primary service (see Chapter 4).

6.4 INTERNET SYSTEM GROWTH PATTERNS IN MAJOR COUNTRIES

This section analyses the different levels of development and performance of the Internet system based on penetration rates of Internet hosts, numbers of networks and volume of traffic, growth rates and changes in indicators. In all, 32 countries were selected to compare Internet system growth between countries during the period January 1992 to January 2000.[15] Press *et al.* (1998) suggest using the ratio of users per capita as a yardstick for comparisons of level of Internet system development between countries. They categorize five levels of the pervasiveness dimension including Non-existent, Experimental, Established, Common and Pervasive. The number of hosts is used to measure development in this analysis. The number of users is estimated to be ten times the number of hosts: it was commonly accepted in the Internet community that, before the Internet became popular, there were about ten users per host.[16]

Growth Patterns

During the early 1990s, most European countries, and especially the Nordic countries, caught up with the USA in terms of penetration rate of Internet hosts. By January 1992, some were forging ahead in terms of number of hosts per thousand inhabitants. For instance, Norway (2.334) and Finland (2.266) had a greater number of hosts per thousand inhabitants than the US (2.065) while Switzerland was level with the USA. Sweden (1.968) and Australia (1.830) exhibited a development of the Internet system similar to that of the USA. Most western countries (Canada, Iceland, the Netherlands, Israel, Germany, New Zealand, Austria, Denmark, the UK and France) had achieved the common stage with over 0.1 hosts per thousand inhabitants. Only one non-western country, Singapore (0.175), entered this stage. Southern Europe (Portugal, Spain, Italy and Greece) and Ireland and Belgium were in the experimental stage along with Asia (Japan, Hong Kong, Taiwan and South Korea), Eastern Europe (Hungary and Poland), South America (Mexico and Brazil) and South Africa.

Figure 6.1 shows the number of hosts per thousand inhabitants and compound annual growth rate (CAGR) between January 1992 and January 2000. In general, countries with a less developed Internet system in 1992 show greater annual growth rates. Average CAGR between 1992 and 2000 of the six countries which had achieved the highest number of hosts per thousand inhabitants was 62.96 per cent, that of 11 countries in the established stage was 88.07 per cent and that of 15 countries in the experimental stage was 124.11 per cent.

As a result of this rapid growth, most countries were in the pervasive stage by January 2000. Only six countries – South Korea, Greece, South Africa, Poland, Mexico and Brazil – were still in the common stage. Figure 6.2 shows growth changes and numbers of hosts per thousand inhabitants. Growth change is calculated by dividing CAGR between 1996 and 2000 by CAGR between 1992 and 1996. In most countries, the Internet started commercialization after 1995. The average growth change for 32 countries is 0.62. In general, the rate of growth in a country decreases as the Internet system becomes more widespread.

Figure 6.2 shows different patterns of Internet system growth across countries. Two different patterns of development can be seen among countries that

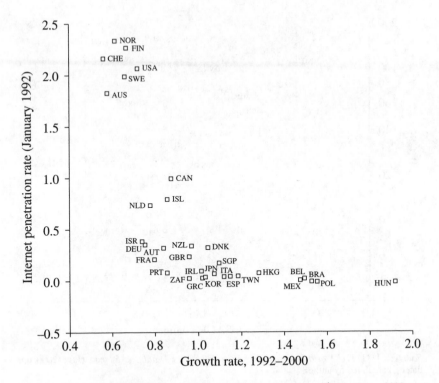

Source: ITU, *ITU World Telecommunication Indicators Database*, 5th edn (June 2000 updated), calculated by the author.

Figure 6.1   Growth rate and Internet hosts penetration

had already reached the pervasive level in January 1996: slowdown and continuous growth. Finland, Iceland, New Zealand and Australia show significant slowdown. For example, annual growth rates between 1991 and 1995 in Finland and Iceland were 107 per cent and 150 per cent, respectively, but fell to 34 per cent and 38 per cent respectively between 1995 and 1999 (see Table 6.6). There was more than one host in these countries for every ten inhabitants. Almost 40 per cent of the total population in Finland and about 54 per cent in Iceland were using the Internet.

Switzerland, Canada, Sweden, Norway and the USA exhibited steady growth. Annual average growth in Canada in terms of Internet host computer penetration between 1996 and 2000 was higher than the average of the total 32 countries. Annual growth in Switzerland in terms of host computer penetration increased from 51 per cent in 1991–5 to 61 per cent during the period 1995–9.

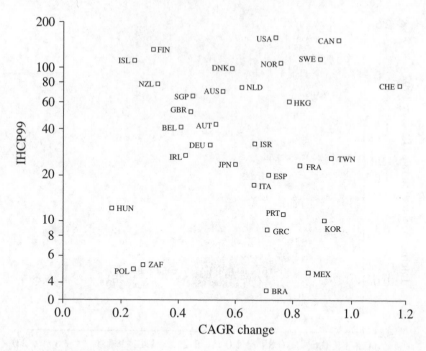

Source: ITU, *ITU World Telecommunication Indicators Database*, 5th edn (June 2000 updated), calculated by author.

Figure 6.2   Growth changes and the number of hosts per 1000 inhabitants of a country, January 2000

Hungary, Poland and South Africa had not reached the pervasive level by January 2000 and their average annual growth measured by number of host computers per thousand inhabitants decreased from January 1996, as it did in Finland and Iceland (Tables 6.7 and 6.8). Annual growth rate of host computers in Hungary decreased from 403 per cent during the period 1992–6 to 69 per cent between 1996 and 2000, which is lower than the average growth rate of the 32 countries (73.57 per cent), during the same period. The annual growth in Internet penetration in Poland and South Africa also fell between 1992 and 1996, from 285 per cent and 163 per cent to 69 per cent and 46 per cent, respectively. This contrasts with Taiwan, South Korea and Mexico (Tables 6.7 and 6.8). Annual growth rates in Taiwan during the periods January 1992 to January 1996 and January 1996 to January 2000 were 124 per cent and 114 per cent, respectively.

Table 6.9 summarizes different patterns of Internet system growth between countries in the periods 1991–5 and 1995–9, based on the above analysis.

Table 6.6   Growth rate change in selected countries, group I

Country	Numbers of host computers per 1000 inhabitants (January 1996)	CAGR 1991–5 (A)	CAGR 1995–9 (B)	Growth rate change (B/A)
Iceland	31.03	1.50	0.38	0.25
Finland	41.67	1.07	0.34	0.31
New Zealand	14.77	1.55	0.51	0.33
Australia	17.13	0.75	0.42	0.56
Netherlands	11.08	0.97	0.60	0.62
United States	23.02	0.83	0.61	0.74
Norway	19.34	0.70	0.53	0.76
Sweden	16.41	0.70	0.62	0.89
Canada	12.70	0.89	0.85	0.95
Switzerland	11.35	0.51	0.60	1.17
Average of group 1	19.84	0.95	0.56	0.67
Average of total 32 countries	8.28	1.35	0.74	0.62

Source: Data calculated by author from ITU, *ITU World Telecommunication Indicators Database*, 5th edn (June 2000 updated).

Some of the information from the above tables is summarized below:

1. Some first movers (for example, the USA, Canada and Sweden) continued to show steady growth even after the Internet became popular.
2. Relatively small countries entered a mature stage of faster growth (for example, Iceland, Finland and New Zealand).
3. There may be different levels of saturation, depending on a country's economic and social context (for example, Hungary, South Africa and Poland).
4. There seem to be different patterns with respect to regions (for example, the Nordic countries, North America, East Asia and Eastern Europe), culture (western civilizations and others) and income.

Comparison of these results with the penetration levels of electronic switching (Antonelli, 1991) yields some surprising results. In Antonelli's study,

Table 6.7   Growth rate change in selected countries, group 2

Country	Numbers of host computers per 1000 inhabitants (January 1996)	CAGR 1991–5 (A)	CAGR 1995–9 (B)	Growth rate change (B/A)
Hungary	1.54	4.03	0.67	0.17
South Africa	1.17	1.63	0.46	0.28
Belgium	3.02	2.24	0.92	0.41
Ireland	3.73	1.48	0.63	0.43
UK	7.51	1.38	0.61	0.45
Singapore	7.62	1.57	0.71	0.45
Germany	5.80	1.01	0.52	0.51
Austria	6.63	1.12	0.60	0.53
Denmark	9.69	1.34	0.79	0.59
Japan	2.15	1.38	0.82	0.60
Italy	1.32	1.36	0.90	0.66
Israel	4.91	0.89	0.60	0.67
Spain	1.31	1.34	0.96	0.72
Portugal	1.19	0.97	0.75	0.77
Hong Kong	2.87	1.44	1.13	0.79
France	2.60	0.87	0.72	0.82
Taiwan	1.21	1.22	1.14	0.93
Average of group 2	3.78	1.49	0.76	0.56
Average of total 32 countries	8.28	1.35	0.74	0.62

Source: Data calculated by author from ITU, *ITU World Telecommunication Indicators Database*, 5th edn (June 2000 updated), ITU (http://www.itu.int/it/).

only four countries, Canada, the USA, France and Norway, had entered the leader category (15 countries were categorized as leaders in terms of electronic switching systems in 1987). Most European countries were slow followers (three countries) or laggards (eight countries). Greece was one of the non-adopters at that time. In contrast, six East Asian countries were in the leader category.

By January 1996, most western countries had reached a pervasive level of Internet development as measured by penetration of Internet hosts. Four

Table 6.8   Growth rate change in selected countries group 3

Country	Numbers of host computers per 1000 inhabitants (1995)	CAGR 1991–5	CAGR 1995–9	
Poland	0.60	2.85	0.69	0.24
Brazil	0.13	1.80	1.28	0.71
Greece	0.74	1.20	0.85	0.71
Mexico	0.15	1.60	1.36	0.85
Korea	0.65	1.08	0.98	0.91
Average of group 3	0.45	1.71	1.03	0.68
Average of total 32 countries	8.28	1.35	0.74	0.62

Source: Data calculated by author from ITU, *ITU World Telecommunication Indicators Database*, 5th edn (June 2000 updated), ITU (http://www.itu.int/it/).

Table 6.9   Different patterns of the Internet system growth

Development of the Internet system in 1995	Slowdown		Continuously growing
Pervasive	Iceland, Finland, New Zealand	Australia, Netherlands	USA, Norway, Sweden, Canada, Switzerland
Common	Hungary, South Africa, Belgium, Ireland, UK, Singapore	Germany, Austria, Japan, Italy, Israel, Denmark, Spain	Hong Kong, France, Taiwan, Portugal
Established	Poland	Brazil, Greece	Mexico, Korea

Asian advanced countries (Japan, Taiwan, Hong Kong and Singapore) were at the common level of Internet system development and South Korea still remained at the established level. Antonelli (1991) and Ernst and O'Connor (1992) point out that the Asian countries were able to catch up with the technological leaders in electronic switching systems thanks to their strong technological capabilities in the electronics sector. So why did these technological capabilities not accelerate the localization of the Internet? First, the Internet system is an almost entirely self-contained system while electronic switching is a sub-system of the telecommunication system. Localization of the Internet system probably calls for much more complex technological adaptation efforts than was the case for the electronic switching system. Second, the technological characteristics of the Internet differ from those of the traditional telecommunication system. This implies that localization of the Internet system requires new technological learning. Third, there are differences between the Internet system and the electronic switching system in terms of social learning. Localizing the Internet, which is a large technological system, involves not only a technological capability building process, but also a social capability building process, including institutional changes through the mechanisms of learning and forgetting (Abramovitz, 1989; B. Johnson, 1992; Lundvall and Johnson, 1994; Gregersen and Johnson, 1997). The time and effort needed for social capability building for a large technological system depends on the institutional similarities and differences in a country compared to the country where it was invented and developed. This is because the transferred technological system often embodies, not only the features of knowledge and production systems, but also often the culture, ideology and values embedded within technologies (Gregersen and Johnson, 1997). For example, the value system embodied in electronic switching is centralized control and integration, while the Internet system was designed for a system of decentralized control and a diversified culture.

6.5 COMPETING TECHNOLOGIES

Scholars working within technoeconomic perspectives argue that the development of technological systems involves complementary technologies or substitution between technologies. In this section, different paths in the transformation process of the online service (videotex)[17] to the Internet system between countries are examined. Historical experience suggests that the exponential growth of the Internet in the 1990s was partly attributable to the well-established commercial online service system. Most major online service providers emerged as ISPs by changing their system to support the Internet platform. However, different paths of online service development between the USA (mainly online services) and other countries, in particular Europe (mainly the videotex system) may have influenced the process of transformation of the online service (videotex) system to the Internet environment.

Development of the Online Services (and Videotex) System

The development of specialized online services took two different paths. In North America, online services were provided, based on a proprietary system, mainly by information service providers. CompuServe launched the first commercial online service in 1979. With the liberalization of the telecommunication market and technological developments, various online services, including CompuServe, Prodigy, Genie and America Online (AOL), were developed during the 1980s (Huber, 1987; Huber *et al.*, 1992). Online services provided various kinds of information services, including information access and retrieval (videotex), messaging (email, voice messaging), computing services (for example, online databases), transactional services (credit card transaction, electronic funds transfer) and other data network services mainly accessed through PCs. Online services were well established by the end of the 1980s. For example, in the USA the revenue from online services reached US$9.6 billion in 1991.[18] Major American online services providers such as AOL and CompuServe[19] expanded their services into Europe and other regions from 1990.

In contrast to the USA, in Europe and Asia, and especially in France and Germany, online services were developed mainly within the videotex environment with PTOs acting as service providers. In France and Germany, Télétel and Bildschirmtext were launched in 1982 and 1983, respectively. Videotex systems made it possible for users to access information data banks, offering news updates, telephone numbers and train schedules, and literature databases using conventional telephone lines and a television set (Bildschirmtext), a special video monitor (Télétel) or PCs. The number of French videotex system users had reached almost 6 million in 1991.[20] One of the important factors in the success of Télétel was a simple and compact terminal, Minitel, which was initially provided free of charge.[21] However, in most other countries, videotex systems had been converted either to PC-based videotex systems or to an online services system by the early 1990s. After successive failures in designing a videotex terminal, the German videotex system was changed to a PC-based system at the beginning of the 1990s (Gilbert, 1996). The Germans enhanced their system during the 1990s to compete with the Internet, CompuServe and AOL in terms of multi-media and network capabilities and both quality of service and speed of access.

Until mid-1990, online services and videotex systems were more popular than the Internet (see Table 6.10). In 1995, there were about 21 million online subscribers worldwide, 44 per cent of whom were in the USA and 31 per cent in France (ITU, 1997b).

Table 6.10   The growth of online services and the Internet system between 1990 and 1995

	1990	1991	1992	1993	1994	1995
Online and videotex services subscribers (millions)	9.7	11.1	12.3	15.0	17.5	20.9
Numbers of Internet hosts (millions)	0.4	0.7	1.3	2.7	5.8	14.0

Source: Adapted from ITU (1997); *ITU World Telecommunication Indicators Database*, 5th edn (June 2000 updated).

Challenges from the Internet System

The landscape of the online information services market has been changed by technological innovations in the Internet system and in PC hardware and software. At the end of the 1980s, user-friendly interfaces and corresponding protocols were introduced, such as Internet Relay Chat (IRC, 1988), Hytelnet (1990), the Wide Area Information Service (WAIS, 1991), Gopher (1991), the World Wide Web (WWW, first implemented in 1990), VERONICA (1992) and the NCSA's (National Center for Supercomputing Applications) Mosaic (1993).[22] These innovations greatly increased the popularity of the Internet. In particular, the WWW had the powerful potential to integrate other protocols and thus more versatile multi-media services.[23]

Technological innovations in the Internet system were facilitated by computer and communication technologies. Computer technology is itself being changed profoundly by the convergence of computer and communication technologies: for example, the new interfaces required by telecommunication applications such as voice and video input and output. Convergence processes such as 'the integration of many human communications media into a single coherent system in itself creates a new technology with opportunities for the development of new products and services' (Gaines, 1998: 20).

There has been positive feedback between telecommunications and information technologies (Gaines, 1998; Shapiro and Varian, 1999). Gaines (1998) argues that advances in existing technologies trigger breakthroughs in new technologies that themselves help to sustain the advance of existing technologies. The widespread use of PCs resulted from a decrease in the price of hardware and advances in software, for example Windows/OS2. This user-friendly and graphic user interface contributed to expanding usage among a wider circle of users. It also facilitated hardware development to enable the capability of the PCs to keep up with the new developments in the software sector. The technological improvements in telecommunication, such as intelligent networks, fibre optics and faster modems, facilitated users' access to the Internet. The technological development of the Internet system created economic incentives for the development of telecommunication technologies to keep up with demand for faster and higher bandwidth for data switching and transmission. In addition to these technological innovations, powerful metaphors for the Internet system such as 'open', 'decontrol or decentralized', 'global' and 'free' contributed to its fast diffusion.[24]

The Continuing Growth of the Videotex System in some Countries

Online services and videotex systems did not fade away (see Tables 6.11 and 6.12). Online service providers were enhancing their systems, benefiting from the interrelated technological innovations, while videotex systems, in particular in France, found it difficult to utilize technological advances in computer systems mainly because of technological and economic obstacles in transforming the Télétel system.[25] Schneider points out that the success of Télétel may have contributed to the relatively limited development of the PC in France as compared to some other west European countries. In the face of the challenge from the Internet system, the development of online service systems and videotex systems started to integrate Internet access into their offerings. Online service providers such as Prodigy and CompuServe switched their systems to the Internet platform and other online service providers progressively moved to Internet platforms from 1995. France Télécom also started to offer the Wanadoo service, which was designed to enable the use of Minitel services with a PC-monitor and special software, and allowed access to the Internet from May 1996. However Schneider (2000) argues that Télétel's strategy of accessing the Internet through Wanadoo services was not a 'real solution' to the problem of being locked into inferior technology.

Most PTOs in most advanced countries and some developing countries had begun to provide videotex services in the early 1990s.[26] Table 6.11 shows 21 countries with more than 1000 subscribers to videotex services.[27] Singapore and South Korea show a greater than 70 per cent annual growth rate and Germany and Finland exhibit growth rates of 36.08 per cent and 23.22 per cent, respectively, during the period 1991 to 1997. In France and Switzerland, the annual growth rate of videotex service subscribers was 3.55 per cent and 7.33 per cent, respectively, in the same period. In most other countries (for instance, Portugal) the number of videotex service subscribers tended to decrease. By the end of the 1990s, South Korea, Singapore and Germany showed similar (or greater) annual growth in videotex service subscribers to rates of growth in Internet hosts (see Table 6.12 and Figure 6.3).

Table 6.11   Videotex service subscribers in major countries (thousands)

Country	1991	1995	1997
France	6 001.0	7 400.0	7 400.0 (3.55[1])
Germany	302.3	965.4	19 19.0 (36.08[1])
Spain	300.0	620.0	N.A.
Italy	169.7	N.A.	N.A.
Japan	139.0	238.6	305.4[2]
South Korea	124.9	718.2	3 117.6 (70.96[1])
Finland	100.0	235.0	350.0 (23.22[1])
Switzerland	85.0	112.5	129.9 (7.33[1])
Sweden	30.6	N.A.	N.A.
South Africa	28.3	N.A.	N.A.
Netherlands	18.2	N.A.	N.A.
Austria	14.1	28.5	N.A.
Taiwan, China	12.3	21.2	N.A.
Belgium	9.4	14.6	10.0[2]
Singapore	7.5	97.2	295.8 (84.50[1])
Norway	6.1	N.A.	N.A.
Denmark	6.0	N.A.	N.A.
Portugal	4.7	1.5	1.1 (−21.85[1])
Brazil	4.0	N.A.	N.A.
Ireland	2.5	N.A.	N.A.
Israel	1.7	N.A.	N.A.

Notes:
1. CAGR between the period 1991 and 1997.
2. 1996.
3. N.A.: not available.
4. Data of the US was not available.

Source: ITU, *ITU World Telecommunication Indicators Database*, 5th edn (June 2000 updated).

Online service (and videotex) providers such as AOL (US), T-online (Germany), Niffy (Japan), Chollian (South Korea), Hitel (South Korea) and Unitel (South Korea) emerged as major ISPs in 2000 (see Table 6.13). The total number of Internet subscribers to the three online service providers in South Korea was about 10.5 million.

While the French videotex system ran the risk of becoming locked into an inferior system, in other countries (Germany, South Korea, Finland and Singapore) videotex (or online service) systems appear to have continued a

Table 6.12 Comparison between the Internet and videotex (or online services) system

	1991	1993	1995	1997	1999
The number of Internet hosts (thousands)					
Finland	11.4	33.1	215.7	486.8	461.8
France	12.0	53.8	151.1	355.0	1 233.1
Germany	27.1	111.6	474.4	1 132.2	1 635.1
South Korea	1.5	9.0	29.3	121.9	283.5
Singapore	0.5	2.8	22.8	57.6	148.2
The number of videotex (online service) subscribers (thousands)					
Finland	100.0	175.0	325.0	350.0	N.A.
France	6 001.0	6 500.0	7 400.0	7 400.0	5 000.0
Germany	302.3	496.7	965.4	1 919.0	4 150.0
South Korea	124.9	354.7	718.2	3 117.6	8 803.0[1]
Singapore	7.5	15.1	97.2	295.8	426.8[2]

Notes:
1. December 1999.
2. December 1998.

Source: ITU, *ITU World Telecommunication Indicators Database*, 5th edn (June 2000 updated); Schneider (2000); NCA (http://www.nca.or.kr).

high rate of growth and to have contributed to the adaptation of the Internet system. One of the main differences between the French system and that in other countries was the terminal: other countries had changed their systems to adopt PCs. Even though the French videotex system eventually changed to a PC terminal, the existence of more than 6 million dumb terminals seems to have been an obstacle to its meeting the challenge from the Internet. There were several reasons for the continuous growth of online services and the videotex system. On the supply side, most videotex and online service providers, in order to justify their charges, began to introduce competitive features such as greater reliability and better performance by enhancing multi-media capabilities and bandwidth (ITU, 1997a). Some online service providers such as AOL, Prodigy and Niffy even offered free subscriptions. The congestion on the Internet also contributed to the continuing growth of the established videotex and online services system. Videotex and online service providers were progressively transforming their

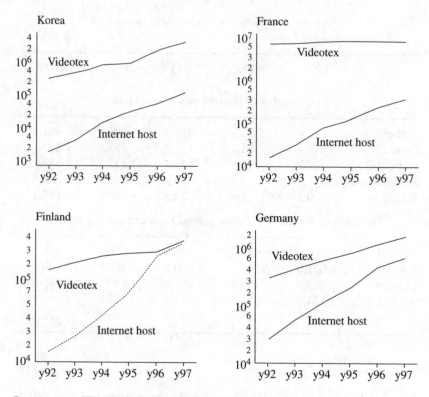

Data sources: ITU, *ITU World Telecommunication Indicators Database*, 5th edn (June 2000 updated); Schneider (2000); NCA (http://www.nca.or.kr).

Figure 6.3   The Internet and videotex growth

systems to offer services that integrated the existing online services and Internet services. The financial arrangements among online service pro-viders, network providers and information service providers made change difficult. For example, there were financial settlement arrangements between online service providers and other network operators for interconnection and the volume of traffic in South Korea.[28] It was not easy to change this arrange-ment until the use of the Internet was well established. In Korea, there was fierce competition between South Korea Telecom and Dacom in providing online services after competition was introduced in the data communication sector.

Users also seemed to need time and to have to make an effort to learn how to use the Internet. The absence of order on the Internet, language barriers and lack of local content in the early stages of the Internet system, seem to

Table 6.13   Top 10 ISPs ranked by subscribers in September 2000

	Country	Number of subscribers (millions)	Name of ISP (Internet Service Provider)
AOL	USA	24.6	Includes Compuserve
T-online	Germany	7.0	Deutsche Telekom
EarthLink	USA	4.6	Merged with MindSpring Feb.2000
Niffy	Japan	4	Fujitsu
Juno	USA	3.7	
Chollian	South Korea	3.7	Dacom
Terra	Spain	3.5	Telefónica
Tin.it	Italy	3.5	Telecom Italia
Hitel	South Korea	3.4	Korea PC Telecom
Unitel	South Korea	3.4	Samsung SDS

Source: Data adapted from ITU (http://www.itu.int/journal/200102/E/html/indicat.htm)

have added to users' difficulties while traditional online services offered users a degree of standardization, for instance the means to search efficiently across a range of available and reliable sources (Ochsner and Thomas, 1996). Users need time to master complex searching techniques, surfing multiple sites and evaluating the resources. The content on the videotex system was locally customized and provided in the national language. However its use was an important learning mechanism for users and suppliers in the adoption of the Internet. Until user-friendly interfaces, applications and content in national languages became available, the advantages of the Internet were confined to specific advanced users, for example those that wanted to access other countries' web sites for research purposes. Also there were already well-established communities using the existing online and videotex systems.

   In some countries (for example, Germany and South Korea) the development of online services (videotex) systems seems to have facilitated the local development of the Internet system. The competition between different technologies appears to have contributed to technological innovations and improvements in the 'using and supplying capabilities' of online information and to the establishment of an 'online culture' in the local context.

6.6   INTERNET SYSTEM DEVELOPMENT

The pervasiveness of the Internet system, in terms of number of users, and disparities in access to the Internet between countries can be grouped by economic strength. The localization of the Internet system involves the transformation of ICTs. Transformation of ICTs focusing on choices between the Internet and the cellular phone is analysed below.

Pervasiveness of the Internet System

To examine the different levels of Internet system development, countries are classified into categories: Leaders, Fast Followers, Slow Followers and Laggards. The pervasiveness of the Internet system in a country is measured by the number of users per hundred inhabitants in 2000.

The following classifications were used by Maddala and Knight (1967), Antonelli (1991) and Press *et al.* (1998).

1.   Leaders: countries in which the number of the Internet users is greater than 10 per 100 inhabitants in 2000;
2.   Fast Followers: countries in which the number of the Internet users is between 1 and 10 per 100 inhabitants in 2000;
3.   Slow Followers: countries in which the number of the Internet users is between 0.1 and 1 per 100 inhabitants in 2000;
4.   Laggards: countries in which the number of the Internet users is less than 0.1 per 100 inhabitants in 2000.

Table 6.14 shows the varying performance of the Internet system's development, measured by the number of Internet users in 147 countries in 2000.[29] 34 countries entered the class of leaders, 42 and 51 countries were classified as fast followers and slow followers, respectively. In the leader countries, about one-quarter of the population use the Internet. In the fast followers, about 4.0 per cent of the population use the Internet. Slow followers have slightly fewer than 0.4 users per 100 inhabitants.

The development of the Internet system shows big discrepancies with respect to regions and the economic strength of countries (Table 6.15). Twenty-five countries out of a total of 34 leaders are advanced wealthy economies. Only one wealthy economy, Greece, belongs to the fast followers. Among the developing countries, four Eastern European countries (Estonia, Slovenia, Hungary, Slovak Republic), one Asian country (Malaysia), one Middle East region (UAE) and three American countries (Puerto Rico, Uruguay, Chile) reached the pervasive level of Internet system development. Most African, Middle East and South Asian countries are in the slow follower or laggard categories.

Table 6.14 Classification of countries by the performance of the Internet system development

Group	Number of countries	Internet users per 100 inhabitants (January 2000)	
		Mean	Std. deviation
Leaders	34	26.58	10.42
Fast followers	42	4.04	2.66
Slow followers	51	0.38	0.26
Laggards	20	0.05	0.03
Total	147	7.44	11.84

Source: Data calculated by author from ITU, *ITU World Telecommunication Indicators Database*, 5th edn (June 2000 updated).

Table 6.15 Internet system development by country group, region and income

		Leaders	Fast followers	Slow followers	Laggards	Total
Advanced countries	Europe	16	1			17
	North America	2				2
	Pacific	2				2
	Asia	5				5
Developing countries	Europe		1			1
	Eastern Europe & CIS	4	13	5	3	25
	America	3	12	7	1	23
	Asia & Pacific	1	5	3	2	11
	Middle East & North Africa	1	5	7	1	14
	Africa		5	24	7	36
	South Asia			5	2	7
Total		34	42	51	16	143

Source: ITU, *ITU World Telecommunication Indicators Database*, 5th edn (June 2000 updated), (http://www.itu.int/it/), calculated by author.

Disparities in Access to the Internet System between Countries

During the 1990s, the information and communication infrastructure across the world improved at a rapid rate. In particular, the Internet and cellular phone systems experienced 67.86 per cent and 54.93 per cent of annual growth rate, respectively, during the period 1994 to 2000. Table 6.16 shows information and communication infrastructure growth in countries grouped by economic strength in 1994 to 2000. Least Developed Countries (LDC)[30] and developing countries (DC) exhibit higher growth rates than the advanced economies in terms of information and communication infrastructure, including telephone mainlines, PCs, cellular phones and Internet systems.

Table 6.16   The growth of information and communication infrastructure, 1994–9, by countries grouped by economic strength

	Number of Internet hosts	Number of cellular phone subscribers	Number of telephone main lines	Number of PCs
Advanced countries	66.71	47.36	3.40	15.13
Developing countries	102.48	84.94	14.78	27.82
Least developed countries	136.78	85.98	9.37	26.88
World	67.86	54.93	7.43	17.01

Source: ITU, *ITU World Telecommunication Indicators Database*, 5th edn (June 2000 updated); ITU (http://www.itu/it/), calculated by author.

The world penetration rate of Internet hosts per thousand inhabitants increased from 0.14 to 13.62 between 1991 and 2000. Cellular phone subscribers also increased, from 0.30 to 12.25 per 100 inhabitants. However these two technological systems show different performance with respect to disparities among countries grouped by level of economic strength. Table 6.17 shows both real penetration rate (grouped by countries' economic strength) and the indicator for examining the relative level of the Internet and cellular phone system measured by the ratio between country group and world average.

The development of the cellular phone system shows continuous reduction in the disparities between the advanced economies and developing economies. The gap between the advanced economies and LDCs has also narrowed, although the levels are far lower than those between advanced economies and developing economies. However there has been very little sign of convergence in access to the Internet system among countries grouped by economic

Table 6.17 Changes in disparities between the Internet and cellular telephone systems

	Internet				Cellular phone			
	Advanced countries	Developing countries	Least developed countries	World	Advanced countries	Developing countries	Least developed countries	World
	Number of Internet hosts per 1000 inhabitants				Number of cellular phone users per 1000 inhabitants			
1991	0.82	0.00	0.00	0.14	1.76	0.02	0.00	0.30
1994	5.21	0.03	0.00	0.85	5.42	0.16	0.01	0.99
1997	30.80	0.30	0.00	5.06	18.72	1.02	0.03	3.68
2000	83.74	1.07	0.01	13.62	53.67	6.09	0.21	12.25
	Index (ratio: group/world)							
1991	6.08	0.00	0.00	1.00	5.76	0.08	0.00	1.00
1994	6.10	0.03	0.00	1.00	5.47	0.17	0.01	1.00
1997	6.09	0.06	0.00	1.00	5.09	0.28	0.01	1.00
2000	6.16	0.08	0.00	1.00	4.25	0.48	0.02	1.00

Source: ITU, *ITU World Telecommunication Indicators Database*, 5th edn (June 2000 updated); ITU (http://www.itu.it/), calculated by author.

Table 6.18 Distribution of information and communication infrastructure (2000)

		Population[1] (million)	GDP[1] (billion USD)	Telephone main lines (million)	Personal computers (million)	Internet hosts (million)	Internet users (million)	Mobile phone subscribers (million)
Advanced countries	Europe	395.3	9 008.3	218.0	115.6	18.4	95.4	251.2
	North America	305.8	9 953.2	213.3	173.0	51.4	108.0	118.2
	Pacific	22.9	449.4	12.0	10.3	1.9	7.4	10.7
	Asia	207.2	5 291.9	114.8	60.5	6.3	76.2	119.6
	Total	931.2	24 702.8	558.1	359.4	78.0	287.0	499.7
Developing countries	Eastern Europe	402.3	649.5	86.0	15.8	1.1	12.4	28.3
	Asia & Pacific	486.6	487.1	24.4	8.3	0.4	10.5	19.4
	China	1 295.3	991.0	144.8	20.6	0.3	22.5	85.3
	Africa	157.7	199.9	7.3	3.7	0.3	3.1	10.5
	South Asia	231.8	664.2	14.1	4.7	0.0	0.5	2.1
	India	1 012.4	141.0	32.4	4.6	0.2	5.0	3.6
	Arab	216.8	520.4	18.8	5.0	0.1	2.5	8.8
	America	499.0	1 790.1	76.0	21.9	2.1	19.1	62.1
	Europe	67.1	215.0	19.3	2.7	0.3	2.2	46.1
	Total 1[1]	4 369.0	5 658.2	423.1	87.3	4.7	77.9	266.2
	Total 2[2]	2 061.3	4 526.2	245.8	62.1	4.2	50.4	177.3

LDC		776.8	184.0	4.4	1.9	0.0	1.0	1.6
World		6 077.0	30 545.0	985.6	448.6	82.7	365.9	767.5
		%	%	%	%	%	%	%
Advanced	Europe	6.50	29.49	22.12	25.76	22.28	26.07	32.73
countries	North America	5.03	32.59	21.64	38.56	62.13	29.53	15.40
	Pacific	0.38	1.47	1.21	2.29	2.35	2.03	1.39
	Asia	3.41	17.32	11.65	13.49	7.59	20.82	15.58
	Total	15.32	80.87	56.63	80.11	94.34	78.44	65.11
Developing	Eastern Europe	6.62	2.13	8.73	3.52	1.33	3.40	3.68
countries	Asia & Pacific	8.01	1.59	2.47	1.86	0.45	2.88	2.53
	China	21.32	3.24	14.70	4.59	0.39	6.15	11.11
	Africa	2.59	0.65	0.74	0.82	0.31	0.84	1.37
	South Asia	3.81	2.17	1.43	1.05	0.03	0.14	0.28
	India	16.66	0.46	3.29	1.03	0.23	1.37	0.47
	Arab	3.57	1.70	1.91	1.11	0.12	0.69	1.15
	America	8.21	5.86	7.71	4.87	2.48	5.21	8.09
	Europe	1.10	0.70	1.95	0.61	0.30	0.61	6.00
	Total 1[1]	71.89	18.52	42.93	19.46	5.65	21.29	34.68
	Total 2[2]	33.92	14.82	24.94	13.84	5.03	13.78	23.10
LDC		12.78	0.60	0.45	0.43	0.01	0.27	0.21
World		100.00	100.00	100.00	100.00	100.00	100.00	100.00

Notes:
1. 1999.
2. Not including China and India.

Source: ITU, *ITU World Telecommunication Indicators Database*, 5th edn (June 2000 updated); ITU (http://www.itu/it/), calculated by author.

strength. Rather the figure for the relative penetration of Internet hosts per thousand inhabitants in advanced economies compared to the world average increased from 6.09 in 1997 to 6.16 in 2000.

Table 6.18 shows disparities in access to the information and communication infrastructure among countries grouped by economic strength and region. In 2000, about 366 million people in more than 200 countries had access to the global Internet system, connected by about 82.7 million computers. However only 15.32 per cent of the total world population (advanced economies) and 94.34 per cent of total computers were connected to the Internet. Disparities in use of the Internet appear to be smaller than disparities in access to the Internet. In 2000, approximately 287 million people in advanced economies used the Internet, which is 78.44 per cent of total world Internet users. There are relatively more users than hosts in developing countries. For example, China has about 6.15 per cent of total Internet users, but only 0.39 per cent of Internet hosts.

Different Choices of Technological Systems

It is worth noting that countries show different choices on advanced communications systems. The Internet system and the cellular telephone system emerged as the most popular advanced data and voice communications systems during the 1990s (OECD, 1999a). The high growth rate of cellular telephone systems is a result of the reduction in prices and advances in technological performance through digitalization. The two systems have some similarities. Both systems were originally developed for military purposes[31] and both are relatively cost-efficient compared to the traditional public fixed network; that is, the PSTN in the long distance segment (see Table 6.19). However they have different technological characteristics. First, the Internet system was designed for data communication while the cellular phone primarily was designed for voice communication. Second, the Internet is controlled by decentralized intelligence while the mobile system is controlled by centralized intelligence. Major innovations in the mobile telephone system have been achieved by network operators, while users have played a critical role in technological innovations in the Internet system.

One of many differences between the two communication systems is their associated technological capabilities. The development of the Internet system mainly involves information processing and communication technologies while the knowledge required to use the mobile system is mainly based on communication technologies. As indicated above, the growth of the mobile telephone system was mostly achieved by a reduction in prices and advances in technological performance mainly stemming from technological innovations, for example, digitalization.[32] However the localization of the Internet system is

Table 6.19   Comparison between Internet and cellular phone systems

	The Internet system	Cellular phone system
Main Service	Data	Voice
Network control	Decentralized	Centralized
Major innovators	Users (research communities)	Suppliers (e.g. network operators and equipment manufacturers)
Network building process	Global → Regional & National	National → Regional & Global roaming
First users	Research communities	Business communities
Technological capabilities	Information processing and communication systems	Communication system
Strength as compared to PSTN	Global reach	Mobility

Source: Elaborated by author.

generally accompanied by more user capabilities and a wider range of institutional changes than that of the mobile phone system.

Regions in advanced countries seem to make different choices in terms of advanced communication systems. The penetration rates for cellular phones are greater in the advanced economies of Europe and Asia than in the North American and Pacific regions. For example, about 64 per cent of Europeans use cellular phones while for America and Canada the figure is only 39 per cent. About 58 per cent of people in the Asian advanced economies use cellular phones, while the figure for Australia and New Zealand is about 47 per cent. In contrast, the advanced economies in North America and the Pacific region have relatively more Internet hosts than in Europe and Asia (see Table 6.20).

It is not possible to state that there is divergence in the growth of advanced communication systems between countries because they are still evolving. However, as Figure 6.4 shows, the choice between the Internet system and the cellular phone system in advanced economies during the period 1991 to 2000 differs. In the advanced economies of Asia and Europe cellular phone use has increased faster than Internet use, particularly since 1997. The advanced economies of North America and the Pacific region show higher growth rates for the Internet.

Table 6.20   Comparison of Internet and cellular phone penetration rates,
by Country group (2000)

	Internet host computers (million)	Cellular phone subscribers (million)
Europe	18.41	251.23
North America	51.35	118.21
Pacific	1.94	10.69
Asia	6.27	119.61
Advanced	77.98	499.74
Developing countries	4.44	266.16
Least developed countries	0.24	1.63
World	82.66	767.53
	Internet host computers per 1000 inhabitants	Cellular phone subscribers per 1000 inhabitants
Europe	46.59	63.56
North America	167.92	38.65
Pacific	84.62	46.63
Asia	30.27	57.73
Advanced	83.74	53.67
Developing countries	1.07	6.09
Least developed countries	0.01	0.21
World	13.82	12.25

Source: ITU, *ITU World Telecommunication Indicators Database*, 5th edn (June 2000 updated); ITU (http://www.itu/it/), calculated by author.

6.7   CONCLUSION

The development of the Internet raises the question of whether it will contribute to reducing disparities in the existing technological and economic strength of countries or will increase the gaps because it is a radical innovation. This chapter has examined this question in terms of 'population dynamics' in the development of the Internet system which involves technological, economic, cultural and geographic factors.

The internationalization and the localization of the Internet appear to be influenced by economic, cultural and regional factors. Analyses of the global

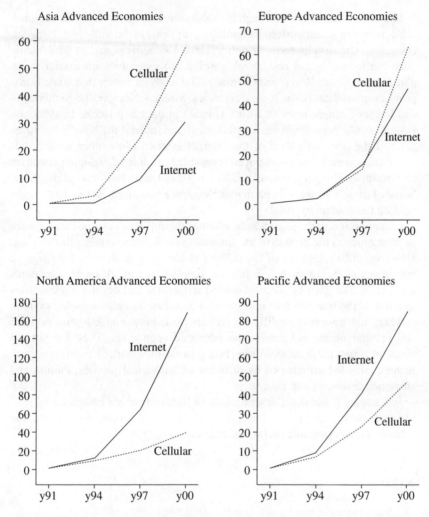

Source: ITU, *ITU World Telecommunication Indicators Database*, 5th edn (June 2000 updated); ITU (http://www.itu/it/), calculated by author.

Figure 6.4   Different growth patterns of the Internet and cellular phone in advanced economies

expansion of the Internet system and growth patterns between regions support this argument. In addition comparison with international diffusion of electronic switching systems suggests that the localizing of the Internet system is likely to need much more complex technological and social learning efforts.

The selection processes through the substitution and complementary mechanism between competition technologies appear to be different between countries. The development of online service systems seems to have facilitated the technological and social learning processes in some countries, in particular in South Korea and Germany. The analysis shows that some European countries (that is, the Nordic countries, Sweden, Norway, the Netherlands and Iceland) caught up with North America in the early 1990s. In 1995, the USA, Canada, New Zealand, Australia, Switzerland and the Nordic countries reached the pervasive level of the Internet system. Most other western advanced economies, Asian developed economies and some developing countries (for example, Hungary, Poland and South Africa) were followers at that time. Some of these followers, in particular Singapore and South Korea, had caught up with the leaders by 2000.

It may be too early to conclude whether there is evidence of convergence or divergence in the growth of the Internet system, because it is still evolving. However, unlike the case of the cellular phone system, there is little sign of reductions in the disparities in Internet access between advanced economies and LDCs. The gaps between advanced economies and developing countries in terms of the Internet have narrowed far less than the cellular phone system.

There also appear to be different choices made between the Internet system and cellular phone systems in the advanced economies. They are not the result of a natural or random selection process of advanced communication technologies but are shaped by different technological profiles, culture and strategies between countries.

In Chapter 7, the main determinants of localization are examined by testing hypotheses about the pervasiveness of the Internet system and the technological, economic and social factors.

NOTES

1. See, for example, Freeman (2001) and Loader (1998).
2. Freeman and Perez (1988) distinguish between incremental innovation, radical innovation, new technology systems and changes in the technoeconomic paradigm, based not only on continuous or discontinuous effects on product or process, but also on constellations of innovations.
3. Bresnahan and Trajtenberg (1995: 84) argue that 'general purpose technologies' (GPTs) are characterized by the potential for pervasive use in a wide range of sectors and by their technological dynamism. They point out that the evolution and advances of a GPT throughout the economy bring about fostering generalized productivity gains. See Helpman (1998) for the definition and measurement of GPTs and economic growth.
4. As Verspagen (2001) points out, in the 1980s and early 1990s mainstream economics was occupied with Solow's paradox, which states that 'we see computers everywhere except in the statistics on productivity growth'.
5. See Fagerberg *et al.* (1994) and Verspagen (1993, 2001) for the controversies over technology, competitiveness and trade.

6. See, for example, Romer (1986, 1990) and Lucas (1988).
7. See, for example, Dosi *et al.* (1990), Verspagen (1993) and Fagerberg *et al.* (1994).
8. On the discussions on the issues of the digital divide and social inclusion, see Loader (1998), Wyatt *et al.* (2000), Compaine (2001) and Warschauer (2003).
9. Kedzie (1995) suggests six regional categories incorporating elements of geography, history and religion, based on Huntington's (1993) work. They are Africa, Asia, Eurasia, Latin America, the Middle East and Western Europe. Western Europe also includes countries that are not on the continent but that have a dominant Western European heritage: the United States, Canada, Australia and New Zealand. Israel is also included in the West European category.
10. This includes North America, South America and the Caribbean.
11. However the cultural and regional factors seem to be more important than the economic factor in understanding the Internet system's global expansion (and localization), although these three different routes overlap to some extent. For example, western countries were connected to the NSFNET earlier than Asian advanced countries. American developing countries and Eastern Europe countries were also connected earlier than developing countries in other regions.
12. See, for example, Kedzie (1995).
13. The Netherlands, Sweden, Taiwan and France also had reasonably well balanced traffic among the 87 countries between 1992 and 1994. The traffic balances in the Netherlands, Sweden, Taiwan and France were 0.98, 0.98, 0.94 and 0.89, respectively. The remaining countries show levels of less than 0.7.
14. Jouanigot *et al.* (1993: CBC-4).
15. Reliable data on the Internet, such as the number of hosts and amount of traffic, are available from the end of 1991. Data are only available on 32 countries out of the total 39.
16. This rough yardstick changed as the Internet system became popular. For example, the number of users per Internet hosts in 2000 was estimated at about 3.02.
17. ITU defines videotex services as services using terminals to communicate with databases over the telephone network (http://www.itu.int/ITU-D/ict/publications/world/material/handbook.html#c24).
18. 'Booker, On-line service Reach \$9.6 billion', *ComputerWorld*, 24 Aug 1992, in Huber *et al.* (1992).
19. In 1998, CompuServe was taken over by AOL, but it remains an independent service, mainly focusing on the business sector.
20. See OECD (1998d).
21. See Mayntz and Schneider (1988) for a comparative analysis of the videotex systems in the UK, France and Germany with respect to technologies, organization and policies. See also Sutherland (1995) for a comparison of the success of the French videotex system and failures of other countries including the UK, the USA, Germany, Canada and Japan.
22. E-mail on the Internet commenced in 1972, news distribution in 1977, Gopher in 1991 and Web browsers with multi-media capabilities in 1993. Email allows users to send text-based messages to each other using a common addressing system. Telnet allows Internet users to log into other proprietary networks, such as library card catalogues, through the Internet, and to retrieve data as though they were directly accessing those networks. FTP allows users to download files from a remote host computer onto their own system. Usenet enables users to post and review messages on specific topics.
23. Developed at the European Centre for Particle Research (CERN), the WWW was first used experimentally in 1989. A graphic browser, Mosaic, was developed at the NCSA at the University of Illinois. In accordance with NCSA policies, this software was made widely available on the Internet free of charge. It led to the exponential growth of the Internet by being able to provide images, sound, video clips and multi-font text in a hypertext system. The WWW has two primary features that provide a method of accessing information through the Internet. First, Web clients (or browsers) can combine text and graphical material and can incorporate all of the other major Internet services such as FTP, email and news in one standard interface. Second, the Web incorporates a hypertext

system that allows individual Web pages to provide direct links to other Web pages, files and other types of information.

24. From a different angle, Stefik (1996) argues the four metaphors have guided the development of the Internet including digital libraries (publishing and community memory), electronic mail (communications medium), electronic marketplace (a place for selling goods and services) and digital worlds (a gateway to experience).

25. For example, Gilbert (1996: 321) points to the three main reasons for the decline of the Minitel system: technological breakdown as users had more and more PCs and the network speed did not evolve; Minitel's connotation of being expensive; and service providers' high expectations on increasing prices. OECD (1998d: 22) also points to the main criticisms of the system: 'it is obsolete and too slow ... its profitability is a factor of the time spent on-line ... the system is suspected of shielding costly services with little added value from foreign competition and of hindering the expansion of personal computers and the Internet in France'.

26. See Shorrock (1988: 7–55) and Jouët *et al.* (1991) for the development of videotex in major countries.

27. Réunion, Guadeloupe and French Polynesia also had more than 1000 videotex subscribers in 1991.

28. This analysis is mainly from the interview with Dr Joo-Young Ok and Mr Tae-Chul Jung, Director of DACOM in South Korea, 27 December 2000. DACOM was a leading video system operator in Korea and started to convert its videotex system to the Internet from 1998.

29. Countries whose population was less than 1 million were excluded from the analysis in order to improve the stability data.

30. Least developed countries (UN classification) aggregate. The 47 economies included are: Afghanistan, Angola, Bangladesh, Benin, Bhutan, Burkina Faso, Burundi, Cambodia, Cape Verde, Central African Republic, Chad, Comoros, Congo Dem. Rep., Djibouti, Equatorial Guinea, Eritrea, Ethiopia, Gambia, Guinea, Guinea-Bissau, Haiti, Kiribati, Lao PDR, Lesotho, Liberia, Madagascar, Malawi, Maldives, Mali, Mauritania, Mozambique, Myanmar, Nepal, Niger, Rwanda, Samoa, São Tomé and Principe, Sierra Leone, Solomon Islands, Somalia, Sudan, Tanzania, Togo, Uganda, Vanuatu, Yemen Rep. and Zambia.

31. Wireless communication was invented by Guglielmo Marconi in 1898, but radiotelephony was further developed for military purposes during World War II. The first commercial mobile radiotelephone service, Mobile Telephone Service (MTS) was introduced by Bell Systems in 1946. See Calhoun (1992), OECD (1999a) and Amendola and Ferraiuolo (1995) for the development of wireless communications technologies and industry.

32. Standardization and subsidies also contributed to the explosive growth of the mobile system.

7.   Co-evolution: localization of the Internet system

7.1   INTRODUCTION

The 'population of dynamics' of development of the Internet system was examined in Chapter 6, where it was argued that the global expansion and localization of the Internet appear to have been influenced by economic, cultural and regional factors. Technological and social learning in the localization of the Internet system appear either to be locked into the existing system or facilitated by competing technologies. The Internet system has been localized through the choice of ICTs made by the advanced economies. There is little evidence of convergence in terms of access to the Internet between rich and poor countries, but there are differences in Internet system development among the advanced economies.

This chapter analyses the development of the Internet system as the outcome of localization across countries in relation to economic, cultural and regional factors. Factors that might influence localization of the Internet can be summarized, on the basis of the theoretical analysis in Chapters 2 and 3 and the empirical findings in Chapters 4 and 5, as follows.

Localization of the Internet system is likely to be influenced by the dynamic interactions between a country's economic, social and cultural characteristics and its science and technological systems. Development of the Internet, not surprisingly, is related to telecommunications and computer systems because of their technological interrelatedness, but the Internet has two features that make it distinctive from other technological systems. It was invented and developed to facilitate communication through the use of computers and telecommunications for the research and academic communities. Even after the Internet system became publicly accessible, these users continued to lead its development. Thus the economic, social and cultural factors that are specific to research and academic communities are also likely to be distinguishable in the development of the Internet. In addition, as discussed in Chapter 4, the localization of the Internet system is likely to be influenced by a country's level of global integration because the Internet system has been extended through the collaborative activities of global research communities and facilitated by regional research network building activities.

Hypotheses, based on the theoretical and empirical findings described in Chapters 2 to 6, along with relevant empirical studies, are all elaborated in section 7.2. Section 7.3 examines the interaction that underlies the Internet system and the factors that appear to influence localization of the system in more than 50 countries using the following techniques. First, a two-stage least squares (2SLS) estimation technique with a system of simultaneous equations is used to examine the relationship and interactions among the endogenous factors underlying the Internet system; that is, Internet host computers, PCs and telephone mainlines. As discussed in Chapter 3, the Internet system consists of host and server computers and uses public and private telecommunications networks.

Section 7.4 presents econometric models for testing the hypotheses, and discusses the results. The characteristics of each country concerned are examined by analysing indicators of knowledge production and distribution capabilities, global integration level, size of the social system, cultural factors (especially those associated with language) and income distribution; also the way such factors vary according to sector policies, Internet access and usage costs is discussed. An ordinary least squares (OLS) regression technique with principal components analysis (PCA) is used to analyse the relationship between Internet system development and the economic and social systems. Finally, some conclusions are presented.

7.2   MAIN HYPOTHESES

Findings from Previous Research

There are a few studies that attempt to explain the interdependency of the Internet system and the socioeconomic environment by focusing on similarities and differences in the system's development across countries. Some studies have attempted to show differences and similarities in the diffusion of the Internet across countries (for example, OECD, 1996c; ITU, 1999a; Hargittai, 1999; the Mosaic Group;[1] ITU[2]). Studies by OECD (1996c), ITU (1999a) and Hargittai (1999) employ mainly statistical analysis, while the Mosaic Group and the ITU studies focus on country-level case studies. Case studies such as these are based on research methods that employ information about industrial structure and the market share of firms, or information about legislation, regulation and policy measures. The empirical results suggest that the diffusion of the Internet is associated with economic and social factors, such as income and human development, and language and technology-specific factors, such as telecommunications infrastructure, policies, computerization and pricing, and interventions in the

Internet's development. However all these studies have some limitations: they provide only rough interpretations of the relationship between economic strength and the penetration rate of the Internet system, based on a simple correlation analysis (see, for example, ITU, 1999a), or they cover only selected, rich countries (OECD, 1996c; Hargittai, 1999).

The case studies for the most part focus on different patterns of Internet development across countries. For example, the Mosaic Group researchers analysed the characteristics of Internet diffusion patterns for 30 countries (Press *et al.*, 1998). Their analysis has four components: dimensions of Internet diffusion, success determinants, relevant government policies and multinational factors. Internet system development in a country is analysed in their study using six indicators: pervasiveness, geographic dispersion, sectoral absorption, connectivity infrastructure, organizational infrastructure and sophistication of use. The Mosaic Group also attempted to analyse the determinants of diffusion of a country's Internet, focusing on the telecommunication infrastructure, personal computing and software, financial resources, human capital, sectoral demand and the competitive environment. The case studies based on this analytical framework provide good country comparisons but they do not offer insights into the dynamic interactions between the Internet system and the economic and social environments. Rather they provide a yardstick for a comparison of Internet system development across countries.

The second set of empirical studies examines the relationship between the Internet system and social and economic factors, using econometric analysis.[3] The OECD (1996c) argues that the number of PCs as a rough proxy for computerization at a national level is strongly correlated with Internet system development in terms of the number of Internet hosts. The OECD (1998a) also argues that liberalization of the telecommunication infrastructure influences Internet system development. Rutkowski and colleagues found a strong correlation between income measured by gross national product (GNP) and the number of Internet hosts.[4] They suggest factors influencing the Internet's diffusion such as the regulatory environment, network competition, availabilities of components (private leased lines, local access lines, computers) cost-based or reasonably priced, skills for designing and operating TCP/IP computer networks, users' capabilities and time of entry into the Internet community. The analysis undertaken by the ITU (1997b) suggests that a country's level of income is the most important factor influencing Internet development.

Other factors identified as relevant are telecommunications infrastructure and policies, ICT development, service pricing and social factors such as age, language and education (ITU, 1997b; Männistö *et al.*, 1998). The ITU (1997b) found that a country's human development level correlates with its level of

Internet connectivity, using the Human Development Index designed by the authors of the United Nations Development Programme (UNDP) 1996 Human Development Report.[5] Most of these results are based on a simple correlation or regression analysis or on descriptive analysis. Hargittai (1999) attempted multiple regression analysis of variables such as income distribution (Gini coefficient), English language competency, telecommunication policy, telephone usage costs and telephone density. Based on these measures, the results obtained showed that neither education level, English language competency nor income distribution appeared to have a significant impact on Internet connectivity.

These somewhat contradictory results suggest that simple correlations of predictor and outcome variables (ITU, 1997b) are not sufficient for a detailed understanding of the relationship between the various factors that may influence Internet connectivity. Anderson *et al.* (1995) argue that cultural differences are more important than the domestic social and economic conditions in explaining Internet system development in different countries. They also suggest that the level of Internet connectivity is a dominant predictor of democracy. However most of these studies consider the Internet as a product (for example, email) rather than as a complex system whose features are influenced by the local telecommunication infrastructure and computer systems, the development of data communication usage in business, the research community and the public.

Hypotheses

This section develops the hypotheses to be tested. A technological system that is developed across countries may be expected to show similarities and differences reflecting its dynamic interaction with the different economic, social and cultural systems. Its development is facilitated or restrained by government policies. Differences and similarities in the technological systems across countries can be explored by country-specific factors and technological system characteristics (Dosi *et al.*, 1990). The co-evolutionary nature of technological systems and other sub-systems in a society can also be observed in the development of the Internet system. For example, historical experience, the legislative environment and traditions in the knowledge production and distribution systems constitute different styles of knowledge and economic systems. Different styles of knowledge systems may be expected to contribute to variance in computerization among countries via different patterns of knowledge transformation. Ernst and Lundvall (1997) argue that western countries have attempted to transform tacit knowledge into explicit knowledge through computerization and in this respect the USA stands at the extreme end of the spectrum:

The Japanese model is explicit in its promotion and exploitation of tacit knowledge, while the American model is driven by a permanent urge to reduce the importance of tacit knowledge and to transform it into information; that is, into explicit, well-structured and codified knowledge. Central to the American model is an attempt to transform tacit knowledge into explicit knowledge through the automation of human skills. This is in line with a strong normative bias in western civilization in favour of explicit and well-structured knowledge and the high priority given to formal natural sciences as the ideal for all other sciences. Economists tend to share and re-enforce this bias also because economic models have even greater difficulties in analysing tacit knowledge than in analysing information (ibid.: 40–42).

From this point of view, the development of the Internet system in the USA can be understood as following its knowledge system style. At least, cultural differences between countries in selecting information and communication technologies and research and academic communities appear to take an important role in designing and selecting the Internet system (see Chapter 5). The localization of the Internet system in other countries has progressed alongside other system changes.

As discussed in Chapters 2 and 3, interrelatedness and interdependence, the channels of knowledge exchange and transfer, the time of system transfer and both technology- and country-specific conditions may influence the localization of the Internet system. In terms of these technological, economic and political aspects of the Internet system, five groups of hypotheses are elaborated below.

Internet System and Computerization and Telecommunication Infrastructure

The penetration rate of PCs and telephone lines in a country is likely to directly influence the localization of the Internet system because they are components of the system.[6] As discussed in Chapter 3, the Internet, computer and telecommunication systems have an extreme level of systemic technological interrelatedness, complementarity and interdependence (David, 1985; Rosenberg, 1994).

The pervasiveness of the Internet system is likely to be determined by the level of computerization and the growth of the telecommunication infrastructure in the country. The level of installed PCs is often taken as an index of the development of the Internet system (OECD, 1996c; US Department of Commerce/International Trade Administration, 1999). The ITU emphasizes the importance of the telecommunication infrastructure for the development of the local Internet system: 'A shortage of infrastructure, notably of telephone lines, is a further big obstacle to increasing Internet access in developing countries' (ITU: 1999a, 35).

In turn, the development of the Internet system influences the level of computerization and the telecommunication infrastructure in a country. The localization of the Internet system is associated with greater levels of computerization and changes in the context of computerization. This may be expected to promote the development of software and hardware of computer systems associated with computer networking and content. As Nora and Minc (1980) point out, these changes involve transforming the role of computer systems in a country from primarily information-processing tools into networking tools. The development of the Internet system also encourages the development of the telecommunication infrastructure because Internet traffic generates demand for greater bandwidth. It is also associated with the reconfiguration of the telecommunication system from a voice-centric and centralized control system under monopoly management into a data-centric and distributed control system operating in an increasingly competitive market. These changes affect the physical infrastructure, pricing, management and governance systems both locally and at the global level.

Hypotheses 1 and 2:   Countries with higher levels of computerization and telecommunication infrastructure achieve faster localizing of the Internet system; the development of the Internet system influences the computerization and telecommunication infrastructure in a country.

Knowledge Production and Distribution Systems and Localization of the Internet

As discussed in Chapter 2, differences in the knowledge production and distribution systems have been found to be primary factors in explaining differences in adopting and using new technology. Acquiring, adapting, transforming and distributing knowledge (both tacit and codified) are supported by particular combinations of the research and education and training systems and the linkages between them. A knowledge infrastructure is not easily built upon, however. Antonelli suggests that the knowledge accumulation of a country depends upon its combined competence 'acquired by means of learning processes and socialization of experience, the recombination of available information and formal R&D activities' (ibid.: 46).

As explored in Chapters 3 and 4, the role of the research and academic communities is particularly important to the development of the local Internet system. The Internet system was invented, developed, transferred and adapted by these communities to achieve efficient use of computers by connecting with the telecommunications systems (McClure *et al.*, 1991). In most developed countries, research networks are seen not only as infrastructures to support researchers but also as important means of developing and implementing new services in advance of what is generally available in the marketplace. Research and academic users have continued to lead the technological development of the Internet: in the USA, research and academic communities have established consortia to develop and deploy advanced technologies .[7]

The role of scientists and researchers in the localization of the Internet system was crucial in that the Internet system was transferred through the global research community network. Scientists and researchers were the first adopters in most countries and contributed to transforming and localizing these new technologies, for example by providing local language support.[8] The characteristics of the first users influenced the extent of 'increasing returns' (Callon, 1995). Universities and other research organizations were the primary sources of initial growth. Net access became routinely available to scholars in the late 1980s and to the general public in North America and parts of Europe in the mid-1990s (Gaines, 1998). Thus the size of the research community may influence the speed of localization of the Internet system.

Hypothesis 3:   Countries with better knowledge production and distribution capabilities are localizing the Internet more quickly.

Global Integration Efforts and Localization of the Internet

As was explored in Chapter 5, the national backbone network was built in advance of regional and local systems through the connection of major research and academic institutions: international backbones were established by connecting these national research networks before national Internet systems were developed. This unique system-building process can be attributed in part to the gateway concept and economies of scale. Countries that were already involved in international academic networks were better placed to build up global connections; thus the global (and regional) integration efforts of a country influenced the development of its national Internet system. In addition, the relative benefits in terms of price of using the Internet system compared with the existing telephone system were greater in international communications. Those institutions with a high proportion of transnational activities had a greater incentive to introduce and develop the Internet system. Therefore the presence of transnational businesses may facilitate the development of the Internet system from the demand side.

Third, Internet technologies were transferred through the seamless global networks of invisible colleges and this reinforced these networks. Furthermore some technological innovations were accomplished through cooperation and non-market competition among network members. The economies of scale produced from using the Internet created the incentive to build regional networks connecting several national Internets and, in turn, these regional network-building efforts facilitated its localization. The existence of regional networks enhanced the efficiencies of the national Internet system, in that expensive international leased lines could be shared and technological expertise and experiences could be interchanged at regional level. As analysed in Chapter 4, those countries that were undergoing strong regional integration and were involved in transnational activities producing relatively high usage of international telecommunications faced greater demand from users for access to the Internet system. One of the main competitive advantages of the Internet system over the public switched telephone network is its pricing system. Pricing is not based on a geographical structure, thus the greater the distance of communication, the greater the benefit (at least in principle).

As seen in Chapter 5, some of the leaders in developing the Internet system, including Singapore, Hong Kong, the Netherlands, the UK and Switzerland, had a common economic characteristic – that of being a main offshore financial centre.[9]

Hypothesis 4:   Countries more closely integrated into the global society and economy achieve a faster process of localization of the Internet system.

Economic and Social Characteristics and Localizing the Internet System

A country's overall economic strength is considered one of the determinants in the localization of the Internet system in that investment in the physical and human capital required for building the technological and organizational systems of the Internet is substantial. Demand for Internet services is also higher in richer countries because the Internet system can be used to build up bigger human and physical systems that are capable of generating economic value. The Internet is also used to produce links between the growing numbers of global information resources and to produce novelty in applications aimed at increasing productivity, strengthening education or creating entertainment products. In fact, advanced ICTs, often considered as a *cause* of economic growth, may be a result of economic growth (Mansell and Wehn, 1998). Furthermore equality of income distribution in a country may influence localization of the Internet system. The equality of income distribution may influence both expansion in capital formation and the domestic market (OECD, 1992; Tylecote, 1991). The more egalitarian and wealthy a society, the greater the number of people that will be able to afford the new technology. A more equitable distribution of income may contribute to the expansion of capital formation through increased saving (Tylecote, 1991).

The importance of the size of countries or social systems in explaining different speeds of localization of new technological systems also seems clear (Antonelli, 1992; Dekimpe *et al.*, 1998). Language is a cultural factor that may influence the localization of the Internet (ITU, 1999a). English language competence is a precondition for the acquisition and use of knowledge about Internet technologies because of its prominence in the computer and telecommunication sectors (Laponce, 1987; Piscitello and Chapin, 1993). Most of the content on the Internet is in English.[10] The Matthew effect[11] in producing content and communicating on the Internet may delay localization of the Internet in non-English speaking countries. Countries where English is not the official language must devote more effort to adapting Internet technologies and making accessible the content available on the Internet.

Hypothesis 5: High-income countries localize the Internet system more quickly.
Hypothesis 6: Countries with greater equality of income distribution localize the Internet system more quickly.
Hypothesis 7: Small countries localize the Internet system more quickly.
Hypothesis 8: There is a positive correlation between localization of the Internet and English literacy and proficiency.

Government Policy and Localizing the Internet system

Sectoral policies such as liberalization and privatization of telecommunication influence the development of technological systems. Since the beginning of the 1990s, most countries have undergone institutional reforms in their telecommunication sector (ITU, 1999c). The introduction of competition in telecommunication markets and the establishment of a regulatory authority are believed to have reduced the cost of provision of Internet services and increased performance. By 1998, 88 countries were in the process of completing or had completed privatization of their incumbent network operator (ibid.). The main policy aim of privatization is improving the telecommunication infrastructure and facilitating the rapid introduction of new products and services by attracting private and foreign investment. These changes in sector policies have influenced the localization of the Internet system. Pressure of competition, together with the local supply of skills and local demand, influences the rate and direction of technological activities (Porter, 1990). In turn, the localization of the Internet system has promoted and enforced these institutional changes in the telecommunication sector. Recently some countries have planned and introduced changes in their sectoral policies in order to accommodate the convergence of the telecommunication, broadcasting and IT industries mainly brought about by the Internet system.

The costs of using Internet services are still high, taking into account the price of PCs, access costs and telephone costs. In most developing countries these costs far exceed the average monthly income. Monthly access charges were in excess of US$20 in African countries in 1998. In Uganda in 1998, the Internet monthly access charge was US$92, equivalent to 107 per cent of GDP per capita (Jensen, 1999). The pricing structure for Internet access and use may influence the localization of the Internet system (Mackie-Mason and Varian, 1995a, 1995b). In fact there are a variety of price structures for Internet access which may encourage or discourage access and use of the Internet. The most popular model is a fixed monthly fee for full Internet dial-up access, either unlimited or for a certain number of 'free' hours (ITU, 1999a).

Finally the development of the Internet system in a country may be influenced by the time that the local system was connected to NSFNET. Connection to the NSFNET allowed a country to start to experience and accumulate expertise in Internet technologies. Early connecting countries followed up with rapid development of the technologies surrounding the Internet by getting access to resources and communicating with the 'club' members who had invented and developed the Internet system. The differences in timing of connection to NSFNET are mainly attributable to the science and technology policies in those countries. The US government controlled the networks being connected to NSFNET and countries (see Chapter 5).

Hypothesis 9:   Countries with a more competitive telecommunication sector have been faster in localizing the Internet system.
Hypothesis 10:   Early connection to the global Internet system has resulted in faster localization of the domestic Internet system.

The next section tests hypotheses 1 and 2.

7.3   ENDOGENOUS MODEL

It is argued that the development of the Internet system is directly affected by the penetration rate of PCs and the level of the telecommunication infrastructure in a country, even though the causal relationship between them is questionable (ITU, 1999a). Figure 7.1 shows that the number of PCs connected to the Internet increased from 0.04 per cent in 1990 to about 19 per cent in 1999.[12] The number of Internet hosts to main telephone lines worldwide also increased, from 0.01 per cent in 1990 to about 8 per cent in 1999.

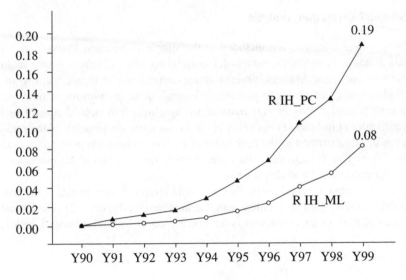

Notes:
1. R IH_PC is the number of the Internet hosts per PC.
2. R IH_ML is the number of the Internet hosts per main telephone line.

Source: ITU, *ITU World Telecommunication Indicators Database*, 5th edn (June 2000 updated).

Figure 7.1   *Relative development of computer and telecommunication infrastructure*

However a relatively high level of PC penetration and telecommunication infrastructure does not guarantee fast localization of the Internet (OECD, 1996c). Nor does a good telecommunication infrastructure necessarily result in a high level of local Internet system growth in a country. So how much do PCs and the telecommunication infrastructure contribute to the development of a country's Internet system? And how much does the Internet system contribute to the development of the telecommunication infrastructure and computer system? To examine the relationships between the main components of the Internet system a correlation technique is used. This allows a simultaneous equation model of the computer and Internet to be estimated using 2SLS estimation techniques to produce an analysis of the interactive relationship between the endogenous factors underlying Internet systems (that is, Internet host computers, PCs and telephone mainlines) and to make limited statements about the 'causal' relations between these factors.

Simple Correlation Analysis

Ninety-nine countries are included in the simple correlation analysis which calculates a Spearman's rank order correlation (rho). There are two main reasons for using Spearman's rank order correlation. First, we want to include as many countries as possible.[13] Second, there are non-linear relations among variables, thus they are transformed by a logarithm method. Spearman's rank order correlation is not sensitive to asymmetric distribution or the presence of outliers because the rank order of each observation is used rather than its value. The Spearman's rank order correlation is robust to all monotonic (order preserving) transformations.

As expected, Internet hosts, PCs and main telephone line penetration show a substantially high correlation with one another (see Figure 7.2). The lowest value of rank order coefficient is the correlation of Log IH 99 with Log ML

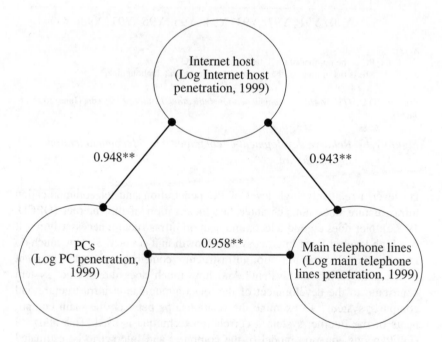

Note: **: correlation coefficient is significant at the level of the 0.01 (2 tailed).

Data source: ITU, *ITU World Telecommunication Indicators Database*, 5th edn (June 2000 updated), ITU (1999b).

Figure 7.2   Spearman's rank order correlations among Internet host, PC and main telephone line penetration (1999)

99, which is 0.943. The correlation of Log ML 99 with Log PC 99 is 0.958. This result supports the argument that countries with higher levels of PCs and telecommunication infrastructure are likely to be faster in localizing the Internet system.

Table 7.1 presents the changes in the correlation matrix for 71 countries between 1995 and 1999. Correlations among variables increased between 1995 and 1998. This result is consistent with the increasing use of PCs for communication.

Table 7.1   Correlation (Spearman rank-order coefficients) matrix (1995, 1999)

1995 (number of cases: 71)

	Internet penetration[1]		
PC penetration[2]	0.939** 0.000	PC penetration[2]	
Main telephone line penetration[3]	0.925** 0.000	0.912** 0.000	Main telephone line penetration[3]

1999 (number of cases: 71)

	Internet penetration		
PC penetration[2]	0.946** 0.000	PC penetration[2]	
Main telephone line penetration[3]	0.936** 0.000	0.944** 0.000	Main telephone line penetration[3]

Notes:
1. Log transformation of the number of Internet hosts per 1000 inhabitants.
2. Log transformation of the number of PCs per 100 inhabitants.
3. Log transformation of the number of main telephone lines per 100 inhabitants.
4. ** : correlation is significant at the level of the .01 (level) (2 tailed).

Source: *ITU World Telecommunication Indicators Database*, 5th edn (June 2000 updated), ITU (1999a).

The more PCs that are installed the more information and knowledge is trans-formed or created in digital form and the more PCs go online (Nora and Minc, 1980). As a result, the price of computers falls and the available content online increases. It is also likely that the price of the telecommunication infrastructure becomes cheaper and performance improves as the telephone network expands, particularly in the light of trends towards market liberalization which either act as comparative indicators for countries with telecommunication systems that remain partially regulated or introduce the effects of potential competition, which tends to reduce prices. If the price of using the telecommunication infrastructure decreases and the performance of telecommunication infrastructure improves as the Internet spreads, then it can be said that the growth of the Internet system induces more computerization and growth in the telecommunication network infrastructure.

Questions of Causality

Simple correlation analysis provides little information about the complex relationship between variables. Simultaneous equation methods are commonly used as a means of testing assumptions about 'causality' when it appears that one set of variables 'induces' changes in another set of variables. In order to estimate simultaneous equation models, a 2SLS estimation can be employed.[14] Table 7.2 shows descriptive statistics for all the variables.

The following sets out the assumptions that underlie the three-equation model: (1) the level of computerization and telecommunication infrastructure predict Internet system development; (2) Internet system development and telecommunication infrastructure predict the level of computerization; (3) Internet system development and the level of computerization predict telecommunication infrastructure.

$$ISI = \beta 0 + \beta 1 \times CPI + \beta 2 \times TID + \beta 3 \times CONLAG + \varepsilon. \qquad (7.1)$$

$$CPI = \beta 0 + \beta 1 \times ISI + \beta 2 \times TID + \beta 3 \times IKD + \varepsilon. \qquad (7.2)$$

$$TID = \beta 0 + \beta 1 \times ISI + \beta 2 \times CPI + \beta 3 \times TIT + \varepsilon. \qquad (7.3)$$

The endogenous variables are jointly determined and the exogenous variables are predetermined. The explanatory variables for the Internet system (ISI) which is measured as the number of hosts per 1000 population are as follows: CPI measured by the number of PCs per 100 inhabitants (1999); TID measured by the number of main telephone lines per 100 inhabitants (1999); CONLAG is connection time lag, the number of years between 1988 and the year the country established a connection to NSFNET (equation 7.1). The use of CONLAG reflects the hypothesis that the development of the Internet system is influenced by the time a country became a member of the global system.

Table 7.2 Descriptive statistics (number of cases: 57)

Variables	Minimum	Maximum	Mean	Std. deviation	Transformation
Hosts per 1000 inhabitants (1999)	0.02	155.24	21.77	39.86	Log
PC per 100 inhabitants (1999)	0.33	51.05	12.13	14.95	Log
Main lines per 100 inhabitants (1999)	2.22	71.20	28.80	21.45	Log
Time lag	12.0	28.0	19.44	5.12	
Paper consumption (ton) per 1000 inhabitants (1997)	0.16	191.76	26.44	36.44	Log
Telecom Investment per inhabitant (average 1995–7)	0.51	287.26	60.07	65.80	Log
Hosts per 1000 inhabitants (1998)	0.02	111.29	14.75	27.25	Log
PC per 100 inhabitants (1998)	0.17	67.93	20.24	21.53	Log
Main lines per 100 inhabitants (1998)	2.11	67.42	27.89	21.18	Log

Source: Data calculated by author from *ITU World Telecommunication Indicators Database*, 5th edn (June 2000 updated), ITU (1999a); UNESCO (1999); Merit (<NIC.MERIT.EDU> nsfnet/statistics).

The explanatory variables for CPI are ISI, TID and the volume of information and knowledge distribution (IKD) measured by printing and writing paper consumption per 1000 inhabitants (1997) (equation 7.2). The volume of information and knowledge may also influence the computerization of a country because the need for computerization mainly comes from the efficient use of the knowledge and information (Nora and Minc, 1980).

The explanatory variables for TID are ISI, CPI and telecommunication investment (TIT) (equation 7.3). TIT is measured by total telecommunication investment per capita (average between 1995 and 1997).

Table 7.3 shows the correlation matrix. The instruments show substantially high correlations with the explanatory variables. The desirable properties of an instrument are relevance, that is, a high correlation with the endogenous regressors that are independent of those regressors' correlation with other instruments, and exogeneity, that is, no absence of codetermination of both dependent variable and instrument (Hall *et al.*, 1996).[15] Donald and Newey (2001) argue that the minimal number of instruments should be used for 2SLS in order to minimize approximate mean square error.

There is a feedback loop between ISI, CPI and TID. Therefore endogenous variables are predicted using instrumental variables or instruments. Using these predicted variables the above equations are estimated. As Johnston (1984) and Johnston and DiNardo (1997) suggest, lagged variables for the three dependent variables are used as instruments. Equation 7.1 uses two lagged variables (CPI98 and TID98) and TIT and IKD as instruments for CPI99 and TID99. CONLAG is included as an instrument on the assumption that the level of education can predict the level of computerization and development of the telecommunications infrastructure, but it is not expected to be predicted by them. In the same way, ISI98, TID98, TIT, EDI and IKD are used as instruments for ISI and TID in the CPI equation on the assumption that IKD can be used as a predictor for ISI and YID but is not likely to be predicted by them. ISI98, CPI98, EDI, IKD and TID are used as instruments for ISI and CPI in the telecommunications infrastructure equation.

The columns of Table 7.4 present the coefficient estimates from the 2SLS estimation of the Internet system, computerization and telecommunication infrastructure equations. The regression coefficients for ISI on CPI (equation 7.2) and ISI on TID (equation 7.3) are substantially high but at different statistically significant levels (above the 0.1 per cent and 1 per cent level, respectively). This result indicates that the Internet system can influence the development of computerization and the telecommunication infrastructure.

The regression coefficient for CPI on ISI in the equation 7.1 model is also substantially high and statistically significant above the 0.1 per cent level, while the regression coefficient for CPI on TID is a not statistically significant. From this result, the hypothesis that the level of computerization

Table 7.3 Correlation matrix

		ISI99	CPI99	TID99	ISI98	CPI98	TID98	TIT	CONLAG	IKD
ISI99 (Log IHP99)	Pearson Correlation Sig. (2-tailed) N									
CPI99 (Log PCPS)	Pearson Correlation Sig. (2-tailed) N	0.966* 0.000 57								
TID99 (Log MLPS)	Pearson Correlation Sig. (2-tailed) N	0.907* 0.000 57	0.905* 0.000 57							
ISI98 Log IHP98	Pearson Correlation Sig. (2-tailed) N	0.994* 0.000 57	0.966* 0.000 57	0.917* 0.000 57						
CPI98 (Log PCPS)	Pearson Correlation Sig. (2-tailed) N	0.968* 0.000 57	0.998* 0.000 57	0.898* 0.000 57	0.966* 0.000 57					
TID98 (Log MLPS)	Pearson Correlation Sig. (2-tailed) N	0.905* 0.000 57	0.904* 0.000 57	0.998* 0.000 57	0.915* 0.000 57	0.897* 0.000 57				
TIT (log investment 95–97)	Pearson Correlation Sig. (2-tailed) N	0.882* 0.000 57	0.898* 0.000 57	0.812* 0.000 57	0.875* 0.000 57	0.895* 0.000 57	0.810* 0.000 57			
CONLAG	Pearson Correlation Sig. (2-tailed) N	−0.840* 0.000 57	−0.807* 0.000 57	−0.729* 0.000 57	−0.833* 0.000 57	−0.806* 0.000 57	−0.722* 0.000 57	−0.762* 0.000 57		
IKD97 (Log Paper Consumption per Inhabitant 97)	Pearson Correlation Sig. (2-tailed) N	0.908* 0.000 57	0.928* 0.000 57	0.818* 0.000 57	0.908* 0.000 57	0.931* 0.000 57	0.809* 0.000 57	0.850* 0.000 57	−0.820* 0.000 57	

Note: **Correlation is significant at the 0.01 level (2-tailed).

193

Table 7.4   2SLS regression result

	Equation 1 model	Equation 2 model	Equation 3 model
Dependent variable	Internet host (1999)	PCs (1999)	Main telephone lines (1999)
Number of cases	57	57	57
Adj. R-square	0.947	0.951	0.821
F-test significance	335.522	359.503	86.363
Internet host (1999)		0.554 (5.294)***	0.817 (3.206)**
PCs (1999)	0.690 (8.102)***		0.129 (0.478)
Main telephone lines (1999)	0.162 (2.205)*		0.174 (2.348)*
Connection time	−0.165 (−3.158)**		
Paper consumption		0.283 (3.857)***	
Telecom investment			−0.024 (−0.180)

Notes:
1. Standardized coefficients (Beta) with significance (t-statistic) reported in parentheses.
2. *** = significance at the 0.1 per cent level; ** = significance at the 1 per cent level;
    * = significance at the 5 per cent level.

influences the Internet system can be supported, while the hypothesis that the level of computerization influences the development of the telecommunication infrastructure cannot be demonstrated statistically. The regression coefficients for TID on ISI (equation 7.1) and CPI (equation 7.2) are statistically significant above the 5 per cent level. With greater than 95 per cent certainty, therefore, the hypothesis that the telecommunication infrastructure influences the development of the Internet and computerization can be supported.

In equation 7.1, CONLAG is statistically significant above 1 per cent and shows a substantial *t* statistic but lower regression coefficient value (−0.165) than that of PCs (0.690). The negative sign of CONLAG shows, as expected, that the earlier a country achieves connection to the global Internet system, the greater is Internet system development.

In equation 7.2, the volume of paper-based knowledge and information shows a statistically high regression coefficient value, 0.283 (significant above 0.1 per cent) but the value is lower than that for the Internet system (0.554).

The volume of paper-based knowledge and information can be considered an important predictor of computerization, although less important than the Internet system. The Internet system can be considered the determinant of the development of computerization. The volume of paper-based knowledge and information also shows a substantially high correlation with the Internet system.

It is not difficult to infer the causality among these three independent variables. In general, the popularization of PCs tends to reduce their price and improve their performance. This reduces the cost and improves the quality of providing and using the Internet system and creates the potential to increase digital content which can be accessed via Internet systems. Again the development of the Internet system directly influences computerization, in that it increases demand for new computer hardware and software. In fact PCs as terminals and servers are indispensable components of the Internet system. Indirectly the development of the Internet stimulates improvements in the performance of PCs in various ways.

Improvement in the telecommunication infrastructure has certainly facilitated Internet system development, as suggested by ITU (1999a), although its relative impact on system development seems to be much less than that of computerization. The expansion of the telecommunication access network does not show strong effects on the Internet system. This is because leased lines (national and international) are more important than access lines for suppliers. The improvement in the telecommunication infrastructure has also influenced the diffusion of computers and computerization. From an early stage of development, computers have been designed to be connected with each other with the aim of supporting an information communication system. For example, the term 'télématique' (Nora and Minc, 1980) reflects the convergence of computer and telecommunication systems. Bell (1980) points out how computers were designed as information devices:

> Behind the term ['télématique'] is an instrument and a concept. The instrument is the computer; the concept, information. The computer is not only a computational machine but also a communications device. It can transmit data; it can store and retrieve information; it can be used to simulate complicated reality. It is also, thus, an information device. (Bell, 1980: vii)

The impact of the Internet system on telecommunication is much higher than that of the telecommunication infrastructure on Internet system development. This can be demonstrated if we divide countries into two groups: (1) countries that already had a relatively high number of access lines when the Internet system took off, and (2) other countries. The effects of telecommunication network expansion on the development of the Internet system may be greater in countries with a relatively low rate of access lines, while the effects of the

Internet on telecommunication network expansion may be greater in countries with a relatively high number of access lines. In fact increases in demand for Internet access are boosting demand for second residential lines and ISDN access in most developed countries (OECD, 1998a). In this sense, the telecommunication infrastructure measured by telephone main lines (fixed access lines) is seen to have less impact on Internet development than its likely actual effects. In addition, not only the number of telephone lines, but also price and performance, are important factors in the development of the Internet system.

The interesting result of this analysis is that the relative impact of Internet system growth on the telecommunication infrastructure is much higher than the effect of telecommunications investment on the telecommunications infrastructure. One possible explanation for this is that a substantial amount of recent telecommunication investment has gone on the expansion of the mobile network. In 1997, 26 per cent of total investment in the telecommunications network in OECD countries went on constructing mobile networks (OECD, 1999a). Multi-collinearities among explanatory variables, in particular between telecommunications investment and computers, possibly reduce the impact of telecommunication investment on the telecommunication infrastructure. Although the levels of computerization and the telecommunication infrastructure show statistically and substantially high correlations, the causal relation between them is not clear from this analysis. In fact the telecommunication systems have been digitized using computers. However the reciprocal effects of the level of computerization and the level of the telecommunication infrastructure may be less than those generated indirectly through various data networks, for example the Internet system.

Comparison of the results of the 2SLS regression with a system of simultaneous equations supports the suggestion that computerization and the telecommunications infrastructure are important predictors of the Internet system. However other factors, for example time lag to connect to the global Internet system and the volume of paper-based knowledge and information are also important in understanding differences and similarities in Internet system development across countries.

7.4   CO-EVOLUTION OF THE SOCIAL AND ECONOMIC SYSTEMS AND THE INTERNET SYSTEM

In this section, the hypotheses about the relationship between country and sector-specific factors and localization of the Internet system are examined using an OLS regression technique with principal components analysis (PCA). First, indicators of knowledge production and distribution capabilities and global integration level are created using PCA. Second, the relationship between social and economic factors and the Internet system is analysed using the OLS regression technique. The social and economic variables include two new indicators representing knowledge production and distribution capabilities and the global integration level, and the size of the social system, cultural factors (language) and income distribution, and the way they vary with sector policies such as liberalization of the telecommunication market and the ownership status of the dominant telecommunication network operator. Finally, the relationship between Internet access and usage costs is examined across a set of countries whose choice was based on availability of data on Internet access and usage costs.

Data and Method

Data were collected from various sources at the aggregate country level. The selection of countries was made on the basis of availability of data. Some data, such as Internet monthly access prices (US$20 hours of off-peak use), are only available in the comparable form for 41 countries.[16] Empirical analyses are conducted for two groups of selected countries. The first multiple regression analysis covers 60 countries, including four low-income countries, 31 middle-income countries and 25 high-income countries. As Table 7.5 shows, the selected countries are located in Africa (2), the Asia and Pacific region (13), Europe (31), Middle East and North Africa (2) and the Americas (12).

The PCA is based on the same set of countries. The unit of analysis is the nation-state. PCA is the appropriate technique for creating new variables to

Table 7.5   Selected countries for OLS and PCA

	Africa	Asia and Pacific	Europe	Middle East and North Africa	America	Total
Low-income	1	2	1			4
Middle-income: lower		5	6	1	4	16
Middle-income: upper	1	1	7		6	15
High-income		5	17	1	2	25
Total	2	13	31	2	12	60

Source: Adapted from *ITU World Telecommunication Indicators Database*, 5th edn (June 2000 updated) and World Bank, *World Development Indicator 1998*, CD-ROM.

avoid multi-collinearity in the data in developing a regression model. New variables are linear composites of the original variables.

The central idea of principal component analysis is to reduce the dimensionality of the data set which consists of a large number of interrelated variables, while retaining as much as possible of the variation present in the data set. This is achieved by changing to a new set of variables, the principal components, which are uncorrelated, and which are ordered so that the first few retain most of the variation present in all of the original variables (Jolliffe, 1986:1).

Principal Components Analysis

The first set of variables is related to the KPDI (knowledge production and distribution capabilities index) which represents a country's knowledge infrastructure and distribution capabilities. However it is very difficult to measure the knowledge production and distribution capabilities of a country. The criteria for the selection of the indicators representing knowledge production and distribution capabilities are mainly based on OECD (1992), David and Foray (1994) and Mansell and Wehn (1998). KPDI is based on four variables: (1) a single measure of educational attainment formed by a combination of adult literacy rate (one-third weight) and the combined gross primary, secondary and tertiary enrolment ratio (two-thirds weight); (2) science and technological capabilities measured by two variables that including the scientists and engineers in R&D per million inhabitants and the number of patents per million inhabitants in the USA; (3) the volume of information and knowledge distribution measured by newspaper and other printing and writing paper consumption per 1000 inhabitants; and (4) the institutional environment measured by a combination of political rights (half weight) and civil rights (half weight).[17]

The second set of variables is the GII which is based on three indicators of the rate of trade measured as the percentage of GDP PPP (purchasing power parity), gross FDI stock as a percentage of GDP and total incoming and outgoing international telecommunication traffic measured by minutes per inhabitant.

Table 7.6 presents descriptive statistics for the explanatory variables for 60 countries. Australia, the UK, Sweden, Finland and Canada achieve more than 100 per cent in terms of schooling, while Pakistan, Nigeria, India, Thailand and Turkey have the lowest level of EDI. Japan, Israel, Sweden, the USA and Norway lead in terms of scientists and engineers, with more than 3600 per million inhabitants, while Malaysia, Pakistan, Colombia and Nigeria have less than 100 R&D personnel density per million inhabitants. For total number of patents granted in the USA during the period 1991 to 1998, the USA,

Table 7.6 Descriptive statistics for data included in principal components analysis

	Minimum	Maximum	Mean	Std. Deviation
EDI (Combined school enrolment ratio, 1998)	43	114	80.52	14.32
SER (Scientists & Engineers in R&D per million inhabitants, 1985–98)	15	4 909	1 595.33	1 287.49
PWP (Other printing and writing paper consumption (tonne) per 1000 inhabitants (1997) (thousand)*)	0.163	191.76	30.83	36.77
PAT (US Patents per million inhabitants, 1978–98*)	0.06	1752.29	208.15	36.77
PCR (Political & Civil Rights Index, 1997)	40	100	81.5	14.32
ITI (International Traffic (minutes) per inhabitant, 1995–7*)	1.48	595.14	91.77	117.85
RTR (Rate of Trade of PPP GDP, 1998*)	3.9	269.1	42.08	41.21
FDI (Gross FDI stock as a percentage of GDP 1997*)	0.5	102.30	23.91	22.16

Note: * Log transformation.

Source: *ITU World Telecommunication Indicators Database*, 5th edn (June 2000 updated); UNESCO (1999); UNDP (2000), World Bank (2000); Freedom House (1997).

Switzerland and Japan lead. Eleven countries have less than one patent per million inhabitants during that period. Most developed countries show the highest level of democracy, although the level of freedom in Singapore appears to be the same as that in Pakistan. Finland, the USA, Japan, Canada and Switzerland consumed more than 80 tonnes of paper per thousand inhabitants in 1997, while paper consumption per thousand inhabitants in Ecuador, Belarus, Nigeria, Bolivia and Armenia was less than one tonne.

For trade in goods as a share of PPP GDP, Singapore, Ireland and Switzerland show the highest figures, at more than 100 per cent, while Brazil, China,
Pakistan and India achieve less than 10 per cent. Looking at inward and
outward FDI as a percentage of GDP in 1996, Singapore shows 102.3 per
cent, the Netherlands 79.5 per cent, Belgium 77.2 per cent and Nigeria 68.5
per cent, while 16 countries show less than 10 per cent. Singapore, Switzerland, Ireland, Canada and Belgium belong to the highest group in terms of
international telephone traffic (sum of incoming and outgoing) measured in
minutes per inhabitant, while Pakistan, Indonesia, China, Nigeria and India
show the lowest figures.

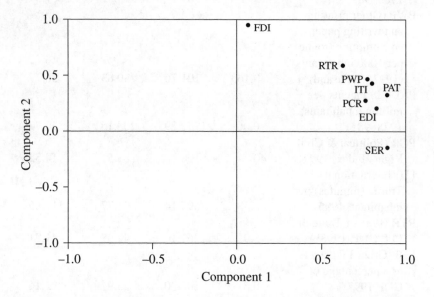

Data source: *ITU, World Telecommunication Indicators Database*, 5th edn (June 2000 updated); UNESCO (1999), UNDP (2000), World Bank (2000), Freedom House (1997).

Figure 7.3   Components plot

The PCA was conducted in two ways: including all eight variables and
separating them into two groups. There are two reasons for this: first, to
analyse differences between KPDI and GII and, second, to compare the
results between two variables with correlation and without correlation in the
OLS analysis. Eight variables were included in a factor analysis using principal components with Varimax rotation. Two components were found to explain
100 per cent of the total variance. Figure 7.3 shows the component plot in
rotated space. Component 2 loads heavily only the FDI.

Table 7.7   Rotated components matrix and component score coefficient, CPs1

	Rotated component matrix		Component score coefficient	
	CP1 KPDI	CP1 GII	CP1 KPDI	CP1 GII
EDI	0.827	0.319	0.213	−0.085
SER	0.894	−0.156	0.335	−0.380
PAT	0.896	0.191	0.199	−0.003
PWP	0.778	0.417	0.122	0.137
PCR	0.765	0.453	0.172	−0.010
RTR	0.628	0.264	0.037	0.282
ITI	0.809	0.582	0.143	0.099
FDI	0.078	0.948	−0.247	0.731

Table 7.8   Component score and coefficient score of variables included in KPDI CP2 and GII CP2

	Component matrix		Component score coefficient	
	CP2 KPDI	CP2 GII	CP2 KPDI	CP2 GII
EDI	0.953		0.230	
SER	0.799		0.210	
PAT	0.953		0.250	
PWP	0.893		0.235	
PCR	0.834		0.219	
RTR		0.949		0.431
ITI		0.911		0.414
FDI		0.687		0.312

Table 7.7 shows the rotated components matrix and component coefficient score for each variable. Because of rotation, the signs of the coefficient of FDI in component 1 and the three variables (EDI, SER, PAT and PCR) are negative. This may not reflect the actual relationship between these variables considering the correlation coefficients among them. To avoid this problem, the knowledge production and distribution capabilities index (KPDI) and global integration index (GII) were created, using component analysis. The estimated variables created by two separate components analyses are used as CP2 KPDI and CP2 GII for OLS regression analysis. Table 7.8 shows the

Table 7.9　　Correlation matrix among KPDI, GII and GDP

	CP1 KPDI		
CP1 GII	0.000	CP1 GII	
GDP	0.856**	0.374**	GDP
	0.000	0.003	
	CP2 KPDI		
CP2 GII	0.735**	CP2 GII	
	0.000		
GDP	0.922**	0.787**	GDP
	0.000	0.000	

Source: *ITU World Telecommunication Indicators Database*, 5th edn (June 2000 updated), ITU (1999a); UNESCO (1999); UNDP (2000), World Bank (2000); Freedom House (1997).

component scores and coefficient scores of eight variables for KPDI and GII. The values of the coefficient scores of the variables for KPDI and GII are the same for the OLS regression coefficient of variables.

Table 7.9 shows the correlation matrix CP1 KPDI and GII and GDP, and CP2 KPDI and GII and GDP. The results of PCA, KPDI CP1 show no correlation with GII CP2. However CP2 variables show a significantly high correlation coefficient (see Table 7.9). As KPDI is considered to be the most important source of economic growth, there is a statistically significant and substantially high correlation between KPDI and income (CP1: 0.856; CP2: 0.922). GII also shows high correlation coefficients with KPDI (CP2: 0.735) and income (CP1: 0.374; CP2: 0.787), but much less than that between KPDI and income. In general, countries with a relatively big economy and surrounded by a relatively low level of regional economic integration tend to show relatively low levels of GII.

Table 7.10 shows countries grouped by the relative level of KPDI CP2 and GII CP2. Most developed countries have relatively high levels of both KPDI and GII. Australia has the highest figure in terms of CP2 KPDI, followed by the USA, Sweden, Finland and Japan. Nigeria, Pakistan, India, Turkey and Egypt belong to the lowest group in terms of CP2 KPDI. Singapore shows the highest figure with respect to CP2 GII and Switzerland, Belgium, Ireland, and the Netherlands follow. India, Pakistan, Russia, China and Belarus exhibit the lowest level of CP2 GII. Singapore shows a very high level of GII but a moderate level of KPDI, while Japan shows a very high level of KPDI but a low level of GII (Figure 7.4). Turkey shows very low levels of both KPDI and GII.

Table 7.10   *Countries grouped by relative values of KPDI CP2 and GII CP2*

GII	KPDI				
	Very high	High	Moderate	Low	Very low
Very high	Sweden, Norway, Canada, Denmark, Belgium, Switzerland, Netherlands, UK	Ireland, New Zealand	Singapore	Malaysia	
High	Australia, Finland	Germany, France, Israel, Austria, Italy, Spain, Slovenia	Estonia, Hungary	Croatia	
Moderate	USA	Korea, Portugal	Czech, Poland, Greece, Slovak, Uruguay, Chile, Lithuania	Mexico	Ecuador
Low	Japan	South Africa	Argentina	Bulgaria, Venezuela, Philippines, Peru, Thailand	Bolivia, Sri Lanka, Nigeria, Senegal
Very low			Russia	Brazil, Ukraine, Romania, Colombia	Belarus, China, Indonesia, Armenia, Turkey, India, Pakistan
	12	12	12	12	12

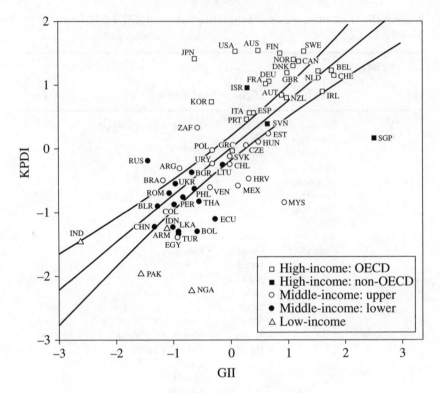

Figure 7.4   KPDI CP2 and GII CP2, by country

Multiple Regression Models

In this section, the relationship between the social and economic factors and the Internet system is analysed. The two new variables created by PCA are included in the multiple regression models.

Dependent variable

The most common indicator used to measure the development of the Internet system is the number of hosts, as provided by Network Wizards (NW) and RIPE. Internet hosts are the individual computers connected to the Internet that can both access and deliver information identified by a domain name that has an associated IP address. However there are some limitations to using host and domain names to compare Internet system development (OECD, 1998a; ITU, 1999a). First, some of the hosts may be unreachable at the particular time when a survey to count the number of hosts in a country is conducted. Also access to some hosts is blocked by company fire walls

(OECD, 1998a). Second, host data do not indicate the total number of users that can access the Internet. Some countries may have few hosts but many users because multiple users can use a single host computer. Thus host data are regarded as the minimum size of the public Internet system in a country. The third and the most serious limitation of host data is that hosts can be registered under generic Top Level Domains (gTLDs) such as .com, .net and .org. In fact the majority of Internet hosts are registered under the .com domain name: in January 1999, the number was 28.1 per cent. However there are no regular statistics on the question regarding countries in which the hosts with three letter domain names are located.

Despite these limitations, data on Internet hosts are considered the most reliable and comparable data available for measuring Internet system development because surveys have been regularly undertaken using a standard method and giving world coverage. For this analysis, the ISI is measured by the number of hosts per thousand inhabitants in January 1999, where hosts are individual computers with network access. The number of hosts is calculated from the way generic Top Level Domains registrations (.com, .net and .org) are distributed between countries, based on registration at September 1997, published by Imperative Inc.[18] This method yields a more accurate distribution of Internet hosts where an increasing share of generic gTLDs has been located outside the USA since the registration for these gTLDs was opened to other countries in 1995 (OECD, 1998a; ITU, 1999a).

. The number of Internet users, an alternative indicator of the Internet system development, is a more meaningful statistic in terms of usage. The reliability and comparability of these data have been questioned because of the lack of a standard definition and methodology, but, thanks to the growing availability and number of commercial and official surveys this problem is being overcome (ITU, 1999a).

Table 7.11 shows a comparison of hosts and users for 60 countries. The average number of users per host is about 7.82, but the data show substantial variance between country groups. Brazil has a 0.7 host density per user while

Table 7.11   Internet hosts and users (1998)

	Minimum	Maximum	Mean	Std. deviation
Hosts per 1000 inhabitants	0.00	111.29	17.54	26.93
Users per 1000 inhabitants	0.04	395.29	66.05	83.62
Number of hosts per user	0.70	41.58	8.14	7.82

Source: ITU, *ITU World Telecommunication Indicators Database*, 5th edn (June 2000 updated); ITU (1999a)

data for Peru indicate that there were 41.58 hosts per user in 1998. Therefore, in this analysis, the number of hosts is used as a proxy for Internet system development.

Explanatory variables
Country-specific characteristics such as social, economic and sectoral factors, including telecommunication policy, are included as independent variables in the multiple regression models. The characteristics of countries are explored with respect to their knowledge production and distribution capabilities, their level of global integration and their economic and social systems.

The first and second sets of explanatory variables are used to create a KPDI and a GII (see previous section). The third and fourth independent variables are the size of population (POP) of a country and cultural factors. A language indicator is used as a proxy for the cultural characteristics of a country, indicating whether English is the dominant language. Countries where English is the dominant language are coded, using a dichotomous dummy variable (ENG).

To take into account the effect of income distribution on technological development, the mechanism influencing both capital formation (through saving rates) and the domestic market (through demand) is used. The indicator for inequality of income distribution in a country is often measured by the percentage share of either income or consumption accruing to segments of the population ranked by income or consumption levels. The Gini index is often used as an indicator for equality of income distribution. This measures the extent to which the distribution of income among individuals or households within an economy deviates from a perfectly equal distribution.[19] However the Gini index has some weakness in terms of comparability, particularly for developing countries because of data reliability. There are also problems in terms of data availability and inconsistencies resulting from differences in timings of surveys. In this analysis, the equality of income distribution (EID) is measured by the ratio of the female GDP per capita (in US$) to male GDP per capita provided by the UNDP Human Development Indicators (1999). This index is calculated using the ratio of female to male wages (non-agricultural). This index also may accurately represent the level of income equality because some countries, for example, Islamic countries, limit female labour force participation. Finally the level of income is coded as three dummy variables (INDUM1, INDUM2 and INDUM3).

To represent policy factors, telecommunication policies and time lag in terms of connection to the NSFNET are used as independent variables. The indicator for the liberalization of the telecommunication market (LOT) is measured by the level of competition allowed in the provision of seven telecommunication markets (local, long distance, international, digital cellular, leased lines, data and cable TV) such that one point is given when the market is open to competition, 0.5 points are given when the market is a duopoly. The status of ownership of the incumbent network operator is coded as a dichotomous dummy variable (OWN) where ownership is controlled by private investors. Time lag (TLAG) is measured by the number of years' lag in connecting the local Internet system to the NSFNET.

Finally the cost of using the Internet (COST) for 40 countries is measured by the average cost in 1998 of a 20-hour (off-peak) monthly Internet access basket including ISP charges and call charges (ITU, 1999a). The average cost is adjusted by monthly GDP estimated as PPP.

Table 7.12 presents the descriptive statistics for all the variables included in the model. China has a population of more than 1.2 billion, India 0.98 billion, the USA 0.27 billion, Indonesia 0.21 billion and Brazil 0.17 billion. Singapore has a population of slightly over 3 million and Slovenia and Estonia each have a population between 1 million and 3 million. The variable for the size of population is transformed into a log. In all, 15 English-speaking countries are included in the analysis. Sweden, Norway, Denmark and Finland have the highest equality of income distribution for gender income equality, while Peru, Pakistan, Argentina, Chile and Ecuador have the lowest level. It is interesting that high-income countries show the highest level of equality in income distribution and middle-income (upper) group countries show the lowest level.

Fifteen countries have fully opened their telecommunication markets to competition while, in 1998, Egypt and Ecuador retained a monopoly on all telecommunication market segments. Twenty-seven countries, including Sweden, Finland and Switzerland, had retained the incumbent telecommunication operator as a state-owned organization in 1998, while the remainder of the countries had started to privatize their telecommunication sector. Seven countries were connected to NSFNET in 1987, while 11 countries did not connect themselves to NSFNET until May 1995.

Singapore, Canada, the USA, Australia and Malaysia had the lowest level of Internet usage costs measured by actual cost adjusted using GDP (PPP). China, Venezuela, the Philippines, Thailand and Brazil were the most expensive countries for Internet use out of the 40 countries included in the analysis.

Correlation Analysis

As Table 7.13 shows, ISI appears to have both statistically significant and high correlation coefficients with KPDI (CP1), TALG and PRICE. Only two variables, ENG and INDUM3, do not have statistically significant correlations with ISI. The signs of the correlation coefficients between ISI and

Table 7.12 Descriptive statistic of original variables (N=60)

	Minimum	Maximum	Mean	Std. deviation
Internet Hosts per 1000 pop (1998)*	0.00	111.29	17.54	26.92
CP1 KPDI	−2.59	1.64	0.00	1.00
CP1 GII	−2.94	2.28	0.00	1.00
CP2 KPDI	−2.21	1.54	0.00	1.00
CP2 GII	−2.62	2.53	0.00	1.00
Population (million) (1998)	1.45	1 255.69	77.90	203.85
Rate of female PPP GDP per capita (1998)	0.24	0.82	0.52	0.13
NSF connection time lag	12	28	18.50	4.62
Internet access and using price (off-peak 20 hours) as the percentage of GDP per capita (per month)**	1.28	25.26	5.25	4.62
Liberalization Index	0	10	6.33	3.20
The ownership status of the incumbent network operator	Dichotomous dummy variable frequency 0 1 15 45			
Income	Dummy variable frequency 0 1 INDUM 1 56 4 INDUM 2 44 16 INDUM 3 45 15			
English	Dichotomous dummy variable frequency English (National language) 15 Non-English 45			

Notes:
*Log transformation.
**Number of cases 41.

KPDI, GI, LIB, EID are positive, as expected. There are positive relation-ships between ISI and KPDI, GI, LIB, EID. For example, the greater the knowledge production and distribution capabilities, the greater the number of Internet hosts. The values of the correlation coefficients between ISI and POP, TLAG, OWN, INDUM1, INDUM2 and PRICE are negative, as ex-pected. This means that there are negative relationships between ISI and POP,

TLAG, OWN, INDUM1, INDUM2 and PRICE. For example, the bigger the population, the fewer the Internet hosts.

Table 7.14 shows the correlation coefficient where CPs2: KPDI and CPs2: GII are included as explanatory variables in the regression. The correlation between ISI and GII has a substantially high value compared to the results for the CPs1 Model. This means that GII based on three factors such as ratio of trade to GDP (RTR), volume of international telephone traffic (ITI) and FDI (CPs2 Model) explain Internet system development better than GII reflecting eight variables (CPs1 Model).

The possible effects of multi-collinearity deserve some attention, in particular between KPD1 and TLAG and PRICE (Table 7.13) and between KPDI, GII, TLAG and PRICE (Table 7.14). In the OLS regression analysis collinearities between the independent variables will tend to reduce the efficiency of predictors, but without bias. Reported statistical significance may be less than the actual because the standard errors will be excessively large, but the estimated coefficients will be neither higher nor lower than they ought to be.

The correlation analysis shows that most of the null hypotheses outlined earlier, except the importance of the English factor, can be rejected with a greater than 95 per cent probability. However, in a complex large technological system such as the Internet system, simple relationships such as these rarely tell the whole story. Multiple linear regression analysis can offer a more powerful technique to provide insights into the convoluted interactions between these variables.

OLS Regression Results

The results of the OLS regression are summarized in Table 7.15 (CPs1) and Table 7.16 (CPs2). All F-values in models are statistically significant. Model 1 includes eight variables indicating the relative explanatory power of each factor in relation to other factors. Model 2 adds information on wealth, coded as three dummy variables. In Model 3, the knowledge production and distribution index is excluded. The effect of Internet access costs on Internet system development for 41 countries is examined in Model 4. The eight variables included in Model 1 explain more than 90 per cent of the variance in Internet system development for the 60 countries. The goodness of model fit is similar when knowledge production and distribution index and global integration are changed from CPs1 to CPs2.

For all the models, KPDI apparently is the dominant predictor for Internet system development. KPDI is the most important predictor in Model 1. After including information on income, the adjusted R increases from 0.938 to 0.951 and 0.937 to 0.951 for CPs1 and CPs2, respectively. Alternatively,

Table 7.13   Correlation Matrix (CPS 1)

		ISI	CP1: KPDI	CP1: GII	TLAG	LIB
ISI	Pearson Correlation					
	Sig. (2-tailed)					
	N					
CP1: KPD	Pearson Correlation	0.887**				
	Sig. (2-tailed)	0.000				
	N	60				
CP1: GII	Pearson Correlation	0.353**	0.000			
	Sig. (2-tailed)	0.006	1.000			
	N	60	60			
TLAG	Pearson Correlation	−0.839**	−0.751**	−0.294*		
	Sig. (2-tailed)	0.000	0.000	0.022		
	N	60	60	60		
LIB	Pearson Correlation	0.430**	0.443**	0.326*	−0.489**	
	Sig. (2-tailed)	0.001	0.000	0.011	0.000	
	N	60	60	60	60	
OWN	Pearson Correlation	0.315*	0.260*	0.190	−0.323*	0.327*
	Sig. (2-tailed)	0.014	0.045	0.145	0.012	0.011
	N	60	60	60	60	60
POP	Pearson Correlation	−0.414**	−0.371**	−0.222	0.061	0.098
	Sig. (2-tailed)	0.001	0.004	0.088	0.641	0.458
	N	60	60	60	60	60
EID	Pearson Correlation	0.411**	0.486**	−0.138	−0.194	0.173
	Sig. (2-tailed)	0.001	0.000	0.294	0.137	0.185
	N	60	60	60	60	60
INDUM1	Pearson Correlation	−0.502**	−0.420**	−0.211	0.321*	−0.154
	Sig. (2-tailed)	0.000	0.001	0.106	0.012	0.239
	N	60	60	60	60	60
INDUM2	Pearson Correlation	−0.580**	−0.437**	−0.345**	0.625**	−0.277*
	Sig. (2-tailed)	0.000	0.000	0.007	0.000	0.032
	N	60	60	60	60	60
INDUM3	Pearson Correlation	0.012	−0.206	0.100	0.004	−0.206
	Sig. (2-tailed)	0.929	0.115	0.447	0.975	0.114
	N	60	60	60	60	60
ENG	Pearson Correlation	−0.068	−0.061	0.136	0.026	0.134
	Sig. (2-tailed)	0.607	0.644	0.299	0.845	0.306
	N	60	60	60	60	60
LPRICE98	Pearson Correlation	−0.834**	−0.724**	−0.294	0.641**	−0.435**
	Sig. (2-tailed)	0.000	0.000	0.062	0.000	0.005
	N	41	41	41	41	41

Note: ** Correlation is significant at the 0.01 level (2-tailed); *correlation is significant at the 0.05 level (2-tailed).

OWN	POP	EID	INDUM1	INDUM2	INDUM3	ENG	LPRICE98
−0.007							
0.955							
60							
−0.199	−0.263*						
0.128	0.042						
60	60						
0.000	0.245	−0.171					
1.000	0.060	0.191					
60	60	60					
−0.348**	0.193	−0.024	−0.161				
0.006	0.140	0.853	0.219				
60	60	60	60				
−0.022	−0.086	−0.153	−0.154	−0.348**			
0.866	0.512	0.243	0.239	0.006			
60	60	60	60	60			
0.228	0.200	−0.149	0.326*	−0.154	−0.137		
0.080	0.126	0.255	0.011	0.239	0.298		
60	60	60	60	60	60		
−0.297	0.532**	−0.194	0.214	0.555**	0.340*	−0.247	
0.060	0.000	0.225	0.179	0.000	0.029	0.120	
41	41	41	41	41	41	41	

Table 7.14   Correlation Matrix (CPs2)

		ISI	CP2: KPDI	CP2: GII	LIB	OWN
ISI	Pearson Correlation					
	Sig. (2-tailed)					
	N					
CP2: KPDI	Pearson Correlation	0.941*				
	Sig. (2-tailed)	0.000				
	N	60				
CP2: GII	Pearson Correlation	0.796**	0.735**			
	Sig. (2-tailed)	0.000	0.000			
	N	60	60			
LIB	Pearson Correlation	0.430**	0.562**	0.417**		
	Sig. (2-tailed)	0.001	0.000	0.001		
	N	60	60	60		
OWN	Pearson Correlation	0.315*	0.333**	0.233	0.327*	
	Sig. (2-tailed)	0.014	0.009	0.074	0.011	
	N	60	60	60	60	
POP	Pearson Correlation	−0.414**	−0.308*	−0.571**	0.098	−0.007
	Sig. (2-tailed)	0.001	0.017	0.000	0.458	0.955
	N	60	60	60	60	60
EID	Pearson Correlation	0.411**	0.407**	0.250	0.173	−0.199
	Sig. (2-tailed)	0.001	0.001	0.054	0.185	0.128
	N	60	60	60	60	60
INDUM1	Pearson Correlation	−0.502**	−0.460**	−0.400**	−0.154	0.000
	Sig. (2-tailed)	0.000	0.000	0.002	0.239	1.000
	N	60	60	60	60	60
INDUM2	Pearson Correlation	−0.580*	−0.509**	−0.507**	−0.277*	−0.348**
	Sig. (2-tailed)	0.000	0.000	0.000	0.032	0.006
	N	60	60	60	60	60
INDUM3	Pearson Correlation	0.012	−0.174	−0.063	−0.206	−0.022
	Sig. (2-tailed)	0.929	0.183	0.635	0.114	0.866
	N	60	60	60	60	60
TLAG	Pearson Correlation	−0.839**	−0.837**	−0.597**	−0.489**	−0.323*
	Sig. (2-tailed)	0.000	0.000	0.000	0.000	0.012
	N	60	60	60	60	60
ENG	Pearson Correlation	−0.68	−0.015	0.052	0.134	0.228
	Sig. (2-tailed)	0.607	0.908	0.696	0.306	0.080
	N	60	60	60	60	60
LPRICE98	Pearson Correlation	−0.834**	−0.734**	−0.703**	−0.435**	−0.297
	Sig. (2-tailed)	0.000	0.000	0.000	0.005	0.060
	N	41	41	41	41	41

Note: ** Correlation is significant at the 0.01 level (2-tailed); *correlation is significant at the 0.05 level (2-tailed).

POP	EID	INDUM1	INDUM2	INDUM3	TLAG	ENG	LPRICE98
60							
−0.263*							
0.042							
60							
0.245	−0.171						
0.060	0.191						
60	60						
0.193	−0.024	−0.161					
0.140	0.853	0.219					
60	60	60					
−0.086	−0.153	−0.154	−0.348**				
0.512	0.243	0.239	0.006				
60	60	60	60				
0.061	−0.194	0.321*	0.625**	0.004			
0.641	0.137	0.012	0.000	0.975			
60	60	60	60	60			
0.200	−0.149	0.326*	−0.154	−0.137	0.026		
0.126	0.255	0.011	0.239	0.298	0.845		
60	60	60	60	60	60		
0.532**	−0.194	0.214	0.555**	0.340*	0.641**	−0.247	
0.000	0.225	0.179	0.000	0.029	0.000	0.120	
41	41	41	41	41	41	41	

Table 7.15   OLS regression results (CPs1)

	Model 1	Model 2	Model 3	Model 4
Dependent variable	ISI	ISI	ISI	ISI
Number of cases	60	60	60	41
Adj. R-square	0.938	0.951	0.918	0.953
F-test significance	111.635	104.460	66.679	136.757
KPD Index (CPs1)	0.656	0.660		0.535
	(7.930)***	(5.826)***		(7.069)***
GI Index (CPs1)	0.313	0.284	0.015	0.222
	(6.499)***	(4.862)***	(0.327)	(4.705)***
Connect time lag	−0.270	−0.212	−0.427	−0.168
	(−3.936)*	(−3.093)**	(−5.728)***	(−3.031)**
Population	−0.037	−0.014	−0.188	−0.137
	(−0.743)	(−0.306)	(−3.964)***	(−2.744)*
English	−0.039	−0.011	0.042	
	(−1.111)	(−0.330)	(0.979)	
Liberalization index	−0.126	−0.105	−0.021	
	(−2.624)**	(−2.576)*	(−0.420)	
Ownership	0.068	0.066	0.089	
	(1.774)*	(1.912)*	(2.002)*	
Income equality	0.102	0.112	0.213	0.080
	(2.437)*	(2.879)**	(4.739)***	(2.087)*
Price				−0.186
				(−3.268)**
INDUM1		−0.081	−0.374	
		(−1.165)	(−6.080)***	
INDUM2		−0.046	−0.346	
		(−0.562)	(−4.129)***	
INDUM3		0.086	−0.146	
		(1.493)	(−2.739)**	

Notes:
1. Standardized coefficients (Beta) with significance (t-statistic) reported in parentheses.
2. *** = significance at the 0.1 per cent level; ** = significance at the 1 per cent level;
    * = significance at the 10 per cent level.

retaining all variables included in Model 2 and excluding the KPDI, the goodness of fit measure decreases from 0.951 to 0.918 (CPs1) and 0.951 to 0.921. In addition the global integration index including information about trade, international traffic and FDI (GII CPs2) again explains more of the variation when the indicator is created using eight variables (GII CPs2).

Table 7.16   OLS regression results (CPs2)

	Model 1	Model 2	Model 3	Model 4
Dependent variable	ISI	ISI	ISI	ISI
Number of cases	60	60	60	41
Adj. R-square	0.937	0.951	0.921	0.953
F-test significance	110.597	104.736	70.054	135.945
KPD Index (CPs2)	0.558	0.564		0.438
	(6.470)***	(5.519)***		(5.847)***
GI Index (CPs2)	0.209	0.176	0.125	0.158
	(3.300)**	(2.746)**	(1.556)	(2.317)*
Connect time lag	−0.266	−0.202	−0.417	−0.154
	(−3.823)***	(−2.905)**	(−5.717)***	(−2.618)*
Population	−0.062	−0.044	−0.135	−0.159
	(−1.181)	(−0.904)	(−2.342)*	(−2.914)**
English	−0.034	−0.007	0.025	
	(−0.946)	(−0.194)	(0.586)	
Liberalization index	−0.127	−0.109	−0.038	
	(−2.845)**	(−2.714)**	(−0.781)	
Ownership	0.062	0.059	0.096	
	(1.596)	(1.701)*	(2.212)*	
Income equality	0.093	0.111	0.212	0.079
	(2.271)*	(2.934)**	(5.072)***	(2.049)*
Price				−0.203
				(−3.553)**
INDUM1		−0.090	−0.326	
		(−1.315)	(−4.835)***	
INDUM2		−0.064	−0.289	
		(−0.788)	(−3.230)**	
INDUM3		0.077	−0.111	
		(1.360)	(−1.944)*	

Notes:
1. Standardized coefficients (Beta) with significance (t-statistic) reported in parentheses.
2. *** = significance at the 0.1 per cent level; ** = significance at the 1 per cent level; * = significance at the 10 per cent level.

In Model 1, presented in Table 7.15, most variables, including KPDI (CPs1), GII (CPs2), TLAG, OWN, LOT and EID, are significant predictors at a greater than 90 per cent confidence level. PRICE also has a statistically significant regression coefficient in Model 4. With these results the null hypothesis that there is no relationship between Internet system development and each variable can be rejected. The signs of KPDI, GII and EID are positive as expected, indicating that development of the Internet system is influenced by knowledge production and distribution capabilities, global integration activities and the equality of income distribution in a country. The values of the coefficients for TLAG, OWN on ISI are negative as expected, indicating that countries that connected earlier and privatized their incumbent telecommunication operators have a more developed Internet system. However the sign of LOT is interesting, in that it is negative, contrary to expectations. This suggests that the liberalization of the telecommunication market has a negative effect on the development of the Internet system. POP is a statistically non-significant predictor in Model 1, but appears to be an important factor in explaining Internet system development in Models 3 and 4. Income dummy variables in Model 2 also appear statistically non-significant predictors, but they show significant regression coefficients in Model 3, where KPDI is excluded because there is a substantially high correlation between KPDI and income. The English language factor is not statistically significant in any of the models.

Two variables, KPDI and GII, explain more than 90 per cent of the variation in the pervasiveness of the Internet across countries (see Table 7.17). OLS regression results confirm that KPDI and GII explain the pervasiveness of the Internet system better than income measured by GDP per capita (PPP US$).

Discussions and Findings

The above results support the claim that the pervasiveness of the Internet system in various countries is influenced by their knowledge production and distribution capabilities, global integration levels and wealth, both directly and indirectly. It is also influenced by the time that their local system was connected to NSFNET. In the USA, the role of scientists and researchers in the localization of the Internet system has been crucial, in that they were not only the first adopters but also the local system builders.

Connection to the NSFNET means that a country could start to gain experience and expertise in Internet technologies. The correlation between TLAG and KPDI, GII, LIB and the income dummy variable in Tables 7.14 and 7.15 suggests that the imitation gap (measured by time lag of countries connecting to the NSFNET) may be related to level of knowledge production and distribution capabilities, global integration levels and wealth. TLAG has the highest correlation coefficient, with KPDI, among the factors included in the analysis. From the analysis of the path of the global expansion of the Internet system in Chapter 5, it is possible to infer the nature of the relationship between TLAG and other factors. One explanation for this is

Table 7.17 OLS regression results (KPDI and GII)

	Model 5	Model 6	Model 7
Dependent variable	ISI	ISI	ISI
Number of cases	60	60	60
Adj. R-square	0.908	0.906	0.782
F-test significance	290.480	284.911	212.507
KPD Index (CPs1)	0.887	—	—
	(22.397)***		
GI Index (CPs1)	0.353	—	—
	(8.907)***		
KPD Index (CPs2)	—	0.774	—
		(13.139)***	
GI Index (CPs2)	—	0.227	—
		(3.862)***	
GDPPC*	deleted	deleted	0.886
			(14.578)***

Notes:
1. — not included.
2. Standardized coefficients (Beta) with significance (t-statistic) reported in parentheses.
3. *** = Significance at the 0.1 per cent level; ** = significance at the 1 per cent level; * = significance at the 10 per cent level.

that the technologies underlying the Internet system were transferred through international academic networks from the early stages of development, as discussed in Chapter 4. To connect with the NSFNET investments were needed to purchase expensive international leased lines. The regional integration of academic networks appears to have facilitated connection to NSFNET and made it possible to share the costs among countries. Liberalization, in particular of the international leased line market, reduced the cost to both ISPs and users who access via leased lines. However, as was explained in Chapter 5, connection to the NSFNET was also influenced by political factors.

The liberalization level of the telecommunication market in a country shows a statistically significant coefficient but its value is negative, contradicting the initial hypothesis. However the status of the incumbent operator is a statistically significant predictor. This can be explained if it is assumed that the development of the Internet system is not greatly influenced by the overall liberalization of the telecommunication market and the status of incumbent ownership, but that it is very much influenced by the specific telecommunication policies that promote a reduction in leased line and local call charges. Data representing these specific telecommunication policies need to be developed.

PRICE shows a statistically significant regression coefficient. PRICE in this analysis measures the ratio of actual Internet access costs to national income (GDP PPP). The level of Internet system development changes according to country income groups. The coefficients for the regressions on INDUM1, INDUM2 and INDUM3 represent changes in the level of Internet system development from high-income countries to middle-income: upper; from middle-income: upper to middle-income: lower; and from middle-income: lower to low-income countries, respectively (Model 3 in Table 7.14). A possible reason for the very small values of the *t*-statistics for the income dummy variables in Model 2 is the high correlation between KPDI and income dummy variables.

The value for the coefficient of EID indicates statistical significance at the level of 10 per cent (CPs2 Model 1). The interesting point here is that average income distribution equality measured by the ratio of female GDP to male GDP shows a linear relationship with level of income. EID increases from 0.440 for the low-income countries group to 0.515 for the 'middle-income: lower' countries. However, 'middle-income: higher' countries exhibit a lower value than 'middle-income: lower' in terms of income distribution equality (Table 7.18). High-income countries have the greatest income equality.

The regression coefficient for ENG is not statistically significant in the models. However this does not mean that language has no relationship to the localization of the Internet system. One possible explanation is that the English dummy variable is simply coded as to whether English is the official

Table 7.18   Equality in income distribution: countries grouped by income

	No. of cases	EID		GDP per capita 1998 (PPP, US$)	
		Mean	Std. Deviation	Mean	Std. Deviation
Low-income	4	0.440	0.159	1 664.75	604.10
Middle-income: lower	16	0.515	0.129	4 325.81	1 520.52
Middle-income: higher	15	0.487	0.127	8 463.33	1 929.63
High-income	25	0.556	0.113	20 888.48	4 143.20
Total	60	0.520	0.126	12 083.90	8 266.51

Source: Data calculated by author from UNDP (2000).

language or not in a country, but most countries are low-income countries. However, in most developed countries, students study English as a second language even if they were coded as non-English speaking countries. For example, more than 90 per cent of high school students study English as a foreign language in eight out of 12 European countries.[20] However it is not easy to measure English language competency. Table 7.19 shows an alternative indicator for English competence measured by the number of publications that are in English in the selected countries. Using this indicator, there is a positive relationship between English competence and Internet development. Countries where English is not the national language show great variation in English competence. For example, some European countries (Finland, Sweden, Switzerland and the Netherlands) show a relatively high level of Internet

Table 7.19   Book production by language and pervasiveness of the Internet

Country	Number of Book Titles by Language[1]					Number of Internet hosts per 1000 inhabitants (July 1995)
	Total (A)	National language (B)	Foreign language (C)	English (D)	D/A	
Finland	11 785	9 858	1 927	1 725	14.64	22.32
Sweden	12 895	10 370	2 525	1 839	14.26	14.58
Switzerland	14 870	12 235	2 635	2 112	14.20	10.50
Netherlands	11 844	9 649	2 195	1 531	12.93	9.93
Denmark	11 492	9 507	1 985	1 350	11.75	8.99
Norway	4 943	4 264	679	380	7.69	16.12
Egypt	2 599	2 320	279	179	6.89	0.01
Thailand	7 626	7 120	506	506	6.64	0.08
Peru	2 106	1 895	211	98	4.65	0.02
Italy	30 110	27 850	2 260	685	2.27	1.10
France	41 234	36 542	4 692	700	1.70	2.47
Korea	30 861	30 814	47	45	0.15	0.74
Argentina	5 628	5 611	17	0	0.00	0.17
Brazil	27 557	10 039	17 518	0	0.00	0.12

Note: [1]1993 and nearest year.

Source: Data calculated by author from UN (1997); ITU, *ITU World Telecommunication Indicators Database*, 5th edn (June 2000 updated); ITU (1999a).

development and published books in English, and account for more than 10 per cent of the total, whereas other European countries, such as France and Italy, show a relatively low level of Internet development and publications in English, that is, only 1.70 per cent and 2.27 per cent, respectively.

7.5 CONCLUSION

The hypotheses about the interactive relationship that underlies the Internet system and the dominant factors that influence its localization have been tested using econometric methods. The main findings and limitations are as follows.

Internet System and Computerization and Telecommunication Infrastructure

1. Strong interrelatedness between the Internet, computer and telecommunication systems can be confirmed.
2. From the results of the test for the strength of relationships between Internet, computer and telecommunication system development, certain relationships can be confirmed.
3. The effect of telecommunication system development on the growth of computer system can be confirmed at the 95 per cent confidence level. However, the influence of the computer system on the telecommunication system was not significant statistically. The Internet system appears to be an important predictor of both computer and telecommunication systems. The computer and telecommunication systems are confirmed to be important predictors of Internet system development. The growth in the telecommunication system appears to influence the computer system but the growth in computer system does not appear to be one of the determinants of development of telecommunication system. The effect of the computer system on the telecommunication system seems to be realized indirectly through the growth of data networks including the Internet. The recent growth in telecommunications, in particular main telephone lines, is attributed to the growth of the Internet.

Internet System and Knowledge System

The results confirm the argument that the knowledge production and distribution capabilities of a country are the most important predictors of the localization of the Internet system. This means that not only the specific knowledge and expertise of the Internet system but also the knowledge infrastructure in a country are important for the localization of the Internet system.

Internet System and Global Integration Efforts

The results support the argument that global integration activities in a country are also statistically significant predictors of the Internet system's localization. This means that global integration efforts in a country influence the localization of the country.

Economic and Social Characteristics and Localization of the Internet System

The results confirm the conjecture that the wealth of a country influences the localization of the Internet. They also support the argument that greater equality of income distribution supports faster localization of the Internet system. The influence of the level of income in the localization of the Internet is also confirmed through the relationship between the pervasiveness of the Internet and income equality. With the exception of 'middle-income: higher' countries, the higher-income countries have the greater equality of income. The size of the social system measured by population is a statistically significant predictor when knowledge production capabilities are excluded. Population size has a negative influence on the localization of the Internet, but its relative importance is less than that of knowledge capabilities, government policy (science and technology), economic wealth and equality of income distribution. English language competency does not appear to be a statistically significant predictor using the index selected in this study. However this does not mean that language has no relationship with the localization of the Internet system.

Government Policy and the Localization of the Internet

Telecommunication policies, measured by extent of market openness and ownership status, appear to be statistically significant factors in the localization of the Internet, but not as important as some other factors. The results support the argument that science and technology policy measured by time of connection to the NSFNET significantly influences the localization of the Internet. This is possibly the result of 'selection bias' which means that earlier connection (that is, higher perceived value of connection) implies more rapid local development.

Overall the results of the econometric tests support the argument that the evolution of a technological system involves complex interactions between technologies and cultural, social, economic and political developments. Knowledge capabilities appear to be core resources in the localization of the Internet. However they cannot shed light on all of the underlying dynamic and complex process of interactions between the Internet system and the economic, social and political systems.

NOTES

1. The global diffusion of the Internet project is a multi-year project undertaken by the Mosaic Group to measure and analyse the growth of the Internet throughout the world. The research approach uses the nation-state as the unit of analysis and includes the development of an analytical framework for capturing the state of the Internet within a country at a particular point in time. Since the project's inception in 1997, over 30 countries have been studied (http://mosaic.unomaha.edu/gdi.html, last accessed in August 2001).

2. The ITU is carrying out a series of case studies on the diffusion of the Internet in countries at different stages of development. The aim of the project is to understand the factors that accelerate or slow down the development of the Internet in different environments and, through comparative analysis, to advise policy makers and regulatory agencies on appropriate courses of action. A particular focus will be on the spread of the Internet in different sectors of the economy, such as health, education and commerce, as well as government. (http://www.itu.int/ti/casestudies/, last accessed in August 2001).

3. Most of these methods are based on existing economic empirical analyses of telecommunications. There are two different ways of conducting empirical work to assess the effect of telecommunications at the macroeconomic or country level: aggregate correlation analysis and structural economic analysis (Saunders *et al.*, 1994). The former uses statistical correlation or regression analysis while the latter relies on the classic tool of input–output analysis. Saunders *et al.* provide discussions on the various studies using these methods.

4. Tony Rutkowski's Internet diffusion graphs (ftp://ftp.genmagic.com/pub/internet/) were last accessed in September 2000.

5. The Human Development Index is based on three indicators: life expectancy, educational level and GDP per capita.

6. However they are independent to some extent because each technological system has a different system goal.

7. Internet2 is a consortium being led by over 180 universities working in partnership with industry and government to develop and deploy advanced network applications and technologies, accelerating the creation of tomorrow's Internet. Internet2 is recreating the partnership among academia, industry and government that fostered today's Internet in its infancy. The primary goals of Internet2 are to 'Create a leading edge network capability for the national research community, Enable revolutionary Internet applications' and 'Ensure the rapid transfer of new network services and applications to the broader Internet community' (http://www.internet2.edu).

8. APCCIRN, Meeting Minutes, 1993.1.12–13.

9. Hampton defines an Offshore Financial Centre as 'a centre that hosts financial activities that are separated from major regulating units (states) by geography and/or by region. This may be a physical separation, as in an island territory, or (a legal separation) within a city such as London or the New York International Banking Facilities' (Hampton, 1996: 237).

10. In June 1997, about 82.3 per cent of content on the Internet, measured by the estimated number of significant Web servers (more than 500 characters of text) in every language, was estimated to be in English (Internet Society: http://alis.isoc.org/palmares.en.html).

11. 'The term "Matthew effect" was coined by R.K. Merton in 1968 for a class of phenomena in science, characterized by a skewed distribution in the allocation of funds, citations, awards and so on in analogy to the gospel parable of the entrusted talents (Matthew 25:14–30)' (Bonitz and Scharnhorst, 1999).

12. However non-PC access devices are also used to access the Internet: 14 per cent of net

users accessed the Web from non-PC devices (television set top boxes, hand-held computers and so on) in 1997 (US Department of Commerce/International Trade Administration, 1999).
13. For the stability of data, countries with more than 1 million population are included.
14. See Johnston (1984), Johnston and DiNardo (1997), Berndt (1991) and, for one empirical study, Kedzie (1995), to examine the causal relation between the Internet connectivity and democracy with 2SLS analysis with a system of simultaneous equations.
15. See Hall *et al.* (1996), Bound *et al.* (1995) and Bekker (1994) for discussion of the two properties of instruments, that is, relevance and exogeneity.
16. In this analysis, data on Internet monthly access prices (US$20 hours of off-peak use) are based on the ITU report, *Challenges to the Network: Internet for Development* (ITU, 1999a). Other sources are also available, for example Jensen (1999), which also provide Internet usage costs for the African countries, but most of them are not comparable because of different methodologies and time periods.
17. The choice of these indicators is made in the light of the discussion in Chapter 2.
18. http://www.imperative.com/.
19. The Gini coefficient is used as a measure of income distribution. It was devised by Corrado Gini and is the ratio of the area between the Lorenz curve, the actual income distribution measured in percentile of population, and the line of absolute equality to the area of the entire triangle below the line.
20. European Communities (1997).

8. Conclusion

The Internet is marching on, opening up a new paradigm of time and space – the *e* world. The most conspicuous demonstration of the potential power of the Internet over our economies and societies is evidenced by its sustained exponential growth. According to the Internet domain survey conducted by the Internet Software Consortium, over 233 million computers across the world were connected to the Internet in January 2004. This was more than double the number in July 2001 and was more than ten times the number in January 1994.

Many authors stress that we are witnessing the second wave of the Internet revolution. For example, Wellman and Haythornthwaite (2002: 6) point out, 'we are moving from a world of Internet wizards to a world of ordinary people routinely using the Internet as an embedded part of their lives'.[1] Some others, such as Tapscott *et al.* (2000) and McKnight *et al.* (2001) claim that there will be no business without knowledge and expertise on the Internet and related technologies.

Recognizing the powerful potential of the Internet to our societies, increasingly numerous scholars are investigating various socioeconomic implications of the Internet and related technological systems. Now Internet scholars from different disciplines have emerged to relate successes in the evolution of the Internet and the revolutionary socioeconomic changes that it is bringing about. Few of these scholars' works, however, reveal the whole truth about the unprecedented success of the Internet and this is mainly because they have assumed that the Internet has triumphed because of its technological and economic superiority.

In this volume we have examined the deep structure of economies and societies in shaping the Internet to uncover the paradigm of the Internet system design and its consequence. Chapters 2 and 3 presented theoretical and analytical frameworks for the analysis of the process and outcome of the Internet system development. 'Sociotechnological' perspectives are applied to examine the negotiations between relevant social groups in the processes of development and global expansion of the Internet. The insights given by the 'technoeconomic' perspectives are used to measure the differences between countries and regions with respect to the performance of the Internet system and to examine the relationship between the Internet and other sub-systems of a country. The political economy perspective is employed to bridge the technoeconomic perspective and sociotechnological approaches. The macro (global) context is not just a background for the micro (local)-level analysis and, in turn, heterogeneous actors' political and economic interests cannot be subsumed into structural power relations. In recognition of this, the concept of epistemic communities is introduced in order to uncover political and economic interests between social groups in the design of the data network and the Internet system.

The concept of localization is articulated in order to integrate the internationalization process and the local development of the Internet and to identify economic and social factors influencing differences and similarities in the development of the Internet system between countries and regions.

Academic discourses on sectoral characteristics and the governance of the telecommunication are discussed in Chapter 3. Economic and technological characteristics such as network externalities, economies of scale and scope, technological interrelatedness, interconnectedness and control of service flow contribute to the understanding of technological and industrial dynamics of telecommunications. The governance of telecommunications has been shaped not only by these economic and technological factors but also by political and legal systems. Differences in the governance of telecommunications between the USA and Europe led to the different technological choices in computer network technologies, but are converging towards a market-oriented one through liberalization, privatization and globalization. Different interests between technological leaders and followers have shaped the globalization of telecommunications and the development of the Internet.

Many authors argue that the role of the state should be minimized in order to stimulate private investment in telecommunications and the Internet systems and it may be the only realistic choice for many developing countries. However we believe that the role of the state is very important to the accomplishment of economic and social goals and may be even more so in the climate of liberalization and globalization of the telecommunications system.

The two main issues that this research raises are how political and economic interests have shaped the evolution of the Internet system and why the outcome of Internet system development varies across countries. Chapters 4 and 5 of this volume were devoted to answering the first question. We have analysed the social and economic processes that allowed the Internet to prevail over competing standards and methods for achieving a global information infrastructure. Of particular note in this analysis was the role of negotiations among social groups with different economic and political interests in the design of the Internet and the influence of US promotion of the Internet as a means of overcoming national differences in the governance of the telecommunications sector. The three different groups of packet switching technology developments: (1) private networks for mainly research and academic purposes; (2) public data networks; and (3) customized private networks reflected, the different economic and political interests of these three distinctive groups. The computer scientists who were involved in developing research networks took the initiative in the battle for control over the development of the emerging computer networking technology. However they contributed to these technological innovations in different ways, either by building public data networks (for example, NPL in the UK) or by constructing specialized private networks (for example, ARPANET in the USA) reflecting their different economic and political contexts. Most of the private networks designed by computer scientists were based on the 'datagram' (that is, a host-oriented design), while public telecommunication operators designed the virtual circuit, that is, a network-oriented design. The latter type of network design was based on open architectures, while computer manufacturer-designed protocols meant to be deployed in private networks were not compatible with other systems. The major computer manufacturers sought to control the development of computer network technologies by using the weight or scale of private networks to promote their own systems, either to maintain or to extend their dominance in the market. The battles were shaped by political, economic and technological power relationships, mainly between the USA and European countries through their competition for technological leadership in newly converging communication and information technologies.

The success of the Internet was arguably achieved by the US government policies which were deliberately designed to promote it. It was seen that the growth of the Internet system could be accomplished, on the one hand, by delaying the implantation of international standards (OSI) in the USA – such delays would have been consistent with strategic motives – and, on the other hand, by promoting the commercialization of Internet technologies. A 'developmental bloc' for Internet technology was created by the US government, which encouraged collaboration between researchers, users and vendors to produce technological innovations through continuous and interactive learning. The technological leadership and financial support of the US government appears to have created a critical mass in the development of the Internet. The Internet was supported either directly by NSFNET or indirectly through grants to users: Internet users paid virtually nothing and service providers received financial support from the government.

The battle of the systems of data network technologies reflected changes in the governance of the telecommunications sector globally. The public data network path was embedded in the PTT regime in Europe, while the Internet path was embedded in the process of liberalization of the telecommunication system in the USA. The Internet system is a typical example of private networks established by the US government which was designed to achieve bypass of the public telecommunication network. In the first place, the Internet system was built by connecting private networks in the USA. The flat tariffs and volume-discounted prices of leased lines created an incentive for use and expansion of the networks. The more use was made of a given bandwidth, the more cost-effective it became. Second, the development of the Internet system was facilitated by the liberalization of the telecommunication market in the USA, in that this reduced prices, particularly for leased lines. In turn, the growth of the Internet opened the market for new entrants.

The incentives for exploiting economies of scale and scope accelerated consolidations in the ICT industry, particularly some of the new actors produced by the expansion of the technology, such as Cisco. The growth of the Internet has been accomplished through the consolidation of players in the ICT industry and the coupling of communication and information technologies. After control of the Internet was handed over by the US government to the major US telecommunication operators, mergers and acquisitions within and between the telecommunication and information-processing sectors in both the domestic and global spheres proliferated.

The globalization of telecommunications has been facilitated by the rapid growth of the Internet. The US government established the rules for commercialization by favouring large telecommunication network operators in the USA. PTOs in the USA could acquire and accumulate technological knowledge through participation in the NREN projects and global connection projects. They had the power to carry out commercialization of the Internet and pursue its global expansion. European PTOs followed by forming global alliances. Liberalization and privatization of telecommunications during the 1990s have contributed to the internationalization of the Internet system.

However the internationalization and localization of the Internet have also been shaped by strategies of market players, in particular incumbent PTOs. The growth of the Internet contributed to the lowering of entry barriers to the telecommunication market. In theory, the growth of the Internet creates favourable conditions for new entrants but, in reality, the role of the PTOs becomes increasingly important because they control the access network to most end users.

One of the distinctive characteristics of Internet system evolution is the process of its internationalization. To avoid possible political and economic conflicts, collaboration on the computer networking technologies between the USA and other countries, in particular European countries, was conducted in the name of cooperation between research communities. There were collaboration channels established between the USA and European countries (and other countries) for military and scientific purposes from the early stages of its development. Computer scientists who were involved in experimental networks, such as ARPANET, NPL and CYCLADES, contributed to the establishment of computer networking communities in which they could exchange their knowledge and experiences. Wider research communities were connected with one another by global computer networks such as BITNET (EARN in Europe) and USENET (EUNET in Europe). Global expansion of the Internet was based on these links.

This feature of the internationalization of the Internet bears foreseeable consequences, in that governance was set up on the basis of the existing asymmetric power structure of global computer networking communities in addition to the existing economic and technological disparities between regions and countries. The internationalization of the Internet was intertwined with the national and regional research network-building processes. For example, international networks were built by integrating existing national networks and these international networks encouraged further national and local networks through the arrangements for cost sharing among international networks. Differences in regional and national research networks between regions and countries contributed to the uneven take-off of the Internet between countries. The internationalization of the Internet was also controlled by the selective financial support for US scientists to connect with those countries that had advanced science and technological capabilities through the Internet while some countries were forbidden access to the global Internet systems for political reasons.

The internationalization and commercialization of the Internet system added to the pressure for change to the US-centric governance of the Internet controlled by computer networking professionals. The global-system building process began with the efforts to accommodate global governance by extending to participants from broader communities, but many issues still remain to be resolved. In reality, the building of truly global self-governance may be unattainable.

Chapters 6 and 7 of this book examined consequences of these trends as well as other causes of the digital divide on a global dimension. We have investigated the processes of internationalization and the outcomes of the localization of the Internet in order to find similarities and differences in the performance of the Internet system between countries and regions.

The Internet system was designed with the logical centre of the network architecture being the USA and this could not be changed easily. Rather the asymmetric traffic balance (reflecting uneven development of the national and regional networks), the uneven costs of international leased lines between the USA and other countries and regions, and peering models for international facilities helped to reinforce and create North American and European core centres.

European countries could catch up with the USA and emerge as new core centres of the global Internet partly by strengthening the international academic collaboration networks with the US. Differences between regions in exploiting economies of scale in both building regional networks and aggregating demand reflecting economic and technological gaps, regional integration and cultural contexts contributed to the Internet divides between regions and countries.

The pattern of the internationalization of the Internet appears to fit reasonably well with the cultural, economic and regional characteristics of countries. In general, cultural, economic and regional factors have been historically intertwined with each other. For example, most advanced countries belong to western civilizations and most are located in Western Europe. The USA, Canada, Australia, New Zealand and Israel also share some cultural, economic and political features with Western Europe. In addition to cultural, economic and regional factors, the size of the country, and its economic characteristics in the global economy, for example offshore financial centres, can account for different patterns in the Internet system (see Chapter 6).

The localization of the Internet system involves complex technological and institutional changes. For example, the international diffusion and growth pattern of the Internet system displays different features from those of electronic switching technologies (see Chapter 5). This implies that a large technological system involves much more complex processes than a subsystem of components. The localization of the Internet involves not only a process of technological capability building but also the social learning process which includes institutional and cultural changes.

The different technological and social characteristics of the Internet system and the cellular telephone system appear to have led to different technological choices (see Chapter 6). However the substitution mechanism between competing technologies in the process of localization of the Internet is not as simple as might be expected. The Internet and videotex (online service) systems are not simply competing with each other. In most cases, they encourage one another's development rather than substituting for one another. For example, the cases of Germany and South Korea show that the two systems co-evolved until the Internet systems took over online service systems (see Chapter 6).

Unlike the case of other ICTs, population dynamics of the Internet show little sign of reduction in the disparities in Internet access between advanced economies and LDCs. For example, the gaps between countries grouped by economic strength in terms of the Internet have narrowed far less than for the cellular phone system.

The co-evolution of the Internet system and sub-systems of a country is very complex, but at least the strong interrelatedness between the Internet, computer and telecommunication systems is confirmed by a sense of models of the growth process. The interactive relationships between the Internet and computer systems and the Internet and telecommunication systems are fairly straightforward, but those between computer and telecommunication systems do not appear to be so clear. The reciprocal effects between the levels of computerization and the telecommunication infrastructure may be generated through various computer networks, notably the Internet. The localization of the Internet system is associated with greater levels of computerization and telecommunication infrastructure and changes in their context. It appears to promote the development of software and hardware in computer systems associated with computer networking and contents. The development of the Internet system also seems to encourage the development of the telecommunication infrastructure because Internet traffic generates demand for greater bandwidth.

It also involves the reconfiguration of the telecommunication system from a voice-centric and centralized control system under monopoly management within a country to a data-centric and distributed control system operating in an increasingly competitive market that is global in scope. These changes affect the physical infrastructure, pricing, management and governance systems of the telecommunication system both within countries and on a global level. Unlike what neoliberalists suggest, however, the governance of the Internet and telecommunications appears not to have been shifted to the open and disintegrated industry structure. Rather it is most likely to be shaped by conflicting interests among actors within a country and the uneven global power structure.

The results of the econometric modelling show that knowledge production and distribution capabilities, global integration efforts, economic strength and equality of income distribution, size of social system, telecommunication policies, science and technology policies, prices for access and use of the Internet all influence the localization of the Internet system (see Chapter 7).

First, the knowledge production and distribution capabilities of a country appear to be the most important factors for the localization of the Internet system. This confirms that the knowledge system is the primary factor in explaining the differences in adoption and use of new technologies and thus their contribution to economic growth. Knowledge production and distribution capabilities also show significant and substantial correlations with the economic strength of a country.

As was examined in Chapters 4 and 5, the research communities have played an important role in the development and localization of the Internet system. The role of research communities in the localization of a new technological system, in particular ICTs, is very important because they have capabilities and, thus, power in selecting which technologies people use.

Major innovations took place within research communities and these were extended to commercial use. Technological innovations were accomplished through learning by using the Internet. In this regard, the Internet system was also transferred through international research communities because they were the main users. Scientists and researchers in other countries were also lead users. They played an important role in tailoring the Internet system to the local context in the process of converting the existing national research network built upon public data network standards to the Internet system. This demonstrates that not only specific knowledge and expertise in computer networking but also the knowledge system of the country itself influence the localization process.

Second, the results show that global integration activities influenced the localization of the Internet. Countries that were already involved in international academic networks were in a better position to build up global connections and to share the costs of international leased lines and had more opportunities to cooperate with other countries in localizing Internet technologies. On the demand side, countries with greater transnational activity had a greater need to introduce and develop the Internet system because the biggest competitive advantage of using the Internet system rather than the existing telephone system was in international communications. For example, the Internet also made it possible to bypass traditional international settlement regimes.

In addition to these two main points, several other conjecturers are supported by the statistical models presented in Chapter 7. Not only the level of income but also the equality of income distribution appear to have had a positive influence on Internet localization. Smaller countries were able to localize the Internet system more quickly. Specific sectoral policies such as liberalization of telecommunication also contributed to the localization of the Internet system. Internet access and user costs adjusted by income level of a country were also found to influence localization.

Language does not appear to have been a statistically significant barrier to localization. There are two possible explanations for this. First, some of the poorest countries make considerable use of the English language; and second, some developed countries, in particular European countries, had already invested in the development of information processing and communication technologies supporting their national language and, thus, relatively less time was needed for adaptation of the Internet to the local context (see Chapters 4 and 5).

This book contests many accounts of the diffusion of the Internet that are based on 'technological inevitability' and the 'universality' of the technical methods chosen. The new economy (or knowledge society) which is argued to have been driven by the Internet and ICTs revolution is unlikely to bridge the existing technological and economic divides between groups of people and societies as their source, the deep structure of economies and societies, will not be eliminated naturally as time goes by. Rather it will likely create a new form of divides. At the same, however, we believe that there is also a real window of opportunity to change the existing economic and technological order. For example, surprisingly enough, South Korea is arguably the leader in the development of broadband access technologies (OECD, 2003).

We believe that the future of the Internet will be built up by the choices of relevant social groups and power relations between them in both local and global dimensions, which in turn are expected to determine their freedom of choice.

NOTE

1. See also, for example, Miller and Slater (2000).

Bibliography

Abbate, J. (1994), 'From ARPANET to Internet: a history of ARPA-sponsored computer networks, 1966–1988' (PhD thesis), University of Pennsylvania.

Abbate, J. (1999), *Inventing the Internet*, Cambridge, MA and London: The MIT Press.

Abdala, M.A. (2000), 'Institutional roots of post-privatisation regulatory outcomes', *Telecommunications Policy*, **24**(8–9), 645–68.

Ablett, S.D. Cleevely and P. Aknai (1994), 'The commercial and economic impact of ATM on the telecommunications market', in W.L. Bauerfeld *et al.* (eds), *Broadband Islands '94, Connecting with the End-User*, Proceedings of the 3rd International Conference on Broadband Islands, Hamburg, Germany, 7–9 June, Amsterdam: North-Holland, pp. 335–42.

Abramovitz, M. (1979), 'Rapid growth potential and its realization: the experience of capitalists economies in the postwar period', in E. Malivaud (ed.), *Economic Growth and resources, Vol 1, The Major Issues*, Proceedings of the Fifth World Congress of the IEA, London: Macmillan, pp. 1–51.

Abramovitz, M. (1986), 'Catching up, forging ahead, and falling behind', *Journal of Economic History*, **66**, 385–406.

Abramovitz, M. (1989), *Thinking about Growth*, Cambridge: Cambridge University Press.

Abramson, B.D. (2000), 'Internet globalization indicators', *Telecommunications Policy*, **24**(1), 69–74.

Abramson, B.D. and M. Raboy (1999), 'Policy globalization and the "Information Society": A View from Canada', *Telecommunications Policy*, **23**(10–11), 775–91.

ACM (1984), 'Access to supercomputers: an NSF perspective – an interview with Edward F. Hayes', *Communications of the ACM*, **27**(4), 299–303.

ACM SIGUCCS (1992), 'Connecting to the Internet: what connecting institutions should anticipate', RFC 1359, August.

Akdeniz, Y., C. Walker and D. Wall (eds) (2000), *The Internet, Law and Society*, Harrow: Longman.

Alcántara, C.H. (2001), *The Development Divide in a Digital Age: An Issues Paper*, Technology, Business and Society Programme Paper Number 4, August 2001, Geneva: UNRISD (United Nations Research Institute for Social Development).

Allan, A. and J. Utterback (1997), 'Responding to structural industry changes: a technological evolution perspective', *Industrial Corporate Change*, **6**(1), 183–202.

Amendola, G. and A. Ferraiuolo (1995), 'Regulating mobile communications', *Telecommunications Policy*, **19**(1), 29–42.

Andeen, A. and J.L. King (1997), 'Addressing and the future of communications competition: lessons from telephony and the Internet', in B. Kahin and J.H. Keller (eds), *Coordinating the Internet*, Cambridge and London: The MIT Press, pp. 208–57.

Anderberg, A. (2000), 'History of the Internet and Web', (http://www.geocities.com/~anderberg/ant/history/).

Anderson, R.H., T.K. Bikson, S.A. Law, B.M. Mitchell (with C. Kedzie, B. Keltner, C. Panis, J. Pliskin and P. Srinagesh) (1995), *Universal Access to Email: Feasibility and Social Implications*, MR-650-MF, Rand.

Andrews, M. (1995), *The Paradox of 'Dual-Use': Slogan of Fundamental Redefinition of the Civil–Military Relationship*, Manchester: University of Manchester Press.

Antonelli, C. (1986), 'The international diffusion of new information technologies', *Research Policy*, **15**(3), June, 139–47.

Antonelli, C. (1991), *The Diffusion of Advanced Telecommunications in Developing Countries*, Paris: Development Centre OECD.

Antonelli, C. (ed.) (1992), *The Economics of Information Networks*, Amsterdam: Elsevier Science Publishers.

Antonelli, C. (1995), 'Localized technological change in the network of networks: the interaction between regulation and the evolution of technology in telecommunications', *Industrial Corporate Change*, **4**(4), 737–54.

Antonelli, C. (1999), *The Microdynamics of Technological Change*, London and New York: Routledge.

Antonelli, G. and N. Liso (eds) (1997), *Economics of Structural and Technological Change*, London: Routledge.

Antonelli, C., A. Guena and W. Steinmueller (2000), 'Information and communication technologies and the production, distribution and use of knowledge', *International Journal of Technology Management*, **20**(1/2), 72–94.

Apostolopoulos T., C. Courcoubetis, S. Cohen and X. Psiakki (2000), 'Multiple incentive internet pricing for national academic research networks: a case study', *Telecommunications Policy*, **24**(6–7), 591–611.

Archibugi, D. and B.-Å. Lundvall (eds) (2001), *The Globalizing Learning Economy*, New York: Oxford University Press.

Arnbak, J. (2000), 'Regulation for next-generation technologies and markets', *Telecommunications Policy*, **24**(6–7), 477–87.

Arthur, W.B. (1983), 'On competing technologies and historical small events: the dynamics of choice under increasing returns', WP 83-090.

Arthur, W.B. (1988), 'Competing technologies: an overview', in G. Dosi *et al.* (eds), *Technical Change and Economic Theory*, London and New York: Pinter Publishers, pp. 590–607.

Arthur, W.B. (1989), 'Competing technologies, increasing returns and lock-in by historical events', *Economic Journal*, **99**, 116–31.

Aschauer, D.A. (1989), 'Is public expenditure productive?', *Journal of Monetary Economics*, **23**, 177–200.

Atkinson, A.B. and J.E. Stiglitz (1969), 'A new view of technological change', *Economic Journal*, **1969**, 573–8.

Audretsch, D. (1997), 'Technological regimes, industrial demography and the evolution of industrial structures', *Industrial and Corporate Change*, **6**(1), 49–82.

Averch, H. and L. Johnson (1962), 'Behavior of the firm under regulatory constraint', *American Economic Review*, **52**(5), 1052–69.

Ayres, R. (1988), 'Technology: the wealth of nations', *Technological Forecasting and Social Change*, **33**, 189–201.

Bailey, J., S. Gillett, D. Gingold, B. Leida, D. Melcher, J. Reagle, J. Roh and R. Rothstein (1995), 'Internet economics workshop notes,' Research Program on Communications Policy, MIT, 30 March.

Bain, A. (1964), *The Growth of Television Ownership in the UK since the War: A Lognormal Model*, Cambridge: Cambridge University Press.

Bar, F. (1991), 'Network flexibility: a new challenge for telecom policy', *Communications and Strategies*, **2**, 113–23.

Baran, P. (1964), 'On distributed communications', Memorandum RM-3420-PR, August 1964, Rand (http://www.rand.org/publications/RM/RM3420/ (accessed Feb. 2000).

Barber, D. (1975a), 'Local data networks' in R.L. Grimsdale and F.F. Kuo (eds), *Computer Communications Networks: proceedings of the NATO Advanced Study Institute on Computer Communication Networks 1973*, University of Sussex, Leyden: Noordhoff, pp. 277–90.

Barber, D. (1975b), 'The Cost Project 11: The European informatics network', in R.L. Grimsdale and F.F. Kuo (eds), *Computer Communications Networks: Proceedings of the NATO Advanced Study Institute on Computer Communication Networks 1973*, University of Sussex, Leyden: Noordhoff, pp. 409–14.

Baron, D.P. and R.B. Myerson (1982), 'Regulating a monopolist with unknown costs', *Econometrica*, **50**, 911–30.

Barrett, N. (1996), *The State of the Cybernation: Cultural, Political and Economic Implications of the Internet*, London: Kogan Page.

Barron, I. (1975), 'The decline and fall of the computer', *Minicomputer*

Forum Conference Proceedings 1975, Online Conference Ltd, Brunel University, pp. 17–29.

Bass, F. (1969), 'A new product growth model for consumer durables', *Management Science*, **15**, 215–27.

Baston, H.E. (1933), 'The economic concept of a public utility', *Economica*, **42**, 457–72.

Baumol, W. (1977), 'On the paper tests for natural monopoly in a multiproduct industry', *American Economic Review*, **67**, 809–22.

Baumol, W. (1986), 'Productivity growth, convergence, and welfare: what the long run data show', *American Economic Review*, **76**, 1072–85.

Baumol, W. and J. Sidak (1994), *Toward Competition in Local Telephony*, London: The MIT Press and Washington, DC: The AEI Press.

Baumol, W. and R. Willig (1986), 'Contestability: developments since the book', *Oxford Economic Papers*, **38** (Supplement), 9–36.

Baumol, W., J. Panzar and R. Willig (1982), *Contestable Markets and the Theory of Industry Structure*, San Diego, New York, Chicago, Austin, Washington, DC, London, Sydney, Tokyo and Toronto: Harcourt Brace Jovanovich Publishers.

Baumol, W., J. Panzar and R. Willig (1988), *Contestable Markets and the Theory of Industry Structure*, rev. edn, San Diego, New York, Chicago, Austin, Washington, DC, London, Sydney, Tokyo, Toronto: Harcourt Brace Jovanovich Publishers.

Beauchamp, K.G. (ed.) (1984), *Information Technology and the Computer Network*, NATO ASI Series. Series F: Computer and systems sciences 6, Berlin: Springer.

Becker, G.S. (1983), 'A theory of competition among pressure groups for political influence', *Quarterly Journal of Economics*, **XCVII**, 371–400.

Behringer, M. (1995), 'Towards a high speed pan-European backbone', INET'95, Dante In Print, No. 11 Hawaii, 27–30 June.

Behringer, M. (1997), 'ATM experiments for Advanced Backbone Services', INET'97, the Annual Conference of the Internet Society, June, Kuala Lumpur, Malaysia.

Bekker, P.A. (1994), 'Alternative approximations to the distributions of instrumental variable estimators', *Econometrica*, **62**(3), 657–81.

Bell, D. (1980), 'Introduction', in S. Nora and A. Minc (eds), *The Computerization of Society: A Report to the President of France*, English translation, Cambridge and London: MIT Press, pp. vii–xvi.

Bell, M. (1997), 'Technology transfer to transition countries: are there lessons from the experience of the post-war industrializing countries?', in D.A. Dyker (ed.), *The Technology of Transition: Science and Technology Policies for Transition Countries*, Budapest: Central European University Press, pp. 63–94.

Bell, M. and M. Albu (1999), 'Knowledge systems and technological dynamism in industrial clusters in developing countries', *World Development*, **27**, 1715–34.

Bell, M. and K. Pavitt (1993), 'Technological accumulation and industrial growth: contrasts between developed and developing countries', *Industrial and Corporate Change*, **2**(2), 157–205.

Berg, S.V. (2000), 'Sustainable regulatory systems: laws, resources, and values', *Utilities Policy*, **9**, 159–70.

Berg, S.V. and J. Tschirhart (1988), *Natural Monopoly Regulation: Principles and Practice*, Cambridge: Cambridge University Press.

Berg, S.V. and J. Tschirhart (1995), 'Contributions of neoclassical economics to public utility analysis', *Land Economics*, **71**(3), 310–30.

Berndt, E.R. (1991), *The Practical Econometrics: Classical and Contemporary*, Reading, Menlo Park, New York, Don Mills, Workingham, Amsterdam, Bonn, Sydney, Singapore, Tokyo, Madrid and San Juan: Addison-Wesley.

Berners-Lee, T., R. Cailiau, A. Luotonen, H.F. Nielsen and A. Secret (1994), 'The World Wide Web', *Communications of the ACM*, **37**, 76–82.

Bernstein, M.H. (1955), *Regulating Business by Independent Commission*, Princeton, NJ: Princeton University Press.

Bijker, W.E. (1993), 'Do not despair: there is life after constructivism', *Science, Technology, & Human Values*, **18**(1), 113–38.

Bijker, W.E. (1997), *Of Bicycles, Bakelites, and Bulbs: Toward a Theory of Sociotechnical Change*, Cambridge and London: The MIT Press.

Bijker, W.E. and J. Law (eds) (1992), *Shaping Technology/Building Society: Studies in Sociotechnical Change*, Cambridge, MA and London: The MIT Press.

Bijker, W.E., T.P. Hughes and T.J. Pinch (eds) (1987), *The Social Construction of Technological Systems: New Directions in the Sociology and History of Technology*, Cambridge, MA and London: MIT Press.

Blanc, R. (1987), 'NBS Program in Open Systems Interconnections (OSI)', in G. Muller and R. Blanc (eds), *Networking in open systems: international seminar*, Oberlech, Austria, 18–22 August 1986, Berlin, Tokyo: Springer-Verlag.

Blokzijl, R. (1989a), 'RIPE terms of reference', ripe-001, 29 November.

Blokzijl, R. (1989b), 'Statement of cooperation', ripe-002, 29 November.

Blokzijl, R. (1989c), 'Letter of introduction', ripe-003, 29 November.

Blokzijl, R. (1990), 'RIPE terms of reference', RFC 1181, September.

Blokzijl, R., Y. Devillers, D. Karrenberg and R. Volk (1990), 'RIPE Network Coordination Center (RIPE NCC)', ripe-019, 28 August.

Bohlin, E. and O. Granstrand (eds) (1994), *The Race to European Eminence: Who Are the Coming Tele-service Multinationals?*, Amsterdam, London, New York and Tokyo: North-Holland.

Bonbright, J.C. (1940), *Public Utilities and the National Power Policies*, New York: Columbia University Press.

Bonbright, J.C., A.L. Danielsen and D.R. Kamerschen (1988), *Principles of Public Utility Rates*, 2nd edn, Arlington, Virginia: Public Utilities Reports.

Bonen, Z. (1981), 'Evolutionary behaviour of complex sociotechnical systems', *Research Policy*, **10**, 26–44.

Bonitz, M. and A. Scharnhorst (1999), 'National science systems and the Matthew effect for countries', presented at the Seventh International Conference on Scientometrics and Informetrics, 5–8 July, Colima, Mexico.

Bostwick, W.E. (1991), 'HPCC: an overview of the U.S. high performance computing and communications initiative with focus on the national research and education network', *Computer Networks and ISDN Systems*, **23**(1–2), 37–9.

Bound, J., A. David, D.A. Jaeger and R.M. Baker (1995), 'Problems with instrumental variables estimation when the correlation between the instruments and the endogenous explanatory variable is weak', *Journal of the American Statistical Association*, **90**(430) (June), 443–50.

Bourreau, M. and P. Dogan (2001). 'Regulation and innovation in the telecommunications industry', *Telecommunications Policy*, **25**(3), 167–84.

Bovio, D. and F. Greisen (1993), 'NJE services to the users ... and more!', *Proc. INET 93*, GEA-1 –GEA –6.

Bozeman, B. (2000), 'Technology transfer and public policy', *Research Policy*, **29**, 627–55.

Branscomb, L. (1995), 'Balancing the commercial and public internet visions of the NII', in B. Kahin and J. Keller (eds), *Public Access to the Internet*, Cambridge, MA and London: The MIT Press, pp. 24–33.

Braun, I. and B. Jorges (1994), 'How to recombine large technical systems', in J. Summerton (ed.), *Change Large Technical Systems*, Boulder, San Francisco and Oxford: Westview Press, pp. 25–51.

Brebner, G. (1997), *Computers in Communication*, London: McGraw-Hill.

Bresnahan, T.F. and M. Trajtenberg (1995), 'General purpose technologies: engines of growth?', *Journal of Econometrics*, **65**(1) January, 83–108.

Bright, R. (1973), 'Experimental packet switching project of the UK post office', in R.L. Grimsdale and F.F. Kuo (eds), *Computer Communications Networks: Proceedings of the NATO Advanced Study Institute on Computer Communication Networks* (University of Sussex, United Kingdom), Leyden: Noordhoff International Publishing, pp. 435–44.

Brinkman, R. (1997), 'Towards a culture-conception of technology', *Journal of Economic Issues*, **XXXI**(4), 1027–37.

Brock, G. (1981), *The Telecommunication Industry: The Dynamics of Market Structure*, Cambridge: Harvard University Press.

Brock, G. (1994), *Telecommunication Policy for the Information Age: from Monopoly to Competition*, Cambridge: Harvard University Press.

Bryant, P. (1984), 'The SERC network – its history and development', in K.G. Beauchamp (ed.), *Information Technology and the Computer Network*, NATO ASI Series. F: Computer and Systems Sciences 6, Berlin: Springer, pp. 65–74.

Buchanan, J.E. (1978), 'Market, states, and the extent of morals', *American Economic Review*, **68**(2), 364–8.

Buchanan, J. and R. Tollison (eds) (1984), *The Theory of Public Choice-II*, Ann Arbor, MI: The University of Michigan Press.

Buchanan, J.M., R.D. Tollison and G. Tullock (eds) (1980), *Toward a Theory of the Rent-Seeking Society*, College Station Texas: A&M University Press.

Burg, F.M. (1992), 'CCITT recommendation X.25: packet switching and beyond', in G.R. McClain (ed.), *The Handbook of International Connectivity Standards*, New York: Van Nostrand Reinhold, pp. 369–410.

Burren, J.W. (1991), 'High speed communications – a tutorial on the jargon and technologies', *Computer Networks and ISDN Systems*, **23**(1–2), 119–24.

Busquin, R. and E. Liikanen (2000), *Research and Education Networks in Europe*, February, Brussels: EC.

Cain, L.P. (1997), 'Historical perspective on infrastructure and US economic development', *Regional Science and Urban Economics*, **27**(2), 117–38.

Cairncross, F. (1997), *The Death of Distance: How the Communications Revolution Will Change Our Lives*, London: Orion Business Books.

Calhoun, G. (1992), *Wireless Access and the Local Telephone Network*, Boston: Artech House.

Callon, M. (1987), 'Society in the making: the study of technology as a tool for sociological analysis', in W.E. Bijker, T.P. Hughes and T.J. Pinch (eds), *The Social Construction of Technological Systems: New Direction in the Sociology and History of Technology*, Cambridge, MA and London: The MIT Press, pp. 83–103.

Callon, M. (1992), 'The dynamics of techno-economic networks', in R. Coombs, P. Saviotti and V. Walsh (eds), *Technological Change and Company Strategies: Economic and Sociological Perspectives*, London: Academic Press, pp. 72–102.

Callon, M. (1995), 'Technological competition, strategies of the firms and the choice of the first users: the case of road guidance technologies', *Research Policy*, **24**(3), 441–58.

Callon, M. (ed.) (1998), *The Laws of Market*, Oxford and Malden: Blackwell Publishers.

Callon, M., P. Laredo and V. Rabeharison (1992), 'The management and evaluation of technological programmes and the Dynamics of

Techno-Economic Networks: The Case of AFME [Agence Française pour la Maîtrise de l'Energie]', *Research Policy*, **21**, 215–36.

Campbell, J.L., J.R. Hollingsworth and L.N. Lindberg (eds) (1991), *Governance of the American Economy*, Cambridge: Cambridge University Press.

Campbell-Kelly, M. and W. Aspray (1996), *Computer: A History of the Information Machine*, New York: Basic Books.

Carlaw, K.I. and R.G. Lipsey (2002), 'Externalities, technological complementarities and sustained economic growth', *Research Policy*, **31**, 1305–15.

Carlson, B. (1987), 'NORDUNET', in D. Khakhar (ed.) *Information Network and Data Communication I*, Amsterdam: Elsevier Science Publishers B.V. (North-Holland), pp. 197–207.

Carlsson, B. (1995), *Technological Systems and Economic Performance: The Case of Factory Automation*, Dordrecht: Kluwer Academic Publishers.

Carlsson, B. and G. Eliasson (1994), 'The nature and importance of economic competence', *Industrial and Corporate Change*, **3**(1), 687–711.

Carlsson, B. and S. Jacobsson (1993): 'Technological systems and economic performance: the diffusion of factory automation in Sweden' in D. Foray and C. Freeman (eds), *Technology and the Wealth of Nations: The Dynamics of Constructed Advantage*, London and New York: Pinter Publishers, pp. 77–92.

Carlsson, B. and S. Jacobsson (1994), 'Technological systems and economic policy: the diffusion of factory automation in Sweden', *Research Policy*, **23**(3), 235–48.

Carlsson, B. and R. Stankiewicz (1991), 'On the nature, function and composition of technological systems', *Journal of Evolutionary Economics*, **1**(2), 93–118.

Carpenter, B. (2000), 'Charter of the Internet Architecture Board (IAB)', RFC 2850, May.

Carpentier, M., S. Farnoux-Toporkoff and C. Garric (1992), *Telecommunications in Transition*, Chichester, New York, Brisbane, Toronto, Singapore: John Wiley & Son.

Carroll, M. and J. Stanfield (2003), 'Social capital, Karl Polanyi and American social and institutional economics', *Journal of Economic Issues*, **XXXVII**(2), 397–404.

Castells, M. (1996), *The Information Age, Society and Culture I: Rise of the Network Society*, Oxford: Blackwell Publishers.

Castells, M. (1997), *The Information Age, Society and Culture II: The Power of Identity*, Oxford: Blackwell Publishers.

Castells, M. (1998), *The Information Age, Society and Culture III: End of Millennium*, Oxford: Blackwell Publishers.

Castells, M. (2000), *The Information Age, Society and Culture I: Rise of the Network Society*, 2nd edn, Oxford: Blackwell Publishers.

Castells, M. (2001), *The Internet Galaxy: Reflections on the Internet, Business, and Society*, Oxford: Oxford University Press.

Cawley, R.A. (1997), 'Internet, lies and telephony', *Telecommunications Policy*, **21**(6), 513–32.

Cawson, A., L. Haddon and I. Miles (1995), *Shape of Things to Consume: Delivering Information Technology into the Home*, Aldershot: Ashgate Publishing Ltd.

Cawson, A., K. Morgan, D. Webber, P. Holmes and A. Stevens (1990), *Hostile Brothers: Competition and Closure in the European Electronics Industry*, Oxford: Clarendon Press.

Cerf, V. (1989), 'Internet Activities Board', RFC 1120, Sep-01–1989.

Cerf, V. (1990a), 'Internet Activities Board', RFC 1160, May-01-1990.

Cerf, V. (1990b), 'Thoughts on the National Research and Education Network', RFC 1167, Jul-01-1990.

Cerf, V. (1990c), 'IAB recommended policy on distributing internet identifier assignment and IAB recommended policy change to internet "connected" status', RFC 1174, Aug-01-1990.

Cerf, V. (1990d), 'Information Infrastructure', *IEEE Network Magazine of Computer Communications*, March, 6–11.

Cerf, V. (1991), 'Guidelines for Internet measurement activities', RFC 1262, Oct-01-1991.

Cerf, V. (1994), 'A view from the 21st century', RFC 1607, Apr-1-1994.

Cerf, V. (1995), 'History of the IETF/ISOC Relationship', ISOC (http://www.isoc.org/internet/history/ietfhis.shtml).

Cerf, V. and R. Kahn (1974), 'A protocol for packet network interconnection', *IEEE Trans. on Communications*, **COM-22**(5), May, 637–48.

Cerf, V. and P. Kirstein (1978), 'Issues in packet–network interconnection', *Proceedings of the IEEE*, **66**(11), 1386–408.

Cerf, V. and K. Mills (1990), 'Explaining the role of GOSIP', RFC 1169, Aug-01-1990.

Cerf, V., P. Kirstein and B. Randell (1991), 'Network and infrastructure user requirements for transatlantic research collaboration: Brussels, July 16–18, and Washington July 24–25, 1990', RFC 1210, Mar-01-1991.

Chamoux, J-P. (1997), 'After privatization: neocolonialism?', in E.M. Noam and A.J. Wolfson (eds), *Globalism and Localism in Telecommunications*, Amsterdam: Elsevier Science B.V., pp. 343–50.

Chandler, A.D. (1959), 'The beginnings of "Big Business" in American Industry', *Business History Review*, **33**, 1–31.

Chandler, A.D (1977), *The Visible Hand: The Managerial Revolution in American Business*, London: Cambridge, MA: Belknap Press.

Chandler, A.D. (1990), *Scale and Scope: The Dynamics of Industrial Capitalism*, Cambridge and London: Belknap Press.

Chandler, A.D. (1997), 'The computer company: the first half-century', in D. Yoffie (ed.), *Converging in the Age of Digital Convergence*, Boston: Harvard Business School Press, pp. 37–122.

Chang, H. (1997), 'Critical survey: the economics and politics of regulation', *Cambridge Journal of Economics*, **21**, 703–28.

Charlesworth, A. (1999), 'The governance of the Internet in Europe', in Y. Akdeniz, C. Walker and D. Wall (eds), *The Internet and Society*, Harlow: Pearson Education Limited, pp. 47–78.

Cherry, B.A. and S.S. Wildman (1999), 'Institutional endowment as foundation for regulatory performance and regime transitions: the role of the US constitution in telecommunications regulation in the United States', *Telecommunications Policy*, **23**(9), 607–23.

Chon, K. (1999), 'Asia–Pacific Advanced Network (APAN)', APAN (http://www.apan.net/documents/paper.html).

Choné, P., L. Flochel and A. Perrot (2002), 'Allocating and funding universal service obligations in a competitive market', *International Journal of Industrial Organization*, **20**(9), November, 1247–76.

Chou, W. (ed.) (1983), *Computer Communications Vol. 1 Principles*, Englewood Cliffs: Prentice-Hall.

Chou, W. (1985), 'Data/computer communications network structure', in W. Chou (ed.), *Computer Communications Vol. II Systems and Applications*, Englewood Cliffs: Prentice-Hall, pp. 1–29.

Chretien, G.J., W.M. Konig and J.H. Rech (1975), 'The SITA Network', in R.L. Grimsdale and F.F. Kuo (eds), *Computer Communications Networks*, NATO Advanced Study Institute Series, Leyden: Noordhoff, pp. 373–96.

Civille, R. (1995), 'The Internet and the poor', in B. Kahin and J. Keller (eds), *Public Access to The Internet*, Cambridge and London: The MIT Press, pp. 175–207.

Claffy, K., H.-W. Braun and G.C. Polyzos (1994), 'Tracking long-term growth of the NSFNET', *Communications of the ACM*, **37**(8), August, 34–45.

Clark, D., L. Chapin, V. Cerf, R. Braden and R. Hobby (1991), 'Towards the future Internet Architecture', RFC 1287, December.

Coleman, J.S. (1988), 'Social capital in the creation of human capital', *The American Journal of Sociology*, **94**, S95–S120.

Comer, D. (1983), 'The computer science research network CSNET: A history and status report', *Communications of the ACM*, **26**(10), 747–53.

Comer, D. (1988), *Internetworking with TCP/IP Principles, Protocol, and Architecture*, Englewood Cliffs: Prentice-Hall.

Comer, D. (1991), *Internetworking with TCP/IP*, 2nd edn, Englewood Cliffs: Prentice-Hall.

Comer, E. (1998), *Communication, Commerce, and Power: The Political*

Economy of America and the Direct Broadcast Satellite, New York: St Martin's Press.

Commission of the European Communities Directorate-General Telecommunications, Information Industries and Innovation (ed.), (1990), *ESPRIT '90 Proceedings of the Annual ESPRIT Conference (Brussels)*, 12–15 Nov., Dordrecht, Boston and London: Kluwer Academic Publishers.

Compaine, B.M. (2001), *The Digital Divide: Facing a Crisis or Creating a Myth*, Cambridge, MA and London: MIT Press.

Constant, E. (1984), 'Communities and hierarchies: structure in the practice of science and technology', in R. Lauden (ed.), *The Nature of Technological Knowledge. Are Models of Scientific Change Relevant?*, Dordrecht, Boston and Lancaster: D. Reidel Publishing Company, pp. 27–46.

Constant, E. (1987), 'The social locus of technological practice: community, system, or organization?' in W.E. Bijker, T.P. Hughes and T.J. Pinch (eds), *The Social Construction of Technological Systems: New Directions in the Sociology and History of Technology*, Cambridge: MIT Press, pp. 223–42.

Cooper (1988), 'EARN', *Network News*, no. 25.

Cowhey, P.F. (1990), 'The international telecommunications regime: the political roots of regimes for high technology', *International Organization*, **44**(2), 169–99.

Crandall, Robert W. (1997), 'Are telecommunications facilities "infrastructure"? If they are, so what?', *Regional Science and Urban Economics*, **27**(2), 161–79.

Crew, M.A. and P.R. Kleindorfer (1986), *The Economics of Public Utility Regulation*, Cambridge, MA: The MIT Press.

Crew, M.A. and P.R. Kleindorfer (1996), 'Incentive regulation in the United Kingdom and the United States: some lessons', *Journal of Regulatory Economics*, **9**, 211–25.

Crew, M.A. and P.R. Kleindorfer (2002), 'Regulatory economics: twenty years of progress?', *Journal of Regulatory Economics*, **21**(1), 5–22.

Crocker, S. (1969), 'Host software', RFC001, Apr-07-1969.

Cronin, F.J., E.K. Colleran, P.L. Herbert and S. Lewitzky (1993a), 'Telecommunications and growth – the contribution of telecommunications infrastructure investment to aggregate and sectoral productivity', *Telecommunications Policy*, **17**(9), 677–90.

Cronin, F.J., E.B. Parker, E.K. Colleran and M.A. Gold (1993b), 'Telecommunications infrastructure investment and economic development', *Telecommunications Policy*, **17**(6), 415–30.

Cukier, K.N. (1998), 'The global Internet: a primer', in TeleGeography Inc (ed.), *TeleGeography 1999: Global Telecommunications Traffic Statistics and Commentary*, New York and Washington, DC: TeleGeography Inc., pp. 112–45.

Czempiel, E.-O. and J. Rosenau (eds) (1989), *Global Changes and Theoretical Challenges: Approaches to World Politics for the 1990s*, Lexington MA: Lexington Books.

Dahmén, E. (1988), '"Developmental blocks" in industrial economics', *Scandinavian Economic History Review*, **XXXVI** (1), 3–14.

Dallaire, G. (1984), 'American universities need greater access to supercomputers', *Communications of the ACM*, **27**(4), 292–303.

Dasgupta, P. and I. Serageldin (eds) (1999), *Social Capital: A Multifaceted Perspective*, Washington, DC: World Bank.

David, O.W. (1992), 'Distributed computing at the European Laboratory for Particle Physics', invited talk presented at the 1992 IEEE Region International Conference Melbourne, Australia 11–13 November.

David, O.W. and B.E. Carpenter (1998), 'Data networking for the European academic and research community: is it important?', CERN/CN/91/10 and CERN/CN/92/4, reissued in online form: August.

David, P.A. (1975), *Technical Choice, Innovation and Economic Growth: Essays on American and British Experience in the Nineteenth Century*, London: Cambridge University Press.

David, P.A. (1985), 'Clio and the economics of QWERTY', *American Economic Review*, **75**(2), 332–7.

David, P.A. (1992), 'Information network economics: externalities, innovations and evolution', in C. Antonelli (ed.), *The Economics of Information Networks*, Amsterdam: Elsevier Science Publishers, pp. 103–5.

David, P.A. and J. Bunn (1988), 'The economics of gateway technologies and network evolution: lessons from electricity supply history', *Information Economics and Policy*, **3**, 165–202.

David, P.A. and D. Foray (1994), *Accessing and Expanding the Science and Technology Knowledge-Base: A Conceptual Framework for Comparing National Profiles in Systems of Learning and Innovation*, DSTI/STP/TIP (94) 4, Paris: OECD.

David, P.A. and W.E. Steinmueller (1990), 'The ISDN bandwagon is coming but who will be there to climb aboard?: quandaries in the economics of data communication networks', *Economics of Innovation and New Technology*, **1**, 43–62. 11–22 September.

David, P.A. and E. Steinmueller (1994), 'Economics of compatibility standards and competition in telecommunication networks', *Information Economics and Policy*, **6**, 217–41.

David, P.A. and E. Steinmueller (1996), 'Standards, trade and competition in the emerging Global Information Infrastructure environment', *Telecommunications Policy*, **20**(10), 817–30.

Davies, A. (1994), *Telecommunications and Politics: The Decentralised Alternative*, London: Pinter Publishers.

Davies, A. (1996), 'Innovation in large technical systems: the case of tele-communications', *Industrial Corporate Change*, **5**(4), 1143–80.

Davies, D. (1994), 'There's no such thing as a free internet', INET'94/ JENC5, Prague, Dante In Print, no. 5, 15–17 June.

Davies, D. (1995a), 'The issues and challenges of ATM', presented at a conference organised by Communications Week International, ATM and the Broadband Future, Brussels, Dante in Print, no. 12, 4–6 July

Davies, D. (1995b), 'European Internet – behind the US and moving more slowly', *Europhysics News*, Dante in Print, no. 16, 26 October.

Davies, D. (1995c), 'Roadblocks on the superhighway – meeting the challenges of setting up a high speed backbone in Europe', The Internet – Threats and Opportunities for the Telecoms Industry, London 11–12 December.

Davies, D. (1996), 'TEN-34: a 34 Mbit/s infrastructure for European research', ATM Europe 96, Paris, Dante In Print, no. 20, 19–21 March.

Davies, D. and C. Stover (1998), *Feasibility and Recommendations for Europe and Asia Pacific*, Cambridge, UK: Dante.

Davies, D.W. (1973), 'A review of computer communication technology', in R.L. Grimsdale and F.F. Kuo (eds), *Computer Communications Networks: Proceedings of the NATO Advanced Study Institute on Computer Communication Networks* (University of Sussex, United Kingdom), Leyden: Noordhoff International Publishing, pp. 1–18.

Davies, D.W. (1986), 'A personal view of the origins of packet switching', in L. Csaba, K. Tarnay and T. Szentivany (eds), *Computer Network Usage: Recent Experiences – Proceedings of the IFIP TC 6 Working Conference COMNET '85*, Budapest, Hungary, Amsterdam: North-Holland, pp. 1–14.

Davies, D.W., D. Baber and L. Derek (1973), *Communication Networks for Computers*, London, New York, Sydney and Toronto: John Wiley & Sons.

Davies, H. (1993), 'Operational network services for the European research community', INET '93, San Francisco, Dante In Print, no. 1, 17–20 August.

Davies, H. (1994a), 'DANTE's plans for high speed services', 3rd RARE/ CEC Symposium on High Speed Networking for Research, Dante In Print, no. 2, 2 February.

Davies, H. (1994b), 'EuroCAIRN and the Trans-European Research Backbone Project', EEOS Workshop, Frascati, Italy, Dante In Print, no. 7, 13–14 December.

Davies, H. (1998a), 'Policy and planning of international internet connections', Euro-Med Net '98 Conference, Nikosia, Cyprus, March.

Davies, H. (1998b), 'The European telecommunications market', NATO Advanced Networking Workshop, Yaroslav, Russia, June.

Davies, H. and J. Bersee (1994), 'International network services in Europe and the role of DANTE', *Journal of Information Networking*, **1**(3), Dante In Print no. 6, Autumn.

Davies, S. (1979), *The Diffusion of Process Innovations*, Cambridge: Cambridge University Press.

Decina, M. and V. Trecordi (1997), 'Convergence of telecommunications and computing to networking models for integrated services and applications', *Proceedings of the IEEE*, **85**(12), 1887–1914.

Dekimpe, M., P.M. Parker and M. Sarvary (1998), 'Staged estimation of international diffusion models: an application to global cellular telephone adoption', *Technological Forecasting and Social Change*, **57**, 105–32.

Dekker, M. (1993), 'Report on the NATO Advanced Workshop "Research Networking in Central and Eastern Europe"', *Computer Networks and ISDN Systems*, **25** (Supplement 2), 87–91.

Derthick, M. and P.J. Quirk (1985), *The Politics of Deregulation*, Washington, DC: The Brookings Institution.

Deuten, J., A. Rip and J. Jelsma (1997), 'Societal embedding and product creation management', *Technology Analysis & Strategic Management*, **9**(2), 131–48.

Dicken, P. (1999), *Global Shift: Transforming the World Economy*, 3rd edn, London: Sage Publications.

Dimock, M.E. (1933), *British Public Utilities and National Development*, London: George Allen & Unwin Ltd.

Dinc, M., K.E. Haynes, R.R. Stough and S. Yilmaz (1998), 'Regional universal telecommunication service provisions in the US: Efficiency versus penetration', *Telecommunications Policy*, **22**(6), 541–53.

Disco, C. and B. Meulen (eds) (1998), *Getting New Technologies Together: Studies in Making Sociotechnical Order*, Berlin: De Gruyter.

Dodgson, M. and R. Rothwell (eds) (1994), *The Handbook of Industrial Innovation*, Aldershot, UK and Brookfield, US: Edward Elgar.

Dolfsma, W. and C. Dannreuther (2003), 'Subjects and boundaries: contesting social capital-based policies', *Journal of Economic Issues*, **XXXVII** (2), 405–13.

Domar, E. (1946), 'Capital expansion, rate of growth and employment', *Econometrica*, **14**, 137–47.

Donald, S.G. and W.K. Newey (2001), 'Choosing the number of instruments', *Econometrica*, **69**(5), 1161–91.

Dordick, H.S. (1990). 'The origins of universal service: history as a determinant of telecommunications policy', *Telecommunications Policy*, **14**(3), 223–31.

Dordick, H.S. and M.D. Fife (1991). 'Universal service in post-divestiture USA', *Telecommunications Policy*, **15**(2), 119–28.

Dosi, G. (1982), 'Technological paradigms and technological trajectories: a suggested interpretation of the determinants and directions of technical change', *Policy Research*, **2**, 147–62.

Dosi, G. (1988a), 'Sources, procedures, and microeconomic effects of innovation', *Journal of Economic Literature*, **XXVI** (September), 1120–71.

Dosi, G. (1988b), 'The nature of innovative process', in G. Dosi, C. Freeman, R. Nelson, G. Silverberg and L. Soete (eds), *Technical Change and Economic Theory*, London and New York: Pinter Publishers, pp. 221–38.

Dosi, G. and L. Orsenigo (1988), 'Coordination and transformation: an overview of structures, behaviours and changing in evolutionary environments', in G. Dosi, C. Freeman, R. Nelson, G. Silverberg and L. Soete (eds), *Technical Change and Economic Theory*, London and New York: Pinter Publishers, pp. 13–37.

Dosi, G. and L. Soete (1988), 'Technological change and international trade', in G. Dosi, C. Freeman, R. Nelson, G. Silverberg and L. Soete (eds), *Technical Change and Economic Theory*, London and New York: Pinter Publishers, pp. 401–31.

Dosi, G., C. Freeman and S. Fabian (1994), 'The process of economic development: introducing some stylized facts and theories on technologies, firms and institutions', *Industrial and Corporate Change*, **3**(1), 1–45.

Dosi, G., K. Pavitt and L. Soete (1990), *The Economics of Technical Change and International Trade*, New York: New York University Press.

Dosi, G., F. Malerba, O. Marsili and L. Orsenigo (1997), 'Industrial structure and dynamics: evidence, interpretations and puzzles', *Industrial and Corporate Change*, **6**(1), 3–24.

Dosi, G., C. Freeman, R. Nelson, G. Silverberg and L. Soete (eds) (1988), *Technical Change and Economic Theory*, London and New York: Pinter Publishers.

Douthwaite, B., J.D.H. Keatinge and J.R. Park (2001), 'Why promising technologies fail: the neglected role of user innovation during adoption', *Research Policy*, **30**, 819–36.

Downey, G. (2001), 'Virtual webs, physical technologies, and hidden workers: the spaces of labor in information internetworks', *Technology and Culture*, **42**, 209–35.

Duff, A.S. (2000), *Information Society Studies*, London: Routledge.

Dunford, M. and G. Kafkalas (1992), *Cities and Regions in the New Europe: The Global–Local Interplay and Spatial Development Strategies*, London: Belhaven Press.

Dutton, W.H. (ed.) (1996), *Information and Communication Technologies: Visions and Realities*, New York: Oxford University Press.

Dutton, W.H., J. Blumler and K. Kraemer (eds) (1987), *Wired Cities: Shaping the Future of Communications*, London: CASSELL Education.

Dutton, W.H., S. Gillett, L. McKnight and M. Peltu (2004), 'Bridging broadband Internet divides: reconfiguring access to enhance communication power', *Journal of Information Technology*, **19**, 28–38.

Dutton, W.H., J. Blumler, N. Garnham, R. Mansell, J. Cornford and M. Peltu (1994), *The Information Superhighway: Britain's Response*, Policy Research Paper, Uxbridge: PICT, Brunel University.

Dutton, W.H., J. Blumler, N. Garnham, R. Mansell, J. Cornford and M. Peltu (1996), 'The politics of information and communication policy', in W.H. Dutton (ed.), *The Information Superhighway, Information and Communication Technologies*, New York: Oxford University Press, pp. 387–405.

Dyker, D.A. (ed.) (1997), *The Technology of Transition: Science and Technology Policies for Transition Countries*, Budapest: Central European University Press.

Dyson, K.H.F. and P. Humphreys (1990), 'European Community in telecommunications policy', in K.H.F. Dyson and P. Humphreys (eds), *The Political Economy of Communications: International and European Dimensions*, London and New York: Routledge, pp. 229–43.

Economides, N. (1996), 'The economics of networks', *International Journal of Industrial Organisation*, **14**, 673–99.

Economist (1995), 'Survey of the Internet (1): The accidental superhighway – The explosive growth of the Internet is not a fad or a fluke, but the result of digital free market unleashed', 1 July.

Economist (1997), 'Survey on telecommunications: a connected world', 21 September.

Edquist, C. (ed.) (1997), *Systems of Innovation: Technologies, Institutions, and Organizations*, London and Washington: Pinter.

Edquist, C. and B. Johnson (1997), 'Institutions and organizations in systems of innovation', in C. Edquist (ed.) (1997), *Systems of Innovation: Technologies, Institutions, and Organizations*, London and Washington: Pinter, pp. 41–63.

Edquist, C. and M. McKelvey (eds) (2000), *Systems of Innovation: Growth, Competitiveness and Employment*, Cheltenham, UK and Northampton, MA, USA: Edward Elgar.

Enslow, P.H. (1972), 'Computer–communications networks and policy', in J. Fox (ed.), *Proceedings of the Symposium on Computer-communications Networks and Teletraffic*, New York: Polytechnic Press, 4–6 April.

Ernst, D. and B.-Å. Lundvall (1997), 'Information technology in the learning economy – challenges for developing countries', DRUID working paper no. 97–12, Aalborg University.

Ernst, D. and D. O'Connor (1989), *Technology and Global Competition: The Challenge for Newly Industrialising Economies*, Paris: OECD.

Ernst, D. and D. O'Connor (1992), *Competing in the Electronics Industry: The Experience of Newly Industrialising Economies*, Paris: OECD.

Esfahani, H. and M. Ramírez (2003), 'Institutions, infrastructure, and economic growth', *Journal of Development Economics*, **70**(2), 443–77.

ESPRIT (1997), 'The Future of the Internet – What Role for Europe? Interim Report of an Advisory Group Background' (http://www.cordis.lu/esprit/src/i2eurepo.htm).

European Commission (1993), *White Paper on Growth, Competitiveness and Employment: The Challenges and Ways Forward into the 21st Century*, COM (93) 700 final, 5 December, Brussels: EC.

European Commission (1994), *Europe and the Global Information Society: Recommendations to the European Council*, Brussels, 26 May.

European Commission (1996), *The Phare Programme Annual Report 1995*, Brussels, 23 July (com 360 final).

European Commission (1997), *Green Paper on the Convergence of the Telecommunications, Media and Information Technology Sectors, and the Implications for Regulation: Towards an Information Society Approach*, Brussels: EC.

European Commission (1998), *Internet Governance Reply of the European Community and Its Member States to the US Green Paper*, Brussels: EC.

European Communities (1997), *Eurostat Yearbook 1997*, Luxembourg: EC.

Fagerberg, J., B. Verspagen and N. Tunzelmann (eds) (1994), *The Dynamics of Technology, Trade and Growth*, Aldershot, UK and Brookfield, US: Edward Elgar.

Farmer, M.K. and M. Matthews (1990), 'Cultural difference and subjective rationality: where sociology connects with the economics of technological choice', Conference on 'Firm Strategy and Technical Change: Micro-economics or Microsociology?' Manchester.

Faulkner, W., J. Semker and L. Velho (1995), *Knowledge Frontiers: Public Sector Research and Industrial Innovation in Biotechnology, Engineering Ceramics, and Parallel Computing*, Oxford: Clarendon Press.

Federal Coordinating Council on Science, Engineering and Technology (FCCSET) (1983a) 'Supercomputer panel', Report to Recommended Government Actions to Provide Access to Supercomputers, Washington.

Federal Coordinating Council on Science, Engineering and Technology (FCCSET) (1983b), 'Supercomputer panel', Report to Recommended Government Actions to Retain US Leadership in Supercomputers, Washington.

Financial Times (1988), 'Technology: academics claim a first for European network', Della Bradshaw, 29 July.

Financial Times (1991), 'Survey of networking and open systems (5): protocol that should survive – the US initiative', Michael Dempsey, 22 October.

Financial Times (1992), 'Survey of computers and communications (14): not prepared to play second fiddle – profile of Cisco', Louise Kehoe, 13 October.

Fischer & Lorenz A/S (2000), *Internet and the Future Policy Framework for Telecommunications: A Report for the European Commission*, 31 January.

Fleck, J (1988a), 'Innofusion or diffusation? The nature of technological development in robotics', Edinburgh PICT working paper, no.4.

Fleck, J (1988b), 'The development of information-integration beyond CIM?', Edinburgh PICT working paper, no. 9.

Fleck, J., J. Webster and R. Williams (1990), 'The dynamics of IT implementation: a reassessment of paradigms and trajectories of development', *Futures*, **July/August**, 618–40.

Fleck, J., J. Webster and R. Williams (1993), 'Learning by trying: the implementation of configurational technology', *Research Policy*, **23**, 637–52.

Fleck, L. (1979), *Genesis and Development of a Scientific Fact*, T.J. Trenn and R.K. Merton (eds), (German edition published in 1935), Chicago and London: University of Chicago Press.

Flynn, R. and P. Preston (1999), 'The long-run diffusion and techno-economic performance of national telephone networks: a case study of Ireland, 1922–98', *Telecommunications Policy*, **23**(5), 437–57.

Foray, D. (1997), 'The dynamic implications of increasing returns: technological change and path dependent inefficiency', *International Journal of Industrial Organization*, **15**, 733–52.

Foray, D. and C. Freeman (eds) (1993), *Technology and the Wealth of Nations: the Dynamics of Constructed Advantage*, Paris: OECD.

Foucault, M. (1973), *The Order of Things: An Archaeology of the Human Sciences*, New York: Vintage Books.

Foucault M. (1980), *Power-Knowledge: Selected Interviews and Other Writings, 1972–1977*, ed. Colin Gordon, Brighton: Harvester.

Fox, J. (ed.) (1972), *Proceedings of the Symposium on Computer–Communications Networks and Teletraffic*, New York, 4–6 April, New York, London, Sydney and Toronto: John Wiley & Sons, Inc.

Fransman, M. (1998), 'Analysing the evolution of industry: the relevance of the telecommunications industry', Department of Economics and Institute for Japanese–European Technology Studies, University of Edinburgh.

Freedom House (1997), Freedom in the World country ratings, http://www.freedomhouse.org/ratings/allscore04.xls.

Freeman, C. (1982), *The Economics of Industrial Innovation*, 2nd edn, London: Pinter.

Freeman, C. (1988a), 'Japan: a new national system of innovation?', in G. Dosi, C. Freeman, R. Nelson, G. Silverberg and L. Soete (eds), *Technical Change and Economic Theory*, London and New York: Pinter Publishers, pp. 330–69.

Freeman, C. (1988b), 'Introduction', in G. Dosi, C. Freeman, R. Nelson, G.

Silverberg and L. Soete (eds), *Technical Change and Economic Theory*, London and New York: Pinter Publishers, pp. 1–8.

Freeman, C. (1992), 'From scientific and technical institutions in the national innovation', in B-Å. Lundvall (ed.), *National Systems of Innovation – Towards a Theory of Innovation and Interactive Learning*, London: Pinter Publishers 2nd edition, pp. 169–90.

Freeman, C. (1994a), 'Critical survey: the economics of technical change', *Cambridge Journal of Economics*, **18**, 463–514.

Freeman, C. (1994b), 'Technological revolutions and catching-up: ICT and NICs', in J. Fagerberg, B. Verspagen and N. Tunzelmann (eds) (1994), *The Dynamics of Technology, Trade and Growth*, Aldershot, UK and Brookfield, US: Edward Elgar, pp. 198–221.

Freeman, C. (1995a), 'History, co-evolution and economic growth', Merit University of Limburg, Maastricht, Netherlands and SPRU, University of Sussex, Falmer, Brighton, UK.

Freeman, C. (1995b), 'The "national system of innovation" in historical perspective', *Cambridge Journal of Economics*, **19**(1), 5–24.

Freeman, C. (2000), 'Social inequality, technology and economic growth', in S. Wyatt, F. Henwood, N. Miller and P. Senker, (eds), *Technology and Inequality: Questioning the Information Society*, London: Routledge, pp. 149–71.

Freeman, C. (2001), 'The learning economy and international inequality', in D. Archibugi and B-Å. Lundvall (eds), *The Globalizing Learning Economy*, New York: Oxford University Press, pp. 147–62.

Freeman, C. and F. Louçã (2001), *As Time Goes By: From the Industrial Revolutions to the Information Revolution*, Oxford: Oxford University Press.

Freeman, C. and B-Å Lundvall (eds) (1988), *Small Countries Facing the Technological Revolution*, London: Pinter.

Freeman, C. and C. Perez (1988), 'Structural crises of adjustment: business cycles and investment behaviour', in G. Dosi, C. Freeman, R. Nelson, G. Silverberg and L. Soete (eds), *Technical Change and Economic Theory*, London and New York: Pinter Publishers, pp. 38–66.

Freeman, C. and L. Soete (1990), 'Fast structural change and slow productivity change: some paradoxes in the economics of information technology', *Structural Change and Economic Dynamics*, **1**, 225–42.

Freeman, C. and L. Soete (1997), *The Economics of Industrial Innovation*, 3rd edn, London and Washington: Pinter.

Frieden, R. (1995), 'Contamination of the common carrier concept in telecommunications', *Telecommunications Policy*, **19** (9), 685–97.

Frieden, R. (1998), 'Falling through the cracks – international accounting rate reform at the ITU and WTO', *Telecommunications Policy*, **22**(11), 963–75

Friedmann, J. and G. Abonyi (1976), 'Social learning: a model for policy research', *Environment and Planning*, **8**, 927–40.

Froomkin, A.M. (2000), 'Wrong turn in Cyberspace: Using ICANN to route around the APA and the Constitution', 50 Duke L. J. 17.

FTS (2000), http://www.its.bldrdoc.gov/fs-1037/dir-017/_2407.htm.

Gabel, David (1995), 'Pricing voice telephony services: who is subsidizing whom?', *Telecommunications Policy*, **19**(6), August, 453–64.

Gabler, H.G. (1986), 'Packet switching in the Federal Republic of Germany (with a view to the situation in CEPT-countries', in L. Csaba, K. Tarnay and T. Szentivany (eds), *Computer Network Usage: Recent Experiences – Proceedings of the IFIP TC 6 Working Conference COMNET '85*, Budapest, Hungary, Amsterdam: North-Holland, pp. 201–14.

Gagliardi, D. (1986), 'ISDN: the concept, its origin & direction', presented at ISDN, Online Publication, Pinner, 1–9.

Gaines, B.R. (1998), 'The learning curves underlying convergence', *Technological Forecasting and Social Change*, **57**, 7–34.

Galbi D.A. (1998), 'Distinctive arrangements for international interconnection?', *Telecommunications Policy*, **22**(11), 945–51.

Galbraith, J. (1973), 'Power and the useful economist', *The American Economic Review*, **63**(1), 1–11.

Garcia-Murillo, M.A. and I. MacInnes (2001), 'FCC organizational structure and regulatory convergence', *Telecommunications Policy*, **25**(6), 431–52.

Garnham, N. and R. Mansell (1991), *Universal service and rate restructuring in Telecommunications*, OECD/ICCP no. 3, Paris: OECD.

Gasmi, F., J.-J. Laffont and W.W. Sharkey (2002), 'The natural monopoly test reconsidered: an engineering process-based approach to empirical analysis in telecommunications', *International Journal of Industrial Organization*, **20**, 435–59.

Gerich, E. (1991a), 'Expanding the Internet to a global environment but … how to get connected?', *Computer Networks and ISDN Systems*, **23**(1–3), (2nd Joint European Networking Conference, Blois, France, 13–16 May. Binst (eds)), 43–6.

Gerich, E.(1991b), 'Management and operation of the NSFNET backbone', *Computer Networks and ISDN Systems*, **23**(1–2), 69–72.

Gerla, M. (1985), 'Packet, circuit and virtual circuit switching', in W. Chou (ed.), *Computer Communications Vol. II Systems and Applications*, Englewood Cliffs: Prentice-Hall, pp. 222–67.

Geroski, P. (2000), 'Models of Technology Diffusion', *Research Policy*, **29** (2000), 603–25.

Giddens, A. (1971), *Capitalism and Modern Social Theory: an Analysis of the Writings of Marx, Durkheim and Max Webber*, New York: Cambridge University Press.

Giddens, A. (1990), *The Consequences of Modernity*, Cambridge: Polity Press.

Gilbert, P. (1996), 'The generation gap: Minitel in the face of the Internet', *Online Information 96 Proceedings*, 321–5.

Gladwyn, M. (1988), 'GOSIP – The UK Government OSI Profile', Network News, no. 26, p. 31.

Gold, B. (1981), 'Technological diffusion in industry: research needs and shortcomings', *The Journal of Industrial Economics*, **XXIX** (3), 247–69.

Gold, B. (1988), 'On the adoption of technological innovations in industry: superficial models and complex decision', *Omega*, **8**(5), 505–16.

Goldberg, V.P. (1976), 'Regulation and administered contracts', *The Bell Journal of Economics*, **7**(2), 426–48.

Gomulka, S. (1971), 'Inventive activity, diffusion, and the stages of economic growth', Institute of Economics, Aarhus.

Gomulka, S. (1990), *The Theory of Technological Change and Economic Growth*, London: Routledge.

Gong, J. and P. Srinagesh (1996), 'Network competition and industry structure', *Industrial and Corporate Change*, **5**(4), 1231–41.

Goode, B. (1997), 'Scanning the issue: special issue on global information infrastructure', *Proceedings of the IEEE*, **85**(12), 1883–6.

Goodman, S.E. (1982), 'U.S. computer export control policies: value conflict and policy choices', *Communications of the ACM*, **25**(9), 613–24.

Goodman, S.E., L.I. Press, S.R. Ruth and A.M. Rutkowski (1994), 'The global diffusion of the internet: patterns and problems', *Communications of ACM*, **37** (8), 27–31.

Gorman, S. and E. Malecki (2000), 'The networks of the Internet: an analysis of provider networks in the USA', *Telecommunications Policy*, **24**, 113–34.

Graham, S., J. Coford and S. Marvin (1996), 'The socio-economic benefits of a universal network: A demand-side view of universal service', *Telecommunications Policy*, **20**(1), 3–10.

Gramlich, E.M. (1994), 'Infrastructure investment: a review essay', *Journal of Economic Literature*, **XXXII**, 1176–96.

Granovetter, M. (1985), 'Economic action and social structure: the problem of embeddedness', *American Journal of Sociology*, **91**(3), 481–510.

Granstrand, O. (ed.) (1994), *Economics of Technology*, Amsterdam, London, New York and Tokyo: North-Holland.

Gray, H.M. (1951), 'The integration of the electric power industry', *The American Economic Review*, **41**(2), 538–49.

Greisen, F. (1990), 'EARN connections to East Europe and regulatory issues', *Computer Networks and ISDN Systems*, **19**, 177–80.

Greisen, F. (1992), 'The operational unit for research and academic networking in Europe', *Computer Networks and ISDN Systems*, **25**(4–5), 521–5.

Grieve, W.A. and S.L. Levin (1996), 'Common carriers, public utilities and competition', *Industrial and Corporate Change*, **5**(1), 993–1011.

Greenstein, S. and T. Khanna (1997), 'What does industry convergence mean?', in D.B. Yoffie (ed.), *Competing in the Age of Digital Convergence*, Boston: Harvard Business School Press, pp. 201–26.

Gregersen, B. and B. Johnson (1997), 'How do Innovations affect Economic Growth? – Some Different Approaches in Economics', IKE-Group, Department of Business Studies, Aalborg University, Aalborg, Denmark.

Griliches, Z. (1957), 'Hybrid corn: an exploration in the economics of technological change', *Econometrica*, October, 501–22.

Grossman,W. (2001), *From anarchy to power: the net comes of age*, New York and London: New York University Press.

Grundmann, R. (1994), 'Car traffic at crossroads: new technologies for cars, traffic systems, and their interlocking', in J. Summerton (ed.), *Changing Large Technical Systems*, Boulder, San Francisco and Oxford: Westview Press, pp. 265–89.

Gurugé, A. (1992), 'SNA – the next generation and peer-to-peer SNA', in G.R. McClain (ed.), *The Handbook of International Connectivity Standards*, New York: Van Nostrand Reinhold, pp. 23–44.

Gutstein, D. (1999), *E. con: How the Internet Undermines Democracy*, Toronto: Stoddart Publishing.

Haas, P.M. (1992), 'Introduction: epistemic communities and international policy coordination', *International Organization*, **46**(1), 1–36.

Hadden, S. (1994), 'Extending universal service through the NII, NITA, and 20/20 vision: the development of national information infrastructure', NITA Special Publication 94–28, 47–54.

Hägg, P. (1997), 'Theories on the economics of regulation: a survey of the literature from a European perspective', *European Journal of Law and Economics*, **4**, 337–70.

Hall, A.R., G.D. Rudebusch and D.W. Wilcox (1996), 'Judging instrument relevance in instrumental variables estimation', *International Economic Review*, **37**(2) (May), 283–98.

Hampton, M.P. (1996), 'Where currents meet: the offshore interface between corruption, offshore finance centres and economic development', *IDS bulletin*, **27**(2) (April), 78–87.

Hanna, N., K. Guy and E. Arnold (1995), *The Diffusion of Information Technology: Experience of Industrial Countries and Lessons for Developing Countries*, Washington, DC: The World Bank.

Harasim, L.M. (ed.) (1993), *Global Networks: Computers and International Communications*, Cambridge, MA and London: The MIT Press.

Harberg, A.C. (1954), 'Monopoly and resource allocation', *The American Economic Review*, **44**(2), 77–87.

Hård, M. (1993), 'Beyond harmony and consensus: a social conflict approach to technology', *Science, Technology, & Human Values*, **18**, 408–32.

Hård, M. (1994), 'Technology as practice: local and global closure processes in diesel-engine design', *Social Studies of Science*, **24**, 549–85.

Harding, R. (2001), 'Competition and collaboration in German technology transfer', *Industrial and Corporate Change*, **10**(2), 389–417.

Hargittai, E. (1999), 'Weaving the western web: explaining differences in Internet connectivity among OECD countries', *Telecommunications Policy*, **23**, 701–18.

Harris, R. (1998), 'The Internet as a GPT: factor market implications', in E. Helpman (ed.), *General Purpose Technologies and Economic Growth*, Cambridge, MA: MIT Press, pp. 145–66.

Harrod, R. (1939), 'An essay in dynamic theory', *Economic Journal*, **49**, 14–33.

Hart, J., R. Reed and F. Bar (1992), 'The building of the Internet: implications for the future of broadband networks', *Telecommunications Policy*, **16**(8), 666–89.

Hart, T. (1998), 'A dynamic universal service for a heterogeneous European Union', *Telecommunications Policy*, **22**(10), 839–52.

Hartle, D.G. (1983). 'The theory of "rent seeking": some reflections', *The Canadian Journal Of Economics*, **16**(4), 539–54.

Hartley, D. (1990), 'Keynote address: policy issues for academic and research networking', *Computer Networks and ISDN Systems*, **19**(3–5), 152–7.

Hauben, M. and R. Hauben (1997), *Netizens: on the History and Impact of Usenet and Internet*, Los Alamitos: IEEE Computer Society Press.

Hawkins, R.W. (1996), 'Standards for communication technologies: negotiating institutional biases in network design', in R. Mansell and R. Silverstone (eds), *Communication by Design: The Politics of Information and Communication Technologies*, Oxford: Oxford University, pp. 157–86.

Haywood, T. (1998) 'Global networks and the myth of equality: tricking down or trickling away?', in B. Loader (ed.), *Cyberspace divide: equality, agency and policy in the information society*, London: Routledge, pp. 19–34.

Heart, F.E. (1973), 'The ARPA Network', in R.L. Grimsdale and F.F. Kuo (eds), *Computer Communications Networks: Proceedings of the NATO Advanced Study Institute on Computer Communication Networks* (University of Sussex, United Kingdom), Leyden: Noordhoff International Publishing, pp. 19–34.

Helpman, E. (1998), *General Purpose Technologies and Economic Growth*, Cambridge: MIT Press.

Henderson, R. and K. Clark (1990), 'Architectural innovation: the reconfiguration of existing product technologies and the failure of established firms', *Administrative Science Quarterly*, **35**, 9–30.

Hills, J. (1989), 'Universal service – liberalization and privatization of tele-communications', *Telecommunications Policy*, **13**(2), 129–44.

Hills, J. (1993), 'Universal service and rate restructuring in telecommunications – OECD', *Telecommunications Policy*, **17**(6), 471–2.

Hirschman, A. (1958), *The Strategy of Economic Development*, New Haven and London: Yale University Press.

Hirschman, A. (1967), *Location of Industry and International Competitiveness*, London: Oxford University Press.

Hobday, M (1998), 'Product complexity, innovation and industrial organization', *Research Policy*, **2**, 689–710

Hodgson, G. (1988), *Economics and Institutions: A Manifesto for A Modern Institutional Economics*, Cambridge: Polity Press.

Hodgson, G. (1991), 'Evolution and intention in economic theory' in P. Saviotti and S. Metcalfe (eds), *Evolutionary Theories of Economic and Technological Change: Present Status and Future Prospects*, Chur, Reading, Paris, Philadelphia, Tokyo and Melbourne: Harwood Academic Publishers, pp. 108–27.

Hodgson, G. (1993), *Economics and Evolution: Bringing Life Back into Economics*, Cambridge: Polity Press.

Hodgson, G. and E. Screpanti, E. (eds) (1991), *Rethinking Economics: Markets, Technology and Economic Evolution*, Aldershot, UK and Brookfield, US: Edward Elgar Publishing Limited.

Hoff, J., I. Horrocks, and P. Tops (eds) (2000), *Democratic Governance and New Technology: Technologically Mediated Innovations in Political Practice in Western Europe*, London: Routledge.

Hoffman, E. and L. Jackson (1993), 'FYI on introducing the internet – a short bibliography of introductory internetworking readings', RFC 1463, May.

Hofstede, G. (1980), *Culture's Consequences: International Differences in Work-related Values*, Newbury Park: SAGE Publications.

Holton, R.J. (1992), *Economy and Society*, London: Routledge.

Holtz-Eakin, D. and A. Schwartz (1995), 'Infrastructure in a structural model of economic growth', *Regional Science and Urban Economics*, **25**(2), 131–51.

Holzner, B. (1968), *Reality Construction in Society*, Cambridge: Schenkman Publishing Company.

Houghton, J. (1999), 'Mapping information industries and markets', *Telecommunications Policy*, **23**, 689–99.

Howells, J. (1995), 'Going global: the use of ICT networks in research and development', *Research Policy*, **24**, 169–84.

Huber, P. (1987), *The Geodesic Network: 1987 Report on Competition in the Telephone Industry*, Washington, DC: Department of Justice.

Huber, P., M. Kellogg and J. Thorne (1992), *The Geodesic Network II: 1993*

Report on Competition in the Telephone Industry, Washington, DC: Department of Justice.

Hudson, H.E. and E.B. Parker (1990), 'Information gaps in rural America: telecommunications policies for rural development', *Telecommunications Policy*, **14**(3), June, 193–205.

Hughes, T. (1983), *Networks of Power: Electrification in Western Society, 1880–1930*, Baltimore and London: Johns Hopkins University Press.

Hughes, T. (1986), 'The seamless web: technology, science, etcetera, etcetera', *Social Studies of Science*, **16**, 281–92.

Hughes, T. (1987), 'The evolution of large technological systems', in W.E.Bijker, T.P. Hughes and T.J. Pinch (eds), *The Social Construction of Technological Systems: New Directions in the Sociology and History of Technology*, Cambridge: MIT Press, pp. 51–82.

Hughes, T. (1992), 'The dynamics of technological change: salients, critical problems, and industrial revolutions', in G. Dosi, R. Giannetti and P. Toninelli (eds), *Technology and Enterprise in a Historical Perspective*, Oxford: Clarendon Press, pp. 97–118.

Hughes, T. (1994), 'Beyond the economics of technology: summary remarks 2', in O. Granstrand (ed.), *Economics of Technology*, pp. 425–37.

Hughes, T. (1997), 'Comparing the development of electric power and computer network', draft of presentation, Abisko Conference 20–23 May.

Hughes, T. (1998), *Rescuing Prometheus*, New York: Vintage Books.

Hulsink,W. (1996), 'Do nations matter in a globalising industry? The restructuring of telecommunications governance regimes in France, the Netherlands and the United Kingdom (1980–1994)', Ph.D. thesis, University of Rotterdam.

Hummon, N.P. (1984), 'Organizational aspects of technological change', in R. Lauden (ed.), *The Nature of Technological Knowledge. Are Models of Scientific Change Relevant?*, Dordecht, Boston and Lancaster: D. Reidel Publishing Company, pp. 67–82.

Huntington, S.P. (1993), 'The clash of civilizations?', *Foreign Affairs*, **72** (3), 22–49.

Huston (1992), IEPG INET 92 Report (http://iepg.isc.org//docs/IEPG-inet92.html).

Internet Architecture Board (1993), 'Correspondence between the IAB and DISA on the use of DNS', RFC 1401, January.

Internet Software Consortium (1999), 'Host distribution by top-level domain name, network wizards', July (http://www.isc.org/ds/WWW-9902/dist-byname.txt).

Internet Software Consortium (2000a), 'Distribution by top-level domain name by host count January 2000' (http://www.isc.org/ds/WWW-200001/dist-bynum.html.).

Internet Software Consortium (2000b), 'Distribution of top-level domain names by host count July 2000' (http://www.isc.org/ds/WWW-200007/dist-bynum.html).

Internet Software Consortium (2001), 'Host distribution by top-level domain name'.

Internet Software Consortium (2004), 'Host distribution by top-level domain name'.

Ioannidis, D. (1994), 'The internationalization of telephone operators: survival in an integrating world', in E. Bohin and O. Granstrand (eds), *The Race to European Eminence: Who are the Coming Tele-service Multinationals?*, Amsterdam, London, New York and Tokyo: North-Holland, pp. 391–400.

ITU (1997a), *World Telecommunication Development Report 1996/1997: Trade in Telecommunications*, Geneva: ITU.

ITU (1997b), *Challenges to the Network: Telecoms and the Internet*, Geneva: ITU.

ITU (1999a), *Challenges to the Network: Internet for Development*, Geneva: ITU.

ITU (1999b), *World Telecommunication Development Report 1999: Mobile Cellular*, Geneva: ITU.

ITU (1999c), *Trends in Telecommunication Reform 1999: Convergence and Regulation*, Geneva: ITU.

ITU and TeleGography (1994), *Direction of Traffic*, Geneva: ITU and Washington, DC: TeleGeography.

ITU and TeleGography (1996), *Direction of Traffic, 1996*, Geneva: ITU and Washington, DC: TeleGeography.

Jacobson, C.D. and J.A. Tarr (1995), *Ownership and Financing of Infrastructure: Historical Perspectives*, policy research working paper 1466: background paper for World Development Report 1994, June 1995, The World Bank.

Jacot, J.-H. (1997), 'A general taxonomic approach to technology policy', in D.A. Dyker (ed.), *The Technology of Transition: Science and Technology Policies for Transition Countries*, Budapest: Central European University Press, pp. 20–27.

Jagger, B., R. Slack and R. Williams (2000), 'Europe experiments with multimedia: an overview of social experiments and trials', *The Information Society*, **16**, 277–301.

Jagger, N. and I. Miles (1991), 'New telematic services in Europe', in C. Freeman. M. Sharp and W. Walker (eds), *Technology and the Future of Europe*, London: Pinter.

Jardins, R. (1986), 'Towards the information society: world cooperation on open system standardization', in L. Csaba, K. Tarnay and T. Stentivany (eds), *Computer Network Usage: Recent Experiences (Proceedings of the IFIP TC 6 Working Conference COMNET '85)*, Budapest, Hungary, Amsterdam: Elsevier Science Publishers B.V, pp. 15–17.

Jasanoff, S. (ed.) (1997), *Comparative Science and Technology Policy*, Cheltenham, IK and Lyme, USA: Edward Elgar.

Jasanoff, S., G. Markle, J. Petersen and T. Pinch (eds) (1995), *Handbook of Science and Technology Studies*, Thousand Oaks, London and New Delhi: Sage.

Jennings, D. (1990), 'The EARN OSI programme', *Computer Networks and ISDN Systems*, **19**(3–5), 234–9.

Jensen, M. (1999), *Africa Internet Status*, July (http://www3.wn.apc.org/africa/afstat.htm), accessed February 2001.

Joerges, B. (1988), 'Large technical systems: concepts and issues', in R. Mayntz, R. and T. Hughes (eds) *The Development of Large Technical Systems*, Boulder: Westview Press, pp. 9–36.

Johnson, B. (1992), 'Institutional learning', in B.-Å. Lundvall (ed.), *National Systems of Innovation – Towards a Theory of Innovation and Interactive Learning*, London: Pinter Publishers, pp. 23–44.

Johnson, D. (1992), 'NOC internal integrated trouble ticket system functional specification wishlist ("NOC TT REQUIREMENTS")', RFC 1297, January.

Johnston, J. (1984), *Econometric Methods*, 3rd edn, New York: The McGraw-Hill Companies.

Johnston, J. and J. DiNardo (1997), *Econometric Methods*, 4th edn, New York: The McGraw-Hill Companies.

Jolliffe, I.T. (1986), *Principal Component Analysis*, New York, Berlin, Heidelberg and Tokyo: Springer-Verlag.

Jones, D.N. (1988), 'Regulatory concepts, propositions and doctrines: causalities and survivors', *Journal of Economic Issues*, **XXII**(4), 1089–1108.

Jones, D.N. and P.C. Mann (2001), 'The fairness criterion in public regulation: does fairness still matter?', *Journal of Economic Issues*, **XXXV**(1), 153–72.

Joskow, P.L. (1989), 'Regulatory failure, regulatory reform, and structural change in the electrical power industry', *Brookings Papers on Economic Activity, Microeconomics*, **1989**, 125–208.

Jouanigot, J-M., O.H. Martin and J. Yu (1993), 'IP traffic measurement and analysis at CERN', Presented at *INET '93* Conference, San Francisco, CA, 17–20 August.

Jouët, J., P. Flichy and P. Beaud (eds) (1991), *European telematics: the emerging economy of words*, Amsterdam: Elsevier Science Publishers B.V.

Kahin, B. (1990), 'Commercialization of the Internet summary report', RFC 1192, 01 Nov 1990.

Kahin, B. (1992), 'Overview. Understanding the NREN', in B. Kahin (ed.), *Building Information Infrastructure*, NY: McGraw-Hill Primis.

Kahin, B. (1995), 'The Internet and the national information infrastructure', in B. Kahin and J. Keller (eds), *Public Access to the Internet*, Cambridge and London: MIT Press, pp. 3–23.

Kahin, B. and J. Keller (eds) (1995), *Public Access to the Internet*, Cambridge and London: MIT Press.

Kahin, B. and J. Keller (eds) (1997), *Coordinating the Internet*, Cambridge: MIT Press.

Kahin, B. and C. Nesson (eds) (1997), *Borders in Cyberspace: Information Policy and the Global Information Infrastructure*, Cambridge: MIT Press.

Kahn, A. (1970a), *The Economics of Regulation: Principles and Institutions, vol. I: Economic Principles*, New York, London, Sydney and Toronto: John Wiley & Sons.

Kahn, A. (1970b), *The Economics of Regulation: Principles and Institutions, vol. II: Institutional Issues*, New York, London, Sydney and Toronto: John Wiley & Sons.

Kahn, R. (1978), 'Scanning the issue', *Proceedings of the IEEE*, **66**(11), 1303–5.

Kahn, R. (1994), 'Viewpoint: the role of government in the evolution of the Internet', *Communications of ACM*, **37**(8), 15–19.

Kaldor, N. (1957), 'A model of economic growth', *Economic Journal*, **67**, 591–624.

Kalin, T. (1997), 'Evaluating Phare 1994 R&D Networking', Dante In Print, no. 27.

Kapoor, A. (1992), *SNA: Architecture, Protocols and Implementation*, New York: McGraw-Hill.

Karshenas, M. and P. Stoneman (1992), 'A flexible model for technological diffusion incorporating economic factors with an application to the spread of colour television ownership in the UK', *Journal of Forecasting*, **11**, 577–601.

Karshenas, M. and P. Stoneman (1995), 'Technological diffusion', in P. Stoneman (ed.), *Handbook of the Economics of Innovation and Technological Change*, Oxford: Blackwell Publishers, pp. 265–91.

Katz, J.E. and P. Aspden P. (1998), 'Internet dropouts in the USA – the invisible group', *Telecommunications Policy*, **22**(4–5), pp. 327–39.

Katz, M. (1996), 'Remarks on the economic implications of convergence', *Industrial and Corporate Change*, **5**(4), 1079–95.

Katz, M. (1997), 'Experience in deregulation: telecommunications – ongoing reform of U.S. telecommunications policy', *European Economics Review*, **41**, 681–90.

Katz, M. and C. Shapiro (1985), 'Network externalities, competition, and compatibility', *The American Economic Review*, **75**(3), 424–40.

Katz, M. and C. Shapiro (1986), 'Technology adoption in the presence of network externalities', *Journal of Political Economy*, **94**, 822–41.

Katz, M. and C. Shapiro (1994), 'Systems competition and network effects', *The Journal of Economic Perspectives*, **8**(2), 93–115.

Kavassalis, P. and W. Lehr (1998), 'Forces for integration and disintegration in the Internet', *Communications & Strategies*, **30**(2nd quarter), 135–51.

Kavassalis, P. and R. Solomon (1997), 'Mr Schumpeter on the telephone: patterns of technical change in the telecommunications industry before and after the Internet', *Communications & Strategies*, **26**(2nd quarter), 371–408.

Kearney, J.D. and T.W. Merrill (1998). 'The great transformation of regulated industries law', *Columbia Law Review*, **98**(6), 1323–1409.

Kedzie, C. (1995), 'Democracy and network interconnectivity', (http://www.isoc.org/HMP/PAPER/134/html/paper.html), accessed September 2000.

Keesing R.M. (1981), *Cultural Anthropology: A Contemporary Perspective*, 2nd edn New York: Holt, Rinehart & Winston.

Kehoe, L. (1992), 'Survey of computers and communications (14): Not prepared to play second fiddle – Profile of Cisco', *Financial Times*, 13 October.

Keller, J. (1995), 'Public access issues: an introduction', in B. Kahin and J. Keller (eds), *Public Access to the Internet*, Cambridge and London: MIT Press, pp. 34–45.

Kelly, P. (1978), 'Public packet switched data networks, international plans and standards', *Proceedings of the IEEE*, **66**(11), 1527–39.

Kennard, W. (1999), *Connecting the Globe: A Regulator's Guide to Building A Global Information Community*, Washington, DC: Federal Communications Commission.

Kettl, D. (1993), *Sharing Power: Public Governance and Private Markets*, Washington, DC: Brookings Institution.

Kiessling, T. and Y. Blondeel (1998), 'The EU regulatory framework in telecommunications – a critical analysis', *Telecommunications Policy*, **22**(7), 571–92.

Kirstein, P. (1973), 'A survey of present and planned general purpose European data and computer networks', in R.L. Grimsdale and F.F. Kuo (eds), *Computer Communications Networks: Proceedings of the NATO Advanced Study Institute on Computer Communication Networks* (Sussex, United Kingdom), Amsterdam: Noordhoff International Publishing, pp. 257–76.

Kirstein, P. (1999), 'Early experiences with the Arpanet and Internet in the United Kingdom', *IEEE Annals of the History of Computing*, **21**(1), 38–44.

Kleinrock, L. (1978), 'Principles and lessons in packet communications', *Proceedings of the IEEE*, **66**(11), 1320–29.

Kleinrock, L. (1992), 'Technology issues in the design of NREN', in B. Kahin (ed.), *Building Information Infrastructure*, New York: McGraw-Hill Primis, pp. 174–98.

Klepper, S. (1997), 'Industry Life Cycles', *Industrial and Corporate Change*, **6**(1), 145–81.

Klepper, S. and E. Graddy (1990), 'The evolution of new industries and the determinants of market structure', *Rand Journal of Economics*, **21**(1), 27–44.

Kline, S.J. and N. Rosenberg (1986), 'An overview of innovation', in National Academy of Engineering, *The Positive Sum Strategy: Harnessing Technology for Economic Growth*, Washington, DC: The National Academy Press.

Klingenstein, K. (1993), 'A coming of age: the design of the low-end Internet', in B. Kahin (ed.), *Building Information Infrastructure: Issues in the Development of the National Research and Education Network*, New York: McGraw-Hill, pp. 119–217.

Krasner, S.D. (ed.) (1983), *International Regimes*, Ithaca, NY: Cornell University Press.

Krol, E. and E. Hoffman (1993), 'FYI on "What is the Internet?"', RFC 1462, May.

Krueger, A.O. (1974), 'The political economy of the rent-seeking society', *The American Economic Review*, **64**(3), 291–303.

Kuhn, T. (1962), *The Structure of Science Revolutions*, Chicago: University of Chicago Press.

Kunze, H. (1986), 'The BILDSCHIRMTEXT service in the Federal Republic of Germany', in L. Csaba, K. Tarnay and T. Szentivany (eds), *Computer Network Usage: Recent Experiences-Proceedings of the IFIP TC 6 Working Conference COMNET '85*, Budapest, Hungary, Amsterdam: North-Holland, pp. 275–86.

Kurisaki, Y. (1997), 'The globalism of public telecommunications operators – towards a new framework of telecommunications policy', in E.M. Noam and A.J. Wolfson (eds), *Globalism and Localism in telecommunications*, Amsterdam: Elsevier Science B.V. pp. 361–74.

Laffont, J-J. (1989), *Fundamentals of Public Economics*, trans. J.P. Bonin and H. Bonin, revised English language edition, Cambridge and London: MIT Press.

Laffont, J-J. and J. Tirole (2000), *Competition in Telecommunications*, Cambridge and London: MIT Press.

Laffont, J-J., P. Rey, and J. Tirole (1997), 'Competition between telecommunications operators', *European Economic Review*, **41**(3–5), 701–11.

Lakoff, S.A. (1979), 'Scientists, technologists and political power', in I. Spiegel-Rösing and D. Price (eds) *Science, Technology and Society: A Cross-Disciplinary Perspective*, London and Beverly Hills: SAGE Publications, pp. 355–92.

Langdale, J. (1989), 'The geography of international business telecommunications: the role of leased networks', *Annals of the Association of American Geographers*, **79**(4), 501–22.

Langlois, R.N. and D.C. Mowery, (1996), 'The federal government of the U.S. software industry', in D.C. Mowey (ed.), *The International Computer Software Industry: A Comparative Study of Industry Evolution and Structure*, New York and Oxford: Oxford University Press, pp. 53–85.

LaPonce, J.A. (1987), *Languages and Their Territories*. Toronto: University of Toronto Press.

LaPorte, T. (ed.) (1991), *Social Responses to Large Technical Systems: Control or Anticipation*, Dordrecht: Kluwer.

Latham, D. (1988), 'A DoD statement on open systems interconnection protocols', RFC 1039, January.

Latour, B. (1999), 'On recalling ANT', in J. Law and J. Hassard (eds), *Actor Network Theory and After*, Oxford and Malden: Blackwell Publishers, pp. 5–25.

Lauden, R. (ed.) (1984), *The Nature of Technological Knowledge: Are Models of Scientific Change Relevant?*, Dordrecht, Boston, Lancaster: D. Reidel Publishing Company, pp. 83–104.

Law, J. (1987), 'Technology and heterogeneous engineering: the case of Portuguese expansion', in W.E. Bijker, T.P. Hughes and T.J. Pinch (eds), *The Social Construction of Technological Systems: New Direction in the Sociology and History of Technology*, Cambridge and London: MIT Press, pp. 111–34.

Law, J. (ed.) (1999), *After ANT: Complexity, Naming and Topology*, Oxford and Malden: Blackwell Publishers.

Law, J. and M. Callon (1992), 'The life and death of aircraft: a network analysis of technical change', in W.E. Bijker and J. Law (eds,), *Shaping Technology/Building Society: Studies in Sociotechnical Change*, Cambridge and London: MIT Press, pp. 21–52.

Layton, E. (1974), 'Technology as knowledge', *Technology and Culture*, **15**, 31–41.

Lazear, W. (1987), 'MILNET name domain transition', RFC 1031, November.

Lazonick, W. (1993), 'Industry clusters versus global webs: organizational capabilities in the American economy', *Industrial and Corporate Change*, **2**(1), 1–24.

Lee, K. (1996), *Global telecommunications regulation: A political economy perspective*, London: Pinter.

Lehr, W.H. and T. Kiessing (1998), 'Telecommunication regulation in the United States and Europe: the case for centralized authority', paper presented to the Twenty-sixth Telecommunications Policy Research Conference, Alexandria, VA, 3–5 October.

Lehr, W.H and M. Weiss (1996), 'The political economy of congestion charges and settlements in packet networks', *Telecommunications Policy*, **20**(3), 219–31.

Leiner, B. (1987), 'Network requirements for scientific research', Network Working Group RFC 1017, August.

Leiner, B. (1994), 'Internet technology', *Communications of the ACM*, **37**(8), 2.

Leiner, B., V.G. Cerf, D.D. Clark, R.E. Kahn, L. Kleinrock, D.C. Lynch, J. Postel, L.G. Roberts and S. Wolff (2000), 'A brief history of the internet', ISOC (http://www.isoc.org/internet/history/brief.html).

Leoussi, A. (2000), 'IT in western culture: a new technology with ancient roots', *Knowledge, Technology, & Policy*, **13**(2), 14–29.

Levi-Faur, D. (1998), 'The competition state as neomercantilist state: understanding the restructuring of national and global telecommunications', *Journal of Socio-Economics*, **27**(6), 665–86.

Levy, B. and P. Spiller (1994), 'The institutional foundations of regulatory commitment: a comparative analysis of telecommunications regulation', *Journal of Law, Economics & Organization*, **10**(2), 201–45.

Levy, B. and P. Spiller (1996), *Regulations, Institutions and Commitment: Comparative Studies of Telecommunications*, New York: Cambridge University Press.

Leydesdorff, L. and P. Besselaar (eds) (1994), *Evolutionary Economics and Chaos Theory: New Directions in Technology Studies*, London: Pinter Publishers.

Lindblom, C.E. (1990), 'Knowledge and social society', *Inquiry and Change: The Troubled Attempt to Understand and Shape Society*, New Haven: Yale University Press, pp. 1–14.

Lipatito, K. (1994), 'Component innovation: the case of automatic telephone switching', *Industrial and Corporate Change*, **3**, 359–78.

Lissoni, F. and J.S. Metcalfe (1994), 'Diffusion of innovation ancient and modern: a review of the main themes', in M. Dodgson and R. Rothwell (eds), *The Handbook of Industrial Innovation*, Aldershot, UK and Brookfield, US: Edward Elgar, pp. 101–41.

List, F. (1841), *The National System of Political Economy*, English edn, London: Longman.

Loader, B. (ed.) (1997), *The Governance of Cyberspace: Politics, Technology and Global Restructuring*, London: Routledge.

Loader, B. (ed.) (1998), *Cyberspace divide: equality, agency and policy in the information society*, London: Routledge.

Lopez-de-Sianes, F. and A.Vishny (1997), 'Privatization in the United States', *Rand Journal of Economics*, **28**(3), 447–71.

Lottor, M. (1992), 'Internet Growth (1981–1991)', RFC 1296, January.

Lucas, R.E. (1988), 'On the mechanics of economic development', *Journal of Monetary Economics*, **22**: 3.

Lucker, M. (1996), '2NSF's new program for high-performance Internet connections', *Communications of the ACM*, **39**(10), 27–8.

Lundstedt, S.B. (1990), *Telecommunications, values, and the public interest*, Norwood, NJ: Ablex Publishing Co.

Lundvall, B-Å. (1988), 'Innovation as an interactive process: from user–producer interaction to the national system of innovation', in G. Dosi, C. Freeman, R. Nelson, G. Silverberg and L. Soete (eds), *Technical Change and Economic Theory*, London and New York: Pinter Publishers, pp. 349–69.

Lundvall, B-Å.(ed.) (1992), *National Systems of Innovation: Towards a Theory of Innovation and Interactive Learning*, London: Pinter Publishers.

Lundvall, B-Å. and B. Johnson (1994), 'The learning economy', *Journal of Industry Studies*, **1**(2), 23–42.

MacKenzie, D. (1990), 'Economic and sociological explanation of technical change', conference on firm strategy and technical change: Micro economics or micro sociology?, Manchester, 27–8 September.

MacKenzie, D. (1996), *Knowing Machines: Essay on Technical Change*, Cambridge and London: MIT Press.

MacKenzie, D. and J. Wajcman (eds) (1999), *The Social Shaping of Technology*, 2nd edn, Buckingham and Philadelphia: Open University Press.

Mackie-Mason, J. and H. Varian (1994), 'Economic FAQs about the Internet', *Journal of Economic Perspectives*, **8**(3), 75–96.

Mackie-Mason, J. and H. Varian (1995a), 'Some FAQs about usage-based pricing', *Computer Networks & ISDN Systems*, **28**(1,2), 257–66.

Mackie-Mason, J. and H. Varian (1995b), 'Pricing the Internet', in B. Kahin and J. Keller (eds), *Public Access to The Internet*, Cambridge: MIT Press, pp. 269–314.

Mackie-Mason, J. and H. Varian (1996), 'Some economics of the Internet', in W. Sichel and D. Alexander (eds), *Networks, Infrastructure, and the New Task for Regulation*, Ann Arbor: University of Michigan Press, pp. 107–36.

Maddala, G.S. and P.T. Knight (1967), 'International diffusion of technical change: a case study of the oxygen steel-making process', *The Economic Journal*, **77**, 531–58.

Madden, G., S.J. Savage, G. Coble-Neal and P. Bloxham (2000), 'Advanced communications policy and adoption in rural Western Australia', *Telecommunications Policy*, **24**(4), 291–304.

Madeuf, B. (1983), 'International technology transfers and international technology payments: definitions, measurement and firms' behaviour', *Research Policy*, **13**, 125–40.

Maher E.M. (1999), 'Access costs and entry in the local telecommunications network: a case for de-averaged rates', *International Journal of Industrial Organization*, **17**, 593–609.

Makarewicz, T.J. (1991), 'The effectiveness of low-income telephone assistance programs – Southwestern Bell's experience', *Telecommunications Policy*, **15**(3), 223–40.

Malerba, F., S. Torrisi and Nick von Tunzelmann (1991), 'Electronic computers', in C. Freeman, M. Sharp and W. Walker (eds), *Technology and the Future of Europe*, London: Pinter, pp. 95–116.

Malerbra, F. and S. Torrisi (1996), 'The dynamics of market structure and innovation in the Western European software industry', in D.C. Mowery (ed.), *The International Computer Software Industry: A Comparative Study of Industry Evolution and Structure*, New York and Oxford: Oxford University Press, pp. 165–96.

Malkin, G. (1994), 'The Tao of IETF – a guide for new attendees of the Internet engineering task force', RFC 1718, November.

Malkin, G. and A. Marine (1991a), 'FYI on questions and answers: answers to commonly asked "new Internet user" questions', RFC 1206, Feb-01-1991.

Malkin, G. and A. Marine (1991b), 'FYI on questions and answers: answers to commonly asked "experienced Internet user" questions', RFC 1207, Feb-01-1991.

Mandelbaum, R. and P. Mandelbaum (1992), 'The strategic future of mid-level networks', in B. Kahin (ed.), *Building Information Infrastructure: Issues in the development of the National Research and Education Network*, New York: McGraw-Hill, pp. 59–118.

Männistö, L., T. Kelly and B. Petrazzini (1998), 'Internet and the global information infrastructure in Africa', *From TamTam to Internet*, May, Geneva: ITU.

Mansell, R. (1993), *The New Telecommunications: A Political Economy of Network Evolution*, London: Sage.

Mansell, R. (ed.) (1994), *The Management of Information and Communication Technologies: Emerging Patterns of Control*, London: Aslib.

Mansell, R. (1996), 'Communications by Design?' in R. Mansell and R. Silverstone (eds), *Communications by Design: The Politics of Information and Communication Technologies*, New York: Oxford University Press, pp. 15–43.

Mansell, R. and W. Steinmueller (2000), *Mobilizing the Information Society: Strategies for Growth and Opportunity*, New York: Oxford University Press.

Mansell, R. and U. Wehn, U. (eds) (1998), *Knowledge Societies: Information Technology for Sustainable Development*, a report for and on behalf of the United Nations, Oxford: Oxford University Press.

Mansell, R., D. Neice and E. Steinmueller (2000), 'Universal access policies for knowledge-intensive societies', in B. Cammaerts and J.C. Burgelman (eds), *Beyond Competition: Broadening the Scope of Telecommunications Policy*, Brussels: VUB University Press, pp. 97–110.

Mansfield, E. (1961), 'Technical change and the rate of imitation', *Econometrica*, **29**, 741–66.

Mansfield, E. (1986), 'Technological change and the industrial diffusion of technology: a survey of findings', in D. McFetridge (ed.), *Technological Change in Canadian Industry*, Toronto: University of Toronto Press, pp. 77–99.

Mansfield, E. (1989), 'The diffusion of industrial robots in Japan and in the United States', *Research Policy*, **18**, 183–92.

Marceau, J. (1994,) 'Clusters, chains and complexes: three approaches to innovation with a public policy perspective', in M. Dodgson and R. Rothwell (eds), *The Handbook of Industrial Innovation*, Aldershot, UK and Brookfield, US: Edward Elgar, pp. 3–12.

Martenson, G. (1998), 'The impending dismantling of European Union telecommunications regulation', *Telecommunications Policy*, **22**(9), 729–38.

Marshall, A. (1920), *Principles of Economics: An Introductory Volume*, London: Macmillan. 8th edn of Marshall (1890a).

Mathison, S. (1978), 'Commercial, legal, and international aspects of packet communications', *Proceedings of the IEEE*, **66**(11), 1527–39.

Mayntz, R. and T. Hughes (eds) (1988), *The Development of Large Technical Systems*, Boulder: Westview Press.

Mayntz, R. and V. Schneider (1988),'The dynamics of system development in a comparative perspective: interactive videotex in Germany, France and Britain', in R. Mayntz and T. Hughes (eds), *The Development of Large Technical Systems*, Boulder: Westview Press, pp. 263–98.

McCormick, R.E., W.F. Shughart II and R.D. Tollison (1984), 'The disinterest in deregulation', *American Economic Review*, **74**(5), 1075–9.

McClure, C., A. Bishop, P. Doty and H. Rosenbaum (1991), *The National Research and Educational Network (NREN): Research and Policy Perspectives*, Norwood: Ablex Publishing Corporation.

McKelvey, M. (1997), 'How do national systems of innovation differ?: A critical analysis of Porter, Freeman, Lundvall and Nelson', in G.M. Hodgson and E. Screpanti (eds), *Rethinking Economics: Markets, Technology and Economic Evolution*, Aldershot, UK and Brookfield, US: Edward Elgar Publishing Limited, pp. 117–37.

McKnight, L.W. (1993), 'European and Japanese research networks; cooperating to compete', in B. Kahin (ed.), *Building Information Infrastructure: Issues in the Development of the National Research and Education Network*, New York: McGraw-Hill, pp. 46–58.

McKnight, L.W. and J.P. Bailey (eds) (1997), *Internet Economics*, Cambridge, MA: MIT Press.

McKnight L.W. and J. Boroumand (2000), 'Pricing Internet services: after flat rate', *Telecommunications Policy*, **24**(6–7), 565–90

McKnight, L.W., P.I.M. Vaaler and R.L. Katz (eds) (2001), *Creative Destruction: Business Survival Strategies in the Global Internet Economy*, Cambridge and London: MIT Press.

Melody, W. (1985), 'The information society: implications for economic institutions and market theory', *Journal of Economic Issues*, **XIX**(2), 523–39.

Melody, W. (1996), 'Toward a framework for designing information society policies', *Telecommunication Policy*, **20**(4), 243–59.

Melody, W. (ed.) (1997), *Telecom Reform: Principles, Policies and Regulatory Practices*, Lyngby: Technical University of Denmark, pp. 13–27.

Melody, W (1999), 'Telecom reform: progress and prospects', *Telecommunications Policy*, **23**(1), 7–34.

Merton, R.K. (1968), 'The Matthew effect in science', *Science*, **159**(810), 56–63.

Mészáros, I. (1986), *Philosophy, Ideology and Social Science: Essays in Negation and Affirmation*, Brighton: Harvester.

Metcalfe, J.S. (1981), 'Impulse and diffusion in the study of technical change', *Future*, **13**(5), 347–59.

Metcalfe, J.S.(1988), 'The diffusion of innovations: an interpretative survey', in G. Dosi, C. Freeman, R. Nelson, G. Silverberg and L. Soete (eds), *Technical Change and Economic Theory*, London and New York: Pinter Publishers, pp. 506–89.

Metcalfe, J.S. (1995), 'The economic foundations of technology policy: equilibrium and evolutionary perspectives', in P. Stoneman (ed.), *Handbook of the Economics of Innovation and Technological Change*, Oxford: Blackwell Publishers.

Metcalfe, R.M. and D.R. Boggs (1983), 'Ethernet: distributed packet switching for local computer networks', *Communications of the ACM*, **19**(7), 395–403.

Michie, J. (1997), 'Network externalities – the economics of universal access', *Utilities Policy*, **6**(4), 317–24.

Miles, I. (1996), 'The information society: competing perspectives on the social and economic implications of information and communication technologies', in W. Dutton (ed.), *Information and Communication Technologies: Vision and Realities*, New York: Oxford University Press, pp. 37–52.

Miller, D. and D. Slater (2000), *The Internet: an ethnographic approach*, Oxford: Berg.

Miller, E.S. (1995), 'Is the public utility concept obsolete?' *Land Economics*, **71**(3), 273–85.

Miller, J. (ed.) (1986), *Telecommunications and Equity: Policy Research Issues*, Proceedings of the Thirteenth Annual Telecommunications Policy Research Conference Airlie House, Airlie, Virginia, USA, 21–4 April 1985, Amsterdam, New York, Oxford and Tokyo: North-Holland.

Miller, R., M. Hobday, T. Lerpux-Demers and X. Olleros (1995), 'Innovation in complex systems industries: the case of flight simulation', *Industrial and Corporate Change*, **4**(2), 363–400.

Milne, C. (1998), 'Stages of universal service policy', *Telecommunications Policy* **22**(9), 775–780.

Minoli, D. (1991), *Telecommunications Technology Handbook*, Boston: Artech House.

Misa, T.J. (1988), 'How machines make history, and how historians (and others) help them to do so', *Science, Technology, & Human Values*, **13**, 308–31.

Misa, T.J. (1992a), 'Theories of technological change: parameters and purposes', *Science, Technology, & Human Values*, **17**(1), 3–12.

Misa, T.J (1992b), 'Controversy and closure in technological change: constructing "Steel"', in W.E. Bijker and J. Law (eds), *Shaping Technology/ Building Society: Studies in Sociotechnical Change*, Cambridge and London: MIT Press, pp. 109–39.

Misa, T.J (1994), 'Retrieving sociotechnical change from technological determinism', in M.R. Smith and L. Marx (eds), *Does Technology Drive History?: The Dilemma of Technological Determinism*, Cambridge and London: MIT Press, pp. 115–41.

Mischa, S. (1977), *Computer-communication Design and Analysis*, Englewood Cliffs, NJ: Prentice-Hall.

Mockapertris, P. (1983), 'Domain names – concepts and facilities', RFC 882, November.

Mosher, R. (1992), 'Digital's networking standard strategy – DECnet, OSI and TCP/IP', in G.R. McClain (ed.), *The Handbook of International Connectivity Standards*, New York: Van Nostrand Reinhold, pp. 45–71.

Moss, M. and A. Townsend (2000), 'The Internet backbone and the American metropolis', *The Information Society*, **16**, 35–47.

Mowery, D.C. (ed.) (1996), *The International Software Industry*, New York and Oxford: Oxford University Press.

Mowlana, H. (1996), *Global Communication in Transition: The End of Diversity?*, Thousands Oak, London, New Delhi: Sage Publications.

Mueller, M. (1993), 'Universal service in telephone history: a reconstruction', *Telecommunications Policy*, **17**(5), 352–69.

Mueller, M. (1999), 'Universal service policies as wealth redistribution', *Government Information Quarterly*, **16**(4), 353–8.

Myrdal, G. (1957), *Economic Theory and Underdeveloped Regions*, London: Duckworth.

Mytelka, L. (2000), 'Local system of innovation in a globalized world economy', *Industry and Innovation*, **7**(1), 15–32.

Nadreau, J.R. (1997), 'NATO's contribution to computer networking in Central and Eastern Europe and in former Soviet Union', Proceedings JENC8, 521-1–521-6.

National Communications System Technology & Standard Division (1996), 'Telecommunications: Glossary of Telecommunication Terms', FED-STD-1037C, General Service Administration Information Technology Service.

National Research Council (1985), Executive Summary of the NRC Report on Transport Protocols for Department of Defense Data Networks, Request for Comments, February, p. 939.

National Research Council of the National Academy of Sciences (1988), *The National Challenge in Computer Science and Technology*, Washington, DC: National Academic Press.

Naughton, J. (1999), *A Brief History of the Future: the Origins of the Internet*, London: Weidenfeld & Nicolson.

NCA (2000), *Informatization White Paper*, Seoul: NCA.

Neggers, K. (1991), 'European Engineering Planning Group (EEPG) – summary report', *Computer Networks and ISDN Systems*, **23**(1–2), 63–8.

Nelkin, D. (1979a), 'Technology and public policy', in I. Spiegel-Rösing and D. Price (eds), *Science, Technology and Society*, London and Beverly Hills: Sage Publications, pp. 393–442.

Nelkin, D. (1979b), *Controversy: Politics of Technical Change*, Beverly Hills and London: Sage Publications.

Nelkin, D. (1995), 'Science controversies: the dynamics of public disputes in the United States', in S. Jasanoff, G.E. Markle, J.C. Peterson and T. Pinch (eds), *Handbook of Science and Technology Studies*, Thousand Oaks, California and London: Sage Publications, pp. 444–56.

Nelson, R. (1988), 'Institutions supporting technical change in the United States', in G. Dosi, C. Freeman, R. Nelson, G. Silverberg and L. Soete (eds), *Technical Change and Economic Theory*, London and New York: Pinter Publishers, pp. 312–29.

Nelson, R. (1992), *The Co-Evolution of Technologies and Institutions*, New York: Columbia University.

Nelson, R. (ed.) (1993), *National Systems of Innovation: Case Studies*, Oxford: Oxford University Press.

Nelson, R. and S. Winter (1974), 'Neoclassical vs. evolutionary theories of economic growth: critique and prospects', *Economic Journal*, 886–905.

Nelson, R. and S. Winter (1977), 'In search of a useful theory of innovation', *Research Policy*, **6**, 36–76.

Nett, L. (1998), 'Auctions: An alternative approach to allocate universal service obligations', *Telecommunications Policy*, **22**(8), September, 661–9.

Network Wizards (1995a), 'Host distribution by top-level domain name, network wizards', January (http://www.isc.org/ds/WWW-9501/dist-byname. html), accessed November 1998.

Network Wizards (1995b), 'Host distribution by top-level domain name, network wizards', July (http://www.isc.org/ds/WWW-9507/dist-byname. html), accessed November 1998.

Network Wizards (1996a), 'Host distribution by top-level domain name, network wizards', January (http://www.isc.org/ds/WWW-9601/dist-byname. html), accessed November 1998.

Network Wizards (1996b), 'Host distribution by top-level domain name, network wizards', July (http://www.isc.org/ds/WWW-9607/dist-byname. html).

Network Wizards (1997a), 'Host distribution by top-level domain name, network wizards', January (http://www.isc.org/ds/WWW-9701/dist-byname. html), accessed November 1998.

Network Wizards (1997b), 'Host distribution by top-level domain name, network wizards', July (http://www.isc.org/ds/WWW-9707/dist-byname. html), accessed November 1998.

Network Wizards (1998a), 'Host distribution by top-level domain name, network wizards', January (http://www.isc.org/ds/WWW-9801/dist-byname. html), accessed November 1998.

Network Wizards (1998b), 'Host distribution by top-level domain name, network wizards', July (http://www.isc.org/ds/WWW-9802/dist-byname. html), accessed November 1998.

Network Wizards (1999), 'Distribution by top-level domain name by name', January (http://www.isc.org/ds/WWW-9901/dist-byname.txt), accessed February 2000.

Network Working Group and Network Technical Advisory Group NSF (1986), 'Requirements for Internet gateways – draft', RFC 985, May.

Niosi, J., P. Saviotti, B. Bellon and M. Crow (1993), 'National innovation systems of innovation: in search of a workable concept', *Technology in Society*, **15**(2), 207–27.

NITA (1999), *Falling through the Net: Defining Digital Divide: A Report on the Telecommunications and Information Technology Gap in America*, Washington, DC: US Department of Commerce.

NITA (2000), *Falling through the Net: Toward Digital Inclusion*, Washington, DC: US Department of Commerce.

Noam, E. (1992), *Telecommunications in Europe*, New York: Oxford University Press.

Noam, E. (1994a), 'Beyond liberalisation: from the network of networks to the system of systems', *Telecommunications Policy*, **18**(4), 286–94.

Noam, E. (1994b), 'Beyond liberalisation II: the impending doom of common carriage', *Telecommunications Policy*, **18**(6), 435–52.

Noam, E. and R. Kramer, (1994), 'Telecommunications strategies in the developed world: a hundred flowers blooming or old wine in new bottles?', in C. Steinfield, J. Bauer and L. Caby (eds), *Telecommunications in Transition: Policies, Services and Technologies in the European Community*, Thousand Oaks: Sage Publications, pp. 272–87.

Noam, E. and A. Wolfson (eds) (1997), *Globalism and Localism in Telecommunications*, Amsterdam, Lausanne, New York, Oxford, Shannon and Tokyo: Elsevier.

Noble, D.F. (1977), *America by Design: Science, Technology and the Rise of Corporate Capitalism*, New York: Alfred A. Knopf.

Noble, D.F. (1979), 'Social choice in machine design: the case of automatically controlled machine tools', in A. Zimbalist (ed.), *Case Studies on the Labour Process*, New York and London: Monthly Review Press, pp. 8–50.

Noble, D.F. (1984), *Forces of Production: A Social History of Industrial Automation*, New York: Alfred A. Knopf.

Noble, D.F. (1999), 'Social choice in machine design: the case of automatically controlled machine tools', in D. MacKenzie and J. Wajcman (eds), *The Social Shaping of Technology*, 2nd edn, Buckingham, Philadelphia: Open University Press, pp. 161–76.

Noll, A.M. (1998), 'The costs of competition. FCC Telecommunications Orders of 1987', *Telecommunications Policy*, **22**(1), February, 47–56.

Noll, R.G. and B.M. Owen (1983), *The Political Economy of Deregulation: Interest Groups in the Regulatory Process*, Washington, DC: AEI.

Nonaka, I., R. Toyama and A. Nagata (2000), 'Firm as a knowledge-creating entity: a new perspective on the theory of the firm', *Industrial and Corporate Change*, **9**(1), 1–20.

Nora, S. and A. Minc (1980), *The Computerization of Society: A Report to the President of France*, English translation, Cambridge and London: MIT Press.

North, D.C. (1994), 'Economic performance through time', *American Economic Review*, American Economic Association, **84**(3), 359–68.

NSFNET (1992), 'The NSFNET backbone services acceptable use policy', June (<NIC.MERIT.EDU> /nsfnet/acceptable.use.policy).

O'Brien, R.C. and G.K. Helleiner (1983), 'The political economy of information in a changing international economic order', in R.C. O'Brien (ed.), *Information, Economics & Power: The North–South Dimension*, London, Sydney, Auckland and Toronto: Hodder & Stoughton, pp. 1–27.

Ochsner, H. and K. Thomas (1996), 'The Internet: the demise of traditional online', Online Information 96 Proceedings, 477–81.

OECD (1979), *The Usage of International Data Networks in Europe*, Paris: OECD.

OECD (1992), *Technology and the Economy: The Key Relations*, Paris: OECD.

OECD (1995), *The Changing Role of Telecommunications in the Economy: Globalisation and Its Impact on National Telecommunication Policy*, OECD working papers, no. 79, Paris: OECD.

OECD (1996a), *Access and Pricing for Information Infrastructure Services: Communication Tariffication, Regulation and Internet*, Dublin: OECD, 20–21 June.

OECD (1996b), *Global Information Infrastructure–Global Information Society (GII–GIS): Statement of Policy Recommendations made by ICCP Committee*, Paris: OECD/GD (96).

OECD (1996c), *Information Infrastructure Convergence and Pricing: The Internet*, OCDE/GD (96) 73, Paris: OECD.

OECD (1997), *Business-to-Consumer Electronic Commerce Survey of Status and Issues*, Paris: OECD.

OECD (1998a), *Internet Infrastructure Indicators*, DSTI/ICCP/TISP (98) 7/FINAL, Paris: OECD.

OECD (1998b), *Internet Traffic Exchange: Development and Policy*, DSTI/ICCP/TISP (98) 7/FINAL, Paris: OECD.

OECD (1998c), *Measuring Electronic Commerce: International Trade in Software*, Paris: OECD.

OECD (1998d), *France's Experience with the Minitel: Lessons for Electronic Commerce over the Internet*, DSTI/ICCP/IE (97)10/Final, Paris: OECD.

OECD (1999a), *Communications Outlook*, Paris: OECD.

OECD (1999b), *Building Infrastructure Capacity for Electronic Commerce Leased Line Development and Pricing*, DSTI/ICCP/TISP (99) 4/FINAL, Paris: OECD.

OECD (2000a), *Local Access Price and E-Commerce*, DSTI/ICCP/TISP (2000) 1/FINAL, Paris: OECD.

OECD (2000b), *A New Economy? The Changing Role of Innovation and Information Technology in Growth*, Paris: OECD.

OECD (2001a), *Bridging the 'Digital Divide': Issues and Policies in OECD Countries*, DSTI/ICCP (2001) 9/FINAL, Paris: OECD

OECD (2001b), *Understanding the Digital Divide*, Paris: OECD.

OECD (2003), *ICT and Economic Growth: Evidence from OECD Countries, Industries and Firms*, Paris: OECD.

Olthoff, R. (1988), 'The cosine project', *Network News*, no. 27, November, 26–8.

Online (1981), *Viewdata '81*, the second world conference on viewdata, videotex and teletext, Northwood: Online Conference Ltd.

Onwumechili, C. (2001), 'Dream or reality: providing universal access to basic telecommunications in Nigeria?', *Telecommunications Policy*, **25**(4), 219–31.

Owen, K. (1982), 'Data communications: IFIP's international "network" of experts', RFC 828, August.

Padlipsky, M.A. (1982a), 'A perspective on the ARPANET reference model', RFC 871, M82-47, September.

Padlipsky, M.A. (1982b), 'A critique of X.25', RFC 874, M82-50, September.

Paltridge, S. (1996), 'How competition helps the Internet', *The OECD Observer*, **201**(August/September), 25–7.

Paltridge, S. (1999), 'Short communication: OECD regulatory and statistical update', *Telecommunications Policy*, **23**, 683–6.

Panzar, J.C. (2000), 'A methodology for measuring the costs of universal service obligations', *Information Economics and Policy*, **12**, 211–20.

Paoletti, L.M. (1973), 'Autodin', in R.L. Grimsdale and F.F. Kuo (eds), *Computer Communications Networks: Proceedings of the NATO Advanced Study Institute on Computer Communication Networks* (University of Sussex, United Kingdom), Leyden: Noordhoff International Publishing, pp. 345–72.

Parulkar, G.M. and J.S. Turner (1990), 'Towards a framework for high-speed communication in a heterogeneous networking environment', *IEEE Network Magazine*, March, 19–27.

Patel, P. and K. Pavitt (1994), 'National innovation systems: why they are important, and how they might be measured and compared', *Economic Innovation and New Technologies*, **3**, 77–95.

Patterson, R. and W.J. Ernest (2000), 'New IT and social inequality: resetting the research and policy agenda', *The Information Society*, **16**, 77–86.

Pavitt, K. (1985), 'Technology transfer among the industrially advanced countries: overview', in N. Rosenberg and C. Frischtak (eds), *International Technology Transfer: Concepts, Measures and Comparison*, New York: Praeger, pp. 3–23.

Pedersen J.S. (1989), 'Continuity and change: central perspectives on organizational change', Institute of Organization and Industrial Sociology and Institute of Industrial Research and Social Development, Copenhagen School of Economics and Social Science, Copenhagen, Denmark.

Peltzman, S. (1976), 'Towards a more general theory of regulation', *The Journal of Law and Economics*, **19**, 211–40.

Peltzman, S. (1989), 'The economic theory of regulation after a decade of deregulation', *Brookings Papers on Economic Activity, Microeconomics*, 1–59.

Perez, C. (1983), 'Structural change and the assimilation of new technologies in the economic and social system', *Futures*, **15**, 357–75.

Perez, C. (1985), 'Microelectronics, long waves and world structural change: new perspectives for developing countries', *World Development*, **13**(3), 441–63.

Perez, C. and L. Soete (1988), 'Catching up in technology: entry barriers and windows of opportunity', in G. Dosi, C. Freeman, R. Nelson, G. Silverberg and L. Soete (eds), *Technical Change and Economic Theory*, London and New York: Pinter Publishers, pp. 458–479.

Perl, L.J. (1997), 'Regulatory restructuring in the United States', *Utilities Policy*, **6**(1), 21–34.

Peterson, J. (1993), *High Technology and the Competition State: An Analysis of the EUREKA*, London: Routledge.

Petrazzini, B. and A. Guerrero (2000), 'Promoting Internet development: the case of Argentina', *Telecommunications Policy*, **24**, 89–112.

Pickens, R. and K. Hanson (1985), 'Integrating data, voice and image', in W. Chou (ed.), *Computer Communications Vol. II Systems and Applications*, Englewood Cliffs: Prentice-Hall, pp. 268–356.

Pinch, T.J. and W.E. Bijker (1984), 'The construction of facts and artifacts', *Social Studies of Science*, **14**, 399–441.

Pinch, T.J. and W.E. Bijker (1986), 'Science, relativism and the new sociology of technology: reply to Russell', *Social Studies of Science*, **16**, 347–60.

Pinch, T.J. and W.E. Bijker (1987), 'The social construction of facts and artifacts: or how the sociology of science and sociology of technology might benefit each other', in W.E. Bijker, T.P. Hughes and T.J. Pinch (eds), *The Social Construction of Technological Systems: New Direction in the Sociology and History of Technology*, Cambridge and London: MIT Press, pp. 17–50.

Piscitello, D.M. and A.L. Chapin (1993), *Open systems networking: TCP/IP and OSI*, Reading, MA: Addison-Wesley Publishing Company.

Polanyi, K. (1944), *The Great Transformation*, New York: Rinehart.

Pool, S. (1990), *Technologies Without Boundaries: On Telecommunications in a Global Age*, London: Harvard University Press.

Porte, T. (ed.) (1989), 'Proceedings of the NATO Advanced Research Workshop on social responses to large technical systems: regulation, management or anticipation', Berkeley, California, 17–21 October.

Porter, M. (1990), *Competitive Strategy: Techniques for Analyzing Industries and Competitors*, New York: Free Press.

Posner, M.V. (1961), 'International trade and technical change', Oxford Economic Papers, XIII, 323–41.

Posner, R.A. (1971), 'Taxation by regulation', *Bell Journal of Economics and Management Science*, **2**, 22–50.

Posner, R.A. (1974), 'Theories of economic regulation', *The Bell Journal of Economics and Management Science*, **5**(2), 335–58.

Pospischil, R. (1998), 'Fast Internet. An analysis about capacities, price structures and government intervention', *Telecommunications Policy*, **22**(9), 745–55.

Postel, J. (1981a), 'Transmission control protocol', RFC 0793, Sep-01-1981.

Postel, J. (1981b), 'Assigned numbers', RFC 0790, Sep-01-1981.

Postel, J. (1981c), 'Internet protocol', RFC 0791, Sep-01-1981.

Postel, J. (1983), 'Official protocols', RFC 840, April.

Postel, J. (1984), 'Domain name system implementation schedule', RFC 897, February 1984.

Postel, J. and J. Reynolds (1984a), 'ARPA–Internet protocol policy', RFC 902, July.

Postel, J. and J. Reynolds (1984b), 'Domain requirements', RFC 920, October.

Pouzin, L. (1973), 'Presentation and major design aspects of the CYCLADES' in R.L. Grimsdale and F.F. Kuo (eds), *Computer Communications Networks: Proceedings of the NATO Advanced Study Institute on Computer Communication Networks*, The Netherlands: Noordhoff Publishing, pp. 231–56.

Pouzin, L. (1982), *The CYCLADES Computer Network – towards layered network architectures*, vol. 2 of Monograph Series of the ICCC, New York: Elsevier.

Pouzin, L. (1985), 'Internetworking', in W. Chou (ed.), *Computer Communications Vol. II Systems and Applications*, Englewood Cliffs: Prentice-Hall, pp. 180–221.

Pouzin, L. (1991), 'Ten years of OSI-maturity or infancy?', *Computer Networks and ISDN Systems*, **23**(1–2), 11–14.

Pouzin, L. and H. Zimmermann (1978), 'A tutorial on protocols', *Proceedings of the IEEE*, **66**(11), 1346–70.

Preissel, R. and N. Higham (1995), 'Liberalization of telecommunications infrastructure and cable television networks: the European Commission's paper', *Telecommunications Policy*, **19**(5), 381–90.

Press, L. (1995), 'Developing networks in less industrialized nations', *IEEE Computer*, **28**(6), 66–71.

Press, L. (1996a), 'Seeding networks: the federal role', *Communications of the ACM*, **39**(10), 11–18.

Press, L. (1996b), 'The role of computer networks in development', *Communications of the ACM*, **39**(2), 23–9.

Press, L., G. Burkhart, W. Foster, S. Goodman, P. Wolcott and J. Woodard. (1998), 'An Internet diffusion framework', *Communications of the ACM*, **41**(10), 21–6.

Prieger, J. (1998), 'Universal service and the Telecommunications Act of 1996 – The fact after the act', *Telecommunications Policy*, **22**(1), 57–71.

Proceedings of JENC 17 (1996), *17th Joint European Networking*, Amsterdam: Terena.

Putnam, R. (1993), *Making Democracy Work: Civic Tradition in Modern Italy*, Princeton, NJ: Princeton University Press.

Quarterman, J.S. (1990), 'The matrix: computer networks and conferencing systems worldwide', Digital Equipment Corporation.

Quarterman, J.S. and S. Carl-Mitchell (1994), *The Internet Connection: System Connectivity and Configuration*, Reading, Melo Park, New York, Don Mills, Wokingham, Amsterdam, Bonn, Sydney, Singapore, Tokyo, Madrid, San Juan, Milan and Paris: Addison-Wesley Publishing Company.

Quarterman, J.S. and J.C. Hoskins (1986), 'Notable computer networks', *Communications of the ACM*, **29**(10), 932–71.

Rai, A., T. Ravichaudran and S. Samaddar (1998), 'How to anticipate the Internet's global diffusion', *Communication of the ACM*, **41**(10), 97–106.

Rastl, P. (1994), 'Coordinating networks in Central and Eastern Europe: CEENet', *Proc. INET '94 / JENC5*, 424-1-424-3.

Rbischon, T. (1994), 'Transformation through integration: the unification of German telecommunications', in J. Summerton (ed.), *Changing Large Technical Systems*, Boulder: Westview Press, pp. 119–39.

Reardon, R. (1988), 'Open systems: will the future ever arrive?' in R. Reardon (ed.), *Networks for the 1990s*, Pinner: Online Publication, pp. 139–45.

Reynolds, J. and J. Postel (1993), 'Official protocols', RFC 880, October.

Rheingold, H. (1994), *The Virtual Community: Finding Connection in a Computerized World*, London: Secker and Warburg.

Rheingold, H. (2000), *The Virtual Community: Homesteading on the Electronic Frontier*, Cambridge, MA and London: MIT Press.

Rip, A. (1995), 'Introduction of new technology: making use of recent insight from sociology and economics of technology', *Technology Analysis & Management*, **7**(4), 417–31.

Rip, A., T. Misa and J. Schot (eds) (1995), *Managing Technology in Society*, London and New York: Pinter.

Ritchie, D.M. and K. Thompson (1974), 'The UNIX time-sharing system', *Communications of the ACM*, **17**(7), 365–75.

Ritchie, D.M. and K. Thompson (1978), 'The UNIX time sharing system', *Bell System Technical Journal*, **57**(6), 1905–22.

Roberts, L. (1978), 'The evolution of packet switching', *Proceedings of the IEEE*, **66**(11), 1307–13.

Rogers, E.M. (1983), *Diffusion of Innovation*, 3rd edn, New York and London: The Free Press.

Rogers, E.M. (1995), *Diffusion of Innovation*, 4th edn, New York: The Free Press.

Rogers, M., M. Hobday, T. Lerpux-Demers and X. Olleros (1995), 'Innovation in complex systems industries: the case of flight simulation', *Industrial and Corporate Change*, **4**(2), 363–400.

Rohlfs, J. (1974), 'A theory of interdependent demand for a communications service', *Bell Journal of Economics*, **5**(1), 16–37.

Roland, A. (1992), 'Theories and models of technological change: semantics and substance', *Science, Technology, & Human Values*, **17**(1), 79–100.

Romer, P. (1986), 'Increasing return and long-run growth', *Journal of Political Economy*, **94**(5), 1002–37.

Romer, P. (1990), 'Endogenous technical change', *Journal of Political Economy*, **98**(5), 571–5102.

Romer, T. and H. Rosenthal (1987), 'Modern political economy and the study of regulation', in E. Bailey (ed.), *Public Regulation*, Cambridge: MIT Press, pp. 72–115.

Rosenau, J.N. (1992), 'Governance, order and change in world politics', in J.N. Rosenau and E-O. Czempiel (eds), *Governance without Government: Order and Change in World Politics*, New York: Cambridge University Press, pp. 1–29.

Rosenberg, N. (1976), *Perspectives on Technology*, Cambridge: Cambridge University Press.

Rosenberg, N. (1982), *Inside the Black Box: Technology and Economics*, Cambridge: Cambridge University Press.

Rosenberg, N. (1994), *Exploring the Black Box: Technology, Economics, and Industry*, Cambridge: Cambridge University.

Rosenberg, N. and C. Frischtak (eds) (1985), *International Technology Transfer: Concepts, Measures, and Comparisons*, New York: Praeger Publishers.

Rosner, R. (1986), 'Networked computers services for universities', in L. Csaba, K. Tarnay and T. Szentivany (eds), *Computer Network Usage: Recent Experiences – Proceedings of the IFIP TC 6 Working Conference COMNET '85*, Budapest, Hungary, Amsterdam: North-Holland, pp. 77–90.

Rosston, G. and D. Teece (1995), 'Competition and local communications: innovation, entry and integration', *Industrial and Corporate Change*, **4**(4), 787–814.

Rosston, G.L and B.S. Wimmer (2000), 'The "state" of universal service', *Information Economics and Policy*, **12**, 261–83.

Rousenau, J. and E-O. Czempiel (eds) (1992), *Governance without Government: Order and Change in World Politics*, New York and Melbourne: Cambridge University Press.

Ruggie, J.G. (1975), 'International response to technology: concepts and trends', *International Organization*, **29**(3), Summer, 557–83.

Russell, S. (1986), 'The social construction of artifacts: a response to Pinch and Bijker', *Social Studies of Science*, **16**, 331–46.

Ruthfiled, S. (1995), 'The Internet's history and development: from wartime tool to the fish-cam' (http://www.acm.org/crossroads/xrds2–1/inet-history.html), accessed November 2000.

Rutkowski, A.M. (1997), 'Factors shaping Internet self-governance', in B. Kahin and J.H. Keller (eds), *Coordinating the Internet*, Cambridge and London: MIT Press, pp. 92–106.

Rycroft, R.W. and D.E. Kash (1994), 'Complex technology and community: implications for policy and social science', *Research Policy*, **23**(6), 613–26.

Sabatino, R. and J. Arce (1999), 'The implementation of pan-European research network TEN-155', presented at the TERENA/NORDUnet Conference in Lund, Sweden, DANTE in Print, no. 39, June.

Sahal, D. (1981), 'Alternative concepts of technology', *Research Policy*, **10**, 2–24.

Sahal, D. (1985), 'Technological guideposts and innovation avenues', *Research Policy*, **14**(2), 61–82.

Samarajiva, R. (2000), 'The role of competition in institutional reform of telecommunications: lessons from Sri Lanka', *Telecommunications Policy*, **24**(8–9), 699–717.

Sanders, E. (1987), 'The regulatory surge of the 1970s in historical perspective', in E. Baily (ed.), *Public Regulation: New Perspectives on Institutions and Policies*, Cambridge, MA and London: MIT Press, pp. 117–50.

Sarkar, J. (1998), 'Technological diffusion: alternative theories and historical evidence', *Journal of Economic Surveys*, **12**(2), 131–76.

Saunders, R., J. Warford, and B. Wellenius (1994), *Telecommunications and Economic Development*, 2nd edn, Baltimore and London: Johns Hopkins University Press.

Saviotti, P.P. and J.S. Metcalfe (1984), 'A theoretical approach to the construction of technological output indicators', *Research Policy*, **13**, 141–51.

Saviotti, P.P. and J.S. Metcalfe (eds) (1991), *Evolutionary Theories of Economic and Technological Change: Present Status and Future Prospects*, Chur, Reading, Paris, Philadelphia, Tokyo and Melbourne: Harwood Academic Publishers.

Schement, J.R. (1995). 'Beyond universal service – characteristics of Americans without telephones, 1980–1993', *Telecommunications Policy*, **19**(6), 477–85.

Scherer, F. and D. Ross (1990), *Industrial Market Structure and Economic Performance*, Boston: Houghton Mifflin Company.

Schiller, D. (1998) 'Social movement in telecommunications – rethinking the public service history of US telecommunications 1894–1919', *Telecommunications Policy*, **22**(4–5), 397–408.

Schneider, V. (1994), 'Multinationals in transition: global technical integration and the role of corporate telecommunications networks', in J. Summerton (ed.), *Changing Large Technical Systems*, Boulder: Westview, pp. 71–91.

Schneider, V. (2000), 'Evolution in cyberspace: the adaptation of national videotex systems to the Internet', *The Information Society*, **16**(4), 319–28.

Schneider, V. and R. Werle (1990), 'International regime or corporate sector? European Community in telecommunications policy', in K. Dyson and P. Humphreys (eds), *The Political Economy of Communications: International and European Dimensions*, London and New York: Routledge, pp. 77–106.

Schott, T. (1993), 'World science: globalization of institutions and participation', Science, *Technology, & Human Values*, **18**(2), 196–208.

Schwartz, M. (1977), *Computer-Communication Network Design and Analysis*, Upper Saddle River, NJ: Prentice-Hall.

Schwartz, M. (1986), 'The nature and scope of contestability theory', *Oxford Economic Papers*, **38**(Supplement), 37–55

Schwartz, M. (1987), *Telecommunication Networks: Protocols, Modeling and Analysis*, Reading, MA, Don Mills, Amsterdam, Sydney, Singapore, Tokyo, Madrid, Bogotá, Santiago and San Juan: Addison-Wesley Publishing Company.

Scitovsky, T. (1954), 'Two concepts of external economies', *Journal of Political Economy*, **62**, 143–51.

Shapiro, C. and H.R. Varian (1999), *Information Rules: A Strategic Guide to the Network Economy*, Boston: Harvard Business School Press.

Shaw, R. (ed.) (1997), *Internet Domain Names: Whose Domain Is This?*, Cambridge and London: MIT Press.

Shenker S., D. Clark, D. Estrin and S. Herzog (1996), 'Pricing in computer networks: reshaping the research agenda', *Telecommunications Policy*, **20**(3), 183–201.

Shepherd, W. (1984), '"Contestability" vs. Competition', *The American Economic Review*, **74**(4), 572–87.

Shepherd, W. (1995), 'Contestability vs. Competition – Once More', *Land Economics* **71**(3), 299–309.

Shorrock, D. (1988), *New Media: Communications Technologies for the 1990s*, Pinner: Online Publications.

Shrum, W. and C. Bankston (1993), 'Organizational and geopolitical approaches to international science and technology networks', *Knowledge and Policy*, **Fall/Winter** (1993–4), 119–33.

Shrum, W. and Y. Shenhav (1995), 'Science and technology in less developed countries', in S. Jasanoff, G.E. Markle, J.C. Peterson and T. Pinch (eds), *Handbook of Science and Technology Studies*, Thousand Oaks, California and London: Sage, pp. 627–51.

Silverberg, G., G. Dosi and L. Orsenigo (1988), 'Innovation, diversity and diffusion', *The Economic Journal*, **98**, 1032–54.

Silverberg, G. and D. Lehnert (1993), 'Long waves and "evolutionary chaos" in a simple Schumpeterian model of embodied technical choice', *Structural Change and Economic Dynamics*, **4**, 9–37.

Silverberg, G., G. Dosi and L. Orsenigo (1988), 'Innovation, diversity and diffusion', *The Economic Journal*, **98**, 1032–54.

Silverstone, R. and E. Hirsch (eds) (1992), *Consuming Technologies: Media and Information in Domestic Spaces*, New York: Routledge.

Silverstone, R. and R. Mansell (1996), 'Conclusion', in R. Mansell and R. Silverstone, *Communication by Design: The Politics of Information and Communication Technologies*, New York: Oxford University Press.

Simon, H.A. (1998), *The Sciences of the Artificial*, 3rd edn, Cambridge: MIT Press.

Singh, J.P. (2000), 'The institutional environment and effects of telecommunication privatization and market liberalization in Asia', *Telecommunications Policy*, **24**(10–11), 885–906.

Sitzler, D., P. Smith and A. Marine (1992), 'Building a network information services infrastructure', RFC 1302, February.

Skocpol, T. (1979), *States and Social Revolution*, New York: Cambridge University Press.

Slevin, J. (2000), *The Internet and Society*, Cambridge: Polity Press.

Slye, W.R (1988), 'Federal government use of telecommunications', *NTIA Telecom 2000: Charting the Course for A New Century*, US Department of Commerce, Washington, DC: Government Printing Office.

Smith, M.A. and P. Kollock (1999), *Communities in Cyberspace*, London: Routledge.

Smith, P. (1996), 'Comment: end of the line for the local loop monopoly?', *Telecommunications Policy*, **20**(9), 637–40.

Smith, P. (1997), 'The NSF partnerships and the tradition of U.S. science and engineering', *Communications of the ACM*, **40** (11), 35–7.

Sobel, J. (2002), 'Can we trust social capital?', *Journal of Economic Literature*, **40**(1) (March), 139–54.

Soi, I. and K. Aggarwal (1981), 'A review of computer–communication network classification schemes', *IEEE Communications Society Magazine*, **19**(2), 24–32.

Solow, R.M. (1956), 'A contribution to the theory of economic growth', *Quarterly Journal of Economics*, **70**, 65–94.

Solow, R.M. (1957), 'Technical change and the aggregate production function', *Review of Economics and Statistics*, **39**, 312–20.

Sørensen, K. (1996), 'Learning technology, construct ring culture: sociotechnical change as social learning', SLIM internal working paper.

Sørensen, K.H. and N. Levold (1992), 'Tacit networks, heterogeneous engineers, and embodied technology', *Science, Technology, & Human Values*, **17**(1), 13–35.

Sorrow, R. (1956), 'A contribution to the theory of economic growth', *The Quarterly Journal of Economics*, **70**, 65–94.

Sorrow, R. (1957), 'Technical change and the aggregate production function', *Review of Economics and Statistics*, **39**, 312–20.

Spanier, S. (1986), 'Emergence of TCP/IP. Localnet '86', San Francisco. New York: Online Publications, November, pp. 21–33.

Spender, D. (1996), *Nattering on the Net: Women, Power and Cyberspace*, Toronto: Garamond Press.

Spiegel-Rösing, I. and D. Price (eds) (1979), *Science, Technology and Society*, London and Beverly Hills: Sage Publications.

Spratt, E. (1987), 'INDC-86: networking development in the U.K. academic community', in D. Khakhar (ed.), *Information Network and Data Communication I*, Amsterdam: Elsevier Science Publishers B.V. (North-Holland), IFIP, pp. 183–90.

Spulber, D.F. (1989), *Regulation and Markets*, Cambridge, MA. and London: MIT Press.

Stallings, W. (1987), *Handbook of computer–communications standards: V.1, The open systems interconnection (OSI) model and OSI-related standards*, New York: Collier Macmillan.

Staudenmair, J.M. (1990), 'Comment: recent trends in the history of technology', *American Historical Review*, **95**, 715–25.

Stefik, M. (ed.) (1996), *Internet Dreams: Archetypes, Myths, and Metaphors*, London and Cambridge, MA: MIT Press.

Stefik, M. (2000), *The Internet Edge: Social, Technical, and Legal Challenges for A Networked World*, London and Cambridge, MA: MIT Press.

Stehmann, O. (1995), *Network Competition for European Telecommunications*, New York: Oxford University Press.

Steinfield, C., J.M. Bauer and L. Caby (1994), *Telecommunications in Transition: Policies and Technologies in the European Community*, Thousand Oaks, London and New Delhi: Sage.

Steinmueller, W.E. (1996), 'The U.S. software industry: an analysis and interpretive history', in D.C. Mowery (ed.), *The International Software Industry*, New York and Oxford: Oxford University Press, pp. 15–52.

Steinmueller, W.E. (1997), 'Empirical opportunities for the evolutionary approach: technological trajectories, diffusion and technological infrastructure', paper prepared for seminar on evolutionary theory and empirical research, Stockholm School of Economics, SPRU, University of Sussex, 10 and 11 October.

Steinmueller, W.E. (2000), 'New information and communication technologies and leapfrogging possibilities for developing countries' for publication in the *Special Issue of International Labour Review* on ICT, INK, SPRU, University of Sussex.

Steinmueller, W.E. (2001), 'Seven foundations of the information society: a social science perspective', SPRU, Information, Networks and Knowledge, University of Sussex.

Sterba, M. (1992), 'An overview of East and Central European networking activities', version 5, Ripe-74, November (ftp://ftp.ripe.net/ripe/docs/ripe-074.txt).

Sterba, M. (1993), 'An overview of East and Central European networking activities', version 6, Ripe-86, May (ftp://ftp.ripe.net/ripe/docs/ripe-086.txt).

Stewart, M. and K. Wallis (1981), *Introductory Econometrics*, 2nd edn, Oxford: Basil Blackwell.

Stigler, G. (1968), *The organization of Industry*, Illinois: Irwin.

Stigler, G. (1971), 'The theory of economic regulation', *The Bell Journal of Economics and Management Science*, **2**(1), 3–21.

Stiglitz, J. (1987), 'Learning to Learn', in P. Dasgupta and P. Stoneman (eds), *Economic Policy and Technological Performance*, New York: Cambridge University Press, pp. 125–53.

Stockman, B. (1991), 'NORDUnet experiences in network management', *Computer Networks and ISDN Systems*, **23**(1–2), 73–8.

Stoneman, P. (ed.) (1995), *Handbook of Economics of Innovation and Technological Change*, Oxford and Cambridge: Basil Blackwell.

Strange, S. (1988), *States and Markets*, London: Pinter Publisher.

Strange, S. (1989), 'Toward a theory of transnational empire', in E.-O. Czempiel and J.N. Rosenau (eds), *Global Changes and Theoretical Challenges: Approaches to World Politics for 1990s*, Lexington, MA and Toronto: Lexington Books, pp. 161–76.

Strange, S. (1996), *The Retreat of the State: The Diffusion of Power in the World Economy*, New York: Cambridge University Press.

Summerton, J. (1994), 'Introductory essay: the system approach to technological change', in J. Summerton (ed.), *Changing Large Technical Systems*, Boulder: Westview Press, pp. 1–21.

Sung, L. (1997), 'Standards competition in wireless: regionalism vs. globalism: the case of the third generation mobile communications systems', in E.M. Noam and A.J. Wolfson (eds), *Globalism and Localism in Telecommunications*, Amsterdam: Elsevier Science B.V. pp. 323–42.

Sunshine, C. (1987), 'Network interconnection and gateways', in D. Khakhar (ed.), *Information Network and Data Communication I*, Amsterdam: Elsevier Science Publishers B.V. (North-Holland), IFIP, pp. 173–82.

Sunshine, C. (ed.) (1989), *Computer Network Architecture and Protocols*, 2nd edn, New York: Plenum Press.

Sunshine, C. (1990), 'Network interconnection and gateways', *IEEE Journal on Selected Areas in Communications*, **8**(1), 4–11.

Sussman, G. (1997), *Communication, technology, and politics in the information age*, Thousand Oaks: Sage.

Sutherland, E. (1995), 'Minitel – the resistible rise of French videotex' (http://www.georgetown.edu/sutherland/minitel/), accessed August 2001.

Tapscott, D., D. Ticoll and L. Alex (2000), *Digital Capital: Harnessing the Power of Business Webs*, London: Nicholas Brealey.

Tarjanne, P.J. (1997), 'Emerging market structures and options for regulatory reform in public utility industries', in W. Melody (ed.), *Telecom Reform: Principles, Policies and Regulatory Practices*, Lyngby: Technical University of Denmark, pp. 29–50.

Tarjanne, P. (1999). 'Preparing for the next revolution in telecommunications: implementing the WTO agreement', *Telecommunications Policy*, **23**(1), 51–63.

TeleGeography Inc. (1992), *TeleGeography 1992: Global Telecommunications Traffic Statistics and Commentary*, New York and Washington, DC: TeleGeography Inc.

TeleGeography Inc. (1999), *TeleGeography 1999: Global Telecommunications Traffic Statistics and Commentary*, New York and Washington, DC: TeleGeography Inc.

Tenkhoff, P.A. (1980), 'Private and public networks: a role for each?', in D. Barber and L. Arthur', *Data Networks: Development and Uses*, papers presented at Networks 80, an International Conference, London, Northwood.

Teske, P. (1993), 'When the public goes private', chapter prepared for the Columbia Institute for Tele-Information book, *Private Networks, Public Objects*, Political Science Department, SUNY Stony Brook, http://www.columbia.edu/dlc/wp/citi/citi496.html/ accessed September 2000.

Tétényi, I. (1996), 'Paving the highway by PHARE', JENC7, the 7th annual Joint European Networking Conference, Budapest, Hungary, 13–16 May.

Thatcher, M. (1999), *The Politics of Telecommunications: National Institutions, Convergence, and Change in Britain and France*, Oxford and New York: Oxford University Press.

Thatcher, M. (2002), 'Regulation after delegation: independent regulatory agencies in Europe', *Journal of European Public Policy* , **9**(6), 954–72.

The Cook Report (1993), 'NSFNET Privatization and the Public Interest', January (http://www.cookreport.com/p.index.shtml.) accessed August 2000.

The Cook Report (1995), 'The international connections manager – an interview with Steve Goldstein', January (http://www.cookreport.com/icm.shtml) accessed August 2000.

The Cook Report (2000), 'Secret meeting shows ICANN–IBM dependence', January (http://www.cookreport.com/icannoverall.shtml), accessed August 2000.

Thomas, G. and S. Wyatt (1999), 'Shaping cyberspace-interpreting and transforming the Internet', *Research Policy*, **28**, 681–98.

Thompson, G. Frances, J. Levačié and R. Mitchel (eds) (1991), *Markets, Hierarchies and Networks*, London: Sage with Open University.

Thompson, M., R. Ellis and A. Wildavsky (1990), *Cultural Theory*, Boulder, San Francisco and Oxford: Westview Press.

Tirole, J. (1994), 'The internal organization of government', *Oxford Economic Papers*, **46**, 1–29.

Tobagi, F., M. Gerla, R. Peebles and E. Manning (1978), 'Modelling and measurement techniques in packet communication networks', *Proceedings of the IEEE*, **66**(11), 1423–47.

Tomer, J.F. (1987), *Organizational Capital: The Path to Higher Productivity and Well-being*, New York: Praeger.

Trebing, H. (1996), 'Introduction to part 2: analyzing public utilities as infrastructure in a holistic setting – the new challenge for public policy', in W. Sichel and D. Alexander (eds), *Networks, Infrastructure, and the New Task for Regulation*, Ann Arbor: University of Michigan Press, pp. 61–72.

Trebing, H. (1997), 'Emerging market structures and options for regulatory reform in public utility industries', in W. Melody (ed.), *Telecom Reform: Principles, Policies and Regulatory Practices*, Lyngby: Technical University of Denmark, pp. 29–50.

Tucker, J. (1975), 'The European informatics network and packet switching', *Minicomputer Forum Conference Proceedings 1975*, Online Conference Ltd, Brunel University, 273–9.

Tullock, G. (1967), 'The welfare costs of tariffs, monopolies and theft', *Western Economic Journal*, **5**, 224–32.

Turnbull, D. (1993), 'Local knowledge and comparative scientific traditions', *Knowledge and Policy*, Fall/Winter (1993–4), 29–54.

Turner, C. (1997), *Trans-European Telecommunication Networks: The Challenge for Industrial Policy*, London and New York: Routledge.

Tushman, M.L. and P. Anderson (1986), 'Technological discontinuities and organizational environments', *Administrative Science Quarterly*, **31**, 439–65.

Tylecote, A. (1991), *The Long Wave in the World Economy: the Present Crisis in Historical Perspective*, London and New York: Routledge.

UN (1997), *Statistical Yearbook 1995*, 42nd issue, New York: United Nations.

UNDP (1996), *Human Development Report 1996*, New York and Oxford: Oxford University Press.

UNDP (1997), *Human Development Report 1997*, New York and Oxford: Oxford University Press.

UNDP (1998), *Human Development Report 1998*, New York and Oxford: Oxford University Press.

UNDP (1999), *Human Development Report 1999*, New York and Oxford: Oxford University Press.

UNDP (2000), 'Driving information and communications technologies for development: a UNDP agenda for action 2000–2001', October (http://sdnhq.undp.org/it4dev/ffICTe.pdf.) accessed February 2001.

UNESCO (1999), *Statistical Yearbook 1999*, Paris: UNESCO.

Ungerer, H. and N. Costello (1988), *Telecommunications in Europe: Free Choice for the User in Europe's 1992 Market: The Challenge for the European Communities*, Brussels: Commission of the European Communities.

US Congress, Office of Technology Assessment (1989), 'High-performance Computing and Networking for Science – Background Paper', OTA-BP-CIT-59, Washington, DC: U.S. Government Printing Office, September.

US Department of Commerce/International Trade Administration (1999), *Industry and Trade Outlook 1999*, New York: The McGraw-Hill Companies.

Utterback, J. and F. Suárez (1993), 'Innovation, competition, and industry structure', *Research Policy*, **22**, 1–21.

Valletti, T.M. (2000), 'Introduction: symposium on universal service obligation and competition', *Information Economics and Policy*, **12**, 205–10.

Veblen, T. (1919), 'Why is economics not a evolutionary science?', *The Place of Science in Modern Civilisation, and Other Essays*, reprint edn, New York: Russell and Russell, pp. 56–81.

Vernon, R. (1966), 'International investment and international trade in the product cycle', *Quarterly Journal of Economics*, May, 190–207.

Verspagen, B. (1991), 'A new empirical approach to catching up or falling behind', *Structural Change and Economic Dynamics*, **2**(2), 359–82.

Verspagen, B. (1993), *Uneven Growth Between Interdependent Economies: An Evolutionary View on Technology Gaps, Trade and Growth*, Aldershot, UK and Brookfield, US, Hong Kong, Singapore and Sydney: Avebury.

Verspagen, B. (2001), *Economic Growth and Technological Change: An Evolutionary Interpretation*, OECD DSTI/DOC (2001) 1, Paris: OECD.

Vickers, J. (1995), 'Concept of competition', *Oxford Economic Papers*, **47**, 1–23.

Vickers, J. and G. Yarrow (1991), 'Economic perspectives on privatization', *Journal of Economic Perspectives*, **5**(2), 111–32.

Vickers, R. and T. Vilmansen (1986), 'The evolution of telecommunications Technology', *Proceedings of the IEEE*, **74**(9), 1231–47.

Villemoes, P. (1996), NORDUnet – A successful collaboration, November, http://www.nordu.net/articles/article1/text.html.

Vogelsang, I. and B. Mitchell (1997), *Telecommunications Competition: The Last Ten Miles*, London: MIT Press and Washington, DC: The AEI Press.

Von Hippel, E. (1988), *The Sources of Innovation*, New York and Oxford: Oxford University Press.

von Tunzelmann, G.N. (1995), *Technology and Industrial Progress: The Foundations of Economic Growth*, Aldershot, UK and Brookfield US: Edward Elgar.

Wade, R. (1990), *Governing the Market: Economic Theory and The Role of Government in East Asian Industrialization*, Princeton: Princeton University Press.

Walker, J. (1994), *Security and Arms Control in Post-Confrontation Europe*, Oxford: Oxford University Press.

Walker, P.M. and S.L. Mathison (1973), 'Regulatory policy and future data-transmission services', in N. Abramson and F.F. Kuo (eds), *Computer–Communication Networks*, Englewood Cliffs: Prentice-Hall, pp. 295–370.

Wallerstein, I. (1974a), 'The rise and future demise of the world capitalist system: concepts for comparative analysis', *Society in History*, **16**, 387–415.

Wallerstein, I. (1974b), *The Modern World System*, New York: Academic Press.

Wallerstein, I. (1979), *The Capitalist World Economy*, New York: Cambridge University Press

Warschauer, M. (2003), *Technology and Social Inclusion: Rethinking the Digital Divide*, London and Cambridge, MA: MIT Press.

Watson-Verran, H. and D. Turnbull (1995), 'Science and other indigenous knowledge systems', in S. Jasanoff, G.E. Markle, J.C. Peterson and T. Pinch (eds), *Handbook of Science and Technology Studies*, Thousand Oaks, London and New Delhi: Sage Publications, pp. 115–39.

Waverman, L. and E, Sirel (1997), 'European telecommunications markets on the verge of full liberalisation', *Journal of Economic Perspectives*, **11**(4), 113–26.

Weber, M. ([1922] 1964), *The Theory of Social and Economic Organization*, reprint, New York: Free Press.

Weber, M. (1968) *Economy and Society: An Outline of Interpretive Sociology*, in G. Roth and C. Wittich (eds), *Wirtschaft und Gesellschaft*, translation, New York: Bedminster Press.

Weingarten, F.W. (1986), 'The new R&D push in communications technology', in W.H. Dutton, J.G. Blumber and K.L. Kraemer (eds), *Wired Cities: Shaping the Future of Communications*, Boston: G.K. Halls Co., pp. 41–58.

Weinrib, A. and J. Postel (1996), 'IRTF research group guidelines and procedures', RFC 2014, October.

Wellenius, B., C. Braga and C. Qiang (2000), 'Investment and growth of the information infrastructure: summary results of a global survey', *Telecommunications Policy*, **24**(8–9), 639–43.

Weller, D. (1999), 'Auctions for universal service obligations', *Telecommunications Policy*, **23**(9), 645–74.

Wellman, B. and C. Haythornthwaite (eds) (2002), *The Internet in Everyday Life*, Oxford: Blackwell Publishing.

Werbach, K. (1997), 'Digital tornado: the internet and telecommunications policy', OPP working paper series 29, FCC (http://www.fcc.gov/Bureaus/OPP/Working–Papers/ oppwp29.pdf).

Williams, D. and B. Carpenter (1998), 'Data networking for the European academic and research community: is it important?', reissued in online form, August (Original references: CERN/CN/91/10 and CERN/CN/92/4), CERN (http://nicewww.cern.ch/~davidw/public/Important.doc).

Williams, R. (1983), *Keywords: A Vocabulary of Culture and Society*, London: Flamingo.

Williams, R. (1997), 'The social shaping of multimedia', in H. Kubicek, W.H. Dutton and R. Williams (eds), *The Social Shaping of Information Highways: European and American Roads to the Information Society*, New York: St. Martin's Press and Frankfurt: Campus Verlag, pp. 299–37.

Williams, R. (2000), 'Public choice and social learning: the new multimedia technologies in Europe', *Information Society*, **16**, 251–62.

Williams, R. and D. Edge (1996), 'The social shaping of technology', *Research Policy*, **25**, 865–89.

Williamson, S. (1993), 'Transition and Modernization of the Internet Registration Service', RFC 1400, March.

Williamson, S. and L. Nobile (1991), 'Transition of Nic services', RFC 1261, Sep-01-1991.

Wilson, K.G. (1984), 'Science, industry, and the new Japanese challenge', *Proceedings of the IEEE*, **72**(1), 6–18.

Winner, L. (1986), *Do Artefacts Have Politics? In the Whale and the Reactor*, Chicago: University of Chicago Press.

Winner, L. (1993), 'Upon opening the black box and finding it empty: social constructivism and philosophy of technology', *Science, Technology & Human Values*, **18**(3), 362–78.

Winston, C. (1993), 'Economic deregulation: days of reckoning for micro-economists', *Journal of Economic Literature*, **31**(3), 1263–89.

Winston C. (1998), 'U.S. industry adjustment to economic deregulation', *The Journal of Economic Perspectives*, **12**(3), 89–110.

Winston, C. and R.W. Crandall (1994), 'Explaining regulatory policy', *Brookings Papers on Economics Activity, Microeconomics*, 1–49.

Wise, R. and J. Steemers (2000), *Multimedia: a critical introduction*, London: Routledge.

Witt, U. (1997), '"Lock-in" vs. "critical mass" – industrial change under network externalities', *International Journal of Industrial Organization*, **15**, 753–73.

Wolak, F.A. (1996), 'Can universal service survive in a competitive telecommunications environment? Evidence from the United States consumer expenditure survey', *Information Economics and Policy*, **8**(3), September, 163–203.

Wood, D. (1975), 'A survey of the capabilities of 8 packet switching networks', *Proceedings NBS, IEEE Symposium: Computer Networks: Trends and Applications*, Giththersburg, MD, June.

Wood, D (1985), 'Computer networks: a survey (chapter 14)', in W. Chou (ed.), *Computer Communications Vol. II Systems and Applications*, Englewood Cliffs: Prentice-Hall, pp. 132–79.

Wood, S. (1989), 'Co-ordinating committee for intercontinental research networking', *Network News*, no. 29.

World Bank (1994), *World Development Report 1994: Infrastructure for Development*, New York: Oxford University Press.

World Bank (2000), *World Development Indicators 2003*, Washington, DC: World Bank.

Wyatt, S., F. Henwood, N. Miller and P. Senker (eds) (2000), *Technology and Inequality: Questioning the Information Society*, London: Routledge.

Xavier, P. (2000), 'Market liberalisation and regulation in Hungary's telecommunications sector', *Telecommunications Policy*, **24**(10–11), 807–41.

Young, O.R. (1989), *International Cooperation: Building Regimes for Natural Resources and the Environment*, Ithaca, NY: Cornell University Press.

Yoffie, D. (1996), *Competing in the Age of Digital Convergence*, Boston: Harvard Business School Press.

Zajac, E. (1996), *Political Economy of Fairness*, Cambridge, MA and London: MIT Press.

NEWSLETTERS (AND MESSAGES)

APIA (Asia and Pacific Internet Association) Newsletters (http://www.apia. org/).

CCIRN Messages (1–22) – (ftp://cs.ucl.ac.uk/ccirn).

EARN, EARN Newsletters – EARNEST (1 May 1992–6 May 1993) (ftp:// ftp.univie.ac.at/netinfo/earn/).

Euronet News (bimonthly supplementary to Euroabstracts) no. 4 (December 1976)–no. 34 (March/May 1984).

IAB meeting minutes (March 1988–August 1994) (ftp://ftp.nordu.net/in-notes/ IAB/).

Internet Monthly Reports (1991, 02–1998, 12) (ftp://ftp.nordu.net/in-notes/ imr/).

Internet Society News: vol. 1, no. 1 (January 1992)–vol. 2, no. 4 (March 1994) (ftp://ftp.ripe.net/isoc/pub/isoc_news/).

JANET Network News (no. 25: March 1988–no. 44: June 1995) (http:// www.ja.net/documents/NetworkNews).

The Work of DANTE (no. 1: December 1993–no. 36: December 1999) (http:// www.dante.net/pubs/works/).

DOCUMENT & DATA SOURCES

APCCIRN and APAN meeting minutes and documents (1992.6.16–1995.01.01) (http://www.apng.org/apng/).

APIA documents (http://www.apia.org/).

CEENet documents (http://www.ceenet.org/).

EU R&D Programs Documents (http://dbs.cordis.lu/).

FNC and CCIRN meeting minutes and documents (http://www.fnc.gov/).

ICANN documents (http://www.icann.org/).

IEPG meeting minutes and documents (http://www.isc.org/iepg/docs/).

INET Conferences and Papers (http://www.isoc.org/isoc/conferences/inet/).

InterNIC documents (http://rs.internic.net/).

Index

Acceptable Use Policy (AUP) 97–8, 99
access
  externalities 38
  Internet 2, 123, 142, 166–70
  market 38, 40
  to PCs 8, 166, 168–9
ACOnet (Austrian Academic Computer
  Network) 112
Actor–Network–Theory (ANT) 16–17
ACTS programme 119
advanced countries 166–9, 172–4, 229
Advanced Network and Service, Inc.
  (ANS) 92, 100
advanced network workshop (ANW)
  112
advanced research networks, global
  network of 117–21
Advanced Research Project Agency
  (ARPA) *see* DARPA
Advanced Research Project Agency
  Network (ARPANET) 129, 228
  development 52, 53, 54, 58–9, 62
  protocols 75–6, 99
  system building 90, 92–3, 98, 101–2
America Online (AOL) 157, 160–61,
  163
American National Standard Institute
  (ANSI) 68
architectural innovation 20
Asia Internet Infrastructure Initiative
  (AI3) 121
Asia-Pacific Advanced Network (APAN)
  121
Asia-Pacific Coordination Committee
  for International Research Net-
  working 114
Asia Pacific Internet Association (APIA)
  105, 116, 125
Asia Pacific Network Information
  Center (APNIC) 114
Asia Pacific Networking Group 104, 114

Asia-Pacific region (Internet system)
  112–17
Asynchronous Transfer Mode (ATM)
  80, 119–20
AT&T 40, 57, 62, 72–5, 128
Automatic Digital Network (AUTODIN)
  51

Backbone Network Service (BNS) 76,
  89, 92, 99–101, 109, 115, 118, 129,
  131–2, 145–6, 183
Bildschirmtext 157
BITNET 70, 90, 103, 107, 111, 114,
  228
Bolt Beranek and Newman (BBN) 62,
  99
book production 219–20
broadband technology 80, 117, 118,
  232
BT 116, 120

cable systems, underseas 115–17
Cable and Wireless 40, 124
Canadian National/Canadian Pacific
  Telecommunications (CN/CPT) 63
capability 142
  building 11–12, 13, 25, 156
  social 141, 156
capital 45
  formation 184–5
capitalism 45, 140, 141
causality 190–96
CCIRN 94, 103, 104, 114
CCITT standards 60, 63, 64–7, 68, 69,
  80, 82
Central and Eastern Europe 107, 110–12
centrifugal technological innovations 34
CERN 107, 109, 110, 111, 120, 147
Chollian 160, 163
CIGALE 54
circuit switching 42, 50, 52, 56, 63, 65